SCIENCE AND HEALTH
1875 Edition

BY
MARY BAKER GLOVER

BOSTON:
CHRISTIAN SCIENTIST PUBLISHING COMPANY.
1875.

Entered according to Act of Congress
In the year 1875
by
MARY BAKER GLOVER
In the Office of the Librarian of Congress at Washington

Published by Audio Enlightenment Press.Com

Giving Voice to the Wisdom of the Ages

Copyright © 2014 by Audio Enlightenment Press
All rights reserved. No part of this publication may be reproduced, distributed, or transmitted in any form or by any means, including photocopying, recording, or other electronic or mechanical methods, without the prior written permission of the publisher, except in the case of brief quotations embodied in critical reviews and certain other noncommercial uses permitted by copyright law.
Printed in the United States of America

First Printing, 2014

ISBN 978-1-941489-12-3

www.ScienceAndHealth1875Edition.Com

www.AudioEnlightenmentPress.Com

A Gnostic Audio Selection

First "AudioEnlightenmentPress.Com" Printing

April 2014

Publisher's Introduction

So, why a reprint of a book over 135 years old when there are so many reprints and new editions of the text? Excellent question and one I will endeavor to answer here.

Since it is our goal to find and reprint spiritual classics on the verge of falling into the vast abyss, we came upon reference to this work while reading "Lifting the Veil" by Lillian Dewaters, and the following is quoted verbatim from "The Sickle" by William W. Walter, during a discussion on the understanding of Christian Science, excerpted from pages 127-129, 1918 edition.

Recently there has arisen a misunderstanding among the students of Christian Science, regarding the correctness of the early editions of "Science and Health, with key to the Scriptures."

Some maintain that merely reading the early editions once gave them a much greater depth of understanding, and consequently greater healing power than years of study spent upon the later editions.

Others maintain that Christian Science, in its complete purity, is not to be found in the early editions, and further state that Mrs. Eddy later repudiated these early editions as being incorrect in Principle. Mrs. Eddy's own words ought to be the best authority on this question. She wrote, page 55, "Retrospection and Introspection," under the chapter heading of "The Precious Volume"-"The first edition of my most important work, Science and Health, containing the complete statement of Christian Science, the term employed by me to express the Divine, or spiritual Science of Mind-healing was published in 1875."

The statement, "the first edition of my most important work, Science and Health, containing the complete statement of Christian Science" was undoubtedly written in 1891, or sixteen years after: the publishing of the first edition. Thus we see that after sixteen years of teaching, writing and practice Mrs. Eddy still maintained that the first edition was "The Precious Volume" and the one that contained "the complete statement of Christian Science"

If Mrs. Eddy repudiated the teachings given the world as proven truth in her first edition of "Science and Health," then she had a mere theory instead of understanding, at the time she wrote her first text-book. How then can we be sure that the present text-book is correct Science, for if she had not passed on she might, in another twenty-five years, repudiated the present text-book as incorrect.

Mrs. Eddy had a correct understanding of metaphysical healing when she wrote the first edition of "Science and Health, "and she at no time repudiated any editions of that work.

Numerous articles written by Mrs. Eddy before and during the time that she was searching for Truth, and in which she merely gave her then unproved opinion to others, had gained wide circulation, and it is these early lispings which Mrs. Eddy repudiated as complete Science.

Having now plainly shown that Mrs. Eddy referred to the first edition of "'Science and Health" as "The Precious Volume" and that she plainly stated that the first edition contained the complete statement of Christian Science, I will give a few citations from it for comparison and comment.

Excerpt from "Lifting the Veil" by Lillian De Waters, page 45:

Millicent uttered an exclamation of astonishment, "Do you mean that they are to be found in old manuscripts of Mrs. Eddy?"

"No. These statements of actual truth are found in Science and Health, published in the year 1875. Also these same statements continue throughout the first fourteen editions of this great work.

After that edition a great change was made."

"I'm certainly having many surprises, Mr. Williams. I have never seen or read the first edition of Science and Health, and I surely never dreamed that that first book would be more enlightening to one than the late book. Why, if she told the truth in the first book, did she change her standpoint of understanding, and why have we been told that the latest editions are the best and purest? How can we be sure that her first discovery was correct?"

..."I have read those words before but I never dreamed of their significance. Why, Mrs. Eddy states plainly that she considers her first book her 'precious volume', and says that it is this first edition that contains her 'complete statement of Christian Science'. One surely need not seek to correct or to amplify that which one considers 'complete'." Then, after a moment's pause, "Will you tell me where I can obtain a copy of this book that our Leader valued as the greatest of all her editions of the text book?"

"You may be able to procure it from the book shops that specialize in buying and selling old and rare books. You may also read it in some of the public libraries."

"I certainly shall not rest satisfied until I read a copy. And, to think that I have always been so particular to get the very latest edition!" "Why?"

"Because I have understood that the latest volume read the clearest and smoothest. Why, I have often heard it remarked that the early editions were crudely written."

Spelling and grammar has been kept true to the original. We hope you enjoy this enlightened original reprint.

Barry J. Peterson

Audio Enlightenment Press

TABLE OF CONTENTS

SCIENCE AND HEALTH
1875 EDITION

Preface.	Page i
Chapter I. Natural Science.	Page 1
Chapter II. Imposition and Demonstration.	Page 45
Chapter III. Spirit and Matter.	Page 109
Chapter IV. Creation.	Page 167
Chapter V. Prayer and Atonement.	Page 215
Chapter VI. Marriage.	Page 239
Chapter VII. Physiology.	Page 249
Chapter VIII. Healing the Sick.	Page 281

i

PREFACE

LEANING on the sustaining Infinite with loving trust, the trials of to-day are brief, and to-morrow is big with blessings. The wakeful shepherd tending his flocks, beholds from the mountain's top the first faint morning beam ere cometh the risen day. So from Soul's loftier summits shines the pale star to the prophet shepherd, and it traverses night, over to where the young child lies in cradled obscurity that shall waken a world. Over the night of error dawn the morning beams and guiding star of Truth, and the wise men are led by it to Science, to that which repeats the eternal harmony reproduced in proof of immortality and God. The time for thinkers has come; and the time for revolutions, ecclesiastic and social, must come. Truth, independent of doctrines or time-honored systems, stands at the threshold of history. Contentment with the past, or the cold conventionality of custom, may no longer shut the door on science; though empires fall, "He whose right it is shall reign." Ignorance of God should no longer be the stepping-stone to faith; understanding Him "whom to know aright is Life" is the only guaranty of obedience.

Since the hoary centuries but faintly shadow forth the tireless Intelligence at work for man, this volume may not open at once a new thought, and make it familiar. It has the task of a pioneer to hack away at the tall oak and cut the rough granite, leaving future ages to declare what has been done. We made our first discovery that science mentally applied would heal the sick, in 1864, and since then have tested it on ourselves and hundreds of others, and never found it fail to prove the statement herein made of it. The science of man alone can make him harmonious, unfold his utmost possibilities, and establish the perfection of man. To admit God the Principle of all being, and live in accordance with this Principle, is the Science of Life, but to reproduce the harmony of being, errors of personal sense must be destroyed, even as the science of music, must correct tones caught from the ear, to give the sweet concord of sound. There are many theories of physic, and theology; and many calls in each of their directions for the right way; but we propose to settle the question of "What is Truth?" on the ground of proof. Let that method of healing the sick and establishing Christianity, be adopted, that is found to give the most health, and make the best Christians, and you will then give science a fair field; in which case we are assured of its triumph over all opinions and beliefs.

Sickness and sin have ever had their doctors, but the question is, have they become less because of them? The longevity of our antediluvians, would say, no! And the criminal records of to-day utter their voices little in favor of such a conclusion. Not that we would deny to Caesar the things that are his, but that we ask for the things that are Truth's, and safely affirm, from the demonstrations we have been able to make, that science would have eradicated sin, sickness, and death, in a less period than six thousand years. We find great difficulties in starting this work right: some shockingly false claims are already made to its practice; mesmerism (its very antipode), is one. Hitherto we have never in a single instance of our discovery or practice found the slightest resemblance between mesmerism and the science of Life. No especial idiosyncrasy is requisite for a learner; although spiritual sense is more adapted to it than even the intellect; and those who would learn this science without a high moral standard will fail to understand it until they go up higher. Owing to our explanations constantly vibrating between the same points an irksome repetition of words must occur; also, the use of capital letters, genders and technicalities peculiar to the science, variety of language, or beauty of diction, must give place to close analysis, and unembellished thought. "Hoping all things, enduring all things:" to do good to the upright in heart, and to bless them that curse us, and bear to the sorrowing and the sick consolation and healing, we commit these pages to posterity.

MARY BAKER GLOVER

CHAPTER I

NATURAL SCIENCE

A few years since we clipped the following from the reports on Science:

"At the University at Oxford, a prize of one hundred pounds was offered for the best Essay on Natural Science, to refute the materialism of the present age, or the tendency to attribute physical effects to physical causes, rather than to a final spiritual cause." This demand for metaphysics coming from the very fount of erudition meets the wants of the age, and is the one question towering above all others, insomuch as it relates more intimately to the happiness and perfection of man. The control mind holds over matter becomes no longer a question when with mathematical certainty we gain its proof, and can demonstrate the facts assumed. This proof we claim to have gained, and reduced to its statement in science that furnishes a key to the harmony of man, and reveals what destroys sickness, sin, and death.

Metaphysical science explains cause and effect; removing the veil of mystery and doubt, from Soul and body, and from man and God; it unwinds the interlaced ambiguities of Spirit and matter, and sets free the imprisoned Intelligence; explains the phenomenon man, on the basis of his Principle, and how to gain his harmony in science, which seems to us more important morally and physically than the discovery of the powers of steam, the electric telegraph, or any other advanced idea that science has revealed. Views taken on trust cause conflicting opinions and beliefs that emit a poisonous atmosphere of mind more destructive to the harmony of body than the miasma of matter. Understanding cools and purifies this atmosphere, and thus invigorates the body; but before this result is obtained, understanding and belief, or Truth and error must meet in a war of ideas, and the thunderbolt of public opinion burst overhead; but when this outburst of opinion is spent of its fury, like the rain-

Chapter I. Natural Science.

drops on the earth it will have moistened the parched thought, whereby the rich buds and blossoms that come from the tree of Life may put forth new beauty.

Because Christendom may resist the word science, we shall lose no faith in Christianity, and because we shall apply this word to Truth, Christianity will lose no hold on us. We shall let the Principle of things alone interpret them, and never take an opinion or belief to steady the altar of science. The Principle of the universe and man embraces the understanding, and explanation of Soul and body, and is the basis of all science; but opinions and beliefs regarding God and man, or Soul and body, are the foundations of all error. There is no physical science, the Principle of science is God, Intelligence, and not matter; therefore, science is spiritual, for God is Spirit and the Principle of the universe and man.

We learn from science mind is universal, the first and only cause of all that really is; also, that the real and unreal constitute what is, and what is not; that the real is Spirit, which is immortality, and the unreal matter, or mortality. The real is Truth, Life, Love and Intelligence, all of which are Spirit, and Spirit is God, and God, Soul, the Principle of the universe and man. Spirit is the only immortal basis. Matter is mortality; it has no Principle, but is change and decay, embracing what we term sickness, sin, and death. God is not the author of these, hence Spirit is not the author of matter; discords are the unreal that make up the opposite to harmony, or the real that emanates Truth and not error. Spirit never requires matter to aid it, or through which to act; no partnership or fellowship exists between them; matter cannot co-operate with Spirit, the mortal and unreal with the real and eternal, the mutable and imperfect with the immutable and perfect, the inharmonious and self-destroying with the harmonious and undying. Spirit is Truth, matter its opposite; viz., error; and these two forces control man and the universe, and are the tares and wheat that never mingle, but grow side by side until the harvest, until matter is self- destroyed; for not until then do we learn ourselves Spirit, and yield up the ghost of error, that would

Chapter I. Natural Science.

make substance. Life and Intelligence, matter. God and His idea are all that is real primitively; all is mind, and mind produces mind only, nature, reason and revelation decide, that like produces like; matter does not produce mind, nor, *vice versa*. We name matter, error, it being a false claim to Life and Intelligence, that returns to dust ignored by Spirit, that is supreme over all, and knows nothing of matter.

Natural history presents the mineral, vegetable and animal kingdoms preserving their original species in reproduction; a mineral is not produced by a vegetable, and vice versa; throughout the entire round of universal nature, this rule relating to genus and species holds good; this therefore is science. But error claims the very opposite, viz., that Spirit produces matter; making Spirit, or God, the author of evil as well as good, and harmony the author of discord, evil presenting as much of God as good, which contradicts self-evident Truth. In the science of being we learn all discord, such as sickness, sin or death, is distinct from Spirit, and not produced by God; also, that God is the Soul, or Principle of man, the Truth, unerring and eternal; again, that matter claiming mind, or making itself the basis of mind, is error, and this error, the so-called intelligent body named man, with intelligent nerves, brain, stomach, and so forth. The only reality of being is the Truth of it, and that Life and Intelligence are in matter, is not Truth but its opposite, error; therefore, illusion.

Mind and matter are opposites; that mind is in matter, or that matter is the medium through which mind is made manifest is not more real than that a tree embraces a rock in the heart of it, and is the natural medium through which the rock grows, and is identified. Nature and revelation afford no grounds for the belief that Spirit, God, created, or is in a body of sickness, sin, and death, and the only excuse for such a belief is, that the falsity of this opinion of Life is not seen until we begin to learn the science of Life, and enter into our God-being, wherein we learn that Spirit and matter no more commingle, than light and darkness, than God and His opposite, called devil, which reduced to their statement in science, are Truth and error; in other words, Spirit and matter, forever distinct, one possessing immortality, the other mortality. Said the Apostle, "The flesh warreth against the Spirit and the Spirit against the flesh."

Mind, the basis of all things, cannot cross its species, and produce matter. But in order to classify mind that is real, from belief or the unreal, we name one mind, and the other matter; but recollect matter is but a belief, and mind the only reality. Error can only be defined as belief, which is not mind but illusion. The belief, that Life, Substance, and Intelligence are where and what they are not, is error. Spirit is the understanding and possession of Truth, Life and Intelligence. Belief and understanding never mingle, more than matter and Spirit; one is error, the other Truth. All discord is what we term matter, and discord is mortal, nothingness; harmony is real and immortal, for it belongs to Spirit, is produced by it and proceeds from it. Immortal mind is Spirit, an utterance of Soul proceeding from harmony and immortality. The mind, that we name matter, is the so-called mind of the body, and what is termed sinful and mortal man; but this man is a myth, neither mind nor matter, but a belief that embraces all error. God, Truth, never produced error; Soul and Intelligence never originated inharmony; and at some future data we shall learn all that is mortal or discordant bath no origin, existence or reality, but is the absence of the real; yea, native nothingness, the chaos and night out of which error would simulate the creations of Truth, from dust instead of Deity.

Error pre-supposes man both mind and matter, but this is not the science of being, but science disputing personal sense beards so relentlessly our belief, we naturally ask what are we, and what is man? We are Spirit, Soul, and not body, and all is good that is Spirit; God and the idea of God are real, and nothing else is real. Harmony and its results are real, but discord and what comes of it are the unreal. It were well to begin from this hour, as you read these pages, to reckon Life only in what is good and true; putting aside evil as unreal, not the offspring of God, and unworthy to be named man,

Chapter I. Natural Science.

him whom Spirit produces "the image and likeness of God," but whom matter claims to create in sin.

Admitting error, produces it; but who or what is it that admits error? Not God, Spirit, for error is not the result of Intelligence; error is a self-admission, and admission of self-hood where man is not, and this is all there is to it; admitting a temptation is the only danger in it. To believe in the possibility of pleasurable sin, makes all that is sin; say then to the whole liturgy of intelligent matter, as Jesus said, "You were a liar from the beginning."

Mind is Spirit, outside of matter, and this is the only mind or understanding; the mind called brains, or matter, is belief only; hence, the more material man is the stronger belief, and the weaker manifestation of Soul, or understanding. Belief is what we term personal sense, and personal sense is a belief. That matter is intelligent, that nerves feel, brains think, and sin, that a stomach makes man cross, limbs cripple him, and matter kills him, is a belief, and this belief, error, opposed to the Truth of being. Sin, sickness and death proceed from the so-called five personal senses that we are taught to revere and cultivate, but which Truth at length destroys, through age, experience or spiritual growth, and in place of sentient bodies, we find sensationless bodies, and immortal Soul, as the recognition of being harmonious and eternal. The body mortal is not man, for man is immortal; but with sensation in the body he is not immortal, and cannot be Spirit, which is Soul,

To admit physical effects is to conclude matter cause and effect, whence it follows there are two causes, viz., mind and matter, else that mind produces matter, or matter produces mind, which contradicts the science of Life in its demonstration, and is like saying dust originated man, and a serpent a dove. Soul is Intelligence, but the so-called mind of body is belief only, the limited and mortal that embraces not the boundless and eternal, for such is Intelligence. Hence we learn that Soul, therefore Spirit,

Chapter I. Natural Science.

which is God, is not in man, and that man is idea, and Soul the Principle, Life, substance and Intelligence of man.

Having drawn the line between immortal man, or the reality of being, and the unreal or mortal, that is but a personal recognizance of Life, God, which is impossible, we also learn that pain or pleasure in matter is equally impossible. Things, as they appear from the stand-point of personal sense, are diametrically opposite to science, or immortal man seen from the standpoint of Soul; hence the difficulty sensuous man has to understand this science, and his opposition to it, for "the carnal man is at enmity with God." Mortal man and personal sense are not mind but belief; mind is understanding, belief is ignorance, even the error that Truth consigns to oblivion.

What is deemed Life in vegetable and animal becomes a self-evident falsehood, when all that is left of it is death. The science of being alone reveals Life or Principle, that reverses every position of personal sense; showing, also that sickness, sin and death disappear with the understanding of being and our real existence, for in this alone are we harmonious, sinless, and eternal.

Will man lose his identity in conscious infinitude of being? It is impossible that he should lose aught that tends to his completeness, in a state through which he gains all; matter, embracing sickness, sin and death, is all that will ever be lost. Life is not structural and organic, for Life is Spirit, Soul, and not sense, and without beginning and without end. Life is Principle, and not person; joy and not sorrow; holiness, not sin, and harmony, without a tone of discord. In science we learn there is but one God, also that God is Spirit; hence there is but one Spirit, for there is not an evil God. To gain the harmony of being, and be perfect even as the Father, God must be understood, which means, the Principle of man must be understood; believing in God never made a Christian.

Chapter I. Natural Science.

The only immortal basis of man is Soul; hence the importance to plant one's self on the basis of being, and work from this to gain our ultimate harmony. Soul and not sense reveals the glorious possibilities of man, even the circumference of his being unlimited by a belief of Life in matter; getting out of material nutshells we get out of error, whereby we learn the last shall be first, and the first last; that which was first in matter will be last, alias, nothing in Spirit. Science puts not new wine into old bottles; we cannot adhere to a belief regarding a subject, and at the same time grasp the Truth of it; we must yield the old, or the new is spilled.

Doctrines and opinions based on a personal God are nothing more or less than beliefs of intelligent matter, that we must yield, or spill the inspiration and wine of Truth that enables man to demonstrate Life higher, and to reach practical Christianity that casts out devils and heals the sick.

We will now consider more minutely the Principle, or Soul of man, named God; learn what it is, and how man is harmonious and immortal. The Scriptures inform us, "God is Love," "Truth and Life," and these certainly imply He is Principle, not person. Again, Principle explains person, but person cannot explain Principle. God interprets man, but man cannot explain God, Spirit explains matter, but matter cannot define Spirit, Soul explains body, but body cannot interpret Soul. We must commence with God to explain immortal man, remembering God is Spirit, and Spirit the only substance, because it is Intelligence; holding the earth in equipoise, marking out the pathway of the stars, forming the minutia of identity, and comprehending the universe and man in the harmony of being. Spirit believes nothing, because it understands all, and is Life, not subject to death because it is exempt from matter.

It is mind alone that embraces sensation, therefore, the senses are Spirit and not matter, and belong to Soul instead of body; they are not personal but Spiritual; Intelligence passes from mind to body, that is, from Principle to its idea, but cannot pass from body to mind, for matter is neither cognizant of evil or good; of pain or pleasure. Soul is not in body, it is the unlimited Intelligence, impossible to limit, and the immortality that mingles not with mortality; as light and darkness are opposites, so are Spirit and matter, without the least affinity; light dwelling in darkness would destroy the darkness; thus would the sinless and immortal destroy the sinning and mortal; but darkness extinguishes not light, and matter cannot destroy Spirit, body cannot destroy Soul, but Soul can and does destroy matter. Man is not matter, brains are not Intelligence, they are not the organ of the infinite. Life and Intelligence are not in matter, nor do they act by means of organization; matter is a creation of belief, a chimera of personal sense that reverses science, as we shall hereafter show.

Idea is inseparable from its Principle; man is idea, and Soul the Principle that produces it, therefore man and his maker are inseparable. Opinions and beliefs have no Principle, they are erring and mortal, neither expressing God nor immortal man; but the offspring of personal sense, embracing sin, sickness and death, yes, the dream of Life in matter. Materia medica, physiology, mesmerism, etc., are opinions and beliefs, predicated on intelligent matter, which is error; and the discord and doubt attending them are owing to the false position they occupy. Ideas, like numbers and notes, admit no opinions or beliefs regarding them, when once their Principle is understood; beliefs are theories that change, and are falsely stated, because they are not understood. The identity of every idea is in its Principle where it is learned; immortal man is harmonious and eternal; matter is the offspring of mortal belief; Soul or understanding, has no part in it.

Philosophy in general, finds cause in effect, Soul in body, Principle in idea, and Life and Intelligence in matter. Materia medica seeking cause in effect, would learn of matter what are the conditions of man, examining the liver, heart, lungs, etc., to ascertain how much harmony they are permitting man; thus admitting matter instead of mind, causation, and producing Life or

Chapter I. Natural Science.

death, pain or pleasure, action or stagnation, without the mind's consent; this would place man and God, or body and Soul, at the disposal and control of matter. Physiology finds mind unequal to matter, cause not master of effect, the so-called laws of nature failing in their fulfillment to give health to man; making the Infinite insufficient to govern the finite, Principle not controlling its idea, and the Intelligence, or Soul of man, unable to govern the body. To prevent disease, or the effects of damp atmospheres, violent exertions, a heavy meal, etc., destroying man; we say, laws of matter are our only hope, leaving Spirit powerless.

Mesmerism, placing Life and Intelligence in electricity, finds matter superior to God, and the governing Principle of man, an aura of brains, the lack or excess, quality or quantity of which, determines his discord or harmony.

Theology would make the supreme Being a person, in other words, matter embracing Spirit; God dwelling in man, Life in the things it creates, cause in effect, Soul in body, the infinite and limitless, within limits. With this theory, to be omnipresent, God must paw in personal identity over earth; or possess a body that encompasseth universal space; in which ewe, what would be the personality of God? Spirit is not matter; nor is it both within and without matter; if such were the case, they would be one in substance and Intelligence, else limited to the range of personal sense, or personal sense raised to the capacity of omnipresence, which is again impossible. Our beliefs of a personal Deity place infinite Life and Love within the stature of a man; make man God, or put God into matter, which is atheism. Error is the basis of all belief; we need, instead, the true idea, based on the understanding of God the impersonal Principle, Truth, and Life of man, which is not body, but Soul.

The artist is not in his painting; the picture is a thought of his, an emanation of Spirit, not matter; the Creator is not what he creates. The potter is not in the clay, but has power over the clay; God

Chapter I. Natural Science.

produces his own personality, and cannot get into it, because it is in Him the circumference and infinite Soul outside of matter and man. The five personal senses are beliefs of Life, substance, and Intelligence in matter, even the fount of error; all discord proceeds from this false source; in reality, there is no personal sense, for matter is not intelligent. The line of demarkation between the Principle that is Intelligence and Life, and the belief of Life and Intelligence in person, is the boundary between belief and science, otherwise, between error and truth. Science contradicts personal sense in every instance, as we shall hereafter show. Understanding is the only admissible evidence of Truth; conclusions drawn from personal sense are foundationless; understanding is a portion of the infinite Principle embracing every idea of Truth. Belief has no Principle; it is a mortal and finite sense of things called knowledge, a lie of limits that would place Soul in body, Life and Intelligence in matter to evolve matter, and call this germination, or nature, seed reproducing itself; not only denying to God the things that are His, but limiting the Infinite, and thinking to fasten Wisdom to discord and decay.

To learn the Truth of things, they must be explained from the basis of Soul, and not sense; personal sense is knowledge, obtained from opinions and beliefs. When our interpretations proceed from the Principle of things, we have them right; but if from observation, or the deductions of personal sense, they are wrong, and beliefs based on the supposition of Life and Intelligence in matter, that are error.

Impressions supposed to proceed from the hearing of the ear, the observations of the eye, from touch, taste, or smell, are these beliefs, but not the ideas of God. Every idea proceeds from Principle, gained through understanding, whereby we arrive at demonstrable Truth. Belief constitutes mistakes, understanding never errs, hence it is necessary to the harmony of mind and body. Inasmuch as belief starts from person, instead of Principle, it is not the Truth of being, but the error called mortal man.

Chapter I. Natural Science.

Knowledge is power, even the force that depends on organizations for strength, it is neither moral suasion, moral might, idea, nor Principle; but a faith, supposition, or belief. Repulsion, attraction, cohesion, and power supposed to belong to matter, are constituents of mind; knowledge gives these properties to matter, but science gives them to Intelligence, the Principle of all; to find inherent properties in matter that act independent of mind is impossible. There is no inertia in Intelligence; but science alone determines whence cometh action, from its harmonious Principle, i.e., from Soul to body, or from belief prolific of error.

Science reveals all action proceeding from God, the universal cause that produces harmony only; and that discord, sickness, sin, and death, are neither action, nor being, but beliefs, or error. The absence of Truth, we name error, but whence cometh error, from God? No; "the same fountain sendeth not forth sweet and bitter water." Error is not an idea, it has neither Principle, nor identity; it is not definable as a person, place, or thing; as an agent, or actor; and being without substance, Life, or Intelligence, and neither Principle nor identity, we learn it came not! but is illusion. Again, what is belief? Nothing real or true, and to understand this is the only fact concerning it. Sickness, sin, and death, all that is the opposite and absence of God, is belief and error presupposing good and evil in matter and man. But is the question answered, whence cometh belief? It has no origin, it is neither Principle nor idea; but illusion, without any real cause or creation.

We say disease is a reality, and identity, but science finds it a belief only; disappearing with mortality, and cognizant only to personal sense; not to Soul. "God made all that was made;" there is but one Principle and its infinite idea; harmony and immortality that belong to man, are perceived through spiritual sense, but not personal. Belief has no Intelligence, having neither Principle nor understanding, therefore it is error, and error is the so-called mind of mortal man! totally depraved, sinning, suffering, and dying; this is the absence of God. Man has no mind in matter; the belief that he

Chapter I. Natural Science.

has, is error. There is but one Intelligence, even God, the infinite Love, Truth, and Life; and God is not man. Matter is not intelligent; brains are not mind; and man is not Soul, a separate God or Intelligence. Jesus laid much stress on this point: "Thou shall have no other gods before Me;" while we daily behold in belief the zeal of error to gain the opposite point, viz.: "I will make ye as gods."

Science informs us immortal mind is Spirit; but personal sense would have mind both Spirit and matter; a moral impossibility. Spirit cannot act through matter, they are diametrically opposed to each other, and never mingle; personal sense is the only foundation for the theory that Spirit and matter mingle, and time and eternity are wearing away this support. Mind is not confined to organization, nor limited by materiality.

Immortal mind is the atmosphere of Soul pervading all space; and regarding even "the sparrow's fall;" no power can compress it within a skull-bone! matter confines it not, the strongest barrier opposed to Intelligence is as nothing; the only clog, or limit given mind, is mortal belief, error's synonym; understanding constructs not, and has no cognizance of limits; it is finite belief that would limit mind; and there is no finite Intelligence. There is finite error, that pre-supposes mind in matter; but this is the evil and not the good, the belief and not the reality; yea, the error, and not the Truth of man.

Spiritual sense belongs to Soul, and is the only real sense; it takes no cognizance of substance in matter, of suffering, sin, or death; Spiritual sense recognizes all that is Truth, Life, and Love; hence there is nothing left personal sense to enjoy or suffer. Personal sense is the dream of Life in matter, a supposition only of reality and substance, of Life and Intelligence, of good and evil, that would limit Soul, and doom all things to decay. Sensation in matter is one of its beliefs, and belief is the opinion, personal, that supports only what is untrue, selfish, or debased; all these mistakes are but the error we name mortal man. God and man will never be understood,

Chapter I. Natural Science.

until we listen alone to the senses attached to Principle instead of person, to Soul instead of body.

Personal sense being error, all evidence obtained therefrom is belief without Principle, or immortal proof. Spiritual, in contradistinction to personal sense, reveals man idea; not substance; his Life and Intelligence, God, in other words, Soul, and not body; and thus secure from chance and change be is harmonious and eternal. The demonstration of this statement will destroy sickness, sin and death, and because of this, it is important to understand at present as well as hereafter, the great Truth which must displace the opposite error that brought sin and death into the world, shutting out the pure sense of immortality; and which ought to be learned to-day.

God is, and was, and ever will be; and if this Intelligence exists, there is also the idea of it, named man, that cannot be separated for a single moment from this, its principle and Soul. We look on a corpse, or the body called man, but is it man? No! Is Soul in it? certainly not; has Soul escaped? No! where was the outside, infinite Spirit, if Spirit was in man? Can Soul be lost? impossible, for the immortal is without end; and Soul is Spirit, and Spirit, God. Is man lost? Not if Soul be left! for Soul is Principle, and man its idea, and these forever inseparable; God would be lost, if man was blotted out, for entity signifies the particular nature of being; and God, without the idea, image, and likeness of Himself, would be a nonentity! Man is the complex idea of God, hence, they cannot be separated.

Contemplating a corpse, we behold the going out of a belief; we have been accustomed to this belief of mind in matter, but not the Truth of man, whose Soul is God and his body the harmonious idea of Him. The belief of Life in matter is all that dies. The Principle, Soul, and Life of man, is not in the body, and cannot die. When Paul's optical sense yielded to science, the vision of Soul, he realized nothing could separate him from God; understanding as he did that the real man is never separated from the sweet sense and presence of Life and Love.

Chapter I. Natural Science.

A sick man is not a sinner above all others; and yet he is not the idea of God; weary of matter that claims so much suffering, the sick become more spiritually inclined, inasmuch as the belief of Life in matter begins to give up its ghosts; all error must finally yield to the Truth of man.

A wicked man is not an idea of God; he is nothing more than the belief that hatred, malice, pride, envy, hypocrisy, etc., are coupled with Life, God! but Life, Love, and Truth, never made a sick man, nor a sinner! the same fountain sendeth not forth sweet and bitter water. Life and its idea, are neither sick, nor sinning, but eternal and harmonious; never mingling with mortal man. The Scripture saith mortal man "is conceived in sin and brought forth in iniquity;" his origin is error, then, is it not? And this error the belief that man is an Intelligence, and creator, after "all was made that was made!" If all that worketh a lie is ultimately destroyed, this man must perish.

The *understanding* of Truth, and its *demonstration*, is eternal Life; a belief can never attain this. Contradicting all accepted theories on this subject, and diametrically opposing the evidences of personal sense, science comes "laying the axe at the root of the tree," and cutting down all that brings not forth good fruit; thence healing the sick, and casting out error. There is no escape from sin, sickness, and death, except on the Principle that God is the only Life and Intelligence of man. So long as we admit Life, sensation, and Intelligence in matter, man will be governed by his body, and at the mercy of death, sickness, and sin.

Harmony is not at the mercy of matter; nor happiness at the disposal of sense; nor Life at the command of death. Do you ask what proof have you there is no sensation in matter, or in other words, no personal sense? We have tested this statement in healing the sick sufficiently to find its Principle invariable. Our position is taken from proofs obtained through our own demonstration; and allowing their Principle to point higher, and acknowledging the relationship between the lower and higher demonstrations with the

Chapter I. Natural Science.

same logic, we say, three and three trillions are six trillions; in that we prove with smaller numbers that three added to three, make six. Because we believe sensation is nerves, it by no means proves this to be the case; the inebriate believes he finds pleasure in alcoholic drinks, and the sinner in sin. The thief believes he has made a gain in stealing; and the hypocrite in hiding himself; but the science of Life contradicts these false positions, and names them simply belief and error; thence, inferring, belief is error, and to understand God and man would destroy all belief, and give us the understanding of what constitutes being.

That pain and pleasure belong to the body is the error of earth, that never enters heaven where nothing is found that worketh a lie. Soul is the only living consciousness, and Soul neither sins, nor suffers; it is immortal, and error is mortal; but sin, sorrow, and sickness, are mortal, destroying themselves, because they are error. sickness and death are not the manifestations of Soul, Truth, or Life, hence they are not of God, and there is no other causation. The tares and wheat must be separated, the real and unreal blend not; happiness is real, and Truth is real, but error is unreal; sin and holiness, sickness and health, Life and death, proceed not from the same source. Life, health, and holiness, together with all harmonies, are Truth; sin, sickness, and death, are error, the opposite of Truth, harmony and Life, and these opposites never blend.

Electricity is not a vital fluid; but an element of mind, the higher link between the grosser strata of mind, named matter, and the more rarified called mind. The so- called destructive forces of matter, and the ferocity of man and beast are animal beliefs, that admit evil because they understand not good. All that is good is Soul; and its opposite is personal sense; the emanations of Soul are purity, harmony, and immortality; those of personal sense, impurity, discord, and death. Science brings to light Truth, and its supremacy, universal harmony, God's entirety, and matter's nothingness.

Chapter I. Natural Science.

Doctrines, theories, and knowledge, are but opinions and beliefs, the impressions and observations of personal sense, based on no Principle or fundamental Truth by which to work out harmony. When we reach immortality, we shall all learn Life is God, that matter is mortal, and that Spirit alone survives the wreck of time. Personal sense will make war on science, until Truth determines the conquest on the side of immutable right. Science reveals Truth; whereas, personal sense takes no cognizance of it; also, it reverses all the positions of sense, and tears away its foundations; hence, the enmity of mankind towards science, until it battles its way up by putting beliefs down. Deductions from a matter-basis are necessarily error; but science taking its positions from Intelligence, reaches man with harmony, and bears the reports only of Truth. These different causes are appreciated better when witnessing the effects of both, and taking science to heal the sick in contradistinction to drugs, electricity, etc., we learn the opposite results of Truth and Error. Systems of medicine, like narcotics, leave man worse, for the stupor they induce; while science demanding demonstration for its proof invites progress, and uses the understanding like a two-edged sword, to amputate error on all sides. After this surgery, mankind will find themselves better.

Doctrines, opinions and belief are the "tree of knowledge" against which Wisdom warned man; knowledge is obtained from false premises, from personal sense, that affords only the mortal evidences of man, presupposing Soul's audience- chamber the brain, falsely claiming the prerogatives of Intelligence, God. Reasoning from such stand-points produces all the discords of mind and body, that must eventually go down, obedient to the mandate, "Thou shalt surely die." Researches after Truth ought to leave matter for Principle, and bring the contemplation of Life outside of sense, thus gathering us nearer harmony and immortality, and proportionately away from sickness, sin, and death.

Soul is not in the body. The belief that Intelligence is in matter is error in the premises and conclusions of man. Life, Intelligence, or

Chapter I. Natural Science.

substance, is not in or of matter, neither can they be aught but Soul, and because we shall ultimately prove this science to individual consciousness, we should begin its first lessons to-clay. In order to gain the understanding of God and man, Soul and body, harmony and immortality, we must base all our conclusions of man on Principle instead of person, on Soul instead of body, or we shall never reach the science of being.

Truth, Life, and Love are God, the Soul of the universe and man, and the only substance and Intelligence: these are not mixed with change, sin, or death, nor with matter, the body mortal; the erring, changing and dying blend not with that which is the same yesterday, to-day, and forever. Life is Intelligence, the Principle that is Soul or Spirit, and there is but one Spirit or Soul of the universe and man. If Life was in man, matter would govern itself, and Spirit would be a portion of matter; therefore, God would be Spirit and matter. No portion of the Infinite can enter the finite; Life and Intelligence that are infinite are not mortal man. But may there not be a portion of God in man and matter? This is equally impossible, for the least part of Spirit would destroy matter, for matter is non-Intelligence, not a power matched against Spirit; it is mortality only, and the immortal is Spirit.

God is Principle, --the Truth, and Soul of man, and man is "the image and likeness of God." Again, God is substance and Life, hence man is but the image and likeness of these; man is not Truth, Life, or Love. God is Spirit, and man the image and likeness of Him; therefore, man is not matter, but idea, and idea no more contains its Principle than figures embrace the rule of mathematics. We have no resort but to reduce God to a level with man, or look away from man for his Substance, Life, and Intelligence, all of which must be outside of matter, or at the mercy of sin, sickness, and death. Darkness may hide the sun, but cannot put it out. Sickness, sin, and death are darkness, or moral ignorance that hide Truth, Life, and Love, but cannot extinguish them, or their idea cannot destroy God or man. The stand-point whence to reckon man is not matter, but

Chapter I. Natural Science.

Spirit. The Soul of man is never lost, insomuch as it is God, Principle, and man its idea, and both are eternal; hence the immortality of Soul and body. Infinite Soul embraces perfect understanding, the light that neither diminishes nor increases, for "no night is there." Day declines, and shadows hide the sun, but darkness flees when the earth has turned on its axis; because the solar centre is the same. Thus the darkness of belief hides, but cannot put out the light of science.

Soul is self-existent and eternal; that immortal man is tributary to Soul instead of body, is the science of being, but we shall never understand it, believing Soul is in the body, or that matter embraces Intelligence and Life. If we understood the Truth of being it would prove Principle and its idea, that is, Soul and body immortal; and instead of requiring laws of health that never yet made man immortal, to save Life, we should be a law of Life and Truth to our own bodies, even that higher law of Soul that prevails over sense, and gives harmony and immortality to all it controls. "Man hath sought out many inventions," but none of them can solve a problem without its Principle; numbers are harmonious only when governed by Intelligence, outside the figures; but ignorance might deny this fact did not self-evident proof force the conclusion. Understanding the science of Life, we gain unfailing evidence of its correctness in healing, etc. Those who obtain even glimpses of it are convinced of its Truth, and those who advance higher are more undoubting than of other proofs.

How can a belief of Life in matter find Life, God? This is not more possible than "for a camel to go through the eye of a needle." To inquire of our bodies what prospect we have for health or Life, is taking the thing out of the hands of God altogether.

To suppose we find pleasure or pain, happiness or misery, Life or death in the body, is not finding God our Life, and "a present help in times of trouble;" also, to admit the same fountain sendeth forth sweet and bitter water, is contrary to our Master's teachings. Life

Chapter I. Natural Science.

supposed to originate in soil and seed, in animality, or the earth, is a belief of Life only, and not the Principle that is Life, without beginning or end of days. Belief is mortality's self, nothing whatever but illusion; we have no doubt but belief could make its mortal man an amphibious animal. Phenomena illustrative of our views will appear as the ages waken from the dream of Life in matter: belief can adopt any position, strange and new, but Life will be found less at the mercy of matter, as belief gives up the ghost, and the science of Life is sufficiently understood to be fairly demonstrated; then man will be found immortal.

Spirit controls matter; when this is fairly understood, phenomena at present so unaccountable to a belief holding Soul pent up in body, will be explained, and mystery and miracle fast disappear. A belief of Life in matter leaves man at the mercy of death, for if this belief should change to one of death he is supposed to die, but the fact remains that man is immortal, and if death in matter or the body, be proved false, Life in matter or the body is proved false also.

The true relation of Soul to body is that of God to man; in other words, of Principle to its idea; these are forever inseparable; and when the true idea, which is the immortal body, is perceptible, we shall have become acquainted with its Principle; "therefore, acquaint now thyself with God."

A sweet combination of sounds informs man this is not governed by chance; that harmony is not accident; we have undeniable proof that the Intelligence producing music, separating light from darkness, etc., guides and controls all. The belief that man is the Intelligence that governs sound, would destroy harmony; for music left to personal sense is at the mercy of misapprehension and discord; controlled by belief instead of the understanding, it would be lost; even thus man would be discord and death without a governing Principle, or left to personal sense. God and man are Principle and idea, and God is the Truth, Life and Love controlling this idea. Then what can separate man from harmony and immortality? St. Paul says: "Neither height nor depth nor any other creature can separate me from the love of God." Love cannot be debarred a manifestation, and is joy and not sorrow, good and not evil, Life and not death; hence the perfect idea God gave of Himself in immortal man, the object of divine affections.

Soul and body are Principle and idea, or God and man united indissolubly, but the man of God is the good and perfect idea of Him governed by Soul instead of sense. This idea expresses the sinless and infinite; not the finite and dying.

Anatomy and theology never defined the man of God; the first, explains the man of man; the second, bow to make this man a Christian, whose life held in matter is separated from God. These are some of the beliefs that serve as mile-stones to point out the rough places science must make smooth. The man of sin, sickness, and death is not, "the image and likeness" of Love, Truth and Life; and all the vanity of the Gentiles, and doctrines preached under the sun, can never make that man immortal, or the image of God. Science lays the axe at the root of error and cutting down the belief of Life in matter, of Soul in body, and God in man, exchanges fable for fact, turns thought into new channels away from personality to Principle, through which alone man is able to reach life.

For Life to be eternal, it must be self-existent, therefore independent of matter; even the "I am" that was, and is, and that nothing can efface. Christ said, "I am the resurrection and Life." Man is not saved in matter, but out of it in God. Denying personal sense, having but one God, taking up the cross and following Christ, Truth, is the only Christianity, but doctrines and creeds have little to do with this.

Life, substance, and Intelligence are Soul outside of personal sense; what appears to be these in man, is simply a belief and dream of Life in matter; the unreal, that is the opposite of the real. The figurative "Tree of Life" was the Principle of man bringing forth

Chapter I. Natural Science.

fruits of immortality. Sin, sickness, and death are the fruits of the "tree of knowledge;" and the Scripture instructs us to judge of the tree by its fruits.

The resistance to metaphysical science will yield slowly but surely; we had sanguine hopes of its present prosperity until we learned its vastness, the fixedness of folly, and man's hatred of Truth. Not through the footsteps of personal sense do we gain Wisdom; the infinite is achieved only as we turn from the finite, and from the personal error to the impersonal Truth of being. Until the scientific relationship between God and man is perceived, and its radical points admitted, we cannot reach the demonstration of which it is capable. Exchange our stand-point of Intelligence and Life, from matter to Spirit, and we shall gain the perfect Life; and the control that Soul holds over body, and receive Christ, Truth, in Principle and not person, and through the understanding and not belief. This is the difficult point, but it must be achieved before man is harmonious and immortal, and to gather our thoughts in this direction to-day is highly important, in view of the vast amount to be accomplished before the final recognition of Life outside of matter. If we make no progress toward the science of Life here, the hereafter will strip off our rags of error, leaving us naked, until we are clothed upon by Truth, the immortality of man.

Not understanding the Principle of being, we shall seek in another world happiness in sense, and then, as now, receive sorrow instead of gladness; because of this error; pain, sickness, sin, and death, will continue so long as the belief remains of Life, happiness, and Intelligence in the body. If the change called death dispossessed man of the belief of pleasure and pain in the body, universal happiness were secure at the moment of dissolution; but this is not so: "they that are filthy shall be filthy still"; every sin and error we possess at the moment of death, remains after it the same as before, and our only redemption is in God, the Principle of man that destroys the belief of intelligent bodies. When we gain the freedom of the Sons of God, we shall master sense with Soul. As progress

Chapter I. Natural Science.

compels this ripening process through which man resigns the belief of Life and Intelligence in matter, there will be great tribulation such as has not been since the beginning.

When pleasures of sense perish, they are taken away through anguish, even the amputation of right hands, and plucking out of right eyes. Man at ease in error, when stricken suddenly down by death, cannot understand Life. Mortal man knows nothing about Life that is learned by relinquishing pleasure and pain of sense; and how long the pangs necessary for error's amputation continue, depends on the tenacity of the belief of happiness in personal sense. When remembering God is our only Life, and contemplating our present adherence to the belief of Life in matter, we may well tremble for the days in which we shall say, "I have no pleasure in them." The false views entertained of pardoned sin, or universal and immediate happiness in the midst of sin, or, that we are changed in a moment from sin to holiness, are grave mistakes. To suddenly drop our earthly character, and become partakers of eternal Life, without the pangs of a new birth, is morally impossible. We know, "all will be changed in the twinkling of an eye when the last trump shall sound," but the last call of Wisdom is not the first call in the growth of Christian character; while man is selfish, unjust, hypocritical and sensual, to conclude the last call of Wisdom has been heard that awakens him to glorified being, is preposterous! Science forbids such feats of imagination, and looks us in the face with reason and revelation.

"As the tree falleth, so shall it lie;" as man goeth to sleep so shall he waken; when the belief of death closes our eyes on this phase of the dream of Life in matter, we shall waken, not to a final judgment or resurrection, not with a single change in character, but for the same judgment of Wisdom to go on in process of purification as before, until Truth finally destroys error. When the final triumph of Soul over sense is achieved, the last trump has sounded, and not until then; this hour "no man knoweth, not the son but the Father;" here prophecy steps and proof is wanting; but science sees beyond

Chapter I. Natural Science.

the grave the certainty of immortality. The science of Life is the only certainty of existence. Truth is harmony and immortality. Universal salvation holds its grounds on the basis of progression, in which case man cannot commence too soon the severest lessons of science, whereby to gain happiness and immortality. Heaven is not a local habitation, but the harmony of mind and body; and we obtain this not of belief, but understanding, not of sense, but science. From the sudden surprise of finding all that is mortal, unreal, a belief only, without creation or Truth, the question arises, who or what is it that believes.

We have before said God is the only Intelligence and cannot believe because He understands. There is neither substance nor Intelligence, in the mountain mirage that seemeth what it is not, and such is mortal man; nor in a face reflected from the mirror; but such is not immortal man the image of God. Intelligence is Soul and not sense, Spirit and not matter, and God is the only Intelligence, and there is but one God, hence there are no believers! So far as this statement is understood will it be admitted, and the true idea of God, which is the only real man, will appear to the understanding, and the old belief of Intelligence and Life in matter, named by Paul "the old man," will disappear or "be put off," for "dust thou art and unto dust shalt thou return;" man never dies, it is only a belief of man.

Apprehending God the only Life and Intelligence of man, is the foundation of harmony, but to gain this understanding of Soul, the Principle that gave man dominion over earth, 'tis necessary to understand one's-self Spirit, and not matter. Jesus established his demonstration in healing the sick, etc., on this very basis, thereby holding all being and prerogative Soul, and not personal sense. Reason is right only when starting from cause instead of effect, from Soul instead of sense; conclusions based on the evidences of personal sense are drawn from mortality.

'Ology and 'ism tend to the conviction that God who is universal cause, is effect also, insomuch as they all make Intelligence moral and physical, or mind and matter. The time has come to separate the belief of personal sense on the one hand, from science on the other; hitherto man has called on man to interpret God, and on matter and its supposed laws, to heal the sick; but as progress compels the change, we shall seek outside of personal sense in the Principle of things, their true interpretation and remedy. To seek Truth through belief is to ask the changing and erring for the immutable and immortal; or to call belief Truth, is ignorance of God. We learn from the Scripture "God is Love," and this certainly is Principle instead of a person; hence God should be understood and demonstrated: belief can neither explain Principle nor demonstrate God. To understand, instead of believe, what most concerns our happiness, is essential, and to know we are right cannot be construed irreverence to Truth.

Our Master ventured to say he was "Truth and Life, and no man cometh unto the Father" (the Principle of his being) "except through me," Truth. Principle is the Father of man, and science alone reveals Principle, hence it is the "Comforter" that leads into all Truth. Jesus regarded himself Principle instead of person: hear his words: "I am the way, the *Truth*, and *Life*."

God is the Soul of man and the only Intelligence, Life or Substance: and man is the reflex shadow of God. Belief is error, and mortal man is a belief: understanding is Intelligence; belief is personal sense, the so-called mind of matter; understanding is Soul, which is Spirit, belief is knowledge and that which said, "I will make ye as gods," is mortal error, alias mortal man. Wisdom said of knowledge, "In the clay thou eatest thereof thou shalt surely die." Christianity is God understood and demonstrated. There is no death in Truth, and *vice versa*. Error is mortal; the very opposite of Truth and its idea which is the perfect and immortal man and universe. Doctrines and theories placing God in man, Soul in body, are founded on belief, and are the offspring of personal sense. We entertain no belief with regard to what we understand, and cannot demonstrate what is not understood. When Soul is accepted as the only Intelligence, we shall depend on this ever-present Truth to

Chapter I. Natural Science.

control its own body; and to understand this Principle of man, is indispensable to his harmony; to know we are Soul and not body is starting right.

Matter is not substance, if God is substance; for matter and Spirit are not one. Which shall be substance, the erring, mutable and mortal, or the changeless, unerring and immortal. Soul is Spirit and Spirit the only substance, insomuch as it is the Principle of man, and the universe. To regard matter a law of itself, or produced by Intelligence is error. Matter is change, decay, and death, and Principle is not in decay, Life is not in death, Soul is not in body. God is not in the things He hath made, and all that he hath made is "good." If Soul was in body, Spirit and matter were one; but Soul is not personal sense, and *vice versa*. God is the Principle, or Soul of all that is real, and nothing is real that does not express Him and is controlled by Him, and immortal. Soul is lost sight of by personal sense, but cannot be lost in science. There is neither growth, maturity, nor decay to Soul: these are the mutations of sense, the clouds before Soul that we call substance, but they are only vapor. Metaphysically speaking, a belief of Life in matter is what might be termed a loss of Soul; for seeking Life and happiness in error, we lose right of Truth.

The idea of God, is the heaven, earth, and immortal man that is unerring, and eternal, because they are controlled by Principle, that is, by Soul, and not sense, by understanding and not belief. That which is mortal, is a dream of Life, Intelligence and substance in matter; a belief that idea creates Principle, and shadow substance! In this error Truth is lost; in other words, error loses sight of Soul or the Principle of man, and a belief of intelligent matter takes the place of the science of man. Soul is self- existent, the forever "I am," that enters not into sin and mortality. The parent of all discord is this strange hypothesis, that Soul is in body, and Life in matter; this error spreads its table with sickness, sin and death, and partakes of its own bounty. In the resurrection of understanding, Life, Soul, and substance will be recognized one and outside of matter, and the

Chapter I. Natural Science.

Intelligence of all that is immortal. The idea of Life is embraced in Soul and not sense, in the immortal and not the mortal.

The most scientific man of whom we have any record, Jesus of Nazareth, called the mortal body that we suppose substance, "ghost"; and his body that others called spirit, "flesh and bones"; showing that substance to his understanding was the deathless Principle that embraces man and is forever inseparable from Soul. But the Jews, strongly material, called the real idea of God, even the body that was not matter, a spirit or ghost; and the body they laid in a sepulchre, substance. By this error they lost logic and Truth, therefore lost sight of Jesus at the very moment when he presented more then ever the real idea of God, and because of this belief, the idea was taken from them. The higher he wrought the problem of being through spiritual science, the more odious he became to the materialistic world that understood him not. Life, Intelligence and substance to them were matter, but to him they were God, the Truth of man; therefore he reckoned himself not matter but Spirit; not sense, but Soul. Said he, "Spirit hath not flesh and bones as ye see me have," but this be said three days after his burial, before relinquishing the belief of substance-matter; after that, his disciples even could not see him. Jesus said, "I and the Father are one," and this separated him from theology and the Rabbis: understanding himself Soul instead of body, and that Soul was God, brought down upon him the anathemas of a world. This statement of himself understood in science, was, that Life, substance, and Intelligence, are not man, but God, not body, but Soul; reversing this, belief could not see the idea of Truth or harmonious man; and the sinning, sick and mortal error that crucified Jesus, occupied the place of God's idea. Mortal and sinful man is not the product of God; sin and death never proceeded from Life, Love and Truth.

Matter being unintelligent, there is no material law governing man and the universe, and Spirit is free by divine right. Soul is the master of man and matter. Truth is not learned through laws of matter; for there are no such laws: matter is not a law-giver. Wisdom

Chapter I. Natural Science.

demanded man "to hold dominion over earth," and all things therein, making him obedient only to higher law. The Truth of man saith be is superior to matter; but the opposite error says, he is inferior to it. Truth says: "I give you power over all things, that nothing shall by any means harm you;" "power to handle serpents, to take deadly drugs," etc. But while our missionaries are carrying the Bible to Hindustan, and explaining it according to a belief, hundreds are dying annually of the bite of serpents. Creeds and ritualism never enable us to follow Jesus' example, and give the demonstration he gave of God. Life cannot be separated from its idea; therefore Soul and body, God and man, are inseparable. All good proceeds from God in the order and harmony of science; evil is its opposite, or knowledge, that proceeds from personal sense, and usurps the place of Wisdom.

The thirty thousand different readings given the Old, and the three hundred thousand the New Testament, account for the discrepancies that sometimes appear in the Scriptures. The science of the Bible is manifest from Genesis to Revelations, and the demonstration that Jesus gave, conclusive evidence of its entire Truth. The opposite of sickness, sin, and death, Jesus knew was alone able to destroy them, and bring to light immortality. This was the platform on which he labored, and cast out devils, viz.; destroy the belief of Intelligence and Life in matter, and it caste out all error, and heals the sick. This was Truth, and "the stone the builders rejected," while yet it must become the head of the comer, this the rock on which Christ, Truth, built its church, that the gates of bell (the beliefs of man) cannot prevail against.

"The image and likeness of God" was lost sight of through belief, and is regained only through understanding. To suppose laws of matter control man, is the error it would be to say that figures govern numbers, when we should find examples wrought on this plan would cause the figures to be erased that the Principle might be allowed to reproduce its own idea. Harmonious man is the immortal idea of God; but the inharmonious is mortal belief. The voice of

Chapter I. Natural Science.

Truth, calls: "Man, where art thou?" and who will meet this inquiry today, with the answer of science? Man is safe in Soul, the Principle of being, but out of this he is "a reed shaken with the wind," the ignis fatuus of belief, tossed about with every wind of doctrine; until the body is sensationless through science, man is not safe; every feeling there betrays where he holds himself; every pain and pleasure of sense, every hope, ambition, and joy that has its foundation in matter, reckons against the science of our course, and must be destroyed. Man, where art thou? is met with reply from the head, the heart, stomach, blood, nerves, etc.; "Lo! here thou art;" looking for happiness and Life in matter, but finding pain and death.

To conclude Life, Love, and Truth are attributes of a personal Deity, implies there is something in person superior to Principle. But nothing is wiser than Wisdom, or truer than Truth; and Life, and Love, have no superlatives, they are primitives and not derivatives. Person is not the Principle of goodness, and the reality, or Spirit, is ours only as we are good. Jesus sought Wisdom of no man, and said: "Call no man Father, for one is your Father, even God," thus regarding man begotten of Soul, and not sense; and controlling matter and triumphing over disease and death, he brought to light his Principle and the immortality of man.

To test our understanding is to put it in practice; if we possess Truth, we shall live truly, but personal sense never aids man in this direction, but wars against spirituality. 'Tis not in all the vanity of the Gentiles to send a drop of rain, or to make a mortal body the idea of God. The example Jesus presented for us to follow, and the Principle he demonstrated in healing, etc. was beyond question, science; but the error of past and present ages is our wrong interpretation, of Jesus and Christ, or man and God. Taught by some doctrine, or belief, that Principle is in person, and Soul in body, we have "gods many," and our standard of Truth changes hands. Our Master taught his students the demonstration of Christianity was not alone in the beatitudes of the Mount, but in healing the sick, also.

Chapter I. Natural Science.

When Moses, the ancient law giver of Wisdom, despaired of making the people understand what God, through science, said to him, the supreme Soul bade him cast down his rod, and it became a serpent, and be fled at first before the serpent, but afterwards took it up, proving his power over it. And "the hand that was made leprous as snow," lie put into his bosom again and plucked it out, and behold it was as his other flesh, and Wisdom said: "It shall come to pass if they will not hear thee, neither harken to the voice of the first sign, that they will believe the voice of the latter;" that is, they will listen to its interpretation, when they see its demonstration in healing. Jesus also said in his answer to John's inquiry, "Art then be that should come?" "Go and show John again these things ye see and hear; the blind receive their sight, the lame walk, etc., and blessed is he who shall not be offended in me; " in other words, who shall not deny that this is the demonstration of Truth. Jesus said to his followers: "Go ye into all the world, heal the sick," etc., and this was enjoined not on his disciples alone, but on all Christendom; wherefore, said he: "Neither pray I for these alone, but for them, who shall understand through the word." "In the beginning was the Word, and the Word was God," the Principle of all being; hence it was not a person, to be understood, or that healed the sick, neither mediumship, mesmerism, nor drugs, but the Principle, that is, Life and Truth.

In the original Scriptures, metaphor abounded, and proper names were significant of spiritual ideas, The authors of Smith's Bible Dictionary say, "The spiritual interpretation of the Scripture must rest upon both the literal and moral." In the original it was written: "Jehovah said, my spirit shall not forever be humbled in man, seeing that they are, or in error they are but flesh." The science of man was not forever to be cast aside in explaining him, seeing that man in error was mortal. But how are we to escape from flesh, or mortality, except through the change called death? By understanding we never were flesh, that we are Spirit and not matter.

Chapter I. Natural Science.

When the belief that we inhabit a body is destroyed, we shall live, but our body will have no sensation. We shall find God in God, that is, Spirit in Spirit, and Intelligence in itself, there will be no loss of science as in mixing different species; and not until the belief that Soul is in body, and Intelligence in matter, is destroyed, will man be found immortal. The so-called man that is mortal, is a compound error made up of many beliefs, and while the science of being is mastering one, another presents itself. In these chemical changes we find it not so easy to overcome sin as sickness, for the dream continues of pleasure in personal sense, when the belief of pain is willingly relinquished, and vice versa. Thus the way is straight and narrow that leads to Life, inasmuch as it is a warfare with the flesh.

The science of the original word not being apprehended by the age in which the Scriptures were written, was not explained; a single misplaced preposition would change its scientific meaning from Principle to person; e.g., wisdom the principle of God; instead of Wisdom, the Principle, God. From the original quotations, it appears the Scriptures were not understood by those who re-read and re-wrote them. The true rendering was their spiritual sense. Before knowledge increased some of the Soul-inspired patriarchs gave good proofs of understanding God. Jacob wrestled with a man, that is, strove against the belief of Life and Intelligence in matter, "until day-break;" until the light of science shone upon his understanding, enabling him to restore the shrank sinew; this was the spiritual sense; the literal-- the hour of dawn. The shrank sinew he restored, understanding simply that he possessed control over matter, and that man is immortal, the image and likeness of God, that cannot lose one jot of its completeness. When Jacob became the demonstrator, even in a limited capacity of this Truth, he was named Israel, the chosen of Wisdom, and thereafter those building on this foundation, were of the house of Israel.

Why Jesus of Nazareth stood higher in the scale of being, and rose proportionately beyond other men in demonstrating God, we impute to his spiritual origin. He was the offspring of Soul, and not

Chapter I. Natural Science.

sense; yea, the Son of God. The science of being was revealed to the virgin mother, who, in part proved the great Truth, that God is the only origin of man. The conception of Jesus illustrated this Truth, and finished the example of creation. Jesus was the idea of this Principle, but born of woman, that is, having in part a personal origin, he blended the idea of Life, that is God, with the belief of Life in matter, and became the connecting link between science and personal sense; "and took upon himself flesh," became apparent as the half-way position of positive science; thus to mediate between God and man; in other words, to present the idea of God that revealed Life outside of matter, in contradistinction to the belief of Life in matter, and demonstrated the Truth that man is idea and not substance, that God is all and in all, and the Principle of man that controls matter. Jesus walked the wave, stilled the tempest, and yet, this idea of God was not comprehended by those who deemed God a person, and Life in matter, and man substance and Intelligence.

"And if Christ (Truth) be not risen, then is my preaching vain;" that is, if it be not understood that God is the only Life, then are the explanations of Jesus vain. Again, the Scriptures saith, "I am the resurrection and Life, he that believeth in me shall not see death;" in other words, he that understands Soul is God, the only Life and Intelligence of man, that the body has not a separate being, but hath Life abiding only in Spirit, shall never die. This idea of Truth was literally scourged by the Rabbis, over eighteen centuries ago; "despised and rejected of men," while yet it bore their infirmities, healed their sicknesses, raised the dead, and sat down at the right hand of the Father, was embraced in the Principle of man, that wrought out the harmony of the universe. As of old, the Pharisees thrust this idea from their synagogues, and the learned Jews sought to kill Jesus; so to-day, church and state unconscious of the re-appearing of this idea of Truth, would silence what cometh, as of old, doing good to its enemies, casting out error, healing the sick and bringing freedom and salvation to man. Prophesying its rejection, Christ said, "when I come again, shall I find faith on earth?"

Chapter I. Natural Science.

To control our bodies, Paul said, was our only reasonable service, but who can presume to reach the sublime bights of our Master, who is begotten of sense, or a servant to it? The time cometh when the true origin of man will be regained, being understood. Truth, like the light, shineth on darkness, that is, first on belief and opinions, and the darkness (or belief) comprehendeth it not, then on the advanced thought, etc., until it is understood. Truth is ruled out by belief, inasmuch as it rules out a personal God, and Life, and Intelligence in matter, and restores the scientific origin of man, and the only true demonstration of God; it is ruled out by materia medica, insomuch as it rules out drugs, one of the errors that saith, Intelligence and Life are in matter. The science of man and the universe understood, would divest drugs of all efficacy, control matter, and bear man over the wave despite the fable of solids and fluids; but alas! who can test the Principle of this saying today; this Truth is the stranger within our gates that is not remembered, while its elevating proof is ready to show practically its honest merit.

Jesus never spake of disease as difficult or dangerous, but of having authority over it. He recommended not obedience to the so-called laws of matter, and in his opposite teachings the Scripture saith: --"He uttered things that had been secret from the foundation of the world," unperceived since knowledge had usurped man's government; hence, Truth cometh to-day bringing not peace, but a sword. Our master forbore not to declare the whole Truth; even the impersonal God, though it severely amputated error, set households at variance, etc. Whosoever, therefore, shall declare what he taught, must accept the hatred of error, and find peace and confidence in the realization that Wisdom is acknowledged only by her children. Realizing all this, the Master said, "If the world hate you, ye may know that it hated me before it hated you." This was the blessed test, benediction and consolation he offered his followers.

Doctrines, opinions and beliefs, the so-called laws of matter, remedies for Soul and body, physiology, theology, materia medica, etc. are error, the very opposites of what Jesus taught and

Chapter I. Natural Science.

demonstrated, regarding Soul and body, or God and man. This may seem severe, but is said with honest convictions of its Truth, with reverence for God and love for man. The door to the sheep-fold through which we gain God shuts them all out. Those who would follow Christ, Truth, heal the sick, etc., through doctrines and beliefs, or matter remedies, are climbing up another way, and unconsciously, though it be, robbing God. Life, Love, and Truth, our Father which art in heaven, teaches man health, happiness, and immortality. Our only rightful law-giver is God, fulfilling all law in righteousness, and visiting not on man the penalty of sin, except for moral transgression; but destroying sin, and death, and triumphing over the grave.

Materia medica, anatomy, and physiology, together with every belief that spake from "the tree of knowledge," would give death and the grave victory over man. But Jesus said to his followers: --"I give you power over all things, that nothing shall by any means harm you;" the true idea of God took away the sting of death, mastered sickness and sin, and caused the lion to lie down with the lamb, even the beliefs that would rob God, to fall at the feet of Love.

If man tarries in the storm until the body be frozen; or rushes into the flames and it be devoured; this is Dot obedience to the Wisdom that gave him "dominion over earth;" unless we understand how to avoid such results, we should keep from their occasion; to do otherwise is the blunder a pupil in addition would make to attempt to solve a problem of Euclid, and because he has not reached this point in mathematics, to fail in his demonstration, and others perceiving this, to deny the Principle of the problem. Jesus taught Truth, and demonstrated it, and the result of this was, it healed the sick, and cast out error.

Christ is God, the Principle and Soul of the man Jesus; constituting Christ-Jesus, that is, Principle and idea. But the person of our Master was not less tangible or real, because "his Life was hid with Christ in God," that is, because he held Life, Soul, and not

Chapter I. Natural Science.

sense; this put all things under his feet, giving him triumph over matter, and the body, over sin, sickness, and death. Holding himself in science, death was lost to Him in infinite Life, and Jesus the idea of Christ, Truth, was as deathless as this its Principle. This scientific understanding of being gave him control over matter, enabling him to heal the sick and cast out the opposite belief that makes matter, or the body, the master of man turned the water into wine; fed the multitude, etc. and finally triumphed over death, and presented to his students the body they thought buried in a sepulchre; that body, however, had not risen, which was their dead belief of him. The print of the nails and spear alone convinced Thomas, who would lean on personal sense instead of Soul, for proofs of immortality; but when partially aroused from the error, or dream of Life in matter, to the scientific understanding of Soul and body, or God and man, exclaimed, in awe, "My Lord, and my God!"

Man is the idea of his Principle, and only as the image and likeness of Intelligence and Life, substance and Spirit, is he beyond the reach of death, in the science of being, where nothing can harm or destroy him; of that which is materialized it can only be said, "dust thou art and unto dust shalt thou return."

When the sharp experiences of supposed Life in matter, its disappointments, and ceaseless woes, turn us from it as a tired child to a home in the bosom of Love, then are we fit to understand Life apart from vanity and lies; but without this weaning process, "who by searching can find out God?" If through the wholesome discipline of chastisement we become His children, understanding in part, righteousness and purity, we behold the Truth of spiritual science, where enraptured thought walks boundless, and conception unconfined has wings to reach its glory. But to gain Truth and Life, we must not only seek, but "strive to enter in;" and the strife consists in destroying the error of personal sense; but here we learn 'tis easier to desire Truth than to get rid of error.

Chapter I. Natural Science.

Theories of a personal God, based on the false premises of Life and Intelligence in matter, must yield to science; and the dream of sense, to the Life that is Soul. We must leave the foundations of time-honored systems, to gain Christ, Truth; come out from the world and be separate, or we have no part and lot in this matter. The so-called laws material, presuppose body and Soul one for a period, until separated by a temporary law of divorcement to come together again at some uncertain future, and in a manner wholly unknown; which is even less logical than annihilation.

To be sure, the Sadducees reasoned falsely on the resurrection, but not more so than the Pharisees! When we admit the immortality of Soul, we have admitted the immortal body, also, for if Soul can be separated from man, Principle can be severed from its idea, which is fatal to a self-existent Intelligence, and equal to saying there may be a time when God is without a single expression of Himself. We ask instinctively for something beyond the things of personal sense, and whence cometh these unsatisfied cravings for immortality?

Pleasures of sense are broken reeds, that pierce us to the heart; but the joys of Soul are imperishable, and attainable even here, for the hereafter commences here; to-morrow grows out of to-day. We cannot realize the Truth of being in a moment; but we can let go somewhat the belief that would fasten immortal Soul within a mortal body. The motive to realize Life and happiness apart from sense, may be gained to-day, and this point won, we have started light to admit a greater influx of light. The realization of Truth is sometimes sudden and severe, as it came of old to Saul of Tarsus, when personal sense was blind he beheld the vision of Soul, "what eye hath not seen or ear heard."

We will specify three of the footsteps that enter in by the door, or enable us to become receptive of Truth. First. To become as a little child in that we are willing to leave the old for the new, and look beyond landmarks, theories, doctrines, and beliefs, pleasures or pains of sense; but here we must watch that we receive not Truth from person, but Principle; the test being, that whatever cometh from Truth is demonstrable, and brings forth good fruits; our lives must testify to this. Secondly. Purity is the foundation of the science of Life; "None but the pure in heart shall see God." Inspiration is the highest means to convey messages from Principle to idea, i.e., from God to man; but these messages are never borne into matter, therefore to be recipient of Truth, we must begin to recognize ourselves Soul, and not body, and receive and impart the teachings of Spirit. Such messages are angels, but not winged messengers; they are the aroma of Soul passing to man, the impressions that guide him aright, and are demonstrable when understood, and not understood unless demonstrated. Thirdly. To rightly apprehend and receive more Truth, we must put into practice what we already possess. This higher understanding of the relationship between God and man will not be recognized by the opposite belief of Life and Intelligence in matter. And the explanations or the wholesome rebukes of our Father, even Wisdom and Love, will often be deemed severity; but we must avoid the yielding to error demanded by error; remembering Love often moves the sinner to hate, in that it stirs this opposite element before destroying it; and not until the sinner and the sick feel their need of Truth to save them from sickness or sin, will they become receptive of it.

It will be seen in scientific statement that gender belongs to Principle, and not person; that all formation is through Intelligence, because Life is Soul outside of sense. This is the stepping- stone to the understanding of Soul which, to know aright is eternal Life; man is immortal only as the idea of God, and not as a belief of Life or Soul in the body. Love is God; but error would couple Love and hate together; vainly thinking to mingle good and evil. Soul's attraction is Truth; but the attraction of sense is error. The former elevates and immortalizes man, the latter debases and makes mortal. The two cannot blend; one rules out the other as light shuts out darkness and darkness light. God is not in matter, and there is neither Life, Intelligence nor Truth where He is not; the body we

Chapter I. Natural Science.

call man is matter. Love is safe in Truth, but not in man, safe in Principle, but not person.

Does Wisdom find pleasure in drunkenness? But personal sense does! and you cannot make the inebriate we call man averse to foul besottedness until this belief is destroyed; when he will turn as naturally from his cup, as the dreamer from incubus. Tell a man intoxication will kill him, cause him to believe this, and possibly it will deter him from listening to this lie of personal sense, viz., that there is pleasure in intoxication; but is he reformed? Abstinence, if it cherishes the desire for intemperance, is not reformation; and this so-called man will fall again whenever the fear is removed. The fear of punishment in time or eternity never made an honest man; it is not a scientific position; moral courage instead of fear is requisite to overcome sin and sickness. But how reform the sensualist through conscience? He traffics little in this commodity; has even less Soul because he has more personal sense than some of the lower animals. They could teach him affection! but convince his reason that is above the brutes, of the nothingness of personal sense, and you have saved him.

Reasoning incorrectly on Soul and body, leads to error of action; understanding the science of being explains personal sense and also destroys it; in science you cannot be a hypocrite in secret even; you will become spiritual, find happiness in the moral resources of being and in Love that is Truth; even as the babe finds peace and nutriment from the mother's bosom. To waken from the dream of personal sense, or pleasure and pain in matter, is the work of time and eternity. The greater your error the harder its struggle will be with Truth when it touches it. The aged are not old when the vail lifts, and sense gives place to Soul. But the hoary error must be met and mastered in time or eternity, and would have been easier controlled in its youth. Man never obtains immortality until the standpoint whence he reckons himself in all the summing up of Life and Intelligence, is Soul and not sense. What a pitiful sight is malice finding pleasure in revenge! 'tis sad to think evil is man's highest

Chapter I. Natural Science.

belief of good until his grasp on goodness grows stronger. We should naturally shrink from madness that rushes forth to clamor with midnight and the tempest. All error is the image of the beast that must be effaced by the sweat of agony, before the crown is laid upon the brow.

A picture on the camera, or a face reflected from the mirror is not substance; then why do we name man substance, and contradict the Scripture that saith man is the image and likeness of God? We know the face and form of a man reflected from the mirror is not man, that he is not in the shadow of himself; hence the error to suppose the Intelligence, substance and Life of man, are man, or in him. Again, who believes that gender belongs to the man in the mirror? Gender is Principle and not person, and man is shadow and not substance; why he is mortal to personal sense, is because it supposes him substance, Life and Intelligence. Mortal man is but a dream of Intelligence, substance and Life in matter, not the man of God, but the man of man, and shadow of shadows, therefore he reflects no Principle, and is without any real basis. To personal sense science is presumptive logic; nevertheless it reveals Truth: the ultimatum of being corroborates the statement that man is shadow and not substance; we are daily hastening to this proof, and must reach its recognition to gain immortality, for the Truth of man alone makes him immortal. The belief, that Soul is in body, turns to matter instead of Spirit for help in times of trouble, and with reluctant consent acknowledges a supreme being.

Theology embraces no creed or faith sufficient to heal the sick, while our master made this the first article of his faith, and proved that faith by works.

It seems ancient Christianity adhered more to Jesus' teachings than modern systems of religion do. Diplomas have rendered it fashionable to appeal to drugs before God; and the result is stereotyped beliefs originating in knowledge, "that forbidden tree,"

Chapter I. Natural Science.

and wanting in the vital point whereby Jesus demonstrated Christianity in the control Soul holds over sense.

The so-called man, born to-day and dying to-morrow, as if something was newly created, and lost, is a dream and illusion! and this definition of him is not more contradictory to personal sense than science demands. The Scriptures inform us clearly on this point. John declares--"All things were made by God, and without Him there was nothing made that was made." This plainly denies any new existence in the past or present, or any creation except what sprang directly from God, the Intelligence that made man; hence we have the authority of Scripture for saying, mortal man and woman since appearing are unreal, a belief only, and illusion.

The question is, did John understand the science that was the basis of his statement? He certainly foresaw its Principle and partly demonstrated it, thus proving his claim to make that statement. The master instructs us, our proof of Truth is the fruit it bears; and the science of being destroying sin, sickness, and death, demonstrates itself Truth.

It is presumptuous to conclude Love, Wisdom and Truth created what is unfit to be eternal. And when did Truth ever destroy its own idea. God cannot destroy man because he is the reflection of God, therefore Christ, Truth, casting out sin, healing the sick, and destroying death, prove these are not of God. The only certainty of immortality is found in the relationship between Principle and idea, i.e., God and man, Soul and body; Life, Love and Truth, the triune Principle, created nothing to be blotted out; because God made man he is immortal. That the sick, sinning, and dying are not "made by Him," we learn of the science of being, and through the demonstrations of Jesus.

There are but two realities, viz., God, and the idea of God; in other words, Spirit, and what it shadows forth. Theology teaches supreme love to God, and this is a glorious privilege, but we cannot

Chapter I. Natural Science.

love God supremely and personal sense or matter more. God is Love, and affections are the offspring of Soul. The understanding of Life outside of matter is the basis of Christianity by which the flesh is denied, the cross taken up, and the guidance of personal sense exchanged for Principle that makes perfect. Doctrines and theories of Life in matter, Soul in body, and God in man, are virtually atheism that must fall to the ground, and those are the days wherein there will be tribulations, such as has not been since the beginning of this belief. Earth will echo back the shock when the cry goes forth, "Why art thou (Truth) come hither to torment me before the time?" The belief of Life in matter results in the belief of death. Life demonstrates Life, and not death, but Life is God, and none but the pure in heart shall see God. Personal sense affords no evidence, not the smallest idea of Truth, Life or Love. Messages of Soul are man's teachers, and these are inspirations not borne into matter, but the outside Intelligence, where Spirit is, and speaks to man. We must recognize ourself Soul, and not body, and outside the body, else Soul is deemed subject to matter, mortality, sin, and death. But in order to do this we must grow away from all that is error and become pure in Spirit to receive or impart the lessons of Spirit.

The messages from God to man, in other words, from Principle to idea, are purity, the atmosphere of Soul, not winged messengers, but that whereby we gain the idea of spiritual man, in the science of his being; the inspirations of truth that are demonstrable when understood, and never understood until demonstrated. Truth is practical, not theoretical, and we shall never have more until we practice what we already have. Not until the sick and the sinner feel their need of Truth that saves from sickness, sin and death, will they apprehend it. Understanding the Truth of Man's being is all that can make him harmonious or immortal, and is the stepping-stone to the understanding of God, the giver of every good, "whom to know aright is life eternal." Man is immortal only as the idea of God, the representative of Spirit and not matter, of Soul and not body. As a belief of Soul in body, or Intelligence and Life in matter, he is only

Chapter I. Natural Science.

mortal. The science of being never mistakes the real for the unreal, or charges Soul with a single belief of personal sense.

Soul is God, for it is Spirit and Intelligence, and there is but one Spirit or Intelligence. To call matter substance does not require Intelligence, but a belief, insomuch as Intelligence understands there is no substance or solidity in matter that can rule out mind from piercing it and reducing it to shadow wherein Soul is found its only substance, and that which holds man, idea, that cannot be lost. It does not require Intelligence to lie, but demands Soul to utter the Truth of man. Intelligence or soul is never in error. Personal sense is the error that embraces all mistakes, wherein falsehood is considered fact until it be understood otherwise and the belief is destroyed. One of the beliefs of personal sense, named sickness, we destroy mentally with the Truth of being, and the sickness is gone; this we have proved by demonstration in hundreds of cases. Belief makes up the sum total of mortal man, but this statement is confounded by those not understanding science, blending the mortal and immortal, and making man God, Intelligence, instead of its idea. Belief is all there is to mortal man, and if this belief is wretchedness only, no circumstance can make it happiness, and if happiness, no circumstance can change it, or make it wretchedness, until the belief of the different conditions are changed; "for as error thinketh so is it."

The science of being is as necessary to those in the belief of health as sickness, for a single change of belief would make the well sick, when, if they understood these conditions depended on mind, instead of matter, they might continue to be well by grounding their belief in the case and letting Intelligence be master of the situation. Ignorance, pride and prejudice close the door on all that contradicts the past or opens it on things not stereotyped. When the science of Life is understood every man will be his own physician, and the doctor's occupation gone, hence materia medica will fight it to the end. But why should the new be scorned when the old has proved incapable of making man healthy or harmonious in mind or body,

Chapter I. Natural Science.

and the new commences at once to do this; the command remains, "Be ye perfect even as your Father is perfect," and yet we must be smitten for insisting on this demonstration. The science of being, that alone can stay the progress of disease and sin, and the atheism that unites matter and God, will be called, in this century, anti-christian.

The belief that man is intelligent matter, subject to birth and death would make Soul mortal, and governed by material laws, God in the things He has made, sin, sickness, and death blending with Truth and Life, and the former having the mastery over the latter. There is but one Spirit, even God, therefore no evil can be in Spirit, there being nothing to make evil of. Jesus cast out spirits, that is, beliefs in other Intelligences and healed the sick with the Truth of being, --he admitted no Intelligence in evil, hence his authority over it. If Spirit sins it must die, for all error is mortal; Spirit is God, and there is but one God; hence to talk of spirits is to believe in gods and demons. We reason wrong on all points relating to God and man, Soul and body, when we start from matter to draw conclusions of Spirit; this renders it impossible for such conclusions to be correct.

Our present stand-point is body not Soul, personality instead of Principle, hence our mistaken views and their consequences in sin, sickness and death. We go into ecstasies over a personal God with scarcely a spark of Love in the heart, when God is Love; and with scarcely a ray from Truth, when God is Truth; and without the understanding of Life, when God is Life, and what is the result? That we have no practical God to heal us; and get out of sin and death only in belief, while they still cling to mortal man; this is not science or the Christianity that heals the sick and demonstrates the harmony of Life. Evil and good never constituted man, for man is the image of God, and all there is to him is the good; evil is not the image and likeness of God, or matter of Spirit; even reason would rescue man from these errors of personal sense were it not silenced by some fatal theory. Action produced by Intelligence manifests harmony only, while action proceeding from mortal minds discords

Chapter I. Natural Science.

until it is finally destroyed. The heavenly bodies controlled by the mind of God, Soul, contradict the supposed laws of sense, and are harmonious. The supposition of Life in matter leaves man at the mercy of sin, sickness, and death, and then would resurrect Spirit from dust! Beginning with dust and returning to dust He who formed the universe! Science undisturbed amid this jargon reveals Soul, the Life, Intelligence and substance that constitutes Spirit, the great forever not in matter nor man. Soul being inside of man would reduce God to man, or make man God; the belief of Soul in body supposes Spirit helpless, sinning, sick and dying. Omnipotence is lost if God is in man, for mortal man is an error through which Truth cannot appear. The mighty arm is crippled when Spirit is made subject to matter. Surely the "tree of knowledge" produced a pigmy race of "gods."

Chapter II. Imposition and Demonstration.

CHAPTER II

IMPOSITION AND DEMONSTRATION

PHENOMENA not understood belong to the things that are, but which we venture not to explain, not having gained their origin and specific character from science. That which is real is not characterized by 'ism or belief; and the understanding grasping a subject is satisfied to name it only as it names itself. Phenomena based on science produce good results only, and never the opposite; this rule is invariable, and should measure every calculation. Whatever can work discord, accomplish a sinister purpose, or harm our neighbor, is not science or the phenomenon of Truth, but the manifestation of some belief and error. What are termed spiritual manifestations, as progress compels the change, will be found not mediumship, but openly defined, and when confined within the limits of harmony and it be found impossible to do evil by means of them, it will be time to consider them demonstrations of science, but not until then. These manifestations at present are the result of tricks or belief, proceeding from the so-called mind of man, and not the mind of God, from the mind of body and not the mind of Soul, from person and not Principle, from belief and not understanding; yea, from matter and not Spirit.

Mind is divided into idea and belief; idea is based on and represents Principle; belief has no foundation in science, and is illusion. What we term the mind of man is belief, forming the visionary basis of matter, therefore matter embraces not the reality of man. Belief is not a manifestation of Intelligence, but of non-intelligence. To distinguish between the mind of Soul and the so-called mind of body, we must remember one is idea, and the other belief, alias the counterfeit and claimant of mind, even as error claims Truth. Mind is immortal, but belief is mortal, it being the so-called mind of mortal body, whereas the mind of immortal Soul is idea, even science revealing Truth. Mediumship overlooks the impossibility for a sensual mind to become Spirit, or to possess a

Chapter II. Imposition and Demonstration.

spiritual body after what we term death, while science reveals this more inconsistent than for stygian darkness to emit a sun-beam. When we are Spirit we shall have gained the high import of this Scripture, "I and the Father are one," and shall find, too, this oneness occasions no loss of identity, but that "I" signifies Spirit and not matter, Principle and not person, Soul and not body, even the Intelligence represented by all ideas, symbolizing harmony from the blade of grass to a star. The question at present is, whether this "I" is Principle or person, Soul or body, yea, God or man? Principle is Soul, Intelligence, the "I am," but where do we place the "I"; is it Spirit in matter, Soul in body, Life in the flower, or the outside Intelligence and Life, that form these; is it man or the Soul of man, outside of matter? The science of being reveals God not in matter, therefore this "I" not body, nor in body, but Soul outside of matter, the infinite, and not finite, yea, Spirit and not person, and through this reckoning, man gains eternal identity.

A suffering, sinning, and dying condition such as must ever remain while the belief of Soul in body and Intelligence in man or matter remains, cannot be preferable to the sinless joy and perfect harmony that a recognition of Life, as Spirit, possessing all beauty and good, without a single demand pleasure, or pain of body confers; why so many called "spiritualists" are very gross materialists is because they make personality Spirit and the only conscious existence, and rejecting a personal God, make a God of persons, which is equally fatal to the science of being; persons called "spirits," instead of Principle that is Spirit and Truth, are their trust, while a belief in "spirits" belongs to the darker ages, and is demonology. There is but one Spirit, viz., God, Truth; in other words, Wisdom, Life, and Love, and nothing is real but what is good or the idea of goodness; evil has neither identity nor individuality, having no Principle.

Charles Sumner was a great man, because of his unswerving adherence to right; he had, more than others, the true idea, and less than others, the beliefs of man. His professions were few, his acts

Chapter II. Imposition and Demonstration.

colossal, his might was mind; not person but Principle, not man but God.

Science never caused a retrograde step in being, or a return to positions outgrown, or that Truth has destroyed. To admit the so-called dead and living commune together, is to decide the unfitness of both for their separate positions, and that a mistake occurs when a man dies to sense or lives to Soul. Any supposed midway between Life outside of matter, or in it, is a myth. We should either see the so-called dead, materially, or they should be advanced beyond our sight.

Conservatism never was right, absolute Truth is all that is right, and absolute error is easier made right than a half-way position. Mediumship assigns to their dead a condition worse than blighted buds or mortal mildew, even a poor purgatory where one's chances for something narrow into nothing, or they mast return to the old stand-points of matter.

"He is not dead but sleepeth." Jesus knew Lazarus was in the dream of a midway condition when Truth wakened him; if we could do this, we might claim his spirituality. Until the imaginary connection between the so-called dead, named "spirits," and those supposed to be living in matter is destroyed, mortal man is not dead, only changed, for the immortal is not gained, and belief can gather itself on the wrong side of the question, and continue the old conclusion of Life in matter; this, however, is far from the science of being. When Life is really gained outside of matter, it is understood, in which case the belief that Life was ever in the body is gone and cannot be resurrected; our friends thus advanced are Spirit, that never rose from dust and can no more return to, or commune with matter than a blossom can return to its bud.

The period required for the dream of Life in matter embracing pleasures and pains of personal sense to vanish, "no man knoweth, not the son but the Father." It will be of longer or shorter duration

Chapter II. Imposition and Demonstration.

according to the period of error, before the reality of being is understood and eternal Life won. What advantage then would it be to us, or the departed, to prolong this state, by prolonging the belief of Life in matter.

There is not as much evidence of intercommunion between the so-called dead and living, as the sick have of their positions relative to disease, which science decides an error, for it denies all identity or reality to discord. The entire phenomena of mediumship are deceptions or delusions; what is capable of error is not science, but destitute of Principle. When the so- called medium understands even in part the science of being, his belief of mediumship is gone, and the result is, be no longer produces the manifestations said to originate with departed "spirits," but which are really contingent on the beliefs of the living, instead of the dead.

The phenomena of science based on a demonstrable Principle, are explainable, but personal interpreters may create an 'ism in which phenomena are not understood, and subject to gross misjudgings. Thus error is engrafted into their net-work, and error is not linked to Truth, hence the gulf impassable that separates the so-called Life in matter, from Life not subject to death, and the mischance and mischief that characterize the so-called spirit-returns; the natural result of the attempt to unite such opposites as Spirit and matter is discord; as soon might fire and frost mingle, for in either case one would destroy the other. That matter communes with Spirit, or that Spirit communes by means of electricity or personality with Spirit or matter, is impossible, and would destroy the order and harmony of progress. If communion is possible between the so-called dead and living, the departed go backward in the scale of being, even as the oak holding on to its primitive acorn, or the so-called medium advances to Life independent of matter, like an acorn, becoming instantaneously an oak. Again, if the medium is on communicable terms with Life, Spirit, independent of matter, there can be no appearance of Life in the body, no action, animal or organic, and to restore this former condition of so-called Life, would

Chapter II. Imposition and Demonstration.

be as impossible as to restore an acorn absorbed into a germ risen above soil, and seed. The seed that has propagated is gone, a new germination having taken place, and until the belief of Life in matter is destroyed, the real Life that is Spirit, is not won; no correspondence or communion exists between these two opposites.

There is but one possible moment when the so-called dead and living commune; the moment called death when the link between them is clasped. In this vestibule more awake to the welcome of those gone before, than to present pains of personal sense; the departing sometimes breathe aloud their vision, naming the face that smiles upon them, and the hand beckoning them; even as a man standing at the falls of Niagara with eyes only for that wonder, whispers aloud his rapture, forgetful of other scenes. The recognition of spiritual Life -- and all Life is Spirit -- comes not at once; even beyond the grave existence is but a belief of personal sense until the science of being is reached, for error brings its own outer darkness and self-destruction, both now and then.

There is but one spiritual communication, and this proceeds from Soul; personal sense takes no cognizance of it; what are termed "spirits," are mere personalities. A shook would not be felt, or sensation held for a moment in the body, if in reality we communed with Intelligence, Spirit, outside of matter. The only living Principle of man speaks through immortal sense, and if mortal sense was touched by this Principle, it would present no appearance of Life, possess no sensation, and the immortal would appear in its stead, and the spiritual take the place of the material; even as light destroys darkness and in its place all is light. Soul is the only truthful communicator with man. Mortal belief and immortal Truth, like tares and wheat, grow side by side until the harvest, but to divide instead of unite these, is the design of Wisdom that separates the wheat, and gathers it away from the tares.

That all things are possible to Truth, is a scientific position; and that all error is possible to belief, is equally apparent. Secretiveness,

Chapter II. Imposition and Demonstration.

jugglery, credulity, superstition and belief, are the foundations of what is termed mediumship. But the so-called mediums have a strong hold on the sympathies of those who mourn the loss of friends; in the sorrows of bereavement, when thought like a fermenting fluid is ready for a chemical change, they turn the gushing emotions into the belief they are not separated, and this consolation comes to the mourner like heaven's benediction, gaining a strong foothold in the minds of millions. Hence the hold mediumship has on community, a belief coming at the hour of individual acceptance, clad with the drapery of heaven, a mystery and marvel, its phenomena not understood, what needeth it more, as the foundation of a new 'ism? Perfection is not expressed through imperfection, therefore Spirit cannot pass through matter; there are no temporary sieves, even, that strain Truth through error.

Matter controlled by Soul, God, is harmonious, and governed by a demonstrable Principle; but when one belief controls another--and this is mediumship--every possible imitation of the real is made by the unreal. The possible to Soul is the impossible to body, so also the impossible to science is the possible to belief. The ideas of God never amalgamate, but retain their distinct identities and are controlled only by the Principle that evoked them. The mineral, vegetable and animal kingdoms have their distinct identities, wherein one creates not or controls the other, all are created and controlled by God. Admitting Life and intelligence in matter, admits mediumship, making man create and control man; beast, bird, and plant create and control each other. But this reverses the order of creation, introducing confusion and discord.

Darkness and light, infancy and manhood, sickness, health, etc., are distinct beliefs that cannot blend. To suppose infancy is uttering the idea of manhood, or thinking its thoughts, would be rejected by reason and revelation; and *vice versa*, that darkness represents light, and sickness health, or that we are residing in Europe when we are on the opposite hemisphere, is simply absurd! Logic would not attempt to bridge over these distinct conditions, and they are not

Chapter II. Imposition and Demonstration.

more markedly distinct than the so-called dead and living, that you think to unite again on planes so different! the one called substance, and the other shadow, matter and Spirit communing together; one would inevitably blot out the other. That Spirit and matter amalgamate is the error progress and science will destroy.

Mediumship pre-supposes one man is Spirit, and controls another man that is matter, while both remain the Same opposites; that bodies which return to dust or new bodies called "spirits" are experiencing the old sensations, and desires material, and mesmerizing earthly mortals; that shadow is tangible to touch, and imparts electricity, etc. Every one of these conclusions are ridiculous; God is not named in them all, and for the best of reasons, viz., that matter is supposed to take care of itself, and mesmerism, and person take the place of idea and Principle, or man and God. Who that has witnessed mesmerism would say it was science, the Truth of being, or that this was electricity? God controls man, and is the only Intelligence, attraction, or Spirit. Any other control, attraction or Spirit supposed to be exercised over mail is a belief and error that ought to be known by its fruits. The caterpillar, transformed into an insect of beauty, is no longer a worm; and to push the conclusion that a butterfly returns again to affinitize with, or to control the worm, is to take mesmerism to befool reason! Change controlled by Principle is science, but some belief may hide its science; progress is the evermore of Wisdom, but nothing save science reveals progress.

Whatsoever utters falsehood is error, therefore, the impossibility for mediumship to be science, and governed by Truth. Our only resignation to a new 'ism or some new disease, is the hope that another stir made in the waters of belief will help to show their muddy foundation.

The electric telegraph is a symbol of mind speaking to mind, that in progress of time will not require wires, for Spirit destroys matter, electricity, etc.; but spiritualism would preserve these to destroy

Chapter II. Imposition and Demonstration.

harmony. Truth pervades all space, needing no material method of transmitting its messages; we only know it blesses man, but "cannot tell whence it cometh"; the sick are healed by it, the sorrowing comforted, and the sinner reformed; these are the manifestations of Soul, not sense, of science, and not mesmerism. Soul sends no despatches on matter; but to-day the electric wire carries to Europe a submarine whisper foreshadowing the science that is to come; little by little the action of thought is losing its matter element, becoming spiritualized, expanding outside of fetters, and science is pushing onward the centuries. The operations of Intelligence teach us God made man upright, but belief has sought out many inventions; Life, Truth, and Love act through no erring medium.

Immortal man communes not with the mortal, and cannot be made manifest through matter; these are distinct and opposite conditions; one is the idea of God, of Spirit outside of matter, and the other a belief of "spirits" and substance in matter; before we commune with Spirit that is immortal, the belief of death must be destroyed. What would be said of an English scholar unacquainted with the classics, before he had entered this department of learning, to claim he understood Greek? You would say he was either an imposter or laboring under some hallucination. What then of believing we are wearing out Life and hastening towards death, communing with immortality! If indeed this communication was possible between the mortal and immortal, the media would never die, or pass the change called death. And if the departed communicate still with mortality, then are they sinning, suffering, and dying still, in which case, wherefore look to them for proofs of immortality and accept them as cracks? Communications gathered from ignorance are pernicious in their tendencies; mediums describe disease, its symptoms, locality, fatality, etc., who know nothing about it, warn people of death, and frighten them into it! This obnoxious practice makes sickness. The case has been proved that a man died from the belief he was being bled to death, showing the cause of his death purely mental; hence the danger of ignorant charlatans dealing with disease. What science finds requisite to

Chapter II. Imposition and Demonstration.

destroy in order to heal the sick, mediumship strengthens and perpetuates.

Jesus cast out "spirits," error did his work, confessed the oneness of God, Spirit, and never described disease, but healed it. If the sick are made more comfortable through some error of process they are ten-fold more the victims of disease in the end. The mysticism of mediumship gives force to its words of doom, enabling it to do more harm than drugs, for the sick are more frightened by what a medium pronounces fatal, than when an M.D. so decides; and this fear is the mental condition that develops disease. Science would have to go over the whole ground and uproot every seed of their sowing to destroy disease. The evidence of belief is all the medium has to rely on, while science repudiates belief with the evidence of understanding, and demands the Principle of being to bring out the harmony of Life.

At one time a medium informed us we were ill, said our brain was overtasked, and we must have rest. To this we filed a vigorous objection, contending for the rights of Intelligence, that mind controlled body and brain, and the views she insisted on were the ones to be rid of, in order to be well. Whereupon she stopped the conversation, exclaiming, Dr. Rush is present, and says you must use valganism; (meaning undoubtedly galvanism,) "and rest or be sick." But even this pretended oracular warning failed to convince us, and the consequence was we went on in a good state of health; having strong doubts that fifty years of post-mortem experience had so demoralized the orthography of that learned man, or perpetuated his old beliefs of matter. Thousands of oar church members who are rational on other topics, are sustaining and believing just this mummery, while yet they send forth the cry against science as dangerous to Christianity.

In the slimmer of 1869, it was stated in the *Banner of Liqht*, published in Boston, that the late Theodore Parker said, through a medium, "there never was and there never would be, an immortal

Chapter II. Imposition and Demonstration.

spirit"! At the same time this paper was repeating weekly that spirit communications were our only proofs of immortality! While we entertain no doubt of the humanitarianism of many spiritualists, we have strong proofs of the incorrect views of spiritualism. A man's assertion that he is immortal, is no more proof of this than we would gain of an opposite condition, were he to say, "I am mortal "; Theodore Parker was beyond such vague hypothesis. Life, Love, and Truth are immortal, and only when these are realized will Life be understood. Truth is eternal Life, and science the only medium of Truth, or Life, hence the saying of Christ, "I am the Way, the Truth, and Life, and no man cometh unto the Father" (the Principle of being) "but through Me."

Though the grass seemeth to wither, and the flower to fade, they reappear; erase the figures that express numhers; shut out the tones of music; give to the worm the body called man, the Principle of these survives despite the so-called laws of matter, and holds its ideas immortal. If the inharmony of belief hides the harmony of Truth, it cannot destroy this Principle, for it is God, supreme over all; "who doeth according to His own will in the army of heaven, and among the inhabitants of the earth, and none can stay his hand or say unto Him, what doest thou."

Matter cannot reply to Spirit, but have you ever ruminated on this heaven and earth expressly declared to be inhabited by man, controlled alone by supreme Wisdom? Did you understand there is no other world, you would be reaching sooner that which is real of Life, where substance is Soul and not matter, and realizing it thus all would be harmonious and eternal. It should never be said, nothing but God; for all that is real comes with God, the substance, Life, and Intelligence of all. Principle and its idea are God and man, co-existent and eternal; there is no substance-matter. The imaginary line called the equator, is not substance, the earth's action and position are sustained alone by Intelligence, that launched the earth into orbit and said to the proud wave, "here shalt thou be staid," that holds the, winds in its fist," "numbers the hairs of the head," and

Chapter II. Imposition and Demonstration.

furnishes sublime proof of the control Spirit holds over matter. Even the simple planchette is made to testify to mind's power over matter, and no longer a mystery and marvel.

The point to be determined is, shall we allow science to explain all action and phenomena, or leave these to speculative belief; to admit one's self Soul instead of body, sets us free to master the infinite idea; it shuts the door on death, and opens it wide on immortality. The belief that God has a separate being leads to multitudinous errors, in which phenomena are ascribed to supernatural and personal causes. Man is the phenomenon of Soul, of Intelligence and not matter, and created by God and not man.

Divest belief of substance in matter, and the movements and transitions possible to mind would be found just as possible to the body; and then would Spirit identify being without the loss of body, that we suppose must occur before this science of being is acknowledged. The final understanding that we are Spirit must come, and we might as well improve our time in solving the so-called mysteries of on this Principle. At present we know not what we are, but hereafter we shall be found Love, Life, and Truth, became we understand them. Do you say the time has not yet come, in which to recognize Soul the only substance, and gain our entire control over the universe and man? Then we refer you to Jesus, who demonstrated this over eighteen centuries ago, and said, "The works I do, ye shall do," and "Behold the time cometh and now is, when they who worship the Father shall worship Him in Spirit and in Truth"; but this method of understanding God and doing good was Dot electricity, materia medica, mesmerism, or mediumship.

Matter is neither Intelligence, nor a creator; the tree is not the author of itself; sound is not the originator of music, or man the father of man. If seed produces wheat, the latter flour, and one animal another animal, etc., who made Intelligence, and how were the loaves and fishes multiplied without meal or monad? Miracles are impossible; they are phenomena not understood, but which their

Chapter II. Imposition and Demonstration.

Principle explains, and we should reach this explanation and understand it as did our Master, who demonstrated it controlling man and matter. The decaying flower, withering grass, blighted bud, gnarled oak, or ferocious beast, together with all discords including sick, sinning and mortal man, were not created by supreme Wisdom; these are the falsities of matter, things of sense instead of Soul, the changing images of mortal mind, not in reality substance, or Life, but only a belief of these. The mind of Soul embraces immortal ideas only, but the so-called mind of body illusion, and not the Truth of being. Personal sense declares matter substance, but what is this sense but a belief of Life and Intelligence in matter.

Eloquence is inspiration, not contingent on erudition, but a scientific phenomenon, showing that all things are possible to Intelligence; sometimes it is supposed to arise from knowledge obtained from books, and again from mediumship. When eloquence proceeds from the belief a departed "spirit" is speaking, and can say what the so-called medium is incapable of uttering, or even knowing alone, the fetters of mind are unclasped, and forgetting her ignorance, by believing others are speaking for her, she becomes eloquent beyond her usual self, and because she thinks some individual, and not the one Spirit, is helping her. Now destroy this belief of aid, and the eloquence disappears, and the old limits personal sense assigns are resumed, and she says I am incapable of "words that glow," being uneducated, proving the fact, "as a man thinketh, so is he." Believing she cannot be eloquent without book-learning, her body responds to this thought, and the tongue grows mute that before was eloquent, loosened on the scientific basis that mind is not confined to the development of educational processes, but possesses primarily all beauty and poetry, together with the power to express them; harmony is caught and not understood by the medium; caught through a belief, and dependent on it; but Soul gives utterance to itself when sense is silent, hence the improvement; she was always capable of this, and a "spirit," or person, had nothing to do with it.

Chapter II. Imposition and Demonstration.

The beliefs of personal sense, of Soul in body, etc., limit mind; Soul sets man free, which explains the phenomena of impromptu poets and uneducated orators; witnessing this in moments falsely called mediumship, 'tis construed supernaturally, which circumscribes the phenomenon by an 'ism. Matter is moved because of mind, through the volition of belief, or the understanding; all harmonious phenomena are produced by the latter, and the inharmonious by the former. Science removes phenomena from mysticism into the hands of interpretation; in which it is no greater mystery that mind moves a table without a hand than that it primarily moves the hand, and secondarily the table, in obedience to the belief that the only method of doing this is by seizing hold of it with the hand. Mind causes all action in the case, through a belief that "spirits" did it, or that electricity caused it, or the more common belief of voluntary muscular power; in other words, matter moving matter. Likenesses of individuals, landscape views, fac-similes of penmanship, certain forms of expression that belonged to the departed, and even sentences of their saying, may be taken as directly from minds as from objects cognizant to personal sense; mind sees what mind embraces, the same as personal sense feels what personal sense touches. Nor is it necessary that the mind embracing the picture, or paragraph, be individually present with the clairvoyant. Any mental link touching mind, though bodies are leagues apart, is sufficient to reproduce these to the clairvoyant; if the individuals have passed away, their aroma of thought is left, which is mentally scented and described. Mind has Senses sharper than the body; this we know from experience, yet we never believed ourself a medium, and always openly avowed this.

Matter is moved solely by mind in accordance with science or belief. But mediumship removes phenomena from rationalism into mysticism, and gives Intelligence to matter, instead of mind. Pictures are formed mentally before the artist gives them to canvas; thus clairvoyants perceiving pictures of thought can copy or reproduce them, even though lost to the recognition of the mind whence they are taken. The strong impressions friendship, or any

Chapter II. Imposition and Demonstration.

intense feeling leaves on mind is ineffacable, except to personal sense, hence another mind can perceive and reproduce the emotion. Clairvoyance is mind-reading alone, whereas science in contradistinction to clairvoyance reveals Truth through the understanding, by which we gain the Principle and explanation of phenomena; these are distinctly opposite stand-points whence to obtain information; and the right interpretation of cause and effect, belongs alone to science. Clairvoyance reaches only the fancied realities of mortal mind, whereas science admits none of these things, but reveals Truth, outside of mortality and error. We can do good to our neighbor through the science of being, but through it we cannot do evil also. Clairvoyance can do evil, accuse wrongfully, and explain unscientifically. If we act from the stand-point of spiritual sense we are right, but if from personal sense, we do evil continually. The sensuous may be clairvoyant, but cannot be scientific, and the scientific cannot be sensual. Foretelling events is to discern them spiritually outside of personal sense, which is prophecy, and accords with the ancient worthies; or through a belief which is clairvoyance, or mind-reading.

If advanced in the science of being sufficiently to blend with the Truth of being, we are seers and prophets involuntarily, not because we are controlled by "spirits," persons, but by Spirit, which is purity, righteousness, and omnipotence. To know the past, present and future, is the office of Intelligence, yea, it is everpresent Truth; and to understand we are not pent up within the boundaries of personal sense, confined to the ear, and eye, for sound and sight, or to muscles, bones, etc., for locomotion, is science, whereby we discern somewhat of being that is real. "Though we take the wings of morning and flee to the uttermost parts of the earth, behold Thou art there." Soul is ever present, embracing its likeness, man, and supporting the idea of Truth to carry out proofs of omnipotence. The science of being enables us to read mind, *foretell events* that concern the universal good, to trace records of Soul, and receive inspirations from God; but not from idle curiosity, or to work evil, or dip into the

Chapter II. Imposition and Demonstration.

experiences of the dead, or connect erring and mortal belief with Principle and its phenomena.

In science, we read mind from the stand-point of Soul, and with all the accuracy of the astronomer calculating the path of the planets. This mind-reading is distinguishable from clairvoyance, in that it is the understanding of being back of personal sense, and possessed by individuals highly spiritual. Its intuitions are from Soul, revealing what disturbs the harmony of man, and what promotes it, and enabling us to heal the sick. We can never learn Christ, as the Principle of healing, except we are able to read mind after this manner, and discern the error we would destroy. The Samaritan woman said, "He told me all things that ever I did, is not this the Christ?" Again, as be journeyed with his students, understanding their thoughts, he rebuked them, etc.

Through this spiritual sense Jesus healed the sick and events of great moment concerning the Christian era and the history of the world were foretold by the glorious old prophets, through spiritual vision. Our Master referred to a lack of spiritual discernment in this direction, when he said, "Ye hypocrites that can discern the face of the sky, but cannot discern the signs of these times"; in other words, whose personal sense was acute, but whose spiritual sense was wanting; he knew it was a wicked and adulterous generation, who seeking material signs, lost the prerogatives of Soul; his cut at the materialism of the age was pungent, but requisite, and he never spared hypocrisy the sternest condemnation. Again, he said to this class of believers, "Ye do the things ye ought not to do, and leave undone those ye should have done." The great Teacher of Christian science knew a good tree sendeth not forth evil fruit; that Soul emits only unerring Truth, while that which proceedeth from personal sense is error; also, that Truth and error cannot mingle; they are the tares and wheat side by side that never blend, but await the harvest, when belief shall yield to understanding, and error be self-destroyed.

Chapter II. Imposition and Demonstration.

At present Truth is trampled upon, while error holds the reins, with virtue at a discount! "Well done, good and faithful villain," is the merit mark for to-day, and youth seems eager for the prize. Such surprising aristocracy of evil is owing to the gilded falsehood of individual character, those whited sepulchres that hold the dead carcasses of conscience ; students of the Science of Life are responsible above all others if false to the teachings of conscience and reason. Said the wicked king, "I hate him because he prophesieth evil continually of me." Reformists are mostly traduced by the class that feel them most: let the good tell the Truth and live it, and the evil publish a lie and live it, and the former will be doubted and the latter believed, until the world advances nearer to what is Truth, when their relative positions will be seen and appreciated.

Those who understand the science of being, bear testimony to Truth, insomuch as they must understand what is indispensable to gain it. Never refute calumny except for Truth's sake; leaving the future years to expose the slanderer and bar, and reward those who wait on God; fear not the individual falsehood, and promulgate Truth sufficiently to gain some balance for the world. Earth holds not a majority of righteous men, and in proportion as we rise in the scale of being, do we learn this, but because evil boasts of greater numbers, this hath no advantage for the sinner. To-day sin offers a premium; let down the bars of morality, and you are society's favorite; put them up higher than society can leap, and you bring opprobrium on the bartender.

Woman especially should hold the standard that rebukes vice, and saith virtue, join us, and though we battle beneath stripes, we will fall in our armor, or lay it down on the field of victory. To ask in prosperity, "am I right?" is wiser than to ask this in adversity. One in a million does this, but can we lessen the number against that one?

Chapter II. Imposition and Demonstration.

Right advances slowly and with bleeding footsteps, but Truth can afford to wait, for "the eternal years of God are hers."

We have investigated the phenomenon called mediumship both to convince ourself of its nature and cause, and to be able to explain it; and have succeeded in the first instance, but may have failed in the second. It is more frequently in company with those who believe in mediumship that mediums narrate something of the departed, describe them personally, etc., showing it to be the effect of mind on this plane acting on theirs. Again, all the information imparted comes from the minds of the living instead of the dead. That some one knew the individual deceased is evident, and it is not more difficult to read mind far away than near. We think of an absent individual as easily as one present; hence the equal ease to discern the absent mind that we visit mentally. The demand to talk of the dead proceeds from the mind of the living, who, believing in this process or yearning for this communion mentally call for it, and this reaches the mind touched to response, and brings on the mood called mediumship. All theories and manifestations growing out of belief are error: and the important era for this age is the awakening or resurrection of understanding through which the unreal yields to the real, and 'isms are given up; the corruptible yields to the incorruptible, and the belief of Life in matter or Soul in sense gives place to the understanding of Life, that Wisdom, Love, and Truth, in which there is no conscious matter.

It follows not that in sleep we communicate with the dreamer at our side, because of his proximity, or that we both are dreamers wandering through the mazes of thought. If Life has become real to the departed, they cannot return to the unreal; or if they are at our side, and Life goes on to them the same as before, we are not in their conscious existence, nor they in ours, hence, we are debarred intercommunion; our dreams being distinct they cannot blend, though we are side by side. If those we call departed have gained a better understanding of Life than ours, they have advanced beyond us; in which case, we would not if we could draw them back to our

Chapter II. Imposition and Demonstration.

ignorance in order to meet us, and we could not if we would; neither can we advance to their plane of understanding except through their footsteps, and these have not yet been taken. If one man dreams he is crossing the Atlantic, and another the Andes, they are not in communion, though they are side by side, and dreamers both. This therefore represents the so-called dead and living who are on earthly planes of error, and have not become Spirit, but cannot communicate, because their beliefs of death have separated them. Again, supposing one man is dreaming and another awake, conscious of his friend's illusion, they certainly do not meet mentally and mingle; even thus the dead and living are parted, either through a belief that they died, or the understanding of Life outside of matter. Memory may repeat the alphabet, and mind here hold the history of the dead, but if we can read, we never in reality go back to the alphabet, or find pleasure in it; thus the advanced mind cannot return to matter.

Soul's vision is independent of optics; but the belief that sight depends on the eye, and thought mast have sound to reach our apprehension, shuts out the understanding of mind, and reverses the order of science. Destroy the belief that we owe to organization, our hearing, seeing, feeling, etc., and we hear without an auditory nerve or typanum, and see without optics, We shall all ere long prove this, and that spiritual senses are true, arid the personal, false. An organ is but the symbol of sight, hearing, etc., the expression only of these; and to hold it thus, would be to retain our faculties by right of Soul's ownership arid government; and to hear, see, etc., with mind instead of matter; which is the only scientific statement of sense and the Principle of immortal man. The real relation between Soul and body reveals the latter without sensation or Intelligence, and the idea of Soul; to understand this opens to view the capabilities of being, untrammeled by personal sense, explains the so-called miracles, and brings out the infinite possibilities of Soul, controlling matter, discerning mind, and restoring man's inalienable birth-right of dominion. Silence the belief we are in the body, and we discern the past and future as readily as the events of to-day; but this is the

Chapter II. Imposition and Demonstration.

science of Life, and not mediumship. The order and naturalness of phenomena that we deem a mystery and marvel, are perceived when we remember mind controls mind, and that matter is only another name for mind; a table or piano is moved by mind instead of muscle, and we should prove our power in this and other directions if we admitted it, but not admitting it, we virtually have it not, like the horse feebly submitting to the rein, unconscious of his power; phenomena that proceed from belief lose their power when we lose the belief that occasioned them; matter is manifest mind.

Misinterpretation hinders the harmony of phenomenon, and leaves it to ignorance and abuse. Clairvoyance foresees the future and repeats the past that is daguerreotyped on mortal mind only, and based on no Principle or Truth; it is mortal opinions unworthy obtaining. A past event is memory, a faculty of mind, and a future one is perception, another mental faculty; all events are mind before matter. Mediumship is a belief of individualized "spirits," also that they do much for you, the result of which is you are capable of doing less for yourself. Why some event, conversation, or even simple circumstance is more readily traced by the clairvoyant than others, is owing to the fact the mental emotions they produced were more vivid, therefore they are more distinctly defined in mind. When told by a clairvoyant something you have long since forgotten, 'tis useless to say they never read it in my mind because I recollected it not. It is by no means necessary the memory of those present retains what the clairvoyant sees. Beliefs, and images of thought are not limited to space or personal sense, that grosser strata of mortal mind. The clairvoyant sees not by means of solar rays, or an object striking the retina; and our proof that mortal mind is the element of all sublunary things is, that they exist to this mind the same as to personal sense. The reader must make due distinction between mediumship and the individual; there are undoubtedly noble purposes in the hearts of noble women and men who believe themselves mediums.

Chapter II. Imposition and Demonstration.

The science of Life, gained by slow and solemn foot-steps, at the expense of all 'isms and 'ologies, will unite being into one silken chord of good-will to man; and there is but one right way under the sun, even the pathway of holiness. We should not hang on the skirts of others, but in our own identity possess, some merit of our own not borrowed from others; and is there any so blind as not to admit individual faults? But mediumship well-nigh disavows all individual responsibility, and literally lays the charge of all good or evil on the shoulders of the dead. While we cherish all charity for our fellow-beings, we have none for a belief that inevitably shuts the door on reason and revelation, and robes the mind in darkness akin to barbarism. But for the misinterpretation of mental phenomena, through a belief of mediumship, the signs of science would have been discerned ere this, in the phenomena of to-day, and what is ascribed to personal agencies, have rested on the basis of Principle. Phenomena not understood had better be let alone, until the explanation is given that deprives humbug and avarice of advantage, and contributes to the general welfare. Principle demands to be understood; but phenomena not based on Principle, you can explain falsely, insomuch as they are creations of sense instead of Soul.

When sensation proceeds from Soul instead of body, the impressions are lucid and pure, and the intuitions correct and harmonious. But when mortal mind, or belief produces them, discord, disease, sin and death are the result. Mesmerism is error that leaves man at the mercy of matter, will, caprice, and mortal mind; God, Spirit, never mesmerized man or matter. The simplest object in the hand of a mesmerized subject may- shock him with a belief of danger; a napkin becomes to him a serpent that stings him; and this is the sensation that is belief, Place in his hand a cold apple; create the belief it is hot, and it produces at once the sensation of pain, the same as fire; destroy this belief of a burn, and the pain disappears. Is not this proof that pain is a belief? Again, whatever object the mesmerizer presents mentally to his subject, he sees; do not these facts prove the so-called senses of the body, mind, instead of organs and nerves? But mesmerism should be put under bonds

Chapter II. Imposition and Demonstration.

not to do evil; at any estimate it is a shameful waste of reason and honesty. That pain and pleasure are produced by belief, in the absence of all conditions to occasion them, is another proof that sensation is mind and not matter. To admit Mind sees, bears, feels, etc., without the agency of matter, is a step toward science.

In genuine clairvoyance there is no sensation in the body during its continuance. But to see in belief is not to see in reality; the basis of the science of being repudiates mesmerism, producing precisely opposite results; it destroys belief, and insists on understanding. Personal opinions or belief cannot be dismissed too soon. To admit that error requires a certain period in which to prepare us for the higher school of immortality, is a grave mistake; there is no necessity "to do evil that good might come"; science begins right, in order to end right, and it cannot begin right too soon. Reasoning from false premises never presented correct conclusions. God never made evil; error produces error, and belief disappears when Truth is understood, even as a cloud passes from before the sun. Science contradicts mortal sense, and reveals in its stead the immortal understanding that gives harmony to man. Wisdom is not gained of knowledge that brought sin and death into the world; neither is it found in pulp, or the brains of man; this so-called mind is but a belief that matter embraces mind.

Magnetism is without a scientific basis; it is one belief or error controlling another one. That Spirit mesmerizes, or vitalizes matter, giving it Life and Intelligence, is the fundamental error of mortal man. Spirit cannot impart Intelligence to non-intelligence, it has no electricity, etc.; emanations of materiality are electricity, and mesmerism is an unmitigated humbug. The immortal basis of man is not matter, electricity, brains, bones, etc., but Spirit that hath understanding; not sense but Soul; and phenomena that proceed from this fundamental Principle of being, are real and harmonious. A desire to do right may mistake the method of doing it, for belief is changing and unreal; intention may be right, but if the Principle of phenomena is misconstrued and assigned to a person, electricity,

Chapter II. Imposition and Demonstration.

etc., its foundation is a belief only, in which case science is not discerned, and phenomena left to misinterpretation and discord. It is not very uncommon to find one's self mistaken in belief. The miser thinks himself rich, but the fact remains he is poor; one individual thinks money makes a man, another, that man is more than money; still another believes man controls man in partnership with God, but these are grave errors; the M. D. thinks his method right, being learned in the school of Hippocrates; but Truth reveals knowledge the cause, instead of the cure of disease, and that there is but one physician that destroys sickness, and never loses a case if the patient observes directions, and yet this doctor is unpopular at present. Would you learn His name? it is the Science of being.

Our false reasoning does all the harm that can be done; it admits power in matter, and divides Wisdom between matter and God, giving them both separate Intelligence and distinct action and power, when there is in reality but one mind, there being but one God; man is not a separate Wisdom or Intelligence. God embraces all Intelligence, and enters not into partnership with man or matter, for this would involve the whole firm in disgrace, and imply at times that Truth is beaten by error. The reign of man is not the kingdom of heaven, or reign of harmony; for the government of God requires loyalty to Soul, and not sense; but manmade views endorse loyalty to sense, and a traitor to Soul; in fine, they have, other gods before me."

Civilization is not without its idolatry; a drug is its Dragon, Principle is prayed to, not worked for, and matter controls mortal man; all inharmonies come from this source. Nerves, brain, lungs, heart, liver, etc., master man; tea, coffee, tobacco, liquor, etc., are idols to which he bows down. There is no other volition, action, or government, but God, and yet the dream of Life in matter denies this, and gives all to personal sense, which would make evil stronger than good. The belief that matter is a power holding the reins of government over man, predominates, and the result is, broken bones, paralyzed limbs, softened brains, disease and death. The Master

Chapter II. Imposition and Demonstration.

healed the sick on the opposite basis of man, and controlled matter to issues worthy Intelligence; primitive Christianity heard the utterances of Wisdom, and cast out "spirits."

The Rochester rappings inaugurated a mockery destructive to order and good morals. Physical signs; that manifest the infinite Wisdom contradict not Truth; manifestations of personal sense in time or eternity are the results of error. Healing the sick is not the entire demonstration of the science of being, but it embraces a better understanding of God, of Soul governing sense than materia medica, or mesmerism. Healing the sick in science, is Truth casting out error; yea, it is taking God the Principle of man to govern the body; but healing the sick with mediumship, mesmerism, drugs, etc., is the greater error overcoming the lesser, and holding forbidden ground stronger because of this. Is it well to expect from drugs a blessing that Wisdom has not? is not God sufficient for the wants of man?

Mystery is the offspring of ignorance, and oppression grows out of governments not understood. Let us choose to-day whom we will serve, and abide the decision; frankly naming our master whether it be God or matter. No sequel is left to disease destroyed by Truth, never a consumption in consequence of measles; for this would take the demonstration out of the hands of Wisdom and give the balance of power to disease. I am, is the Intelligence that touches the chords of man to every harmonious issue, but the dream that Life and Intelligence are in matter would make this "I" both matter, and Spirit; a thing impossible.

Healing the sick through Intelligence, is science in obedience to Wisdom, that gave man dominion over serpents, deadly drugs, etc., and is the natural and normal control that Soul holds over sense. One of the greatest absurdities of human reasoning, is to admit person, or matter, better doctors than the Principle of man and the universe, learned of science. Would we not blush to say, man is a better musician than the Principle of music? Physiology, hygiene, or materia medica has no claims in common with Intelligence, the

Chapter II. Imposition and Demonstration.

Principle of being; and mediumship, galvanism, mesmerism, etc., are the right bands of humbug. The remark was once made in our bearing, "My guardian spirit is nearer to me than God." This was undoubtedly true, understanding literally nothing of the science of being, personality was more to him than Principle; and any change of belief would erect a new standard of conscience.

The theory called spiritualism objects to a personal God, but no 'ism so directly depends on personality. The individual exceptions to this error will reach a higher standard, sooner or later; and leave their material basis, such as electricity, matter conditions, mediumship, dark seances, etc., for the science of Life. The word spiritualism, is comically misapplied when made to designate a sect supposed to hold commerce with "spirits," not Spirit, but personality, in some instances, "sensual and devilish." The true significance of spiritualism, is a reign of Spirit over matter, of Principle over person, in which Soul, instead of sense governs man. Any error is a belief of matter, and cannot proceed from Spirit, God; when the departed become Spirit, those of earth who believe in substance-matter can no more communicate with them than darkness can enter light, that would destroy it. When you reach communion with Spirit, you will gain the utterances of Truth only.

What is called mediumship, tends to destroy all reliance on understanding and science. Admitting intercommunion between evil, here and there, both in time and eternity, we are afloat on the breakers of error, where nothing can stop its flood-tides breaking perpetually on the shores of time.

We learn Truth from divine revelation and our own demonstration; what we cannot understand and demonstrate with scientific certainty and harmony we had better let alone, for it leaves us at the mercy of a belief. The illustration of mediumship is a circle inside of which waits a material body to be mesmerized by a spiritual one, under the table, or perhaps in it, who informs you he rotates eternally back to things of time, and this is progress, through

Chapter II. Imposition and Demonstration.

which he becomes Spirit, God (?) while in glorious rapport with matter, sensuality and sin!

In contradistinction to the 'ism of Spiritualism, let it be remembered other doctrines name the name of God with reverence; hold the Bible the book of books; teach our infant lips the Lord's prayer; and bid man obey the ten commandments, that are perfect in Wisdom. Its military drills on Sabbath, the aboriginal vernacular of its oracles, its rites and ceremonies that choose darkness rather than light, and above all its loose morals, do not entitle spiritualism to the standing it has gained in society; hence aside from these its worst features, it has a humanitarianism and liberality that should redeem it from under the infatuation of mediumship. Spirit has neither Life, nor Intelligence in matter; and if our departed friends are Spirit, and we believe ourselves in matter, we cannot commune together; or if they are yet in matter-beliefs, we have shut them out of our consciousness by a belief of the change death has wrought, making them no longer tangible to personal sense.

Again, if we would commune through the affections, we must be on the same plane of belief, or understanding with them, to make this possible; and if their body is changed to us (as is manifest by its burial), so are their affections changed; and we cannot commune on former terms of personal sense and sympathy. We are separated mentally according to our own views, and on our own grounds, as effectually as distance here separates our bodies. Mediumship is mind-reading on this plane, and nothing more. Some one here knows all the mediums tell; the imagery with which they clothe expression is but futile conjecture and imagination, else thoughts let loose from the limits of personal sense, and the regret is that in this step they should not understand it.

Mediums describe sickness, sin, and death; and this description is supposed to come from Spirit that is wholly unconscious of matter or error, thus perpetuating the error that needs to be dissected and destroyed. Mediums have a certain circumference, and never go

Chapter II. Imposition and Demonstration.

outside of these limits; at the same time protesting mediumship is progress that takes hold of immortality. But the majority of what is termed mediumship, is simply imposition, not even clairvoyance, or mind-reading, but a catch-penny fraud. Until the so-called communications between the dead and living are stopped, sickness, sin, and death will continue; talking error and believing it, make all the reality there is to it. What is termed mediumship rises no higher than personal opinions and mortal views. A ball propelled upward or onward and subject to gravitation, will never pierce immensity. The gravitation earthward must be withdrawn, or the ball stops. So with mind that would leave matter; and would you fetter the unbound with ties of earth to matter conditions? But you cannot if you would; we commune together only as Spirit with Spirit, the immortal with the undying; or matter with matter, the mortal with mortality; and do you hold yourself free from mortal fetters, or your dear departed bound with you?

The dream of Life and Intelligence in matter is destroyed when heaven, man's harmony, is reached. The dead to personal sense are alive to Soul, and preserve all the prerogatives of being, but because personal sense buries their bodies it loses sight of this fact, showing virtually we are separated, and they no longer in sympathy with us, for there is no conscious change to themselves; hence we lose sight of each other. We are holding a belief of them as dead, in one sense, and pursuing it, and they the opposite, understanding, and pursuing that, therefore our directions commence from that hour apart, if they commence in science, for ours is error, else we would not bury the body, and the old and familiar faces would not disappear; a new field of action should be taken by the so-called dead, and the old left to us. Any departure from this natural result in progress is but a belief and. error.

Some mind here retains the image of the departed, or they have left this image in the atmosphere of mind in general; the words and acts of great men other minds may repeat, at least in part. Belief says the departed produce the phenomenon of Spirit communing with

Chapter II. Imposition and Demonstration.

matter, but all there is to mediumship, is belief To say the dead assert the reality of sickness and death after the falsity of these are proved by those who have learned disease did not kill them, while we say it did, is a very erroneous effort through post-mortem evidence to confirm an error of personal sense, that ought to be fading away to the departed and to us. The science of Soul destroys the dream of Life in matter, consequently of sickness, sin, and death, saying, "let the dead bury their dead," that is, let the error of personal sense be destroyed and not resurrected through mediumship and "follow thou Truth," the Life of man.

Intercommunion between the so-called dead and living is a belief only and not a reality; it is another 'ism that makes war on science and opens wide a Pandora box on mankind. Just as the age is getting ready to emerge from dogmatical error, to have the fountains of thought poisoned and dammed up with such mystery and madness is a miserable catch-penny plot, or an ignorance worthy the dark ages. As mind throws off its cruder beliefs of matter and becomes more spiritualized, phenomena resulting therefrom will become more wonderful, and should be understood on the basis of Soul, throwing off its own idea of Intelligence and Life, and opinions of mountebank and charlatan, that perpetuate sickness and sin, discord and mortality, be held back. But here the advanced thinker must wait before some 'ism, and the vain pause before caste, so the vultures that prey on the hour have it much in their own hands. Supineness and hypocrisy on the one hand and persecution on the other, are porters at the door of error to shut out glimpses of Truth. Although the science of being is greatly in advance of to-day as our iniquities declare, it is demanded even more for this, and he that layeth not down all for Truth, is not worthy of it. Every step of spirituality is linked to Wisdom, but it carries us thither through much tribulation; greater violence will be done Truth as the capacities of mind develop, until mind is better understood, and can be met and restrained with science.

Chapter II. Imposition and Demonstration.

Penal law may restrain the manifestations of error, and punish them, but cannot reach the subtle thought before it is manifested; but the higher law of science destroys the mental error before it results in deeds; thus avoiding the penalty, and affording a remedy for dismay and wickedness between the periods of materiality and spirituality. The contest between error and Truth whereby all 'isms will finally disappear, and the age pass into science, has been going on with pen and tongue for centuries, and yet, sin, sickness and death abound, because science that called the battle has been suffocated with opinions and theories. We boast of material law, but find it fails to save from sickness, sin and death; what we need is spiritual law, the Soul's jurisdiction over sense, more potent than man to work out salvation in obedience to the command, "Work out your own salvation," for God worketh with you. Mankind have wrought centuries on material platforms, now let us labor on a spiritual one for succeeding generations, and the body will become harmonious and immortal.

Any mode of treating the sick through manipulation, will-power, or mesmerism is a very poor substitute for science; in the first place it is morally wrong. Because it does wrong by inoculating error, and it is better to take the inanimate poison, than the evil of some people's nature. The less limited the power of an evil mind, the more sin it commits; it is the escaped felon that ventures on more daring crimes according to opportunity. Unless the moral growth equals the knowledge you obtain of the powers of mind, to meet and restrain them, confining them to doing good only, this developed power is to be dreaded. Stealing is not worse physically than metaphysically, and you have no more business to control your neighbor's mind except to do him good, than to control his body, or his household; any attempts to do this should be exposed and punished; mind should be protected as well as body, and any interference therewith outside the moral law of science, is a flagrant wrong. The higher law of justice forbids this evil action, and in spiritual science your quickened sense of right makes it impossible. We may know how a felon steals on the sleeper, and for his purse plunges a dagger in his

Chapter II. Imposition and Demonstration.

breast, but a common moralist even could not do this. To bring the Truth of being to the consciousness and understanding of the sick, is the science that heals them, and lifts its possessor above such a crime; but to control minds for purposes of avarice or revenge, sinks a practice to the committal of any error.

The law of Truth written on the Soul is the governing motive in science, and he who pours into the minds of patients falsehoods for his own sinister purposes, has made a fatal mistake that will be seen in his patients; it will not only hinder their recovery, but render the practitioner unfit to name the name of Christ, and thus make Truth powerless in his bands; all he accomplishes after this, is through mesmerism. Any interference in practice with the mind's free and unbiased action, farther than what relates to disease, and bearing one another's burdens, "and so fulfilling the law of Christ," is averse to science, and leaves the wrong-doer only the alternative of talking science and practicing mesmerism; if sentence against an evil work be not executed speedily, this sin is not without a witness. The mischievous link between mind and matter, called planchette, uttering its many falsehoods, is a prototype of the poor work some people make of the passage from their old natures up to a better man.

We are accustomed to think seeing without optic is second sight, but this is first sight; even our normal condition of being. He that formed the eye, did He not see? hath not Spirit every faculty of Intelligence? That sight is not in the eye is apparent when the mesmerized subject sees through different portions of the head, leaving this optional with belief. The question is at issue with mankind, whether we begin to demonstrate being in science, or leave it longer in the bands of belief, and at the mercy of theories, -- to heal the sick with Intelligence, or hold on to lifeless drugs to do the work of Wisdom, and call on departed personalities to direct our lives. What we need is understanding the Spirit that is Truth, and not "spirits," for there is but one Spirit, even universal Soul, that knoweth all things. Moving matter, mentally seeing, feeling, etc.,

Chapter II. Imposition and Demonstration.

has its scientific explanation thus; but phenomena not understood are at the mercy of belief, and their true interpretation will not be gained until the belief be destroyed.

Again, the understanding of Truth is not gained by what we see, hear, or feel, for a personal sense of things depends on belief alone; therefore the starting-point for the evidence of mediumship is unscientific. If the belief was as positive that we converse with the dead, see, bear, and feel them, as our belief of Life in matter is, they would be as apparent to us, and yet this would not present the Truth of being, a body without sensation. Soul and its manifestations are all that is real; whatsoever can make discord, or utter a lie is proved without Principle, and not the idea of Truth; when the science of our being is gained, tricksters will lose their occupation. In the onward march of Truth, error will bury its dead and never resurrect error; but before this hour, it may take to itself seven beliefs more erroneous than at first, and launch deeper into the dark. This Babel has already begun; mediumship helps becloud the way of Truth; greater discord is inaugurated because of it; a link formed between the error of another plane of existence and this, would be another error for Truth finally to destroy.

We say of matter, it is opaque or luminous, but this should be said of mind that is transparent, its images readily perceived, or that absorbs, and reflects but little. A mind transparent, reflects the thoughts of other minds, and reproduces them, and this is supposed to be the work of the departed. Legerdemain, or slight of hand, has produced more remarkable manifestations than mediumship, and what is done understandingly is better than mysteriously; skill is more rational at this age than superstition. Matter is moved, history repeated, and pictures drawn by mind on this plane; and that which we understand not, we know nothing of; we say matter moves matter here, but that Spirit moves it there; let us have the interpretations of science on these points, and link not error to error throughout time and eternity. Lacking the basis of science, we say, Intelligence is in matter, that mind alone cannot produce

Chapter II. Imposition and Demonstration.

phenomena; also, that body is diseased independent of mind; that matter is self-acting, etc.

A circumstance was related to us by an old gentleman, a distinguished mesmerist. He said to a mesmerized subject under control of his will, "You have a burn on your hand," and he immediately appeared to suffer; the flesh rose up in a blister that was opened and discharged a watery fluid. Then, continued the narrator, I destroyed the belief that he was burned, and the cuticle became smooth and natural as before. We did not witness this test of belief, but having seen the mesmerizer's performances on other occasions, and knowing the man's veracity, and the power of belief, we could not doubt it.

The evidence of one of the personal senses is not more improbable than that of another; mentally to see another's mind is not more impossible than to feel it; then wherefore doubt that we see what mind contains, as well as feel it? We can feel the pain of the sick, and the sorrow that is not ours causes us to weep; the fact is we both see and feel, hear, taste and smell, because of mind and not matter, and from sympathy with mind; all is mind, and matter one of its beliefs. But for the interpretations of ignorance, the basis of all physical manifestations would have been discovered long ago, and given a scientific explanation; thought awake to this subject would have discerned the signs of science in phenomenon, had not a belief, as usual, misinterpreted it.

An absence of eloquence is caused by the belief that schools and colleges possess alone the key to it, or that some especial endowment is wanting; destroy this belief, and you break the shackles of mind that imprison its faculties, and set the captive free to utter the beauties of being. Flowers, birds, waves, mountains and storms are eloquent, and so is man; even the sons of the forest are sometimes orators beyond their learned neighbors, for the reason the nearer we approach our native being, the more we give utterance to Soul; and it is this universal Intelligence outside of language, that

Chapter II. Imposition and Demonstration.

supplies all that is sublime, or beautiful in words. It was inquired concerning Jesus, "bow this man knew letters, having never learned?" Eloquence is the voice of Soul, the God-utterance untrammelled by books, conventionality, or the fear of man; even the self-accusing reminder he is unlearned, cannot disturb the inspired man. I have seen learned men at the mercy of books, and the unlearned eloquent beyond them; the so-called mediums let go their beliefs by supposing somebody else is talking for them, and thus speak beyond the admitted limits of their own capacities. Soul is infinite in eloquence, as in all else, but sense is finite in this as in all else; the Soul- inspired are not comprehended by the man of sense, and the sense-inspired are mediums deceived in the origin of what they say. The victim of delirium sees objects through the shadowy evidence of delusion, and so does the sleeper, the medium, or clairvoyant, and mortal man. Where neither certainty of phenomena nor evidence of Principle exists there is no real foundation.

All theories founded on the belief that Soul is in body, God in man, and Intelligence in matter, therefore, that we must develop from within outwardly, are false, and fatal to science. Wisdom is from without, development is to learn this, to leave the belief of Wisdom within a skull-bone, and take hold of our God-being outside of matter. There is no "inner life;" for Life is God, and God never migrated from man! cause was never in its effect. In common practice we make no attempt to put the greater into the less; and if Soul is superior to body, it is outside of it; and if God is superior to man, he is not in man; and furthermore, man must get out of six feet of Intelligence before he is immortal in Soul. Wisdom cometh from without; Principle is circumference, and idea centre; Soul is Principle, and man the central idea of Soul.

Science reverses the conclusions of personal sense in every instance, and abides by a given statement of man to bring out the harmony and immortality, that theories have failed to do. No condition of matter can change the fact in numbers that four times

Chapter II. Imposition and Demonstration.

three is twelve; science should govern thought, and nothing can mar or destroy man controlled by science. Mediumship is without a scientific statement or proof, and claims to gather Wisdom from "spirits," personalities, outside of matter, while the basis of its evidence is admitted to be matter conditions. The theory called spiritualism admits that God is Principle, but leaves this admission without practical proof. If God is Principle, science alone reveals God; then wherefore ask personalities of another plane to explain Life, Truth and Love? why not strive to reach these beatitudes through science, and hold them your own instead of another's to bestow on you. Person cannot interpret Love, for Love alone explains itself; science reveals and explains Principle, but man cannot explain God; six feet, nor the stature of ancient giants can represent "the fullness of the stature of man in Christ," in other words, the idea of Truth. Measurement may represent the man of personal sense, but this is not the man of Soul.

Mediumship communes with person instead of Principle, the only Intelligence, Life and Love; and accepts a personal version of Principle, praying God to be God, as if Love was idle, and omnipotence uninformed. To call on light for light, is absurd. "Let there be light," is the will of Wisdom; and this full effulgence has nothing to do with mortal stint, but shines for 0. Universal Love bestows all good without respect to persons; and man receives, or rejects it; but a prayer or tear changes not divine economy, or eternal order. Sin shuts out light and blessings, and is the author of all tears and prayers. Wisdom helps those only who help themselves, and cannot bless evil; it destroys sin only as man gives up sin, acting in this direction only as we act. We have seen patients who could not be healed through science, until they gave up the belief of mediumship, and controlled their own bodies; for man is not governed in science except by his own Spirit.

Harmonious man is governed by the Principle of being; the inharmonious by a belief of personality; therefore, the folly to desire

Chapter II. Imposition and Demonstration.

personal control that leads into all error; there is no Truth except Principle, the one God, and thou shouldst have no other."

We learn in science that God and His idea are all that is immortal; but mediumship would establish the immortality of error. Science reveals progression only, but mediumship retrogression. Should a pupil continue in the primary school, when fitted for a higher school? If the departed are unfit for the advanced understanding of Life through which they take a spiritual place in the scale of being beyond us, why impose their ignorance on us as oracular; and think mediumship privileged to be a strainer for error. That the so-called dead return to torment us, or to comfort us, or to seek aid from us, is but a belief and error. When wandering in Australia, are you seeking comfort, or giving support to another, dwelling in the snow-caverns of the Esquimaux? Two different dreams, or different awakenings, separate consciousness. What is named mediumship is a phenomenon of belief, without reality, or science; and we ought to know the consequences of launching into new and stronger fellowship with error, when we are already in it up to our necks.

In an age of sin and sensuality hastening to greater development of power, 'tis fearful to consider the influence of belief without more honesty and understanding to steer clear of the fearful shoals on this dangerous and unexplored coast. The peril of Salem witchcraft even is not past, until that error be met by the understanding and destroyed; not the gallows, but explanation, destroys error. Science must be allowed to explain this phenomenon of belief, in contradistinction to that of Truth and Intelligence controlling man. An evil and artful mind is all the satan there is; and this is the fallen angel, or abused capacity; such a mind learning its control over other minds, will take the reins into its teeth, and Truth alone must take them out and guide it; as of old this mind works its spell in some manner on all it would harm, because the barriers against evil influences from such a source are not understood by the world in general, and the door is not readily closed against them. To this end

Chapter II. Imposition and Demonstration.

metaphysics are important; study mind more and matter less, for we must find refuge in Soul, to escape the error of the latter days; and mediumship and mesmerism more than all else contribute to a terrible future development of discord. We should strongly insist on the majesty of Truth, and its control over error; and begin to-day denying right or reality to aught but God, and the true idea; saying, "depart from me all ye that work iniquity;" and thus break up the reign of error, and let the world of harmony and Truth re-appear. If spirit-returns were possible, they would grow beautifully less at every advanced stage of existence; for the departed would pass away from our ignorance, and we away from the belief of mediumship, until the beliefs of matter were gone, and we united through science; and the will of God "done on earth as it is done in heaven."

The mind of Soul has no fellowship, or communion, with the so-called mind of the body; the changing, sinful and erring thought is not immortal Spirit; matter and brains are not mind, notwithstanding opinions and beliefs to the contrary! But we welcome the increase of knowledge even though it never has borne the fruits of harmony and immortality, and never will approach the demonstration that Jesus gave, because knowledge must have its day, and we want that day over. The so-called mind of body, is belief and error, but the mind of Soul is understanding, even the science of being. Paul learned that to be present with Truth, we must be absent to the body; but Cain concluded very naturally if man gave life he bad the right to take it away, and attempted to kill his brother, showing this belief of Life in matter, or man, was error from the beginning. We name a mistaken thought, mind, while it is error only, without intelligence, but imitating it; without Principle, but claiming to be Truth. Mistakes are impossible to understanding, and understanding is all the mind there is; ignorance and evil are not Intelligence. Soul is the only Intelligence, and a creator not at the mercy of its creation; we see, hear, feel, etc., not because of eyes or ears, these faculties are symbols or expressions of understanding, which is the mind of Soul; the mind of body loses them if an organ be destroyed; but they cannot perish, or be marred in Spirit. The senses of Soul are not matter, but Spirit, that apprehend and reflect Intelligence, and Life; hence, their immortality. Inspiration is the utterance of Soul, giving forth its own idea, or spiritual sense. It is safe to trust this communication; but it would no longer be so if matter, or personal sense interpreted it. The garment in which belief, error, hides itself is, that Soul is in matter, holiness in unholiness, and literally God in man.

Midnight foretells the dawn; and beholding a solitary star the wise men of old were led by spiritual vision to foretell the hour of Truth. But what shepherd-sage today, seeing the light is allowed to explain the darkness. The world is asleep! lulled by stupefying beliefs; in the cradle of infancy dreaming away the hours under its spell. Entering upon an unknown eternity, personal sense will be found as an outlaw escaping to a foreign land, where he is doomed to an unlooked-for death. The footsteps of belief have not advanced man a single league toward immortality; and the unwillingness to learn man and God of science, holds christendom in chains. So much hypocrisy swells the catalogue of society, the honesty that demands demonstration is not desired, and incurs the enmity of mankind. Science never plays the hypocrite. To claim you understand a problem of Euclid, and fail to demonstrate it, would exhibit folly or dishonesty; but to solve the simple problem according to its rule proves you perceive the Principle. Science is the rule of harmonious and immortal man; Jesus the example, and Christ the Principle. This rule of man is embraced in Life, Love and Truth; and the spiritual sense of the Scripture reveals the science of being.

The prophets did anciently what the worshippers of Baal failed to do, yet in some instances, artifice and the faith of belief feigned the work of Wisdom. Necromancy and legerdemain are the inventions of man that originate in brains, or the so-called mind of matter, while science is the mind of God; one proceeds from Soul and the other from sense. The beliefs of man manifest error only; but this is sometimes called a phenomenon of Truth, that proceeds from

Chapter II. Imposition and Demonstration.

"spirits"; the phenomena of Principle are outside of matter, and not in the least dependent on person. Mesmerism hod mediumship are dependent wholly on belief or the so- called person of man. Mind evolves images of thought, and these are the apparitions seen by the so-called medium; it is not more mysterious, only because it is less common, for us to see, than to feel a thought. To feel the grief of another's mind is not unusual, but we think, to see the mind's images of departed friends, is to see them in reality; here are two equal senses, seeing and feeling, that we separate in power. There are those that feel another's pain as quickly as their own; the sick may not have touched them, or spoken on the subject, and yet they feel their pains and can tell their locality, and this because of sympathy the same as yawning is produced. Seeing belongs no less to personal sense, or belief, than feeling; then why more difficult to see a thought than to feel it? Education alone determines the difference, and in reality it is not more marvellous. Haunted houses, unusual noises, voices, apparitions, dark- seances, etc., are tricks produced by tricksters; else they are images and sounds evolved by mind on this plane. The mind of Soul embraces all that is real and immortal, and the so-called mind of body which we name the mind of man, embraces all that is unreal and mortal.

Truth proceeds from Spirit; error from the material body. The mind of Soul, Spirit, is science giving only the idea of Truth; but the so-called mind of body, or man, is belief giving false appearances. Because there is no mind of man, that is, no material mind, thoughts said to emanate from body or brain are delusions. How may we determine the ideas of Truth from belief? By learning their origin; thoughts from the Soul are ideas, and from the brain beliefs; the former proceed from spiritual sense, are not substance, and are harmonious; the latter are the product of personal sense, and are supposed substance at one time, and spirit at another, and are inharmonious; the former are understanding, the latter, beliefs begotten of error. To love our neighbor as ourself is an idea from Soul, yea, from Wisdom, Love and Truth; and this idea personal

Chapter II. Imposition and Demonstration.

sense cannot see, feel, or understand, but the spiritual sense can; "the carnal mind cannot discern spiritual things."

Matter is but a grosser strata of mortal mind, wherein one belief introduces and destroys another in Darwinian process. As before stated, Spirit is Intelligence, whereas the basis of matter is belief; the former is science, the latter mesmerism. The body that is mortal is an individualized belief that germinates, grows and decays, "dust unto dust," and mortal man is just this belief; even a phenomenon of mesmerism, an error construing man matter. Excite the organ of veneration or the religious tone of this belief, and it manifests the most profound adoration; but change the action to an opposite development, and it blasphemes. Mesmerism is a belief, constituting mortal mind, error is all there is to it, which is the very antipode of science, the immortal mind. The former is hallucination, the latter reality; one a wholesale mistake, the other the Truth of being. Mesmerism assures the sick they are recovering, when there is no evidence or basis for this conclusion, turns belief whithersoever it wills, and is the blind leading the blind. Nothing can be more antagonistic to science; it bides the Truth that man is the image and likeness of God, and as such cannot be sick, sinning, or dying, and claims that mortal mind and substance-matter constitute man, thus admitting through personal sense what Soul denies in science.

Mesmerism is a direct appeal to personal sense, proceeds from it, and derives its only prestige from belief; it is predicated on the supposition that Life is in matter, and a nervovital fluid at that; whereas science reveals man's Life, God, and therefore dwelling not in matter. Mesmerism is error and belief in conflict; but science masters error and belief with the understanding of Truth, and reveals man immortal, sinless and undying. Mesmerism is one error at war with another, "a kingdom divided against itself that cannot stand;" but science is harmonious and eternal. Mesmerism is personal sense giving the lie to its own statements, denying the pains but admitting the pleasures of sense; whereas science denies all sensation to matter, and holds the reins in the hands of Spirit. The gulf fixed

Chapter II. Imposition and Demonstration.

between science and mesmerism is impossible. Vitalized matter is a grave mistake. Electricity is the last boundary between personal sense and Soul, and although it stands at the threshold of Spirit it cannot enter into it, but the nearer matter approaches mind the more potent it becomes, to produce supposed good or evil; the lightning is fierce, and the electric telegram swift. The more ethereal matter becomes according to accepted theories, the more powerful it is; e.g., the homeopathic drugs, steam, arid electricity, until possessing less and less materiality, it passes into essence, and is admitted mortal mind; not Intelligence, but belief, not Truth, but error. But the nearer belief approaches Truth without passing the boundary, where it is no longer belief, but understanding, the more plausible and dangerous is the error. Mesmerism attracts man to matter, science attracts to Principle, therefore to Spirit, or God.

The more material man is, the more mesmerism he possesses; but the more spiritual, the less mesmerism and the more science, and the higher his demonstration of Truth. In reality brains and matter are one; but we call them mind and matter; but if the brain be the organ of mind, and to destroy this organ, destroys mortal mind, how can you distinguish between them? What we call mind and matter-man is mind only, but this mortal mind grows finer towards the core, and we name its exterior matter, and the interior mind, in contradistinction to the Truth of being that reveals all Intelligence outside of matter.

The generic name of matter is mind; its different species are the beliefs that say Intelligence, Life, sensation, Substance, good and evil are matter, and the body called man; also, that Spirit and matter commingle, and form mortal man, on the foundation of sickness, sin, and death; this theory is not the Truth of being, but its opposite, viz., error. Life is not organization, and Intelligence takes no cognizance of matter, these are God, Spirit, and to Spirit there is only Principle and idea. The so-called man of matter together with every material belief of a material world, must pass away before sorrow, sickness, sin, and death can disappear. The millennial glory

Chapter II. Imposition and Demonstration.

cometh only as science reveals Intelligence and Life outside of matter. Alas! that man should take a material sword to slay error when the two-edged sword of Truth destroys it so much more effectually.

The history of the Chinese Empire derives its antiquity and renown from the truer idea the Buddhist entertains of God, contrasted with the tyranny, intolerance and bloodshed based on the belief that Truth, Life, and Love are in matter, and the great Jehovah formed after error's pattern of mortal man, or intelligent matter. To suppose matter and Spirit mingle, is the error that hides science on which to base our conclusions of God and man, of Soul and body, and our proof of immortality. At one time, we define law, Intelligence, and again, matter, over which Intelligence holds no control, as in sickness, sin, and death. The law of Spirit is the only law, and this is Truth, destroying the so-called laws of nature, and its idea is walking the wave, destroying error, healing the sick, and raising the dead. This is Soul triumphing over personal sense, putting to fight belief, walking over sin and matter conditions.

Jesus taught and proved this Truth the prerogative of Spirit, and left his example for us, saying, "The works that I do ye shall do." Paul was not one of his disciples, or cotemporaries, and yet he tested these teachings, and demonstrated their Principle. To conclude man and the universe are governed in general by material law, but occasionally that Spirit walks over this law, and holds the control in its own bands, is to divide the capacity of Omnipotence and Wisdom with matter, and to give the latter the more general claim. These are the false conclusions of belief; understanding rebels at such folly, mortal belief produces and governs all that sins, suffers and dies. There is but one law and but one law-giver, the former is science, the latter God, Soul, the only Life, substance, and Intelligence of man and the universe; and not in the least dependent on matter conditions, or acting by reason of them, but destroying them all. This Truth knocks at the door of history; it is for us to say whether we will open and receive it.

Chapter II. Imposition and Demonstration.

Materia medica, hygiene, physiology, creeds and ritualism will lose their power for good or evil, when man loses his belief in them, and makes Life its own proof of harmony and God. That which is right is immortal, and the opposite of right is mortal. When Truth lays its hand on error to wipe it out, all will be growing immortal; but before the final doom of error there will be interruptions in what we call the order of nature, and earth will become dreary and desolate. Not that summer and winter, seed-time and harvest shall utterly cease, before the final spiritualization of all things, but that their order will be interrupted, owing to the change in belief.

The next step in progress is to learn how mind controls matter, and how to destroy error. The science of being emancipates man from belief, giving him understanding, through which his harmony and immortality are obtained. There is neither mortal mind, nor substance-matter; mind is the emanation and atmosphere of Principle, and not person; it proceeds from God, and not man, from Spirit, and not matter, from Soul, and not sense; therefore mind is not in mortality, and man has not a separate mind from Deity, for that would make other Intelligences, and there would be more than one God. When Truth is admitted, and thinking brains and intelligent bodies are found a myth, then will the harmony and immortality of man and the universe appear. When we learn matter has neither Intelligence, substance, nor Life; and neither suffers nor enjoys; disease will be found a belief only, and healed by destroying this belief, and giving man the understanding of himself. Personal sense contradicts the science of being, and so do dreams contradict the daily experiences of sense; personal sense and science are opposites, that dispute each other. In dreams you fly, or meet a far-off friend, and hold your body with your mind, carrying it through the air, or over the ocean, and this dream of sleep is nearer man's being in science, than the waking dream of Life in matter; because personal sense governs it less.

The era of science comes in on this statement and its proof; viz., that all is mind, and there is no matter. Sickness, sin, and death are

Chapter II. Imposition and Demonstration.

creations of mortal mind, that Life, and Truth destroy. Order and beauty emanate from the mind of Soul, that is immortal; and the scientific statement that all is mind, will gain its first proofs in healing the sick on this Principle. A single demonstration of this is important evidence.

A lady having an internal tumor, and greatly fearing a surgical operation, called on us. We conducted her case according to the science here stated, never touched her person, or used a drug, or an instrument; and the tumor was wholly removed within one or two days. We refer to this case to prove the Principle. We have stated all is mind, but the distinction between what we call substance and essence, is made by naming one matter, and the other mind.

Christ understanding that Soul and body are Intelligence and its idea, destroyed the belief that matter is something to be feared, and that sickness and death are superior to harmony and Life. His kingdom was not of this world, he understood himself, Soul, and not body, therefore he triumphed over the flesh, over sin and death. He came to teach and fulfill this Truth, that established the kingdom of heaven, or reign of harmony on earth. The demonstration he made of this Principle and Truth of being, is the strongest proof that God is the only Intelligence that produces a perfect man, and is the Life that is without death, and holiness without sin. Only the science of being reveals the possibility of meeting the command, "Be ye perfect even as your Father in heaven," (the Principle of man) "is perfect." Let us then yield the belief that man is a separate Intelligence from God, and reach his unerring Principle of being, and be governed by Life and Love, outside of matter.

As music is harmonious controlled by its Principle, so man governed by his Principle of being, by Soul and not sense, is harmonious, sinless and immortal. The error of belief regarding Soul and body, and God and man, introduces discord into the demonstration of man, even the sickness, sin and death of which we complain. The idea of Life is obtained only from its perfect

Chapter II. Imposition and Demonstration.

Principle, and gained through science in which man is sinless and immortal.

Sickness, sin and death belong not more naturally to immortal man than to God, to body than to Soul, for it is morally impossible that these should adhere to either, and what gave Jesus authority over sickness, sin and death was the understanding of his scientific being. He stood boldly up in the face of all accredited evidences of personal sense, Pharisaical creeds, etc., and refuted them all with his healing. We never read of his saying a creed or a prayer makes a Christian, or searching into disease, to learn of discord, if it was acute or chronic, recommending laws of health, giving drugs, etc., or even asking the will of God regarding man's Life, for this he already understood. He reckoned sickness, sin and death, "liars from the beginning," and destroyed them with the truth of being that was self-evident to him and his only physician. He kept the commandment, "Thou shalt have no other gods before Me," and we must do likewise and adopt this Truth of being before we obtain its harmony or immortality.

While Jesus rendered to Caesar the things that were Caesar's, he also rendered to God the things that were His, viz., Truth, Life and Love, and we, too, should acknowledge these God, and sufficient to destroy every discord of man. Jesus paid no homage to diplomas, to forms of church worship, or the theories of man, but acted and spake as he was moved by Spirit, the Principle of being. To the believing Rabbi and Pharisee he said, "Even the publicans and harlots go into the kingdom of heaven before you," not that he scoffed at Christianity, but he knew there is neither Spirit, Life, nor Truth in mere forms of religion, and that a man can be baptized, partake of the sacrament, support the clergy, observe the Sabbath day, and make long prayers while yet a sensualist and hypocrite. Forms of personal worship may not be voluntarily wrong, but involuntarily so, inasmuch as they hinder the Spirit. To be a hypocrite in the science of Christianity is morally impossible, for here Christianity is based on demonstration, or proof, and yet many will come falsely in its

Chapter II. Imposition and Demonstration.

name as predicted. When God is understood, man will need nothing besides God to make him healthy and harmonious. Jesus established his church on this very understanding, and taught his followers it cast out error and healed the sick. Instead of believing Christ a person, he said, Christ is "Truth and Life," and "I and the Father are one," thus claiming no separate Intelligence, action or Life from God, and despite the persecution and cross this earned from a Pharisee, he wrought out on its Principle harmonious being.

The question was then as now, at issue with mankind, how did Jesus, through Christ, his God-being, heal the sick? Jesus answered this question in the explanation that the world rejects, when he appealed to his students, thinking they would better understand him; and asked "whom do men say that I am?" referring to the "I" that healed and cast out error, and they replied, "Some say Elias, others Jeremiah," etc.; but these men were dead, therefore, their answer implied that some thought Jesus a medium controlled by the so-called "spirits" of the departed. We cannot doubt the belief of mediumship prevailed to some extent at that time, for Herod had before given the same definitions of Christ's healing; saying, "John the Baptist has come back, and therefore mighty works show forth themselves in him." That this wicked king and debauched husband should gain no higher interpretation of the science of being and the great work our Master (lid, was not surprising; a sinner could not be supposed to comprehend this science if the disciples understood it not fully. They comprehended his spiritual explanations better than did others, but the connection they had with man's physical harmony or their application to heal the sick, they did not yet fully understand, so their Master patiently persisted in teaching and demonstrating to them that the Truth of being healed the sick, cast out error, and raised the dead. This science of Life was not comprehended by his students, until his final demonstration, when their great teacher stood before them the victor, not only over sickness and sin, but over death.

Chapter II. Imposition and Demonstration.

In secret yearnings to be better understood, the Master turned in confidence to Peter, saying, "But whom say ye that I am?" This inquiry meant simply, who or what is it that casts out error and heals the sick? And because he turned from the other disciples' answer and put anew the question to Peter, it plainly indicated he disapproved the belief he was a medium as he bad before signified, saying, "I and the Father are one." Peter's reply so unlike the others admitting He was "Christ," Truth, that healed the sick and cast out error, called forth the answer, "Our Father in heaven," that is, the Principle of man "hath shown thee this," in the science of being, and also that Jesus is the "Son of God," the offspring of Soul and not sense. On this Principle and with this Truth he wrought all his so-called miracles. It was not man, or medicine that healed the sick, but God; not matter that controlled man, but Spirit that controlled matter. This, his interpretation of God and man was the rock or foundation on which Jesus built his church, that is, established his demonstration of Truth, God, against which the gates of error could not prevail, but there was neither a creed nor rite named in it, and mediumship plainly denied.

To be Christ-like is to triumph over Sickness, sin and death, to open the prison doors to the captive; that is, to break the fetters of personal sense, and give to being full scope and recompense. This is the ultimate of the command to love our neighbor as ourself, and an idea from Soul, yea, from Wisdom, Love and Truth; but this idea personal sense cannot see, feel, or understand, whereas spiritual sense can; "the carnal mind cannot discern spiritual things." This idea is vague to personal sense, but to spiritual sense it is harmony. To favor his faults, conciliates the man of error; but it prolongs discord; belief produces all the errors of personal sense, and Soul condemns them. Those hated by personal sense are loved of Soul, and for the very things sense hates them.

The foundation error that makes a mortal man is, that personal sense is Truth; the next that it is pleasure; the third that it is pain; but from this point dates its destruction; hence the so-called pain of

Chapter II. Imposition and Demonstration.

personal sense is comparatively encouraging, it being productive of less sin than its pleasure; but personal sense suffers only from imaginary self-hood; its pleasures and pains are all unreal. The belief that matter has Life and substance is the error that produces all suffering, sin and death; the chemical action of Truth on this error will destroy it. Truth gives the idea of Spirit-substance, and destroys all supposed matter-substance, while error gives the belief of matter- substance, and hides the idea of Spirit-substance.

Immortal man is an idea of Spirit-substance, Life and Intelligence; but the mortal is a belief that Intelligence, Life and substance are in matter. The idea of substance guided by understanding, becomes the infinite idea, even as the Soul of immortal man is the infinite Principle. Mortal man is a belief of Intelligence, substance and Life in the body, therefore of a limited Infinite!

To let oneself out of this nutshell, we must understand the scientific relationship between God and man, or Principle and its idea; but before this is really understood, the interval will be filled with approaches to it through belief; and this will be attended with doubt, discord and sin.

The material world, at a future date, will become a spectacle of disorder and dismay on one hand, and of science on the other. There will be convulsions of mind and consequently of matter, spasms of error, earthquakes, famine and pestilence. Sickness will become more acute, and death more sudden: but to those who understand this hour, as explained in the science of being, length of days will increase, and harmony and immortality be near, even at the door. Knowledge will then diminish and lose estimate in the sight of man; and Spirit instead of matter be made the basis of generation. At this period phenomena will be spiritually discerned, but there will be strong conflicting opinions and results. Those understanding Life scientifically will hold in check those, letting go of old opinions, who would hang an M. D., a mesmerist, or a medium, -- thus

Chapter II. Imposition and Demonstration.

curbing the violence of old beliefs exercising retributive vengeance. The truly scientific will be a law to themselves of Love, Wisdom and Truth, and "do violence to no man, neither accuse any falsely." Sin will make deadly thrusts at the science of Life, as penal code goes out to give place to higher law. But those controlled by Soul will spare the rod contrary to the religious persecutions of past history, and save the erring from the gallows and gibbet. The martyrs will be the adherents to Science, in the coming centuries, and to-day their fate is foreshadowed. In coming years the person or mind that hates his neighbor, will have no need to traverse his fields, to destroy his flocks and herds, and spoil his vines; or to enter his house to demoralize his household; for the evil mind will do this through mesmerism; and not in *propria personae* be seen committing the deed.

Unless this terrible hour be met and restrained by *Science*, *mesmerism*, that scourge of man, will leave nothing sacred when mind begins to act under direction of conscious power. Sensuous man makes war to the death on his enemies; but the spiritual pours blessings on them unseen and unacknowledged; like the chamomile, that crushed, yields the sweetest odor, spiritual minds emit an atmosphere of Truth that blesses their enemies and destroys error while it is persecuting them; but stir the evil sensual mind, and worse than the deadly Upas are the plagues it emits. Those who gain the essential points of the science of Life will Buffer from the sensual world more than even the primitive prophets and disciples did; but the science of being supports its followers amid shoals and quicksands.

Spirituality is the only Christianity; and its basis is, to be absent from the body and present with the Lord; "sensuality is personality ever present with the body. We have already sufficient professions of goodness without the Spirit: too many religions and not enough Christianity is the genius of the age. Man knows already too well how "to make long prayers, to be heard for his much speaking," and to enlarge the pharisaical borders, to steal in private and give in

Chapter II. Imposition and Demonstration.

public, but this is political, not Christian economy. What we want is, "Christ and Him crucified," in other words, Truth and the cross-bearing that attends it, to make mankind better.

Because a man has uttered the law and ten commandments to fashionable audiences some quarter of a century, it does not follow that he can demonstrate the Christianity of the prophets, and of Jesus who cast out error and healed the sick. Sometimes people resort to a cup of tea or coffee to help them preach, as if matter was superior to Truth in this direction. Is the Truth we utter matter, or God? and if the latter, "giving does not impoverish nor withholding enrich; " have we less of the Spirit that is God for having given utterance to it, and is matter or Spirit our strength? Because a man has obtained a high social and public position, are we to conclude he must be a good man? The soft palm upturned to a lordly Salary, and architectural power -- making dome and spire tremulous with beauty, that turns the poor and stranger from the gate, shuts the door on Christianity. It is a skeleton of religion that requires a doctor of physic to save the body and a doctor of divinity to save what? immortal Soul that is already saved. This is not having "Christ in you the hope of glory," nor does it cast out devils and heal the sick; the manger and cross tell in vain their story to pride and prejudice. Taking wealth, popularity and sensuality by the right band, takes God by the left, and palsies that hand, making moral lepers instead of Christians.

Hear our Master's words on this subject, "Ye cannot serve God and <u>mammon.</u>" Ministers should make the pulpit the rostrum of Truth, whipping creeds and pride out of their synagogues to let in humility and the science of God, using those strong arguments, cords, that Jesus twisted together to scourge out of synagogues the money changers and make them temples of Truth. The prophet of to-day beholds in the spiritual horizon the bow of promise; the demonstration of Christianity that our Master gave, is again required, and no other "sign shall be given you." Christianity brings with it a phenomenon that will be misinterpreted by the material age

Chapter II. Imposition and Demonstration.

in which it appears, because it is the phenomenon of Soul, and not matter, that personal sense cannot comprehend, but when spiritually discerned will be found to destroy sickness, sin and death. Creeds, doctrines and beliefs do not express it, much less can they demonstrate it; we must understand God to demonstrate Truth. Jesus of Nazareth, the fittest teacher of mankind, possessed this understanding; but the scorning Rabbi, the rival Pharisee, Gethsemane and the cross were ready to devour him.

Over eighteen centuries ago the mere religionist was willing to hail Christ, Truth, with pomp and sceptre, but it came not thus, and though the modern scourge is a scoff, instead of the lash, the doors of some churches are quite as effectually closed against Christ today as then. Truth bids man watch, but is there guard or control held over personal sense by mere religionists? The Christianity of Jesus was the science of being; it destroyed sickness, sin, and death, denied personal sense, bore the cross, and reached the right hand of God, even the perfect Principle of man. Our Master, meekly, and yet as a victor bore the mockery of his self-conscious God-being. "He maketh himself as God," was the foundation of all accusations against him; and the indignities he met, his followers must now meet, until this Truth is understood. He overcame the world, temptations and sins, proving their nothingness. He wrought through the science of being, the example of salvation from sin, sickness, and death, and established the proof that he was Christ, and that Christ is God, the Soul and Life of man.

Every good word and work of our Master evoked but denial, ingratitude, and persecution, from sensualism and malice. Of the ten lepers be healed, but one returned to give God thanks, that is, to acknowledge the Principle that healed him, therefore, but one interpreted his healing aright; and yet he wrought on for his enemies. He felt their sicknesses, but more he felt their sins. Despised and rejected of men, yet returning blessing for cursing, his spirituality must destroy their materiality, and through his stripes must they be healed; because error had felt the blow Truth gave it,

Chapter II. Imposition and Demonstration.

the scourge and cross awaited Jesus. The man of sorrows was not in danger from salaries or popularity; deserving the homage of a world, and sharing pre-eminently the approval of Soul, brief was his triumphant entry into Jerusalem, and followed by the desertion of all save a few mourners at the cross. This is what it means to be spiritual in an age of materiality. The impossibility for worldly favor to attend Christianity is seen in its great moral distance from it. When personal sense approves, Soul condemns, and where man praises, God receives no thanks. One of the evidences of materialism and error is when the belief of Life in matter is full of worldly prosperity.

History informs us that Jesus, feeling the gross materialism that surrounded him, at times experienced a momentary weakness, and turning, asked "Who hath touched me?" The more material, thought this inquiry was occasioned by contact with his body, but he knew it was mind in the multitude that called on him for aid to destroy its beliefs, and make it more spiritual, even as himself. His quick apprehension of this arose from his spirituality, and their misconception, from their materiality; not that he deserved less the advantages of adroitness, because of his goodness; but possessing the insight and honor that cometh from Soul, only, he had less personal sense; these two come from opposite directions, and the treasures of our Master were laid up in Spirit, not matter. Christianity turns from sense to Soul, as naturally as the flower turns from darkness to light; those things eye hath not seen, or ear heard, neither hath it entered into the heart of man to conceive, belong to it.

Paul and the loving John had a very clear sense of the science of being; they knew a man achieves not worldly honors except he labors for them, and lays a sacrifice upon the altar of mammon, by giving his affections to the world. And they also knew to make this offering to wealth or fame, was not to leave all for Christ, Truth, that comes from the opposite direction, and from opposite means and aims; also, that a man walks in the direction he is looking; and that, "where his treasure is there is his heart also." If our hopes are

Chapter II. Imposition and Demonstration.

spiritual, we are not looking, or yearning for the material, but will wear the "image and likeness of God," at any worldly cost; in reality we are coming out from the world of sense, and being separated from it. The favor of sectarianism, the homage of wealth, and smiles of ambition flee before Christianity; but Wisdom crowns its brow.

If my friends are going to Europe and I am making my way to California, we are no longer journeying together; but have separate time-boards to consult, and different routes to pursue; in fine, our paths have parted, and we have no interests in common, to help each other on in opposite directions; but if they will pursue my course, I will give them my railroad guide, and interest myself to make their passage pleasant; or if will take theirs, they will help me on, and our companionship will continue. Thus the scientist must choose his course, and be honest, acting consistent with that choice; his route lies not with the world of sense, and if he gravitates thitherward, he is like a man who travels one day east and another west, but thinking the passage west a more fashionable route, the company more alluring and its pleasures more enticing, changes tactics and journies six days westerly, and the seventh day toward the east, vehemently protesting he is traveling in one direction only. You would say of that man he is untrue and cannot be trusted; and don't let him cajole you into the belief he is really going east because he produces from his pocket a ticket earned by some toil-worn pilgrim, who had explored the way, and from whom he begged it, and with this passport means to make his passage. Unless a man advances spiritually, he is not scientific; and if he is scientific he must start honestly, and journey some every day; and however long he is in reaching the desired goal, if his honesty be preserved, he will finish his course. Many starting with the letter of science, will omit the Spirit, and make shipwreck of their course. We must not only seek, but strive, or we cannot enter the narrow path of science; for broad is the opposite one of sense that leadeth to destruction, and many go in thereat.

Chapter II. Imposition and Demonstration.

Jesus experienced few of the so-called pleasures of personal sense; perhaps she knew its pains, for "he bore our infirmities that through his stripes we might be healed;" Truth in contact with error produced chemicalization. Hence our Master's sufferings came through contact with sinners; but Christ the Soul of man never suffered. Jesus mapped out the path of the science of being, and through poverty of sense was enriched by Soul; but to those buried in the belief of Life in matter, and insisting that we see alone with eyes, and hear with ears, and feel through nerves, he said, " Having eyes ye see not, and ears ye hear not, that ye might understand and be converted and I might heal you." Their belief of personal sense shut out the communications of Soul; hence the saying, "Ye cannot serve two masters." Jesus adhered to one only, was guided by spiritual sense; therefore the sensualism of the age separated from him, and hated him. His affections were pure; theirs carnal; his senses were Truth; theirs but error, therefore Love with him was spiritual science; with them it was material sense; their imperfection and impurity felt his perfection and purity an ever-present rebuke; hence the worlds hatred of the just and more spiritual Jesus; and the prophets' foresight of the reception it would give him.

The people knew not how to interpret their uncomfortableness arising from his presence with them; and the chemical changes he instituted in their being. When those opposites met, had they understood the meaning of the stir it produced, they would, like Peter, have wept at the warning, and begun a warfare with personal sense that opposed Truth. They in their ignorance of the science of Life, never regarded the fact that the good are hated only by the evil, while the former suffer for the latter in life-long sacrifice. He bore their sins in his own person; that is, he felt the suffering their error brought, and through this consciousness destroyed error. Had the Master utterly conquered the belief of Life in matter, he would not have felt their infirmities; he had not yet risen to this his final demonstration, or bad he partaken equally of their sensuous being, he would not have so suffered from them, nor they from him. By overcoming his own temptations he had measurably conquered for

Chapter II. Imposition and Demonstration.

them, even while they knew it not; he demonstrated purity and Truth, and their power to heal the sick, and assured others they might give his demonstration, but for their disbelief in its science. Though they saw not his righteousness, they must all gain the harmony of being from the Truth he taught, and plant their demonstration on the foundations he laid, on what he had experienced for them, and poured liberally into their ears. This was the cup drank by the pioneer of the science of Life, by him who came with those higher proofs and practices of Truth and Love unperceived by the age in which they appeared; they neither understood him, nor his works, and would not accept his explanation who did understand them.

Anomalous though it seems, I have no doubt that Jesus was shunned, and deemed a bad man at the period of his public labors, by all, save the few unpretentious ones whose Christianity enabled them to understand him. This was the cup drank to the dregs, by our Master; he also spake of those who followed him, drinking this very cup; which must indeed be the case if they are in advance of the public sentiment. Referring to himself as doing nothing beyond the ability of others to do, he said, "The works I do, ye shall do, and greater." Before this he had established the platform that "a tree is known by its fruits," indicating, if they healed the sick on the Principle that he healed, they must be Christians. Though it is in vain we stretch our weary wings to the full realization of that saying to-day, yet in centuries to come I look for its fulfillment. Whosoever shall triumph over personal sense, and lay down his earthly all on the altar of the science of being, will drink his cup, and be able to give the demonstration of healing the sick, casting out error, raising the dead, and triumphing over the grave, that our blessed Master gave for our example. But earth hath no recompense for such a life; personal sense can neither give nor receive this reward; the understanding of God is its only recompense that lifts being above mortal discord and gives it immortal harmony.

Chapter II. Imposition and Demonstration.

A person may reward unjustly, but Principle cannot. That we receive all deserved punishment on earth, is quite as false as that all our rewards are mundane; and who that toils and sacrifices unceasingly bearing the cross only to see their existence mocked, will say this is sufficient from the hand of Love? Or again, that those have suffered all they have to experience, who still gloating in sensuality and hypocrisy, or murder and rapine, succeeding in all villainies up to the time they pass suddenly from sight in this loathsomeness, are pardoned, and pushed straight into glory? Their punishment here was certainly insufficient to reform them, which is the design of Wisdom, and the good man's heaven would be to them a hell. How can they find bliss in purity and Truth, to whom these are the very opposites of themselves. There is nothing in mercy or Love, that can pardon the necessity in science for sinners to suffer after death. To destroy the penalty due to sin, would be for Truth to pardon error; in which case, the sinner is no wiser for what he has experienced; for if he escapes the punishment he deserves, it is not according to God's government, in which justice is the handmaid of mercy. For sin to produce suffering is the only way to destroy it to him who believes in the pleasures of sin. When man admits there is no pleasure in sin, he has begun to save himself.

Contemplating history from every moral data, down to the present, we learn the faith in Christ, Truth, that caused our martyrs to be burned, and the rights of man to be christened on a gallows, repeats itself in the just suffering for the unjust; then how has God pardoned sin? We all suffer because of sin, and must until science destroys sin and its sufferings. Did the martyrdom of John Brown make one of the crimes of Jefferson Davis less, or less deserving its reward? What awaits the God-inspired martyr is the crown of thorns here, and the victor's palm hereafter; but what awaits the pampered hypocrite, is the laurel here, and the thorns there.

The demonstration Jesus gave of God, did for the world more than a problem wrought and explained in mathematics does for the learner; it taught the human race how to demonstrate aright the

Chapter II. Imposition and Demonstration.

Principle, that is God; and if this demonstration had been understood, man would have reached the example of Jesus, and solved his being harmoniously ere this. The martyr-spirit is the stepping-stone from the human to the divine; martyrs are the luminaries of Soul that go down to personal sense, like the sun to appear again in the amplitude of their being, when sensuality shall give place to spirituality, and the leaders' stand-point is reached. Truth is self-conscious right that brings its own reward, but not amid the smoke of battle is it seen, or appreciated.

The personal belief of God that holds Spirit person instead of Principle, making Soul intelligent matter, and possessing all the tyranny and passion a belief of Life in matter manifests, was the very error that crucified Jesus; and that to-day is shutting out the reign of harmony. Jesus knew there was but one God, hence that man's Intelligence was God, and not man; Principle, and not person; therefore, said he, "I and the Father are one; " and because of this scientific statement, and the demonstration it brought with it, the rulers cried out, "Crucify him, *he maketh himself as God*," " and what further witness need we against him."

To-day this very statement is met with the same opposition from sensualism it ever was, and why? Because it cuts off right hands, and plucks out eyes by denying personal sense; and lays the axe at the root of the tree, cutting off the medium of all sin. God is perfect; and if there be no other intelligence, we can have no imperfection; the only way to destroy error is to divest it of supposed Intelligence, by which it can give pain or pleasure. Now to admit there is a separate Intelligence from good, called evil, is the error that admits two powers, namely, God, and devil, simultaneous, but gives superiority and all worldly success to the latter; this error is waning somewhat, and to-day his Satanic majesty is not deemed so much a distinct individual as a universal power. The next step in progress is to learn there is no devil; that error and sin have no Intelligence; the Scriptures deny aught but God, and his creation; and assert there "was nothing made without Him," while "out of the mouth of the

Chapter II. Imposition and Demonstration.

most high proceedeth not good and evil;" in other words, that God never made a demon, for a pure fountain sends not forth corrupt streams, and nothing but God is self-existent; Jesus stripped all disguise from this error, had he only been understood; he explained it impossible to have another Intelligence than God, or for Him to create evil, and demonstrated this by healing the sick, and casting out devils, showing that God destroyed satan instead of making it; in other words, that Truth destroys error by proving its nothingness. The personal belief that man is a separate mind from God, and that this mind comprehends, feels, and exists, an entity within the cranium, and sins, and suffers, *ad libitum*, is the only personal devil there is, and the one we should begin to cast out.

This error is not the result of brains, but is a belief that brains are Intelligence; in other words, that God is in matter: it is not the result of Intelligence in matter, but a belief that matter is intelligent; not the product of man's mind, but a belief there is mind in man, and this belief is delusion, and delusion, error. Do you ask who or what is it that believes? Insomuch as you admit God is not the author of error, and that "all things were made by him and without him nothing was made," we answer no one believes: it is only that error is a belief, and a belief is error. The prerogative of Soul is understanding, but personal sense has no claims whatever to this. We need not cite anatomy, physiology, materia medica, etc., that place Intelligence in personal man, but will cover the ground with the Scripture metaphor that named belief the "tree of knowledge," whence sprang sickness, sin and death. A belief is not Intelligence, nor its result, neither God, nor the result of this Principle; it is not Soul, nor its manifestation. What then is it? The opposite of Soul, called brains, and personal sense. Error is the opposite of Intelligence and imitates it only by falsehood, calling Principle, person, God, man; thus pre- supposing man intelligent matter. Is it an error to believe Truth? It is impossible to do this; all we receive of Truth comes through the understanding, The so- called mind of man can be deranged or destroyed by a blow on the cranium; but Intelligence, that governs man and the universe, is not lost.

Chapter II. Imposition and Demonstration.

Intelligence is Life, Love and Truth, and by no means personal sense, sin, sickness and death. The mind of Intelligence understands and never believes, and the body of Intelligence is spiritual not material; idea, and not substance; yea, it is the reflex shadow of Soul, even man that is "the image and likeness of God;" what besides this we name man, is but a belief and error, dust to dust. Hereby we learn a lie is all the satan there is, and marking its footsteps we gain this proof, all the discords of earth proceed from false conceptions of God and man; besides, falsehood preys on harmony in society, and hides individual character. Truth is generally unperceived, because a lie is a more natural conclusion for the wicked. Expose sin, and it turns the lie on you; a sinner for the time prospers in secret wrong-doing until the final hour that "whatsoever is hidden shall be revealed." We must tell the Truth concerning sin and sinners, because of the moral necessity not to cover iniquity; they will deny what we say, of course, but at the same time it produces the desired effect, and we receive our reward, for it introduces new light and makes sinners afraid to repeat the offence when they are found out. The higher you rise in the scale of Truth, the more intense and multiplied are the lies concerning you; the louder God speaks, the higher the devil lifts its voice to be heard above Him; the more Truth you bring, the more error is stirred by it, until the final conquest on the side of right.

Jesus taught his students the science he understood, but they never reached his demonstration, and rose toward it only as they followed implicitly his directions. It is of little importance whether self-abnegation and faithfulness are rewarded in the present or future; their recompense is sure. There must be a going out of personal sense, and coming in of the spiritual, to understand the science of being, and to give a higher sense of Omnipotence whereby to control man and matter. Jesus taught and practiced the science of being, tested the reception it would meet before it was understood, and notwithstanding the malice that error aimed at Truth, fulfilled his Soul-mission, triumphed over sense, and sat down at the right hand of the Father, having solved being on its

Chapter II. Imposition and Demonstration.

Principle, which is Truth, Life and Love. He who was God, and not in man, was "no respecter of persons;" therefore, claimed no personal worship. Persecuted from city to city, he went about doing good, for which he was maligned and stoned. Jesus taught us Principle is God, and God is Love, but Pharisee and Priest affirmed God is person that can love and hate. Truth that is felt is hated by the sinner; for it cuts off right hands, plucks out the eyes, and calls on him to become wise. The belief of God in matter, or a personal Deity, never yet made a Christian, and will go down in a moral chemical that has already begun arid will continue until God is admitted Soul outside of sense, and the only Intelligence.

The basis of all health, sinlessness and immortality is the one great Truth, that God is the only Intelligence, and for this Truth, the great Teacher of the science of Life was martyred. The reward of our Master was not on earth, and not in matter, but Spirit, while all his sufferings came from the materiality of the age, and were not because of his own sins, but the sins of others. Then was it just for him to suffer? No, but it was inevitable in this wicked world where the good suffer because of the evil, even as the evil derive blessings from the good. Jesus taught us, that the way of Truth is the way of salvation, which is spiritual; material religion consists of rites, ceremonies, a personal God, etc., but this is not Christianity. Seventy students Jesus sent forth whom he had faithfully taught; but of twelve only have we any especial record, and one of those had a devil. His final crucifixion drew near, the hour of triumph over personal sense, and all the pangs this world could occasion-the boar that gave the highest proof of the science of being, proof so important to mankind.

Judas thought to take advantage of the world's ingratitude to his teacher, and betray him into the hands of his enemies for thirty pieces and the smile of a Pharisee. Well did the pitiful traitor know his time, for the world was then in mystery concerning him and his teachings. Perhaps Judas feared the period approached that should reveal the great goodness which enabled his Master to demonstrate

Chapter II. Imposition and Demonstration.

above him, and to rebuke the sinner as none other could; the moral distance between himself and his teacher had already created his enmity, wherein greed for gold held empire over gratitude. He also knew the sensuous world loved a Judas better than it did a Jesus, and this was another point through which to victimize his Teacher, and raise himself with the people. Judas had all the world's weapons, Jesus none of them; therefore he chose not to defend himself before those who understood not that defence, so "he opened not his mouth." The great exponent of Truth and Love silent before error and hate! They to whom he had given the highest proofs of the science of being, misinterpreted them, and said deridingly, "He maketh himself as God." Those "who turn aside the right of a man before the face of the most high," esteemed him "stricken and smitten of God," he was "brought as a lamb to the slaughter, and as a sheep dumb before her shearers," and "who should declare his generation," who in future should say whence cometh Truth, and answer the question, what is Truth?

The Rabbis could not decide this momentous inquiry; they must wait on the centuries; but the women at the cross clued say he was right who had inspired their devotions, winged their faith with understanding, healed the sick, cast out error, and caused those he sent forth to say, "Even devils are subject to us through thy name." But where were the seventy whom he had taught, were all conspirators, save eleven; had they forgotten his weary years of explanations and patient waiting, all his labors of Love as clay by day he taught them the science of Life, and spake to them the Truth of man; could they not give him even a cup of cold water in its name, and satisfy for a moment his yearning for one proof of their fidelity to what he had taught? >From early boyhood, he had been about his master's business; and they about theirs; but their masters were unlike; one was Spirit, and the other matter; one God, the other man, one was Soul, the other personal sense. He had suffered and experienced for them, to give liberally his dear-bought bounty unto their famine; but what was his reward? Forsaken of all save a loving few, who knelt in woe at the scene of his crucifixion. Peter would

Chapter II. Imposition and Demonstration.

have smitten the enemies of his master, but he bade him put up the sword, and take not the world's weapons to defend Truth. Jesus disdaining artifice or brute courage, when Truth could not protect him from the false accusation, was able to submit to a felon's death. His mission was to vindicate a Principle, and not a person, while their highest ambition was the applause of man.

Jesus could no doubt have withdrawn from his enemies, but he permitted them the opportunity to destroy his body mortal, that he might furnish the proof of his immortal body in corroboration of what he had taught, that the Life of man was God, and that body and Soul are inseparable. The opposite belief was the error he came to destroy. Neither spear nor cross could harm him; let them think to kill the body, and after this, he would convince those he had taught this science, he was not dead, and possessed the same body as before. Why his disciples saw him after the burial, when others saw him not, was because they understood better his explanations of this phenomenon; he had given them the Principle of it, in healing the sick; hence the unsatisfied malignity of his foes, that he was not dead, but furnished a higher demonstration than ever of the Principle he taught, and for which they had hoped to kill him. Another important feature was, that he sought not the protection of law from their unjust wrath, but chose in every instance to demonstrate the higher law that governed being, that cast out error, healed the sick, and was about to prove its triumph over death, over the beliefs of personal sense and Life and substance in matter. Jesus knew the body is but a reflex shadow of immortal Soul, also that it is impossible to lose this, for, as the Scripture saith, it is the image of God.

Alone, the meek demonstrator of God and fittest teacher of man, met his fate; no eye to pity, no arm to save; he who had saved others, a solemn, faithful sentinel at the threshold of the great Truth he would establish, unprotected by man, was ready to be transformed by its renewing. He had taught what he was about to prove, that Life was God, and superior to all conditions of matter,

Chapter II. Imposition and Demonstration.

above the wrath of man, and able to triumph over the cross and grave. In the garden night-walk, that hour of gloom and glory, the utter error of supposed Life in matter, its pain, ignorance, superstition, malice and hate, reached him in their fullest sense. His students slept. "Can you not watch with me one hour?" was the supplication of their great spiritual Teacher, but receiving no response to this last human yearning, he turned forever away from earth to heaven, from sense to Soul, and from man to God. The triumph of Soul over sense demanded by the great Principle of being must be proved, and Jesus availed himself of Life and glory outside of matter, in this supreme hour, and final demonstration of the science of being; and yet viewing its utter magnitude, and feeling the lack of all human sympathy, he momently exclaimed, "Hast thou forsaken me?"

Had this appeal been made to a person, we might have doubted the justice or affection of that father, who for an instant could withhold the clear recognition of his presence to sustain and bless so faithful a son. But it was not made to a person, it was made to Truth, Life and Love, the Principle he was to prove: and the momentary fear was, that his understanding of these was not sufficient to meet that hour of the world's hate. Jesus knew God is Love, that He, not man, was Love, insomuch as Love is Soul, and not personal sense; but suppose this recognition should falter under stress of circumstances, what would his accusers say? Even what they did, that Truth should be confounded, and there should be no re-appearing of Jesus.

The weight of mind bearing on him at that hour from the throng of disbelievers in the great Principle for which he was crucified, weighed heavily; not the spear, nor the cross, but the ingratitude of the world drew forth the half suppressed "*ali sabacthani*," that unpinioned for a moment the wings of faith. The world's hatred of Truth caused that moment of agony, harder to bear than the crow, up the hill of grief. A Life that was Love, all the good he did, rewarded with a cup of gall! Behold the sweat of blood falling in holy

Chapter II. Imposition and Demonstration.

benediction on the grass of Gethsemane, and say, was Christianity then the privileged of earth, and can the followers to-day of that Truth so persecuted then, expect the world's approval? Principle bestows few palms until we reach through demonstration, its fullness. Love must triumph over hate, and Truth and Life over error and death, before the thorns are laid off for the crown of glory, and "well done good and faithful," bestows immortal honors. Our Master had realized and demonstrated the science of Life when he was found talking with his disciples after the burial; and whom the Rabbis had hoped to bury in a sepulchre, to-day is acknowledged God! and this God, and this Truth that Jesus taught and proved over eighteen centuries ago, in days to come will be understood.

Soul triumphed over personal sense, and said to death, where is thy sting, and where thy victory, grave? But many who saw this phenomenon misconstrued it; his disciples even, called him a "spirit," but his reply was, Spirit hath not flesh and bones as ye see me have; Jesus demonstrated man's unchanged condition after what we call death, also that Spirit is not person or man; and to convince Thomas of this, he caused him to examine the prints of the nails and spear; he proved for time and eternity that death is but a belief of personal sense, because Life is Spirit, alias God, and God the immortality and Soul of man; but those consenting to the martyrdom of a righteous man were only willing out of their wicked work to make a doctrinal platform for saving souls? His students, not sufficiently advanced to understand the lesson of that hour, performed not their wonderful healing until their Master reappeared, and talked with them of its science, and at length rose out of their sight, that is, his third demonstration was so beyond their understanding, we have no farther record of him to explain. Then received they the holy ghost, in other words, the fuller interpretation that science gives of God, and wrought after the example of their Teacher, when they had no longer a person, but a Principle to lean upon.

Chapter II. Imposition and Demonstration.

In the crucifixion of our Master, human error and divine Truth met, and Truth conquered through "the man of sorrows," who best understands the nothingness of Life in matter, and the substance of Life, Truth and Love. Because Jesus was the fuller manifestation of Spirit therefore, the higher representative of God among men; the world of sense hated him. Fully comprehending this, he said to his disciples, "You hath it loved, but me hath it bated;" proving that mortal man is not allied to Life, Truth, or Love, that personal sense is the very opposite of Soul, in its attractions, joys and sorrows. Herod and Pilate could lay aside old feuds, to unite in putting to derision and death the best man on earth; they could take up common cause against the exponent of Truth, because they both secretly hated it, and were united in their malice against him that upheld it. To get rid of Jesus and his accusing Wisdom, was the design of them both. Said the Rabbi, and Pharisee, "He stirreth up seditions," "he maketh himself as God," "he is a glutton, and a winebibber," "he casteth out devils through Beelzebub," "and is the friend of sinners." The last was the only correct view taken of him. Because his life was nearer Truth, he was more belied than all other men; and because he was the friend of sinners, he failed not to rebuke them pointedly and unflinchingly; hence they regarded him their strongest enemy; and so he was, the strongest foe to error, but the friend of man. Through demonstration Jesus established the foundations of the science of Life, controlled matter, and proved Intelligence, neither matter, nor man, but the Principle of man, able to hold and govern the body, and to destroy sin, sickness, and death.

People's opinions of Jesus were the very opposite of the man, and mark you wisely what will be said to-day of the science he taught and its followers, and see if there be no resemblance between the reception it received in the past, and that accorded it at present. We have few demonstrators to-day in part even, of the great Truth taught by Jesus; but we hesitate not to say it is the privilege and possibility of all Christians to follow his example, and what they claim to do, but they must keep his first command, "to heal the sick," as proof they understand this example, and the Principle that

Chapter II. Imposition and Demonstration.

healed. We see some amelioration of the stake and gibbet in this age, but the vengeance with which doctrines and beliefs pursue Truth, has not ceased in this century.

When the science of being's purity, confronts the impurity of sense, and humanitarianism lifts a voice above sectarianism, blows will fall liberally on science, its true followers will be traduced and persecuted, and imposition and malice will smite their destroyer. Doctors in general will trample on it, insomuch as it heals the sick without drugs, and must ultimately destroy sickness, when their "occupation will be gone." But shall we serve the old masters because Truth has enemies, and disturbs the tranquillity of error? Wisdom has given us more foresight than this; to the advanced thinkers perceiving the scope and tendency of Truth we may look for support; while others will say to the science of being, as did one of old, to please the Rabbis, "Go thy way for this time."

The highest stand-point of being, is its science, but opinions, doctrines and beliefs afford no demonstrable Principle to reach it, and enable man to work out his own salvation; 'tis Truth, the Principle of man that does this. But is there not a smoother and broader path to harmony or heaven; and cannot Christianity lie coupled with worldly peace and prosperity? The very nature of it is peace and blessedness, but its joys and triumphs are not earthly, they are passing away from matter to Spirit. By this we do not mean death, nor a sudden ecstasy; but the gradual fading out of material things, of earthly desires, possessions and pleasures, and the coming in of purity, Truth and immortality. The demands of personal sense will grow less, the appetite become simple, pride, malice and all sin yield to meekness, mercy and Love, until finally the belief of Life in matter yields to the consciousness that Life is Spirit, and Spirit, God. AM good thoughts and deeds are science that proceeds not from a doctrinal basis, but is soul subduing sin, personal belief, personal pleasure, or pain; and revealing all harmony, righteousness and blessedness in our God-being.

CHAPTER III

SPIRIT AND MATTER

IF happiness and Life are of the body, personal sense is man, and man is matter, an intelligent body, but sickness, sin and death do not constitute immortal man, neither are these Spirit.

Nothing false or impure is for a moment embraced in immortal Soul; these are mortal, the destructive elements of matter-mind. The best sermon ever preached is Truth demonstrated on the body, whereby sickness is healed and sin destroyed. Knowing that one will be supreme in the affections, and take the lead of our actions, the Master said, "Ye cannot serve two masters," well knowing that which determines our place in Christianity proves also whether man is the servant of Soul, or sense, of God, or man. If Spirit governs man, sin does not tempt him, the so-called laws of matter make him sick, or limit his Life and usefulness. Straight and narrow is the path of science, and few there be who go in thereat.

The Truth of man makes a new creature; "old things have passed away, and behold all things have become new." When personal sense is exchanged for the science of being, "all things become immortal and harmonious; every belief of matter as substance, Life, or Intelligence, must be destroyed before man is found the image and likeness of God; Christian perfection is won on no other basis. In the scientific unity between Soul and body, or God and man, Soul is not in body, but man is embraced in Spirit, even as Principle contains its idea and is controlled by it. Intelligence embraces and governs the harmonious heavens and earth where His "will is done."

Man controlled by Wisdom, Truth and Love has no physical suffering, his body is harmonious; but the belief of Soul in body and Spirit in matter is governed alone by personal sense, by beliefs of sickness, sin and death, doctrines, theories, etc., hence it is ever getting wrong, and finally goes down, and this man is proved mortal. The man of sense is instinct with lies, and is the "old man to be put off" before God's idea the immortal man is understood; as Paul has it, before the "new man is put on." What the apostle called the "new man," is what the science of being, so new to the world of sense, will bring out when not strangled by error and persecution.

Theories and doctrines that presuppose Soul in body, and God in man, by grafting holiness into unholiness, make sickness, sin and death Truth, or God error; giving the lie to science, and constituting a barren stereotyped belief, straining at gnats and swallowing camels. Why man is not realized perfect, "even as his Father," his harmonious Principle "is perfect," is owing to the belief an Intelligence other than God can direct him away from Truth, Life and Love, when it is but the error of personal sense that does this, and not all intelligent evil; there is but one Intelligence, anti this is God.

Our beliefs of a supreme Being commence, saying, He hath almighty power and is a present help in times of trouble, and end with a drug or a rainy day superior to Him; the understanding of God changes this position, giving omnipotence to Spirit, and no power to matter. Intelligence in matter would negative the omnipotence of Spirit. Mortal error is at war with immortal Truth, and is the sick, sinning and dying belief named mortal man that saith, death is the master of Life.

Error abounds where Truth would much more abound, were God understood, and the scientific relationship of Soul and body as Principle and Idea, and the impossible union of Spirit and matter fully apprehended. Jesus said, "I and the Father are one," that is, I am Soul and not body, Spirit and not matter, hence there is but one Intelligence or Soul because there is but one God; recollect "I" signifies God, and not man; Principle, and not person; Spirit, and not matter; and this is the science of Soul and body that enables us to heal the sick on the Principle or Truth of man; viz., that "in God we

Chapter III. Spirit and Matter.

live, move and have being"; Spirit and not matter hold the issues of Life.

The accusation most denunciatory to Jesus, the great demonstrator of the science of being, was this: "He maketh himself as God"; but this, also was the point that made him all he was more than other men. When this fundamental Truth is understood, it will be found to induce not only more exalted worship, but self-abnegation, a higher spiritual apprehension of the supreme Being, and the ability to bring out all the possibilities of being; it destroys also the belief in matter, and finds man in God; the mistaken opinion that Soul is in the body, or any portion of God in man would rob the All-wise of some omnipotence and Wisdom. Theories and beliefs either admit more than one God, or less than a God; we must break the bars of personality and let go the belief of God in matter, and get out of man into God, to reach the science of Life and be rid of sickness, sin, and death; so long as Life and Intelligence are supposed to be in matter, man will be mortal. The belief that is fatal to science, to man's harmony, and to God's omnipotence supposes a portion of Jehovah is imprisoned in a body of sensuality and death, to escape thence when this body has gone to ruin in His keeping, mastered Omnipotence, and destroyed itself, or when God the Life of man has killed the body, to get out of it, into the science and circumference of being.

The smallest portion of holiness was never inside of sin, or mixed in any manner with it. The good we see, and say it is in man, is outside of him; mortal man, or mind in matter, is morally and scientifically impossible, even to God. The belief that good and evil, God and devil, Spirit and matter mingle in the least, or take the same individuality, is the error called mortal man. There are degrees of comparison, however, in error, the lesser one is the less material man, hence the more transparent to Truth, outside this error the good in connection with mortal man, is outside of him, instead of inside. The idea of God outside the belief of Life in matter is immortal man; we catch glimpses of him when the clouds of error are less dense,

Chapter III. Spirit and Matter.

and at times melt into such thinness we perceive the image and likeness of God in some word or deed that reveals somewhat of the true being, even the immortal man, sinless and eternal. Not, however, that a mortal man embraces one atom of goodness; all is sin and sense there, but that the good outside of him at times shines through him like the sunbeams that the vapory cloud cannot hide. The less we admit matter intelligent, and cease to call the body "I," the more we gather ourself in the good, outside of evil, and the sooner will God be understood, and man will be found the image and likeness of God.

Admitting Soul is in the body, and Life and Intelligence matter, as well as God; the infinite gets into the finite, and even then cannot control the body in which He dwells; contending bodily conditions are beyond the control of Intelligence; we employ matter remedies to do what is not even expected of Omnipotence, and mortal man limps with lameness, droops with dyspepsia, or consumes with pulmonary disease, etc., until this so-called man yields up the ghost.

We should hesitate to say God sins and suffers, although the logic of such reasoning would be this; if God dwells in person or man we must confess to atheism and Submerge Intelligence in matter. How far is the belief removed from infidelity, that unites Spirit and matter, and employs the latter to heal the sick, thus tacitly acknowledging matter superior to God. This error cannot be understood, or it would not be tolerated.

There are evil beliefs, and these falsely called evil "spirits." There is but one Spirit, viz., Life, Love, and Truth; and this is sufficient for all things, and a "very present help in time of trouble"; but when knowledge takes the responsibility to say matter is more potent than man's Maker, is it well to suppose Christianity can mix with this belief, so opposite to Jesus' teachings, and demonstrate as he did the science of being, casting out error, and healing the sick.

Chapter III. Spirit and Matter.

To understand that "I" is Intelligence, and this the one God, enables man to gain the immortality of Soul, and to destroy the errors of sense, and make the body harmonious and eternal, because it is governed by Spirit; but to believe ourself nerves, bones, brain, etc., is to accept the aid of matter to control the body, virtually admitting God incapable of the entire government of man. If brains, nerves, etc., are intelligent, then Spirit and matter commingle, and sin and holiness, sickness and health, Life and death, good and evil, are mixed, and who shall say which is one or the other, for this would be a matter of opinion. Our Master destroyed this doctrine when He said, "there is no fellowship between God and Belial." If man is Intelligence, there are gods many; or if Intelligence is in man, the greater enters into the lesser; and God becomes less than man, and there is no God; 'tis in vain we insist on such self-evident error! Those self-conscious of any goodness are also conscious of Love and Truth, outside of matter.

If man would pay due allegiance to God, what stronger argument has he by which to overcome sickness and sin, than to regard these not made by God, "who made all that was made;" and because they were not, that they are without creation or reality. To trample on sin by holding yourself superior to it, is wisdom; but to fear it, bringeth a snare, because you acknowledge some power or Intelligence superior to God. To trample on the belief of sickness, and to regard yourself superior to it, is wise; but to fear sickness, causes it, by acknowledging its supremacy over you. If you possess Love, Wisdom, or Truth, you have Life, that is superior to death, sickness, or sin, and you ought to prove this fact by demonstration.

If thought is startled at the strong claims of the science of being, and doubts them, are we not surprised also, by the claims of evil? but admit them, although discord is unreal and Truth not as surprising or arbitrary as error.

When sound is interpreted by personal sense, it is but a belief that may be lost with a single change of opinion regarding it, but

Chapter III. Spirit and Matter.

where it exists in its Principle, we hold it in Soul, and a self-conscious capacity undying. The belief that the so-called dead speak audibly to the living, gives a mental impression the same as other beliefs, and has no more reality than those. Sound is produced by mental impressions, and not by the action of air on the mechanism of the ear. Hearing is not dependent on matter, but depends either on belief or the understanding. Those believing in "spirits," may produce to personal sense the impression of sound that has the same reality to them as the more common *modus operandi* has to others. It is mind alone that hears, and mind that gives the impression of sound; and this is proved by clairvoyance.

One individual believes he must use his hands to bring a rose in contact with the olfactories; and another, equally sincere, believes legerdemain can do this; and a third, that the so-called dead handle the rose for him; but each one has produced this phenomenon by his belief, and only because the method is more common to let limbs, lips, and ears express the mind's volition, and sound to sense, other methods we call miracles. As a man thinketh, so is he in error; but as a man understandeth, so is be in Truth. A belief of sickness, coming in contact with another belief of health, is sometimes negatived, and the sick feel better, and this is the only point of science that the malpractitioner adheres to. The supposed sensations of body are the impressions of one's own mind, or that another mind produces, in no case do they proceed from matter; at length they may become a belief of inflammation, suppuration, paralysis, stiffness, etc.; but in no instance do they originate in matter.

Again, one mind coming in contact with the grief of another is depressed, and a tear starts; now has not mind in this instance produced an effect on the body, upon the lachrymal glands? and not more readily, or distinctly on the eyes, than an internal organ. Mind produces diseased bones, and governs alone the entire internal viscera, and this is the explanation of all disease. The excellent author, John Young of Edinburgh, says, "God is the father of minds, and of nothing else;" surely this is the voice of Truth, crying in the

Chapter III. Spirit and Matter.

wilderness, prepare ye the way of moral science, even the reign of Spirit over matter. Scourging Truth out of synagogues will not hide it forever. The signs of to-day point to the era when all that really is, will be understood Spirit and its phenomena; and already the shadow of this right hand rests upon the hour.

The inquiry should no longer be, can mind produce sounds, faces and forms? but what is the best method of training mind here, to produce good instead of evil, that materialism, which depends wholly on mechanical construction and matter conditions for cause and effect, and the evil results from mediumship, may cease forever.

The Jews' determination to recognize God only as person and a king, has not forsaken this age; nor have our creeds and ritualism in other respects quite washed their hands of Rabbinical error. To-day echoes back the cry of bygone centuries: "Crucify him that maketh himself as God," Spirit, and let matter have dominion over man.

Because Jesus understood God better than did the Rabbis, he arrived at the conclusion in advance of them he was Spirit and not matter, and that these never blend; also, that there is but one Spirit, or Intelligence, therefore but one God, one Life, Love and Truth. All forms of belief deny this in the main, and contend that Intelligence is both God and man, that there are two separate entities or beings exercising antagonistic powers; also, that matter controls Spirit, that man is both matter and Spirit, and the supreme Being is God and man; also, that a third person named devil, is another Intelligence and power, and that these three different personages, viz., God, man, and devil blend in one person. When we possess a true sense of our oneness with God, and learn we are Spirit alone, and not matter, we shall have no such opinions as these, but will triumph over all sickness, sin, and death, thus proving our God-being. That we are Spirit, and Spirit is God, is undeniably true, and judging by its fruits, (the rule our Master gave) we should say this is not only science, but Christianity; but the shocking audacity that calls itself God, and yet demonstrates only erring mortality, surprises us! Some one has said

Chapter III. Spirit and Matter.

Christianity must be science, and science Christianity, else one or the other is false and useless; but neither of these is proved thus, hence they are inseparable in demonstration.

When looking to mortal man for evidences of Life and Truth, we find sin and death stronger than either of these, hence we must look away from body to soul; not in mortality is Spirit that is infinite and blest. It is impossible to shut up the infinite in man; we cannot be both Spirit and matter, for these are opposites. Again, if God is both within and without all things, then all is God. When we say the body is matter, we say with Paul, then you must certainly be "absent from the body, to be present with the Lord," even Spirit. But to be absent from the body, materia medica calls death, yet Jesus and Paul knew Life is not in the body. The belief that Life and intelligence blend with matter is the foundation of all misapprehensions of God and man; and we shall prove we are Spirit that mixes not with matter, when this opposite error or belief goes down in death, until it is finally destroyed; yet we shall see, hear, feel, &c., all the same, and independent of matter organizations, which we now deem indispensable to these faculties of Soul. Sooner or later we shall all learn the fetters of our infinite capacities are forged by belief only, and that matter is not substance, Life, or Intelligence. When we understand Spirit better than to think it person or man, or to call it matter and place --life that is supreme in mortality, we shall clothe our bodies with immortality, and not until then.

In science we find Spirit and idea harmonize, and man's existence in Soul, the substance and Principle of the idea we name man. There are no personal senses in Spirit, where thy neighbor is as thyself; thus the command to hold no Intelligence in matter, but to love God, Spirit, with all thy heart, Soul and strength, and thy neighbor as thyself, Jesus said, embraced all law and prophesy. In this relationship of Soul and body otherwise of God and man, what is one man's meat is not another's poison; but what feeds one feeds all, even as Jesus illustrated with the loaves and fishes, when Spirit instead of matter supplied food for the multitude.

Chapter III. Spirit and Matter.

How long before we arrive at the full understanding of the science of being, no man knoweth, not the idea but the Principle, not the son but the Father; yet one thing is certain: we shall destroy sin, sickness and death only as we gain this understanding of science, the Truth of man.

We talk of evil spirits, but there is no evil in Spirit; all discord proceeds from the belief of Spirit in matter; but our slow progress from material stand-points today, portends a long night to the traveller. Whoso opens the way with science is a stranger and pilgrim at present, that marks out the path for future generations.

On the Western Hemisphere, some immortal sentences broke the fetters, and demolished whipping-posts and markets for man, but tyranny would go down in blood, and the breath of freedom must come through the cannon's mouth. The abolition of negro enslavement, however, did not destroy slavery. We have slaves to personal sense, that are hopeless servants, knowing not how to obtain their freedom. The lame, the deaf, the dumb, the blind, the sick and sensual are wearing out years of servitude, dragging their slow length along, chained to the belief the body is their master; and this belief must be abolished, or mankind submit hopelessly to the worst form of slavery. This state of man, however, is not legitimate, and cannot continue forever; even now, in prophetic vision, we see man free as the sons of God, and matter no longer his master; the abolitionists of negro slavery, in discerning the rights of man, foresaw the doom of slavery. Sickness, sin and death belong not to the government of God; neither are we their helpless slaves; they could not conquer man in a single instance, did he understand his authority over them, and assert his freedom in the name of Almighty God, adopting the scientific position that InIelligence controls matter.

A few sentences of the science of being, understood, would enable man to grasp the standard of liberty. Citizens of the world, accept their glorious import and gain your freedom! This is your

Chapter III. Spirit and Matter.

divine right; a belief and not law has bound you, and to a condition of mind and not matter; all the sickness, sin and death on earth are caused by mind, even the belief of man; matter is not cause, and when you destroy the belief that it is, its power over you will flee; you possess your own body and make it harmonious and immortal, or discordant and mortal. You, the Intelligence, embrace the body in comprehension and completeness; put away, then, the error of belief that matter embraces you in mystery and disease; "*you*," the Soul and circumference of being, (for the body is but the idea of "you,") are a law to your members, and the law-giver that makes your body discordant or harmonious, according to the ignorance or understanding, the error or Truth that governs it. Matter has no Intelligence to rule over you; say then to the error whereby you submit to your body, "Depart, ye that work iniquity."

Truth will establish the kingdom of heaven on earth, even the reign of harmony wherein is neither sickness, sin, nor death, and trample out this trio of error; bad God constituted laws of matter with power to male man sick, Christ would not have abrogated those laws by healing the sick, contrary to them. All evidence of physical law and personal sense is destroyed in the science of being.

Personal sense, takes no cognizance of the earth's motion, and beholds the sun making a diurnal round. Science, contradicting personal sense, taught the olden astronomer the sun is our solar centre, and the earth turning on its axis, revolves around it. So at the focus of optical vision when sky and earth appear to meet, and clouds and ocean join hands, science proves them remote as at the nearest points of vision. Again, the barometer, that little prophet of storm and sunshine, declares it fair when personal sense sees nothing but murky clouds and drenching rain-drops. To personal sense, severing the jugular vein takes Life, and destroys man; but to science, Life goes on the same as before, it being indestructible and eternal; for man cannot be destroyed. Science takes all proof out of the hands of personal sense, and makes void this error, interpreting phenomena with reason and revelation based on their Principle.

Chapter III. Spirit and Matter.

Science destroyed Ptolemy's vague theory that earth is the centre of the solar system; and revealed the harmony of the spheres, on a reversed plan.

Personal sense declares Life is in man, and matter is intelligent; that brains, nerves, etc., are seats of pain or pleasure, also, of disease and death; therefore Soul is tributary to the body and in mortality. Theories of anatomy, physiology, etc., make the same blunder with Soul and body that Ptolemy did with the sun and earth; he made the sun tributary to the earth, they make Soul secondary and tributary to the body; but science has destroyed one, and in time will master the other error, overruling the evidence of personal sense altogether, and thus reveal the harmony of man and the universe, on a reversed statement. The Principle of man is Soul, and Soul is Spirit, and this is the only Life, Intelligence, or substance of the universe; all is tributary to Soul. Earth borrows light and heat from the sun, the body borrows Life and Intelligence from Soul. As earth is opaque, having Do light of her own, so the body material is a lifeless, unintelligent belief; but the Spiritual body reflects Life, Love and Truth.

Copernicus marked out the pathway of science in the heavens, and we at a later date would point out the science of Life or Principle of harmonious being; but before Copernicus spake, astrography was a mystery, and the geography of the heavens a myth. The Chaldean shepherd saw in a comet the fate of empires, and read the fortunes of man in a star; no higher revelations than the horoscope hung out upon empyrean, yet earth and heavens were bright, and bird and blossom glad in the sunshine. So to-day we have Truth, Life and Love to gladden man, but leaving him to the interpretations of a belief or personal sense makes him as the wandering comet and desolate star.

"Man never is, but always to be blest."

Chapter III. Spirit and Matter.

The Ptolemic system, or error regarding the heavenly bodies, could not effect the vital interests of man, like the error of belief, relating to our body, that reverses the order of science and assigns to matter the prerogative of Spirit; making man the most inharmonious phenomenon of the universe. When we admit Spirit governs man, and demonstrate this, in our control over the body, sickness, sin and death will disappear; for nothing evil or mortal comes from Spirit; but if we would divide Spirit into persons called "spirits," putting Soul in science of being. The senses of Soul are without pain, and forever at peace; nothing can hide from them the beauties of Truth; but what a transient trust is the eye, when the power of light and lens may all end with a prick of the retina. To understand our being is to hold sight immortal. The science of Soul preserves the sight, and there is no physical science; the Principle of all phenomena is Intelligence and Life, unconfined to matter; where the altitude of the eye need not be perpendicular to the geometrical plane; whatsoever is governed by Soul instead of sense, is never deprived of the action or blessing of Intelligence.

We should never ask after the condition, structure, or economy of the body, but take no thought about it; Soul governs man better than sense, and for the body to be sensationless is science. The compound minerals or aggregate substances that compose the earth, the relations constituent masses bear to each other, or the magnitudes, distances, revolutions, etc., of the celestial bodies, are of no real importance, for all this must give place to the spiritualized understanding, that matter is not substance, and when we admit this, man will be found harmonious and eternal, even the idea of God, that expresses the harmony of being.

Material substance, geological calculations, etc., will be swallowed up in the infinite Spirit that comprehends and evolves all idea, structure, form, coloring, etc., that we now suppose are produced by matter. The spiritual perception of man and of the universe constitutes the true idea of both. While Columbus was putting down one of the errors of personal sense, and giving freer

Chapter III. Spirit and Matter.

breath to the globe, the bands of ignorance and superstition were chaining the honest limbs of the brave old navigator; starvation and disgrace looked him in the face, but sterner still had been the fate of him whom history has since immortalized, had his discovery embraced a Principle, undermining sensuality. Age nor accident interferes with the senses of Soul; the body has no sensation; it cannot see, bear or feel, notwithstanding the belief to the contrary. Understanding this truth, the Master knew no loss of our faculties can occur except to belief; therefore he knew how to handle personal sense, by putting it under his feet, which enabled him to restore sight to the blind, hearing to the deaf, and speech to the dumb.

If it be true that sensation is in nerves, hearing in the ear, sight in the eye, etc.; when these organs are lost our faculties are gone, therefore they cannot be immortal in Spirit, when the reality is they are immortal only thus; personal sense returns to dust, and gives place to spiritual sense, wherein we find not a faculty lost, and nothing gone except sin and suffering. Because the so-called personal senses are mortal we must admit them error, a belief, and not the Truth of man.

What we call laws of nature are as able to destroy the immortality of Soul, as body, or take from man one jot of what God hath given. "To the unknown God, whom therefore ye ignorantly worship," be these laws inscribed. Idolatry keeps pace with civilization, when instead of wood or stone we bow to drugs, fleshbrush, flannel, etc., etc. Thou shalt have no other gods before Me, is the command of Wisdom; no Intelligence in matter, no imaginary physical law, but the one supreme spiritual law of being, namely, the Truth of Soul and body.

Discord and suffering proceed not from God, from Soul, but sense; should man obey Intelligence alone, happiness and harmony would be universal. In the days of Jesus and his students, Truth healed the sick, and would to-day do this, and make man perfect; admitting this Truth, there is but one Intelligence, and this God,

Chapter III. Spirit and Matter.

governing man, yea, Spirit triumphing over matter. Man worships material forms of religion, cringes to popular favor, delves deeper into matter, straining at gnats and swallowing camels; popular humbug is the more merited name for modern knowledge, that like the ancient "tree," greatly multiplies our pains, sin and mortality.

An absolute and perfect Principle, named God, governs man and the universe harmoniously; belief, and personal sense never yet made a harmonious man, or universe. Jesus taught and proved by demonstration, our dominion over matter; also, that a sinless and immortal existence is obtained only through triumph over the body. The Scripture saith, all things are possible to Spirit; but our theories practically deny this, and make healing the sick possible only to matter; but theories are false and the Scripture true. Beliefs rob God and slay man, then spread their table with cannibal titbits and give thanks. Christianity is not dishonest, but our religions axe; to rule mankind and conciliate society at the expense of Truth, yea, to be popular is the weakness of the world. He that leaves all for Truth, and is falsely accused and hated because of Christianity, is wise; the world will believe error and be slow to admit Truth. In this manner the man of sorrows gave to a mocking world the demonstration of the science of being. The cross is the central emblem of history, individually and collectively; all must take it up, and deny pleasure or pain, of personal sense. The history of science over eighteen centuries ago, will repeat itself; persecution for righteousness sake has begun, and those very sects that bore the lash in the past, are the first to flog progress to-day. Jewish rites and ceremonies, and the more modern creed, and ritual, as types and shadows, point to the coming of the Truth of being when the substance or Spirit of those emblems shall appear in demonstration; hence when their Spirit or Truth is gained, all forms should be laid aside; we cannot serve two masters, and keep the commandment, "Thou shalt have no other gods before Me."

We worship spiritually only as we cease to worship through material forms; the material must and will give place to the spiritual;

Chapter III. Spirit and Matter.

let it be so then, and not as in the fable, because the wind blows that would take off the cloak, hug more closely what the wind should remove. Displace the belief of God in matter, or Soul in body, and happiness and immortality will be understood, and never can be until this is done. We gather not grapes of thorns; nor fill vessels that are unemptied.

To empty mankind of error so that Truth may flow into the mind, is the work before us; and those commissioned for this work will suffer tribulation such as has not been since the beginning. When Truth advances, error must recede, but will cry out as it goes: "Why art thou come hither to torment me before the time;" persecution, however, advances the true idea, for it sets thought at work on the subject at issue. Our individual sufferings for Truth, serve to spiritualize us; hence the benediction on those persecuted for righteousness sake, "For theirs is the kingdom of heaven."

Christianity is not a creed, doctrine, or belief; but the demonstration of Life, Love, and Truth; it is not a special gift from a personal Jehovah, but the understanding of God, that is gained through much tribulation in the world, but great peace in Truth; error must and will make war on Truth, because it is proof, and not profession. The Principle of being that makes man harmonious we cannot reach through material rites or the worship of a personal God. The one scientific statement of being, is that neither man nor matter has substance, Life or Intelligence. There is a wide difference between the interpretation belief and opinions give of Christianity, and that *which the* science of Life demonstrates. Jesus and his students healed the sick, because of their spirituality: they healed with Christ, Truth, and not in the name of Christ, but in the practice-thereof. We have no need of creeds and church organizations to sustain or explain a demonstrable platform, that defines itself in healing the sick, and casting out error. The uselessness of drugs, the emptiness of knowledge that puffeth up, and the imaginary laws of matter are very apparent to those who are rising to the more glorious demonstration of their Godbeing.

Chapter III. Spirit and Matter.

The mistake the disciples of Jesus made to found religious organizations and church rites, if indeed they did this, was one the Master did not make; but the mistake church members make to employ drugs to heal the sick, was not made by the students of Jesus. Christ's church was Truth, "I am Truth and Life," the temple for the worshippers of Truth is Spirit and not matter, even the Principle of man and the universe that calls on those professing godliness, to understand God, and to be absent from the body to be present with Him, and to claim their right of membership by destroying sickness, sin, and death. Is there any higher Christianity than this?

No time was lost by our Master in organizations, rites, and ceremonies, or in proselyting for certain forms of belief: members of his church must answer to themselves, in the secret sanctuary of Soul, questions of the most solemn import. First, am I surely gaining a victory over matter, and present with Spirit, present with Love and Truth, supping with them and they with me, gaining this oneness with God, of which Jesus spake, thus rising superior to personal sense, and conquering sickness, sin and death; am I caring less and less for earthly pleasures or pains, and getting out with the sinner and in with the saint? The true answer to these inquiries will set us all right; they are the only signs significant of the burial of the body with Christ, and its resurrection with God, Truth, compared with which rites and ceremonies sink into insignificance. We have no record that forms of church worship were instituted by our great spiritual teacher, Jesus of Nazareth, and we learn the improbability of this, in the science of God, that he taught and demonstrated. Said he, "The time now is when they that worship the Father should worship him in Spirit, and no longer in Jerusalem," (the wealth and learning) "of our temples "; a magnificent edifice was not the sign of Christ's Church.

Anciently the followers of Christ, Truth, measured their Christianity by the control it gave them over sickness, sin and death; whereas the more modem forms of religion leave out the first proof,

Chapter III. Spirit and Matter.

and substitute observances for a test of the latter; but we are learning slowly, as the centuries paw, to leave forms and doctrines, and require the primitive tests of Christianity. If we accept the mere letter of moral and spiritual science and omit the Spirit, we shall not gain the great Truth that destroys sin as well as sickness, but omit the important point that heals the sick. We must watch and work more for the Christianity of the science of being than its other points, and must make our first proof if we would succeed in healing, for this more than all else gives success.

When its science is made clear to the understanding, it presents a thorough explanation of the Principle whereby Jesus and his disciples healed the sick, cast out error, and raised the dead. We may not hope to explain in this limited volume his great Truth and science of being to the full understanding of our readers, insomuch as our own and their beliefs hide its quick perception, and to change their views with Truth is the labor of teaching. It requires experience and time for the spiritual advancement of some students, while others assimilate Truth as the great want of their being. We can only sow the seed in this book, and trust the Lord of harvest to give the fuller sense of harmonious being.

In centuries past, Jesus founded Christianity on the spiritual basis, that neither ritualism, doctrine nor belief, but Wisdom, Truth and Love make Christians, and cast out error, and heal the sick; but to-day church forms are held responsible for Christianity, and drugs and matter-laws to heal the sick.

To ascertain what our progress is and what our state of Christianity, we have only to learn what God we acknowledge and *obey*. If we are progressing, God will become less personal and material to our understanding, and more practical, matter will be yielding to Spirit, and the Spirit we manifest will reveal us; personal sense, that is the basis of all sin and error, cannot judge of Christianity. Admitting matter capable of good and evil to man, robs God of supremacy, and would despoil his dominion, making it a

Chapter III. Spirit and Matter.

kingdom divided against itself that cannot stand. When we get right in regard to Deity, motives and deeds, not professions, will be the standard of Christianity, and we shall gain continually in its proof and practice. Many a rank hypocrite at heart makes clean the outside of the platter. Out theories of God and man admit incapacity in Spirit which robs God, and is the impediment to man's harmony. Those that peruse this book with prejudice, or who will not read it at all, must fail to understand our purpose or Principle; but many, we trust, will read carefully, and if the seed falls into good and honest hearts, those will eventually bear fruit, and understand how the science of God heals the sick; sooner or later all will feel the need of this Truth. When you attempt to demonstrate healing according to the Principle herein stated, you will see every point in our statement is needed to help you; but not until you prove this will you admit it; and alas! little Truth is demonstrated healing the sick by our rules, without the Spirit.

We are Soul, Spirit, and not matter; and it is quite as impossible to be both as to serve God and mammon. Let science interpret God, and man will become harmonious and immortal. You can rest assured of the impossibility to enter into the understanding of science by any other door than Truth that emanates from Principle, and all the opinions and beliefs of man can never change this unerring standard. When God revealed to us the science of being, and it became necessary to test it, we healed in every instance. When an individual highly spiritual comes in contact with us, we feel refreshed and strengthened, and vice versa. But our experiences will reveal fully the inevitable persecutions, false accusations, unworthy students, etc., that hinder the footsteps of science; "our heritage is unto us as a speckled bird; and birds round about would devour us." When we became as it were an involuntary detective, the good drawn to us and the evil repelled, we took this loving hint from our Father to work out a rule for understanding individual character, the evil of which was at first well-nigh hidden from us, and now recognize the hand that has bestowed all these experiences.

Chapter III. Spirit and Matter.

Motive and act are not appreciated until the general thought reaches their stand-points, and sees the earthly sacrifice they demand, or until the individual we bless is ready for the blessing.

The science of being not more palpably reverses the evidences of personal sense than unspiritual individuals put a false construction on its explanations; but the time cometh when all, from the least unto the greatest, must understand the Truth of being, and bring their bodies into harmony with its requirements. Though error has both field and forum to-day, Truth is gradually changing the material universe; understanding this we yield patient obedience to a patient God, and labor on, for the redemption of man is precious. Those in former years inspired of God, healed the sick and cast out devils, error, but the point is unsettled in our own mind whether they really understood how they did this, having left no explanation of it; perhaps like natural musicians they caught the tones of moral and spiritual science without being able to explain them. The Bible that contains it all has been our only text-book; we found, also, the Scriptures have both a literal and spiritual import, but the latter was the especial interpretation we received, and that taught us the science of Life outside of personal sense.

We learned the Principle of being must be understood to make man right, and that this was a step infinitely beyond the power of faith; it was "to know in whom we have believed," to comprehend through Christian experience the way to health and holiness, to Truth and Life. To reach this Horeb height where God is understood, even in part, we must be growing purer; we cannot perceive the Principle of Science without this, "for none but the pure in heart shall see God." Purity is the baptism of Soul, -- "the answering of a good conscience," for a clean Spirit washes the body of all foulness, and signifies such only as understand Truth. As soon may a camel go through the eye of a needle, as man carry the filth of the flesh into the kingdom of heaven, the reign of harmony; we cannot learn harmony of discords; then wherefore seek in mortal bodies the glorious sense or proof of Truth, Life and Love? These are riot in

Chapter III. Spirit and Matter.

matter, not in the body, or personal sense, and it is only a question of time when we shall all learn this; eternity will reveal it to all.

"Cutting off right hands and plucking out eyes" means to become spiritual. Denying sense is the way to the joys of Soul, and until belief gives place to the spiritual understanding that Intelligence is not in matter, we shall not advance many steps towards harmony or heaven. The sensualist's happiness consists in things of sense, his God is matter, person instead of Principle, and body instead of Spirit; his affections are imaginary, whimsical, and unreal; passion, falsehood, malice, hypocrisy, etc., are, alas! what it is to be sensual. Strip the sensualist of his cloak, and what a loathsome spectacle he becomes; he would shrink from beholding himself, and blush to be identified with such being. Talk not of making scientists of elements such as these, the very basis of error must be changed before we can unloose the sandals of Truth. Either in time or eternity a sense of desolation must come to the wicked, darkness and unutterable woo before they lay down matter for Spirit.

Mind is the seat of motive and action, and forms individual character; if this source be corrupt, it sends forth impure streams. Take away wealth, fame, and the organizations of society that weigh not one jot in the balance of God, and we get the view of a man. Break up clans, equalize wealth with accessions of honesty, and worth will be decided by Wisdom; evil is predominant now, the wicked man is master of his more upright neighbor, but success in error is defeat in Truth. "Let the wicked forsake his way and the unrighteous man his thoughts, for lo! I come quickly, and my reward is with me," is the watchword of science. The voice of Sinai and the sermon of the mount are pursuing man, and will overtake the age. Truth has been uttered in its application to every want of man, but the world slumbers; when will the wakening be?

Peals, that should startle the dream of error, are sounding in our ears; marvels, calamities, perils and sin much more abound now that the understanding is making higher demands on man; and if its voice

Chapter III. Spirit and Matter.

be not suffocated, longevity will increase, sin diminish, and the world feel the alterative effects of Truth through every pore. Aggravation of error foretells its doom, and because of the madness of sin we know Truth is nigh, even at our doors, and 6 will overt-urn until He whose right it is shall reign." What is Truth? is the question that convulses the world to-day; hence its throes to put down radicalism and free thought which purge better than a doctor's pills, and to have this question decided permanently in favor of some 'ism. The march of time we cannot stay, for progress is engraven on its banners; those whose kingdom is of this world will fight for their positions, and furnish their sentinels with orders "not to let Truth pass their guard unless it subscribes to their sect;" but Truth has passed already beyond the pointed bayonet; and there is a little tumult still, and rallying to its standard; we must labor in faith many long years, still hoping the hour is not far off of a higher and practical Christianity. Truth is liberty; its followers hoist the standard of freedom; engraven on its banners we read, slavery is abolished, my body is no longer my master, I claim the freedom of the Sons of God. What power opposed to divine Wisdom is it that binds man to conditions of sickness, sin, and death? Is it not the body material? Then is not this body an enemy to man? But this foe is not stronger than Omnipotence, and is not a tyrant without a master.

The humble Nazarene rebelled against its power, and through his demonstration of healing proved matter a fable; showing, despite the Rabbi's pride, his understanding of God exceeded theirs. Intelligence is the master of sickness and sin, else these are immortal, and evil equal to good. Away with the belief that something outside of himself, over which he has no control, makes man sick and a sinner, and finally kills him, but must stop here for it proposes to carry him no further than perdition. If man is hopelessly at the control of matter, of sin, and death, he is annihilated; for error is not immortal. But we have no faith in the necessity of sin, of sickness, or death, because God has no part in these. It is impossible to bide behind the plea, "I am not advanced to this science and higher understanding of

Chapter III. Spirit and Matter.

Life, therefore I cannot triumph over sickness, sin, and death." Then quicken your experiences, for your tardiness is without excuse. Every day and hour has its demands on man, saying, "where art thou? hast thou gained some conquest over error to-day, or resigned thyself more contentedly to its slavery?"

We do not stand still, but are moving forward or backward, as time glides on and the centuries repeat history. If not progressing, we must live over the past until its poor work is erased. If we are satisfied with being wrong, we must become dissatisfied with it; or if content with having done nothing, we must learn to loathe our leisure. Undoing, in time or eternity, the errors of sense, we learn to improve every opportunity to do our work well, and bring our bodies into subjection to Soul. This unwinding one's ways, learning from experience, and partitioning between error and Truth, means something. Nothing short of the suffering that comes of sin will turn man away from it; therefore, "He chasteneth those whom He loveth." Wisdom lets alone the "greatest sinner" for a period, until the awakening cometh, when he must pay the uttermost farthing. Those perceiving the demands of the science of being, and refusing obedience thereto, "will be beaten with many stripes." To heal the sick with Truth, we must understand what is right, and what is wrong; hypocrisy is impossible in science; be master of sin, to control your own or another's body in science. Neither a mere mental process of healing, nor manipulation is the science of being; it is sheer folly and ignorance of its Principle to say you can heal scientifically, and be a hypocrite; this is the greatest mistake of all.

Graham's system, hydropathy, physiology, etc., were considered improvements on allopathy, because they employed less drugs; but if drugs are abstractly the antidotes for disease, why consider it a step in progress to diminish their quantity, especially when sickness increases? Surrendering, in any direction, the control we should hold over our bodies causes disease, and a demand for drugs does this, by giving reins to matter instead of Spirit. To transfer our own power into the bands of matter is destructive to the science of being that

Chapter III. Spirit and Matter.

employs Intelligence alone to control the body, and remedy all the ills that flesh is heir to. The science of being purifies mortal mind, even as impurity is destroyed in matter by the introduction of some cleansing agent. When Truth reaches the mind, the body manifests the effects of an alterative, proving it is mind that moves matter even though we place this mental weight in the belief that drugs, air, exercise, and so forth, are benefiting us, calling it these things only that affect our bodies. When Truth reaches the understanding it stirs individual error to a change of base; and the wrong and right strive together until victory is decided on the part of immutable harmony. This chemicalization, or change, often follows our explanations of science, the effect of which is that the patient recovers; disease comes to the surface during the chemicalization, like a fermenting fluid, and throws itself off, sometimes in violent perspiration, eruptions, increased secretions, and discharges. We have observed with our students, and with the sick, a constant recurrence of morbid symptoms, moral and physical, till the conflict is decided on the part of Truth. We never witnessed as much effect from what is termed a change of heart, or from cathartics or alterative medicines, as we have seen follow the introduction of the science of being into the minds of the sinner, or the sick; like the little leaven, it leavens the whole lump.

These undeniable facts establish the Principle that mind controls the body. Patients with certain mentalities, or students with wrong tendencies and habits, are more difficult to heal or to teach, than others differently constituted. Three classes of students honor Science least, and give the teacher most trouble. The first, whose bigotry and conceit are fixed facts, and the central views, a mysterious God, and natural devil; the second, so early depraved they impersonate innocence, never failing to utter a falsehood, looking you blandly in the face, or to stab their benefactor; the third, so iron-clad with a belief or doctrine, that the bullets of Truth roll off without making an indenture. Errors are the least perceived that lie not upon the plane of your own experience, and sink so deeply

Chapter III. Spirit and Matter.

into the nature of others that you never realize a serpent lies in your path until you feel its bite.

Society is often a silly juror, that judges according to testimony on one Bide; and honesty often agrees too late on its verdict, for fear of wronging the criminal; hence people with work on hand have little time to furnish gossip with law and evidence. To reconstruct timid justice and let Truth be heard above falsehood, is the work of time; a good cause cannot be popular at first; to live wrong and talk right, avails little in benefiting one's self or others. The spiritually-minded, and honest man, although his beliefs are built in solid masonry of thought, is open to the approach and recognition of Truth; therefore he is the only apt student of the science of Life; we have no task in teaching him, nor does he persistently turn back to error; or avenge himself on us. Such an one should be a Paul to the modern Romans; his treasures are Truth, not laid up on earth. Aspirations pure and God-ward, steadfast purpose, honesty, understanding, and independent action, alone fit us for the science of Life.

The evil deceive the good, but putting aside the vail that falls between goodness and depravity; one has a more unerring guide than the other; this guide is repugnance to evil, and their first impressions with regard to individual character, When the good suffer from contact with certain individuals, it is a hint that something is wrong in those individuals; but this hint is not always heeded, and then comes the irresistible conflict and separation between them, for good can never join hands with evil to gain peace, place, or power. The impure are at peace only with the impure, virtue is a rebuke to vice; and Truth to falsehood, etc. Whosoever, therefore, has drank at the fountain of Soul to the purification of sense, is in the harmony of science that blends not with sin. Let him come in contact with the sick, or sinner, a tobacconist, or an imbiber of alcoholic drinks, and though a word be not exchanged between them, in a majority of cases the scientist will exterminate sickness and the bad habit; but in some instances an individual is too

Chapter III. Spirit and Matter.

opinionated, or dishonest, to yield without a struggle, or to acknowledge when he has yielded, and only in case he does this, will the good done be recognized above the evil. The meeting of opposite minds, is a spontaneous separation when this commences, the unconscious individuals are enemies without the preliminaries of becoming such; else they unite on a new base, and the evil yield to the good or the subtlety of error, conquers even the latter; this separation of tares and wheat is obedience to Science.

Never soil your garments with *conservatism*, or let soother's error dim the lustre of your own Truth; always separate yourself from evil. Right is radical, and those walking in the light are like eyes accustomed to the light, that must have it, for they cannot see in darkness. while those accustomed to darkness, like it, and push boldly on. Flowers turn to the sun, or fade and lose fragrance in the darkness. If you have grown out of former things, hesitate not to put them away, and fear not, for conscience' sake, to overstep the boundaries and break the strong chains of old opinions. You must take up this cross if you follow Christ, Truth, and never hold on to what you cannot understand, or breathe an immoral atmosphere that you cannot purify. When error confronts you, spare not the rebuke, or the explanation that destroys it, if you would benefit yourself or others; but if, "having ears they hear not, neither will they understand, that they might be converted and you might heal them," thereafter let them alone, but be sure you drop into no conservative position; always keep well burnished your own armour. To sustain yourself in Truth, you must meet error with a protest, and once beholding the beauty of holiness, you are willing to leave all for it. To gather yourself with sinners hardens the heart. When the spiritual sense of being unfolds Life's harmonies, you will take no risks in the policy of error; far better is a frugal meal with contentment and virtue, than the many gods of luxury and sense. If you are not a Christian to-clay, delay not to become one, for no opportunity equals the present. We are not neutral; all have some weight; then let the influence we exert be thrown in the right scale.

Chapter III. Spirit and Matter.

Nothing is mortal that deserves to continue; therefore decay belongs not to Truth; all that dies is the offspring of belief, and not understanding. Left to the government of Truth, all would be found harmonious and eternal. Nothing in matter equals the power of mind; the baneful effects of an evil associate are more terrible than earthquakes or pestilence. The influence one mind holds over another should be understood and guarded with stronger keepers than it is. The following rules, observed, would open the way for science.

Teachers of primary and high schools should be selected as much for their morals, as learning; these nurseries of character should be strongly garrisoned, and parents demand a faithful fulfillment of such high trusts. The examination of schools should embrace this thought, paramount to all others, that education is both classical and spiritual, to lift one's being higher; schools should not be applauded for a good show, while the thoughts of teachers constantly imparted to their pupils are disregarded, and any thing but pure and uplifting. Physicians, whom the sick employ under circumstances of great helplessness, should be the guardians of virtue, and spiritual guides, when Life and death tremble in the balance; not only should they be able to impart soundness of body, but a higher moral tone of being. Clergymen, standing on the watchtowers of the world, should grasp most firmly, and hold more fearlessly the standard of scientific Truth; they should be teachers that turn the sinner from his way, heal the sick, and cast out error from the land. Husbands and wives should fulfill their tender trusts wisely and well; yielding faithful obedience to the law of spiritual Love, aiding each other to gain its harmonies through the blessing of mutual affection lifting the being higher. Children should obey their parents; insubordination is a growing evil in the nursery and through the land; parents should teach their children Truth through precept and example, and love them, if they would be loved in return. Abstain from secular labor and frivolous amusements, on the Sabbath, observing it as a clay of rest and spiritual improvement.

Chapter III. Spirit and Matter.

Human will is capable of much evil; by gaining the mind's consent against the convictions of conscience, it may turn the judgment whithersoever it wills. To guard and govern the action of mind, enables you to hold the body in subjection. The world is better for all those honest Soul-inspired ones. who govern sense, and sit down at the right hand of Wisdom. The hypocrite can do little with Truth, and cannot understand the Principle of scientific healing: in discord himself he cannot impart harmony to others. You may learn the letter of this science that enables you to gain its Spirit, but the next question is, have you improved your opportunity, and gained its Spirit? if not, you are unfit to heal the sick metaphysically.

Touched by the Principle of his grand symphonies, a Mozart or Beethoven experienced much more than he ever expressed in music; each was a musician before the world knew it; so to catch the divine harmonies of Soul, we must rise in the scale of being through the understanding of science, and experience, in order to demonstrate. Love gives forth its own concord, to correct the discords of sense; and whatsoever inspires us with Love, Wisdom or Truth, whether it be song, sermon, or science, will bless the human family; let us gladly welcome every crumb that feeds the hungry; and every drop that bears to the thirsty, living waters.

The literal meaning of the Scripture is not its highest sense; its spiritual signification is what explains God and man. Church rites and ceremonies have nothing to do with Christianity, and more than this, they draw us towards material things; hence away from spiritual Truth, and all Truth is spiritual. To depend on medicine or the so-called laws of health, prevents the sick being healed by Truth; and to observe rites and ceremonies prevents the Spirit that is Truth. We shall all learn we cannot serve two masters. Physics act against metaphysics, for these opposites produce different results; and if we trust one we mistrust the other. When the metaphysics of the science of being are understood, we shall not believe in physics; in which case we cannot produce the effect through medicine we did before. All seeming effects from matter are effects of mind, that constructs

Chapter III. Spirit and Matter.

the aeriform, liquid, or solid; matter is inertia; all action is mind. Certain forms of belief we call substance, and name matter, others more rarefied, mind; the discordant, mutable and mortal, are not realities, they are beliefs and illusion; the harmonious and undying are all that is real; Principle, and its idea is the only reality.

To depend on personality is error; words cannot always be depended upon, and are sometimes less real than thoughts; treasures in matter are all lost. Persons are riot to be trusted; Principle, is all there is to trust; hence, the greater reliability of science, than all else; but this word, *science*, will not be appended to humbugs, when once we catch its meaning. "Absent from the body and present with the Lord," were Paul's directions for a scientist, for this is spiritual understanding reaching outside of personal sense, and material things. Life, Truth and Love displace the material with the spiritual, but they are self-expressed, and self-existent; nothing is wanting in them. Not that Soul is voiceless, but that it is incapable of jargon, or words "such as hypocrites use." "Let us lay aside the weights that so easily beset us," for the better proofs of Christianity in love to our neighbor, and a perceptible gravitation toward Spirit, and away from matter, whereby man is governed by Soul, instead of sense, by God, instead of man. As religion yields creeds and rites, it will build on the great corner-stone, Truth, the church of Christ. Creeds are beliefs instead of understanding, products of man instead of God. A higher state of existence will be attained only as we lose the beliefs of personal sense, and gain spiritual sense. When we lose our opinions and theories that are false, We shall find God the Principle of being, and the only antidote for all the ills of mind and body; Truth makes man harmonious as nothing else can.

To help us ascend the scale progressive, we naturally appeal to the pulpit, so efficient on the side of right, in all our mighty struggles; and rejoice that in some instances already, it is preaching away creeds, and in their place preaching "Christ, and him crucified"; in other words, Truth, and the persecution it meets from error.

Chapter III. Spirit and Matter.

Already we find materia medica losing matter, and gaining mind, and the latter more potent to heal the sick. Homeopathy is a step in advance of allopathy simply because matter is fading out of its doses, and mind supplying its place; it takes the moral symptoms largely into account in diagnosing disease, whereas allopathy consults only the physical; the former method is a step toward spirituality, and the science of life. Homoeopathy proves the more you exterminate the drug, the more potent becomes the dose, and its pharmacy is your process of mentalizing the vehicle, as you shake and count; the higher attenuations become more potent, as mind, instead of matter, and with spiritual natures, the less matter and more Truth is the grand secret of success in healing.

The ages are passing from the material to the spiritual, and to make this passage more pleasant and beneficial we should welcome the fact, and aid it with the understanding. As the cruder foot-prints of the past disappear, let us retain primitive simplicity as much as possible in our customs and habits; resting assured that no imaginary pleasure of sense is lost without its higher recompense in Soul. For being to quicken into Truth and Life, outside of matter, is not a trance, nor the change called death; nor is there anything in it to awaken dread, or superstition; it is the foot-steps of progress, that we all must take to be immortal; in science, it is as natural and painless a development, as the unfolding of buds into blossoms. When we shut out the belief of Life in matter, the transition from matter to Spirit, will not be through death; but Truth and Life, brought to light; the Master Said, "I will not leave you comfortless, I, Truth, will come unto you."

Life is not realized in the belief of death, nor of Life in matter; we must empty the mind of all this error, before Truth can flow in. Life in matter is but a dream that must be exchanged for reality, by awaking to the science of Life, wherein Spirit is found the only real being. If we would gain the harmony of being, we must begin by admitting the delusion of personal sense, otherwise error will continue until the awakening comes with the tortures of "the rich

Chapter III. Spirit and Matter.

man," and the dream of Life in matter ends in suffering, thus proving itself error.

Life is harmony and immortality, impossible to harness to sickness, discord, and death. Love is universal goodness and blessedness, that mixes not with suffering and sin. Truth is infinite understanding, without an error to obscure its perfect peace, and these three are one in Soul, but many to sense-; then do you lose happiness or caste by finding yourself Soul, instead of sense. Material man loses his individuality, but the spiritual, never; his identity is as immortal as the Soul of man. The man of personal sense loses his identity with all its pleasures and pains, but the man of Soul possesses his individuality on this safe platform, to wit: that there is no personality; being is spirit.

Man gives neither shape or comeliness to beauty; it has these before he perceives them; distinct outline, coloring, etc., are of Soul, else their idea were not given in the universe and man; therefore, beauty is a thing of Life, the offspring of Intelligence, and not matter. The world would collapse without Intelligence and its idea; there is no chance for argument here, philosophy nor skepticism can change the scientific fact that God is and was; and that man, His reflex shadow is, and was forever. We find no diminution of happiness in learning we are Spirit and not matter, Soul and not body; but a vast increase of all that elevates, purifies, and blesses man. Sickness, sin, and death are all that is mortal, and these come only from ignorance, that clings to personal sense and silences the voice of Soul; therefore science reveals the so-called pleasures or pains of personal sense, illusion, and that there is no sensation in matter; the opposite belief that denies this is not the utterance of man's Principle, not the true tone, but the discord. Spirit is concord, matter discord. If it was understood that Life is Wisdom, Truth and Love, and not sickness, sin, and death, things of sense, man would be immortal, and spared the experience of sin. We find the so-called pleasures of sense nearly unknown in infancy, and well nigh lost in age; showing us at both extremities they are nothingness -- things of

Chapter III. Spirit and Matter.

belief alone. Nutriment, one of the parent's beliefs of personal sense, that is first transmitted to their offspring, is nothing but instinct in infancy, instead of pleasure, for appetites and their gratification grow through education into many demands, that instinct forbids. In both biped and quadruped we find belief develops only error, and that instinct is better than reason misguided. Birds, governed by instinct, sing and soar; drenched with the shower, they dry their plumage without having catarrhs, or wetting their feet, are not victims of pulmonary disease; instinct procures them summer residences, even with less difficulty than wealth affords.

Every pleasure we lay up in the storehouse of personal sense, is lost; sickness, sin, or death, destroys it; but joys of Soul are laid up in the immortal storehouse of spiritual sense, where thieves cannot break through and steal. A happy Spirit (and there is none other,) is independent of circumstances, accident, or age; optic nerves never robbed it of light, nor a broken bone of limbs, nor disease of a sound body. Matter may break through sense and steal, but it cannot through Soul, nor take away joys that are spiritual. A sick, crippled, or dying man is not the image of God, of Life, and Truth. Nerves have nothing to do with pain or pleasure; nerves may be destroyed, and pain be left. We suffer physically in dreams, but nerves are not the occasion of this pain. Sometimes a tooth that has been extracted, aches again, in belief. After a limb has been amputated a sense of pain is felt in the old spot; and we find a limb lost, according to one belief, and aching according to another; we have seen an unwitting attempt to scratch the end of a finger that had been cut off for months. When the nerve is gone that we say occasioned pain, but the pain is left, we naturally conclude sensation is mind and not matter; now reverse the case and let mind be absent from the body, or lulled by an opiate, and sensation is lost and nerves are of no avail. The so-called pleasures, or pains, of personal sense, are beliefs only, instead of nerves. Learning the nothingness of personal sense, is the basis of science; this point proved, was our scientific standpoint for healing the sick through mind instead of matter; physical effects, we

Chapter III. Spirit and Matter.

learned, are not the result of physical causes; that diseases are beliefs, that, ruled out of mind, are ruled out of the body.

Most forms, or stages of disease that the body manifests, is remedied on this scientific mental basis; we have tested this in too many instances to doubt it. When medicine is taken and the sick recover, faith and not the medicine, has done this, whereas the almost universal belief is that medicine, or laws of health heal the sick; and because doctor, nurse, patient, and people believe this, according to their faith so is it unto them. But take from this weight of mind and belief some mental power, destroy some confidence in these means, and they will do less for the sick, and destroy all faith, and they are powerless. The cure wrought through the science of being is not the result of faith, but understanding. I never found a quotient proving numbers divided according to the rule of mathematics, more unquestionable than my tests of this science; but to gain prominence for this Truth until it is understood, is impossible; perfection, in the midst of imperfection, is slow to be seen, and slower to be acknowledged. The mental opposition to it at present, throws the great weight of universal belief, (the only prop of materia medica) against the science of Life: but notwithstanding all this, it will live, because its Principle is Truth, independent of belief. The Principle that made harmless the poison viper in the hands of Paul, and from the boiling oil delivered the Evangelist unharmed, that healed the sick, triumphed over sin and death, and crowned the meek brow of Jesus, is immortal; therefore we need not fear what man can do unto it.

Setting aside personal sense, the error that so easily besets man, let us strive to attain this demonstration that Jesus set before us. Enough already has been accomplished, by prophet and apostle, to shut all lips in regard to its Truth; but one thing is sure, that whose learns the letter only of science, without possessing its Spirit, will not be able to repeat their demonstrations. The age will at length require demonstration, in place of doctrine and belief, and the Christian will at length preach only what he practices. As mortal

Chapter III. Spirit and Matter.

man, and the mist of knowledge enveloping man in darkness disappears, the first appeal will be to reason or philosophy, to plant our next footstep, before we understand the higher and spiritual resources of being; but when this period arrives, and before former things have passed away, the reaction of mind will be fearful. Theology, (I say this not with reference to Christianity,) and materia medica have failed to demonstrate what Jesus taught and demonstrated; and why we have not followed his precepts and example is not so much from lack of desire, or willful disobedience, as lack of understanding.

In earlier periods, even the cross that should symbolize a denial of personal sense, was made an instrument of torture. Error is sometimes deceit; again, it is a misconception of Truth, and the desire to grow better is attended with more sermons and ceremonies than understanding and practice. A clergyman once adopted a diet consisting of bread and water, to increase his spirituality, and continued it six weeks, but finding his health failing, he gave it up, advising others never to try fasting to grow in grace. But we will add a leaf of experience here, showing how personal sense, or belief of any sort, shuts out harmony and science. When quite a child we adopted the Graham system for dyspepsia, ate only bread and vegetables, and drank water, following this diet for years; we became more dyspeptic, however, and, of course, thought we must diet more rigidly; so we partook of but one meal in twenty-four hours, and this consisted of a thin slice of bread, about three inches square, without water; our physician not allowing us with this ample meal, to wet our parched lips for many hours thereafter; whenever we drank, it produced violent retchings.

Thus we passed roost of our early years, as many can attest, in hunger, pain, weakness, and starvation. At length we learned that while fasting increased the desire for food, it spared none of the sufferings occasioned by partaking of it, and what to do next, having already exhausted the medicine men, was a question. After years of suffering, when we made up our mind to die, our doctors kindly

Chapter III. Spirit and Matter.

assuring us this was our only alternative, our eyes were suddenly opened, and we learned suffering is self- imposed, a belief, and not Truth. That God never made man sick; and all our fasting for penance or health, is not acceptable to Wisdom, because it is not the science of being, in which Soul governs sense. Thus Truth, opening our eyes, relieved our stomach, also, and enabled us to eat without suffering, giving God thanks; but we never afterwards enjoyed food as we expected to, if ever we were a freed slave, to eat without a master; for the new-born understanding that food could not hurt us, brought with it another point, viz., that it did nut help us as we had anticipated it would before our changed views on this subject; food had less power over us for evil or for good than when we consulted matter before Spirit, and believed in pains and pleasures of personal sense. As a natural result, we took less thought about "What we should eat or what drink," and, fasting or feasting, consulted less our stomach and our food, arguing against their claims continually, and in this manner despoiled them of their power over us to give pleasure or pain, and recovered strength and flesh rapidly, enjoying health and harmony that we never before had done.

The belief that fasting or feasting enables mail to grow better, morally or physically, is one of the fruits of the "tree of knowledge," against which Wisdom warned man, and of which we had partaken in sad experience; believing for many years, we lived only by the strictest adherence to dietetics and physiology. During this time we also learned a dyspeptic is very far from the image and likeness of God, from having "dominion over the fish of the sea, the fowls of the air, or beasts of the field"; therefore, that God never made one; while the Graham system, hygiene, physiology, materia medica, etc., did, and contrary to His commands. Then it was we promised God to spend our coming years for the sick and suffering; to unmask this error of belief that matter rules man. Our cure for dyspepsia was, to learn the science of being, and "eat what was set before us, asking no questions for conscience sake;" yea, to consult matter less, and God more. When we govern our bodies by the understanding of this great Truth, that Spirit forms its own conditions of body, we

Chapter III. Spirit and Matter.

shall be perfectly harmonious; we should not hold the body a seat of pain or pleasure, but be able to dictate terms to it, even as to a muscle that we admit is dependent on mind for its action. But to attain this government over the body requires more instruction and explanation than we have space for in this book; we always advance slowly with students, requiring them to digest one part of the science before giving out another, and so on. We hear it said, "I go into the open air daily to overcome a predisposition to take cold; and yet I have continual colds." Yes, and you will not listen to the explanation that frees you from catarrhs and makes you better in mind and body, if it conflicts in the least with old opinions or beliefs. The freedom of the sons of God you persecute because it is a step outside some 'ism, or the favorite "tree of knowledge" proscribed by Wisdom. Your teachers inform you, God sends sickness, when the Scriptures say, He cures it; also, that His laws are carried out through drugs, food, air, exercise, etc., which would make matter intelligent, and the law of God that walks over matter of none effect.

The peril to the professions, if your eyes are opened to the science of being, is regarded by your leaders, and the laws of God disregarded, so far as health is concerned. They have not discerned, yet, the governing Principle of being. The Bible teaches us to transform our bodies by the renewing of the Spirit; explaining the Scriptures without understanding their application to heal the sick, does little more towards making man harmonious than moonbeams to melt a plane of ice. If you understood the science of being, your thoughts, resting on the sick and afflicted, would do more toward their recovery than all the drugs, manipulations, and long prayers ever adopted. The error of the age is teaching without proof, and not practicing what you preach. Personal sense is error; but the Principle of all being is infallible; therefore, the nearer we approach unto it, the nearer we are to God, that appoints us more solemn trusts as we advance higher, but if false to His commissions, in vain do we attempt to cover it from Wisdom. You may bide your ignorance of spiritual things from the eyes of the world, but can never gain the

Chapter III. Spirit and Matter.

understanding and demonstration of the science of Life, without an honest, high, and God-given purpose.

Sin is thought before it is deed, and you must master it in the first, or it conquers you in the second instance. Jesus said, to look with foul desire on forbidden objects, breaks a moral precept; hence, the stress he laid on the character of a man that is hidden from our perception. Evil thoughts reach farther, and do more harm than individual crimes, for they impregnate other minds and fashion your body. The atmosphere of impure desires, like the atmosphere of earth, is restless, ever in motion, and calling on some object; this atmosphere is laden with mental poison, and contaminates all it touches. When malicious purposes, evil thoughts, or lusts, go forth from one mind, they seek others, and will lodge in them unless repelled by virtue and a higher motive for being. All mental emanations take root and bear fruit after their own kind. Consider, then, the guilt of nurturing evil and impure thoughts, that send broadcast discord and moral death. Sooner suffer a doctor infected with small-pox to be about you, than come under the treatment of one that manipulates his patients' heads, and is a traitor to science.

These points are so vital to the success of all learning to heal the sick in the science of being, we hesitate not to name them, even as we urge their importance when teaching, and we never withdraw aid or interest from a student unless we have found him unworthy his, place. Through a metaphysical mode of healing, patients cannot be made harmonious by a dishonest or impure-minded practitioner; it is the Truth of being that heals in science, and who will say this doctor possesses it? We have classified sickness, error, and to destroy another's error we must conquer our own. If you are fettered by sin you are unfit to free another from the fetters of disease; could you break the manacles from other wrists, with your own hands bound? and yet this would be equally easy. A little that is true regarding man's being, does wonders for the sick, so infinite are the resources of Truth; but alas! how much more good could be done by the good and honest practitioner, with more Truth. When a student learns the

Chapter III. Spirit and Matter.

rules of this science we expect him to use them according to their Principle, or not parade his poor example before the world as a demonstrator. Our hands have been made weak by this mal-practice; we must not seek the approval of man, but of God, leaving futurity to explain us and our motives.

It is science to do right, and nothing short of this can lay claim to it. The injunction to "come out from the world and be separate " has its inevitable fulfilment in Christianity, not only from the natural tendency of opposites to separate, but because the abuse it receives from sinners who verily believe they do right to wrong Truth, or cannot see the wrong they do, separates them. The spiritual are apart from the material from the necessity of opposite natures. The immortality of man is only gained by his spirituality, hence material things are not what he needs; besides, all things are finally resolved into Spirit, their ultimatum for Life and heaven are of Spirit. What fellowship, then, hath light with darkness, and matter with the kingdom of heaven that shall come on earth? Mortal man is but a dream; even the belief that Life, sensation and substance are matter, all of which the ultimatum of being proves illusion. A dream comes in darkness, and this belief comes from error, an ignorance of real existence; but the light of science will awaken us all to the understanding of Life that is real, and the grave is not its goal; sickness, sin, and death, enter not into Life; they are mortality's self. The dream that Life or Intelligence is in matter, Soul in body, and God in man, is fatal as it is false. To admit Spirit in matter is an attempt to limit the limitless, and make immortality a myth; like saying frost is in fire, and with this belief dream you get into the fire, but are glad to waken to live and recognize Life independent of your illusion or matter.

Science reverses every belief of personal sense, for every condition of mortality is destroyed in immortal man. Socrates understood this when pledging the superiority of Spirit over matter in a cup of poison hemlock, refusing to care for the body mortal. The malice of that age would have killed the venerable philosopher

Chapter III. Spirit and Matter.

because of his high regard for spiritual things and indifference to the body. When nothing that loveth or maketh a lie is left, the reign of Spirit will come on earth; science will not always wait, but lifting its voice far above the centuries, will be heard, and old things be done away, and all become new. Who can say that man is alive to-day and tomorrow dead? What has touched Life to such strange issues? matter may destroy itself, but cannot destroy Spirit. What, then, has unstrung this harp of many strings? Theories stop here, and science alone rolls back the mystery and solves the problem of immortal man. Error bites the heel of Truth, but cannot destroy it; Truth bruises the head of error and kills it; error is mesmerism; one lie scaring off another and taking the rule itself; but Truth is science walking over all lies.

Christianity is open seige with the world; on which side are you fighting? Popularity gained by dishonesty, is smoking flax ready to perish. The wrong you (To another weighs most heavily against yourself, for at some time Truth will adjust the balances. As soon think to make evil good, as to benefit yourself by injuring others. If the balance of your character is wrong you lose the weight of Truth, and work not in science; if you treat the sick mesmerically, or with medicine, you are calling on your gods, like the worshippers of Baal, but they are not the Prophet's God, the Principle of being; the moral mercury is what rises or falls your demonstration, according to the amount of Truth you possess. Worshipping in temples made with hands; loving the world and listening to the demands of personal sense, is not the true worship. Then let the Christian who has grown away from forms and ceremonies, enjoy his worship in the right way, viz., Spirit and in Truth. If we come out from the world, as the Scripture demands, and are separate, we shall have its frowns instead of flatteries, and they will enable us, more than its favors, to be a Scientist. Losing her crucifix, the poor Catholic said, "I have nothing left now but Christ," and this was not greater ignorance of God than to fall away from Truth because of persecution. It we have God on our side, what Deed we more? Loving error more than Truth we shall not separate ourself from the

Chapter III. Spirit and Matter.

world, but wait on its approval until sickness comes to dull this false sense of happiness. When we silence the demands of conscience, at some future hour we shall hear the reply, "darkness leadeth not into the guest-chamber of Wisdom; ye cannot enter now." Our unimproved opportunities gone, are not easily reproduced; nor can we borrow Wisdom, therefore we must then learn from suffering.

The hour of darkness will come to those who improve not the preparatory school of the present, to fit them for the future, but would step suddenly into all the benefits of experience; alas! what were the science of being to them in that hour? -- a blessing? yea, a blessing infinite. The dream of Life in matter, based on the evidence of personal sense, will vanish ere long, when we would gladly turn from its fading vision and the pains of sense, to peace and immortality; but the accumulated error of years dies slowly, and sometimes with severe struggles. As a general rule, man will not seek Truth until suffering shows him the need he has of it, or science opens the eyes of his understanding to see it; for science guides man safely over the quicksands and shoals, making Life what it is, harmony, and not discord. Personal sense is a broken reed that leaves man to fall to the earth; but science raises him up to the resources within himself. The very logic of Truth declares the higher and more enduring claims of Spirit over matter in all our experiences, showing that something besides the body, and perishable things of earth, demand our care and must furnish our support. Soul is heard above the din of sense, saying to error, "Depart from me, ye that work iniquity." Man should obey the voice of Wisdom outside his body, that calls him away from a sense or contemplation of sickness, sin, and death, to harmony, health, and Life.

It is not from matter, personal sense, or from doctrines and beliefs, that we catch divine echoes. We must be "absent to the body to be present with the Lord;" only by caring less and less for the body, shall we attain harmony and Life. Our Master's command "Take no thought what e shall eat, or what drink," etc., means

Chapter III. Spirit and Matter.

something. We must seek God, Spirit, outside of our bodies, and through a disregard for them, and not until we find Truth thus, shall we ever obtain it. Looking to the body for pleasure or pain, for Life or death, is error, and asking amiss to consume it on our lusts. After severe toil, we say, I am fatigued, naturally concluding the muscles have been overtasked and need repose; but our only safe and permanent method to overcome a sense of fatigue is to deny the ability of personal sense, to make us weary, and let mind triumph over matter, with the opposite argument that saith, I am not tired, for the "I" is Spirit, and not matter; bid the physical report depart, even as you would a temptation to sin. It is science, to put down the arguments of personal sense, with the higher ones of Soul. Why this mental method of curing physical ailments is better than yielding to the feeling of tired, and taking a respite from labor, is because it is the science of being, that Spirit should control matter; action or sensation belongs not to matter, independent of mind, and when you conquer through mind, the next occasion for fatigue will find you less apt to feel it, and you will not suffer from fatigue as you did before; the belief that body has a sense of fatigue independent of what mind says, is error, that the opposite Truth of being will destroy.

Your body is as unconscious of action, or weariness, setting aside what mind says in regard to this, as a wheel, and to understand this point in science, will rest you as hours of quiet would not. Make a scientific test of this, if you please, and you will find it true; but in order to do this, you must understand how to hold and strengthen the mental argument against the physical, and guard against the influence of other minds, that embrace opposite beliefs. When through the Truth of man you gain one victory over the error, it will bring out a faint understanding of the Principle that controls being harmoniously. A disposition is often manifested to get rid of this physical part of science, by saying the fatigue did actually occur, but you psychologized the individuals to think they were not weary; this argument, however, is weak in behalf of the old positions regarding mind and body, for it admits the power of mind over matter, and this

Chapter III. Spirit and Matter.

is just what you need to admit first, and next to understand its Principle, and not to mesmerize a man to make him wise, or yield to the error that belief is superior to understanding.

The difficulty to understand science is, personal sense comprehends it not, that wars against it, for belief will not and cannot accept a Principle understandingly. We hear a sweet melody, and not knowing how it is produced, may explain it superstitiously, and leave the thing in mysticism. The sick often recover through the science of being; but not comprehending the Principle of their cure, misinterpret it, and do not render to God the things that are God's; but give them to Caesar, saying, medicine, a change of air, or some supposed law of matter, did it. How often have we seen, in chemicalization, produced by the introduction of the Truth of being, relating to disease, given a misinterpretation by an ignorance of its real cause. We look for cause and effect in matter; whereas science finds all causation, mind; that which is produced by the mind of Soul, harmonious, and by the so-called mind of matter, inharmonious. The belief from infancy to age, that muscles are tired and body inharmonious, is error, and this error in the premises, leads to the error in conclusion, viz., that they are tired. Admitting fatigue a sensation of matter that belongs to muscles and nerves, we find rest only in respite from toil, thus admitting matter intelligent; but when we understand a sense of fatigue is one of mortal mind's beliefs, and not a sensation of matter, we begin to master it, and can continue the exercise without the same fatigue or injury.

To gain entire immunity from suffering and sin, and perfect control over the belief of personal sense, or our bodies, we must be perfect in science; a thing not to be looked for at this period; but if we abate the demands and sufferings of personal sense, on the Principle laid down, it is sufficient for a beginning. In doing this even, it will be found that in science we cannot multiply where we should divide, and the answer be right; that we cannot say to muscles, you have strength, and to nerves, you have sensation, and to matter, you hold sway as well as Spirit, and then control our

Chapter III. Spirit and Matter.

body, with the opposite Principle of being; we must deny all sensation or Intelligence to matter or the body, with the understanding that Spirit is all that possesses Intelligence, before we can demonstrate in harmony the science of being. We are tired according to one belief, and rested according to another, and we should understand that every condition, or supposed sensation of the body is but a belief of the mind, and not Truth, the reality of Life.

Understanding this, we remove the condition of mind, that affects the body, by destroying the belief producing it, whatever this may be, and the effect will immediately be seen on the body. On this Principle we bring our bodies into subjection to Soul, the immortality of man; and this makes them harmonious and immortal, because it takes them out of the hands of personal sense and mortality. When matter or muscles claim, "I am tired," let Spirit contradict this; first, because matter cannot feel, nor report a feeling; and secondly, that mind can, and that mind, and not matter is what suffers. Soul, instead of sense, controls the universe and immortal man; but reverse this order of science, and we say man is controlled by mortality. There is but one God, or Intelligence, and our bodies are not this Intelligence, and cannot say, I am tired, or sick. Again, there is but one Spirit, to utter Itself, or report for man, and this voice is Life and Love that never produces suffering, and never made man sick, nor a sinner.

The Truth, that neither Intelligence, Life, nor Substance dwelleth in matter, is the basis of harmony in the universe and man. Even the desolate regions of the cold North, the sunny tropics, the everlasting hills, the winds and mighty billows, the vale, the flowers and heavens, all point to Intelligence, outside of matter; whereas sickness, sin and death are our only evidences of Intelligence, God, in matter, and these do not represent God. In the science of creation, man is harmonious and eternal; but go attempt to put Soul in body, and sensation in matter, and we loose the key of harmonious being, and discord continually. The head says I am diseased, or the stomach, I am deranged, and the body, I am sick, or filled with lusts,

Chapter III. Spirit and Matter.

hatred, malice, envy, and all manner of concupiscence; and what renders the case hopeless, is the belief that Spirit cannot stay all this jargon. Error has another shift, that God created this state of things, and that sickness, sin and death, are His messengers, sent by Wisdom who is not able or willing to destroy them. Then wherefore pray for the recovery of the sick, or that God will turn the sinner from his evil way, and employ a doctor to do what Omnipotence refuses to do? "In Him we live, move, and have being"; what, then, is this power independent of God, that causes disease and then cures it? Does God make man sick, and leave him to cure himself, Spirit send disease and leave its remedy with matter?

Life, Love, and Truth never produced disease and death, nor caused man to sin, and then punished him for sinning, nor made man sick, in order to heal him. Alan is not supreme, and God secondary, body first, and Soul last; and evil stronger than good; this is not the science of being, but the error of sense. The clay cannot reply to the potter, why bast thou made me thus? head, heart, lungs, etc., cannot say we are sick, sinning and mortal, and Spirit, the immortal and unerring Principle of man has made us thus, and is the author of all this discord, He that made man in his own image and likeness. Man that God created is the offspring of Spirit, and not matter, the product of God and not man, and is immortal and harmonious. The base, the foul, and mortal, malice, lust and lies, God has nothing to do with, nor do these belong to immortal man, who is the representative of Spirit and Truth; they are what we term mortal man, but are in fact nothing but error; for man is not mortal, and error has no reality; it is neither God, nor His idea.

Perfection acts not through imperfection. God has nothing to do with the belief of Life in matter. The Principle of being never produced sin and discord, therefore they never were produced. "God made all that was made," and God has nothing to do with sin, sickness, or death, only to destroy these beliefs. Jesus demonstrated this for man. Spirit is cause, and there is no effect from any other cause; hence there is no reality in what proceedeth not from this

Chapter III. Spirit and Matter.

great and only cause. Sin is error, and error the absence of all that is real or true; sickness and death are error; therefore they are neither real nor true. Matter has neither action nor Intelligence of its own; it can dictate no terms to man, and because God sends not sickness, sin and death, that surely never came from Life, Truth and Love -- they never were sent, and are but the dream and illusion of personal sense, or Life in matter. We know this Truth will not be seen and acknowledged until this dream be disturbed by it, or broken up, nevertheless it is Truth, and the science of being. The only evidence we have of sickness or death is from personal sense, that is inadequate to recognize Soul, or the immortality of man, that alone reveals his harmony.

Again, sickness, sin and death are without evidence in truth, which is the immortality of man; there they disappear; the only evidence we have of their reality is in mortality or error; but nothing real is mortal. If matter can heal the sick, and mind cannot, it is more powerful than mind, and if God %ends sickness, it is opposed to His government to heal it; and if matter produces its own conditions, it acts against itself, and will be self-destroyed. Our opposite views abuse the science of being, and give the lie to Truth. Has the clay power over the potter, is matter self-acting and independent of God, thug prior and superior to Spirit? To reap where Truth hath not sown, is to gather error; such contradictory statements as these "soweth the wind and reapeth the whirlwind." It is belief alone or mortal man, that holds matter as God, intelligent, self-creative, and self- acting; Truth finds it unintelligent, neither living nor dying, sick nor well. God has no part in suffering, sin or death, and there is no reality where God is not. If God made man to be sick, it is right that he should be so, and wrong to heal him; man cannot if be would, and should not if he could, annul the decrees of Wisdom. If sickness is a reality, it is a condition of Truth; and do you claim that drugs can destroy a condition of Truth? But if, as is the case, sickness is but a belief, therefore but a dream and illusion, the waking must come from Truth and understanding, that alone can destroy it; and this is Christ healing the sick.

Chapter III. Spirit and Matter.

If man is at the disposal of man and matter, of drugs and worms, he is not "the image of God," and

it is nothingness, the sooner gone the better, for reason and revelation repudiate it. Man is immortal, but be is not Intelligence in matter, else he were mortal; man is the idea of God, the idea of Spirit, therefore he is not subject to laws of matter, to sickness, sin or death. Science reveals the fact that there is no Intelligence in matter, and that all righteous government is Spirit that speaks and it is done; never for a moment admitting matter controls man. The belief that God is the author of sickness, sin and death, or that an opposite power named devil or matter is the father thereof, implies a power independent of and over and above God; while there is no separate might or Intelligence from Spirit, and to talk of "spirits" is narrating ghost stories. There is but one Spirit, even God, and this is always right because it is Life, Truth and Love; matter is but a belief of Spirit, Substance and Life where these are not, and out of this error and belief, we make all suffering, sin and death. Does Wisdom commit mistakes to be rectified by man, does God send sickness and man destroy it, thus undoing what he has done? That which is perfect cannot produce sickness, sin or death; and if God cannot destroy these, they are immortal. Nothing to my understanding exceeds the power of omnipotence, and the sick are never really healed except through God, Intelligence; the power of drugs, electricity and matter is but a belief: it is mesmerism and not science that claims Truth, Life or Intelligence in matter bestowing a blessing that God cannot; and the so-called cures of these agents continue only so long as the belief lasts.

Truth, Life and Love have got it all to do sometime, for they alone accomplish all that continues and is harmonious. If God heals not the sick it is because He cannot or will not, and in either case what chance would there be for matter, or man to heal? Can drugs do more than Wisdom, or change the unalterable Truth? or if God can heal the sick and does not, wherefore should man presume to do it. The error of sickness ought to be as apparent as the error of sin. When a man is sick, has God made him sick? No! Can He heal him?

Chapter III. Spirit and Matter.

Yes. But does He that creates wisely destroy his own creation, or what are we to conclude? "That all things were made by Him, and without Him there was nothing made that was made "; in other words, that all that he created was "good," and what is not good has no creation, and therefore no reality. To really understand that pleasure and pain belong not to matter, heals the sick. Cold, heat, exercise, study, food, infection, etc., etc., never caused a sick nor a healthy condition of man. Nerves, brain, blood, bones, liver, lungs, heart, etc., never determined the Life of man; scrofula, fever, consumption, rheumatism, small-pox, or any other disease never produced pain or inharmony; not one of these can make a single hair white or black, mar or change the creation of God; they are not creators in the smallest sense. If God produced disease, it is good, for all was good that God made.

Mortal man is improved, oftentimes, by sickness because it is error destroying itself; a fermenting stage in which it throws itself off to some extent; again what is named dying is but one belief destroying another; a belief of death destroying a belief of Life in matter. Belief saith an ulcer becomes more painful as it hastens to its end in suppuration, for error grows more imperative before it kills itself. Death is but a chemical change, in which some disease that is supposed to kill a man, reaches its own self-destruction; and we admit certain diseases, such as measles, whooping-cough, etc., never recur a second time; even thus when we say consumption has killed a man, he has only wakened out of the dream of Life in matter, that was never a reality, to live on as before, and find himself not dead, and consumption beaten ever thereafter. This is just what Truth finally does with all sickness, sin and death; lets them prove their own nothingness, that the science of being may appear. Man is not dead when the body mortal is admitted lifeless; the Life of man was never in the body, and to admit this, is the first step towards immortality. Heaven, earth, and man, all the eye seeth, will pass away, and personal sense yield to spiritual sense, which is the only real Reuse; and the supposed life of matter, to Life that is God. To understand that Spirit and its immortal idea, the universe and man,

Chapter III. Spirit and Matter.

are all that is real, is the kingdom or reign of harmony that is to come. The only reality of Life or Substance, is Spirit.

The different phases of error, or mortal belief, are the conception, birth, and death of man and matter, together with the pleasure, pain, sickness and sin of personal sense; all of which are discords, and harmony proves discord not the Truth of man. Once understanding the nothingness of error, we should never again regard it with fear or submit to its false government. Sin is the strongest error, because it embraces a belief of pleasure in matter, that a belief of suffering alone can destroy. Wisdom allows sin to commit suicide. That sickness, sin and death are error and illusion, and that the happiness and Life of man are undisturbed by this error, is science. We should not regard our bodies the source of happiness and being, but find these Soul, and not sense; even the Principle of being that produces harmonious and immortal man. Opposed to this science are the vast array of beliefs, saying lo! here, and lo! there; that would reach perfection and immortality on the merit of another's suffering and experience, instead of the higher understanding of God. We have no schools of healing on the Principle that Jesus taught; yet he required of his followers, all, to preach the gospel, heal the sick, and leave all for Truth.

A religion privileged through wealth and fraternity of interests, is not the first step towards Christianity. A popular 'ism was not what our Master pinned his faith upon; he taught taking up our cross, denying sense, and living Soul, to follow Truth; and this did not include sickness, sin, and death, nor pre-suppose that, brain, nerves, stomach and so forth, hold the issues of Life. Truth made man upright; it was error that sought out the invention of sin, sickness, etc., of wrong- thinking and wrong-acting, saying man is both a sinner and saint, dust and Deity; these were the beliefs of personal sense or different phases of mesmerism. Children were blessed by Christ, Truth, because of their emptiness of these beliefs by which they were better able than adults to enter into the science of being. While age is halting between two opinions, or battling with

Chapter III. Spirit and Matter.

some personal sense, children make easy and rapid strides towards Truth. A little girl who bad listened to our explanations, severely wounding her finger, proved this, concluding, "it cannot hurt me, for there is no sensation in matter," this result followed to the delight of all, and the next day she came running to her mother with laughing eyes and cheeks aglow, informing her "my finger is not a bit sore, and you have done nothing for it." It might have taken months or years for her parents to have gained her position, and laid aside their drugs. We see, through the daily proofs of this science, the power of education on the mind, and how "out of the mouth of babes hast Thou perfected praise." The older and stubborn beliefs of adults may even choke this good seed in the minds of their offspring; like unto the "fowls of the air" they carry it away, because of their want of understanding, before it can take root.

As in mathematics a reversed statement proves the rule, so, also, in the science of life, for example:

There is no pain in Truth, and no Truth in pain; no matter in mind, and no mind in matter; no nerve in Intelligence, and no Intelligence in nerve; no matter in Spirit, and no Spirit in matter, etc. That man should lose his identity because Soul is not in body, and Intelligence in matter, is quite as impossible as that tones of music should be lost in their Principle. Theories and doctrines have never yet explained Spirit and matter, but the Scriptures have, and as science demonstrates them, namely, Life and its idea. "Thou shalt surely die," is the sentence of Wisdom daily executed on the belief of Life and Substance in matter, and yet man is not dead; then wherefore doubt belief is error, and man idea and not Substance, and Spirit the only Substance, because it is the Principle of man and the universe. This science of being cannot be seen at once in the midst of so many beliefs that deny all explanations of man, spiritually, and accept only a material anatomy of him, calling bones, sinews, head, beat, etc., man. These theories cannot be true, if man is immortal, and science and revelation reveal him the "image and likeness of

Chapter III. Spirit and Matter.

God"; man, therefore, is immortal, and that which is mortal, is not man.

If we understood God we should have reached nearer the Principle that proves him immortal; our grand mistake is to suppose man both mortal and immortal. The question arises at every point of theories, what is Truth? and the answer to this, Christ built his church upon over eighteen hundred years ago, namely, I am God, and man is the offspring of Soul and not sense; but this answer was not understood then, and has since been interpreted variously. His garment of truth we have rent and cast lots for, but the answer Jesus accepted as explaining man and God is the unchanging and eternal science of being; "Thou art Christ, the son of the living God," for "I am the Truth and Life," takes all Intelligence out of matter, and yields no homage to personality, making Christianity the foundation of right-thinking and right-acting, and through which we reach our God-being, and not rites and ceremonies, nor the persecuting clans that would stereotype progress. Peter said, "Thou art Christ," and on this statement that Intelligence is Spirit, and not matter, and that "I," is God, and not man, was built the church of Christ, the superstructure of Truth and its demonstration, which was, casting out error and healing the sick. Jesus reiterated this when saying "I and the Father are one "; in other words, that "I" signifies Spirit and not matter, Principle and not person, and "no man cometh unto the Father" (the understanding of this Principle), "but through Me," Truth.

Sin has no foundation when we admit our bodies are not intelligent Sickness is without a foothold on this platform; it is the Truth of man that destroys personal sense; therefore, that alone can destroy sickness, sin, and death. The mission of Jesus was to separate material belief from spiritual understanding, and to show that Truth never mixes with error. Good and evil, Spirit and matter, are separate now and forever. Jesus knew we must understand this, or never reach the harmony of being. This is the science of Life that enables us to come out from the world and be separate; to reach the

Chapter III. Spirit and Matter.

moral distance between Life that is Spirit and the supposed life of matter, and live apart from all that is sickness, sin, or death.

This is the Truth that brings to light immortality. Jesus knew personal sense was error, and that there is no personal sense or Intelligence in matter; therefore that all the reports of this sense are chimeras that the Truth of being overthrows. This advanced standard of being is not yet understood, although it is over eighteen centuries ago that Jesus taught it, and they received not his sayings. Science, not personal sense, Principle and not person, understanding and not belief, must interpret Jesus' demonstration; for Truth and not error, Life and not death, health and not sickness, is its Principle. In order to follow Christ, Truth, we must show by our example, what Truth demonstrates; namely, that it casts out error and heals the sick; and then shall we fulfill the prediction of Jesus when he said, "The works I do ye shall do." The doctrines of man are not built upon the Rock of Truth; theology leaves in mystery the science of God that Jesus not only explained but demonstrated. There is no Life or Principle in man that proves him immortal, hence we have no resource but to annihilate the belief of Life and Intelligence in matter, and understand God, the Principle of man and his immortality.

Beauty is eternal; but the beauty of matter passes away, fading at length into decay and ugliness. Custom, habit, opinions and belief form the transient standard of material beauty; but beauty is a thing of Life, exempt from age or decay, and to be this it must be a thing of Spirit. Immortal man and woman (and there are none other), are unfading perfection, models of beauty that reflect all loveliness insomuch as they are "the image and likeness of God", of Soul and not sense. But in order to reflect beauty the body must represent only the perfect and immortal. To become less sense and more Soul, is the recipe for beauty; but to reach its standard we must put all sin, sickness and sorrow under the feet of our God-being, and rise superior to them; retreat from the belief of pain or pleasure in the body, to the unchanging quiet and glorious freedom of impersonal

Chapter III. Spirit and Matter.

bliss. The embellishments of person are a poor substitute for the beauty of Spirit shining resplendant and eternal, over age and decay. Measuring Life by solar years robs youth, and hourly gives uncomeliness to age. The rising sun of virtue and Truth is the morning of being, and its manhood eternal noon, unmarked by a setting sun. When beauty fades to personal sense, it is not lost to Soul, and affection marvels our friend could seem aught but beautiful.

It is the belief of sickness, sorrow, and of solar years, that mars the face and form. I say the belief, because science admits no reality in aught but God and His idea. To Spirit a thousand years are as one day; hence, a man of years and experience is ripening into higher beauty and excellence instead of growing old; mind is feeding the body with immortality, if it supplies it with Truth, and taking away the error of personal sense that says a day points to a nearer tomb; our body neither suffers nor enjoys. When will it be understood that "I" is impersonal, even mind and not matter? Until this point is gained in the science of being, man will go on in belief, a pendulum between joy and sorrow, sickness and health, Life and death, even as at present. Is man tottering and ready to perish, or sick and sinning, the likeness of Omnipotence? are Life and all our faculties measured by calendars, and beauty a thing of decay? or is there a mortal man that grows, matures and decays, out of which springs the perfect and immortal man?

Verily such admissions leap headlong into error. Science proves a corrupt fountain sendeth not forth pure streams, and the same fountain both sweet and bitter water. Solar years, that stamp the wrinkle on the brow, are the effect of man's reckoning, and not God's; they are a belief of personal sense and not the understanding of Soul. Mortal man is old only by admitting be is thus; for it is mind and not matter that makes the body what it is. Intelligence without beginning and without end is the data (if such it can be called), of Life; man is not young or old; he is and was eternal as the idea of God. Man has neither birth nor death; he is not a vegetable

Chapter III. Spirit and Matter.

animal, nor a transmigrating mind, passing first into a mortal body, and thence to the immortal; this belief is a relic of heathenism; we have no beliefs that are not. Personality is not man, therefore the body mortal is but a belief of man, and not the reality of him. Life, Truth, and harmony are the reality of being, and man is the idea of these; hence the body mortal is but belief and error, discord and death. Shakespeare's description of age presents a picture of mortal man; our bodies are not the repositories of *us*, else all would go down to dust. *I* is Spirit and not matter, and Spirit never for a moment entered or animated matter. If happiness is personal sense, joy is a trembler and builds on sand; or if materiality is man the very worms do rob us.

To understand Intelligence nor Life are in the body, is to conquer age and hold being forever fresh and immortal. The error of growing old is seen in the history of an English lady, as narrated in the London Lancet.

In early life she was disappointed in love, became insane, in which she lost the calculation of time, and lived only in the hour that parted the lovers, never afterward recognizing the lapse of years, and speaking only from that sad hour. The effect of this was, she literally grew no older, and when seen by some of our American travellers at seventy-four years of age, presented the entire appearance of youth, not a wrinkle or gray hair marred the picture, but youth sat gently on cheek and brow. Before being informed of her history the visitors were asked to judge of her age, and each placed her under twenty. This instance of preserved youth suggests a point in science not to be overlooked, and which a Franklin might have built upon, or a Newton, with more certainty than the falling apple; years had not made her old, and wherefore? because she did not believe she was growing old, but lived according to another belief in the hour of youth, the result of which was, time could not make her aged, for the body represented the belief. Mind must say she was growing old, or the body would not present the aspect of age. She was young because during all those years she had never believed she was

Chapter III. Spirit and Matter.

becoming old, therefore time fell powerless at her feet. Impossibilities never occur, and one such instance as the above, proves it not impossible to be young at seventy-five years of age, but the Principle of this proof is worth more than the bare fact; it explains the cause of decrepit age, and how to avoid it.

Never record years and keep time tables of births and deaths, if you would preserve the full faculties of womanhood and manhood. It is only because every hour of our years, mind is admitting we are growing old, that it is difficult to present three score years and ten unmarred by age. It is not the years but the belief that years make man infirm, that brings the infirmity of age; "as a man thinketh so is he." A belief of acute disease -- and all disease is belief -- is more readily destroyed than the chronic, because mind has not settled the question so decidedly, nor admitted the belief as long; the mental force of habit is not as strong in one case as in the other. The belief that man has birth, maturity and decay, is simply saying he is a vegetable animal, the animal not fit to live, and the vegetable incapable of Life. Soul is Spirit, and Spirit Life; God, neither an infant, adult, nor decrepit; and man is "the image and likeness of God," then what precedent have we for the growth, maturity and decay of man. If man were matter, a tree, or a monkey, in his earlier stages of existence, we might admit his growth and decay; but he is the reflex shadow of Spirit, and Spirit knows neither infancy nor age. If man goes out in decay or death, there is a time when Jehovah is left without a likeness or representation, and Soul is without even an image, and Principle loses its idea.

Reasoning from the premises that Soul is in body, and Spirit and matter mingle, our only logical conclusion is, that man goes down with matter, and is annihilated. But Spirit forms man, and is not in that which it creates; can the sculptor bury himself in the statue he is chiseling, and inside the marble work out his model, at every point of progress giving it new outlines and touches? Nor is God, the Soul and Intelligence of the universe and man, divided into larger or smaller proportions, or "gods" which enter man and matter.

Chapter III. Spirit and Matter.

There is but one God, even the Intelligence outside of matter, that is a unity and not integral parts, neither mixed up with error, decay, or death. The Principle of man is outside its idea; mortal man would possess no ponderability if permeated by Spirit, and Spirit be ponderable if it dwelt within matter. Reason permitted scope, and guided by revelation repudiates theories so suicidal to the science of being; for theories are false, and science is true. Take away the belief, that limits, and sensation in matter constitute man, and you have immortal man the idea of God, and remove personality from your belief of God, and you have the infinite principle, even God that is Love. If Intelligence is in man and matter, what is there outside of these to govern the heavens and earth that "declare thy glory." Intelligence in matter, and outside of it, also, would be two powers, the unerring and immortal, and the erring and mortal in perpetual warfare; there is no Omnipotence, or Omnipotence is all there is. "Dust to dust" was not spoken of man; we know all that God produces needs no erasure, and cannot be blotted out, for it is the idea of Spirit and not matter.

Life is the same yesterday, to-day and forever; anachronism and organization have nothing to do with it. Life gives immortality to all it creates; what is not Life, Wisdom, Truth or Love, and their idea, is but a fading error, and empty dream. We say, "I dreamed last night"; would that we understood better than this the wide difference between Soul and sense. "I," signifies Intelligence, the Principle of man, that never slumbers nor wanders into illusion; belief is the only dreamer, and its dream says, Life and Intelligence are in matter; to be sure sleep is one of the phases of this dream, also the nightly thoughts get nearer the Truth of being, that silence the waking dream of substance matter, and yet convey the body whithersoever you will, for this comes nearer the reality of man's existence than the waking dream of Life in matter; and is sometimes prophetic. We have no occasion to find fault with science because it repudiates personal sense, if we would not quarrel with a man for waking us from a nightmare, that produces suffering real to belief, but unreal to science.

Chapter III. Spirit and Matter.

Our past and present views of man and God, have not made man harmonious or immortal, nor God, Love; hence the need of a change of views, as in the science of man. The man intoxicated would be let alone, because he thinks inebriety is enjoyable, but waking out of this error changes his belief, and this error of personal sense becomes apparent. So at the final demand of Wisdom, understanding will comprehend the falsity or nothingness of the claims of personal sense. We say mortal man is born to suffer and die, but mortal man is matter, and does matter suffer? Science will at length destroy this ignorance relating to Soul and body, and teach us the harmony of both never yet gained on the old platforms, and never can be. Why not, then, begin in this direction to-day, and not scoff at demonstrative Truth, because you cannot see it with eyes, feel it with nerves, etc., "for having eyes, you do not see."

Children should be taught this science, the first lessons they receive, and the education of personal sense kept out. Never discuss the so-called laws of matter, food or raiment; rule out of mind sickness, sin and death, give not error all your thoughts; looking in opposite directions, and away from such thoughts, is all that will ameliorate the sharper and longer experiences of getting out of them, either in time or eternity. To be out of an imaginary existence in matter, and realize one's self not body but Soul, is the ultimatum of being. When the belief of happiness in personal sense wanes, and the enjoyment of the intellect and affections increases error is fading out, and Truth is lifting its glad voice above the centuries; yea, above the horizon of animality and sense. If we part not with the imaginary joys of personal sense, appetites, passion, malice, pride, etc., at the suggestions of science, we must at some future time suffer from these sufficiently, to be glad to relinquish them. Leaning on error proves it a broken reed that pierces to the heart; but do you ask, why should we suffer for innocent enjoyments? Because pain or pleasure of the body is not a reality, it is a belief only; and this belief is error, opposed to the Truth of being, and at some time we must learn this. It is not through enjoyment, but suffering, we learn the

Chapter III. Spirit and Matter.

error of Life in matter, and outside of suffering it can only be learned of science; which do you choose for a teacher?

A farm, a merchandise, a husband, wife, etc., may hide this science from individual perception; therefore said our Master, we must leave all for Truth, or we are not worthy of it; and this leaving all means much, even the relinquishing of the belief of personal sense, for the understanding of the science of Life. 'Tis folly to scoff at what is not understood, or to deny the claims of science; rather should we test the Principle of its statements by the rules laid down, and so sure as this Principle is sufficiently understood, to apply its rules to man, we shall bring out his harmonious being in accordance with it. The loving discipline our Father gives to teach us the science of being, in the nothingness of material things, is the schoolmaster that leads us to Christ, Truth. We know the desponding reply personal sense makes to the demands of Soul; but we also know, "Thou shalt surely die," is Soul's verdict on sense; but error dies not at once either in time or eternity.

When the miser loses his gold he has little left, and when the sensualist loses his five personal senses, what he has left is Soul, not understood by him, and the body is mortal until Life is understood, therefore, be wise to-day; willful ignorance culminates in outer darkness, and the future will reveal the great error of leaving the work of time for eternity. The end and aim of being is happiness; but this can only be attained through righteousness; we cannot possess the love of this world and be right, for it shuts out God, that is Love; one will be master in the affections, and personal sense tramples on the pearls of spiritual sense. Adhere to the latter and you will be able to govern the former, but yield to the former and the latter will leave man to sickness, sin and death. If you have stripped sin of its disguises, you have done well; but expect your good to be evil spoken of, or if you have pointed out the straight and narrow way of science, remember you will be persecuted for righteousness sake. This is the cross, take it up; it wins the crown, then wear it. Pilgrim

Chapter III. Spirit and Matter.

on earth, thy home is heaven; stranger here, thou art the guest of God.

CHAPTER IV

CREATION

THE evermore of Truth is changing the universe; thought is expanding beyond words; we are losing our swaddling clothes, asking for more light; yea, reaching forth to the stature of Soul outside the body. "Let there be light," is the demand of Life and Love, changing chaos to order and discord to the music of the spheres. Progress takes off all shackles, and the finite yields to the Infinite. Advancing to a higher plane of action, thought grows new, and rises from the personal to the Impersonal; from the mortal to the Immortal, which is from the material to the spiritual idea of God. We have the authority of holy writ that God is Spirit, therefore it is not personality that demands our ignorant worship, and holds sway over man and the universe. There is but one God: yet there are many persons, and to worship personality would be to have "gods" many. That three persons are united in one body suggests a heathen Deity more than Jehovah; integral molecules are no portions of Wisdom and Love, "that spake and it was done;" and whose "word was God." Life, Truth, and Love, are the triune Principle of man and of the universe; they are the great Jehovah, and these three are one, and our Father, which art in heaven.

What is the person of God? He has no personality, for this would imply Intelligence in matter; the body of God is the idea given of him in the harmonious universe, and the male and female formed by Him. The reflection of an object is by no means the opposite of that object, and we cannot fail to see material man does not reflect Spirit, nor the finite, the Infinite; therefore material and finite man is not the image and reflex shadow of God. Intelligence is Substance, and nothing can hold or embrace Intelligence, because it embraces in itself all things. Soul is outside of matter, and not a person but Principle; unlimited and infinite, beyond all boundaries, it is not pent up in person or man. Intelligence repels error and attracts Truth; holds the universe in space; is diffusive, and extends through

Chapter IV. Creation.

all extent. There is but one Principle and its idea, hence, the oneness of God and Soul, and the brotherhood of man; this idea is named man, it has infinite expressions, all of which are members of the body of Christ, Truth, the Intelligence outside of matter. Principle is expressed in one entirety or full idea.

Take the microscope of Spirit to discern animism, and then only can you comprehend the generic term, man. The compound idea named man, is unintelligent; it is a lifeless image and reflection of Principle, or Soul, which is the Life, Intelligence, and Substance of this idea. A belief of matter separates man from God, and from his fellow-man. The science of being gives harmony to man. Loving God supremely is simply admitting Soul above sense in all things, and loving our neighbor as ourself, because, all have but one Soul, and should recognize themselves Soul, and not personal sense. Understanding ourself and neighbor one in Principle, we shall hold no divided interests, and find it good to keep the two commandments that our Master said out-weighed all sacrifices and burnt offerings, religious rites and ceremonies, and fulfilled the prophecies, ushering in the reign of harmony that is to come on earth, even as in heaven. To love God supremely is to hold no Intelligence in matter, neither pleasure nor pain in the body. Truth, Life, and Love, are not in their idea, but are the Principle of this idea; are not in man, but are God, outside of man.

This science of being alone enables us to love God with all the heart, and our neighbor as ourself. To reach its harmony, we must look away from the supposed Life of matter, and find happiness in Soul and not sense. Man is not distorted into shocking dimensions, because be is the infinite idea, nor is be but a solitary thought, disembodied and alone. When realizing Life as it is, namely, Soul, not sense, or the personal man, we shall expand into Truth and self-completeness that embrace all things, and need communion with nothing more than itself, to find them all. But this statement of Soul and body, or God and man, we shall understand, only in proportion as we lay up our treasures in heaven, and not on earth; that is, in

Chapter IV. Creation.

Spirit, and not matter, and approach the broader interpretation of being, where we gain the glorious consciousness and proof of Life and happiness. The sensuous and material man is slow to gather this meaning. Constantly looking away from the body to the good and true, we shall gravitate towards Spirit and immortality; but ever referring to the body, talking and supposing incessantly, some pain or pleasures there, we shall never become harmonious, but return, "like the sow to her wallowing," and "the dog to his vomit." The freedom or blessedness of the sons of God, is not communing with the body, but away from it with the impersonal Life, Truth, and Love. Regarding the body as the seat of Intelligence, Life, etc., is to hold one's self liable to be annihilated; and believing God a person, robs Omnipotence, clothing it with vestments of mortality.

If Deity is personality, the forever "I am," or God with us, is not Spirit, but matter, bounded by and narrowed into six feet of stature. If God is a person he dwells in a body, in which case matter and Spirit are God; this is impossible, for Spirit and matter are opposites. It is of little consequence what our educated views are on this subject; it is morally impossible for Principle to dwell in its idea; for Soul to inhabit a body; the unchanging to dwell in change, and the undying with death, or the Infinite with the finite, the perfect with the imperfect; yea, for Spirit and matter to unite, and Soul and personal sense to join hands. Soul cannot exist both within and without the body, else matter is gone, and all is found Principle and idea, in which case personality disappears. There is a wider difference between Spirit and matter than between light and darkness, that surely are not min-led into one. We know better than to say Deity is the shadow of matter, but if matter is Substance, God is shadow, and shadow never produced Substance; hence, matter must have created itself, The body of Spirit is spiritual and not material; but Principle, or Soul, cannot be compressed into one of its ideas, into what it has made. If God is in a body He is person, and not Principle, hence man is not his likeness or reflection. Again, the discord that comes from the belief of Soul in body, and intelligent matter, at once proves this theory of being a belief only, and error.

Chapter IV. Creation.

Mortal man is a very unnatural image and likeness of God, immortality. Turning from the contemplation of Soul in matter, we shall not call on drugs, laws of health, etc., for health or happiness, but obtain these by losing sickness, sin and death; in the science of being Soul meets all wants spiritually, giving not a atone for bread. "The flesh lusteth against the Spirit and the Spirit against the flesh," hence the natural antagonism between Spirit and matter. St. Paul called the body of Soul a spiritual body, and the flesh a "natural body"; or what is more probable, some one else translated it thus, when he longed to "lay off this body," i.e., to destroy this belief, he must have thought it a very unnatural body, as he gained life, that is God, Spirit; the personal man and woman is neither- us" nor our local habitation. Who is safe leaning on man, or the body, or finds sufficient Life or Love in man to make him happy? we feel this lack, and the great need of resting on something higher. There is no lack in God, but we do not avail ourself of Spirit, but of personality or matter. Joint heirs with God are the partakers of an inheritance where there is no division of estate; we are Spirit, but, knowing this not, we go on to vainly suppose ourself body, and not Soul. God is not a personality, and Soul is not in body; the immortal is not within the mortal, nor Life in death. This belief has hidden the glorious Truth of man's being, and turned him away from his original selfhood; hence the great need we feel for something better, higher, and holier, than personal man.

The material man depends for happiness and Life, on sense instead of Soul; on matter, rather than Spirit, hence the insufficiency he finds in himself, or personal man. But looking away from sense to Soul, and taking the Principle of Life to demonstrate man, we regain the understanding of our God-being, and instead of vain repetitions, such as heathen use, made to a far-off, personal Deity to aid this hour, we must put our finger to our lips, remembering that Spirit knoweth, while personal sense knoweth not, what man hath need of. "The Father of the rain, who hath begotten the dew, and bringeth Mazzaroth in his season, and guides Arcturus with his sons," knows the wants of every one of its ideas, and controls man

Chapter IV. Creation.

and the universe in harmony and immortality. If only we realized this glorious Truth, it would silence sense, and leave the body in the hands of Soul, where all would be well with it. Man has no Intelligence wherewith to govern man, however much he may say, "I have made a covenant with my eyes" etc. Personal views of the Supreme Intelligence are so bigoted, or narrow and inverted, they neither reach Principle nor represent it, but appeal to a personal God of whom we have beard through the hearing of the ear. Eye hath not seen Spirit, nor hath ear heard its voice.

Reverse this order of things, and above the appeal to a man-God, lift thyself to the Wisdom and Love that maketh the God-man, and you will at length reach Christianity. Denying sense, and holding no Intelligence in matter, we have the guidance of Spirit leading in the way everlasting, where the belief of supreme being changes from person to Principle. Job said, after the withdrawal of all his matter-treasures, "I have heard of Thee by the hearing of the ear, but now mine eye seeth thee." Personal man is only an atom in immensity, therefore the impersonal Life and Love, that embrace all things, cannot be found in him; we must look outside of man for Life and Love, for, "it is not in man that walketh to direct his steps." Reckoning ourself from the standpoint of Soul, instead of personal sense, we progress as spontaneously as light emits light: but reversing this order of science, in which man begins in the body, and looks there for both pain and pleasure, yea, for Life and for death, he retrogrades hourly, until he finally disappears in what is termed death.

The evidence of personal sense, or Life in matter, is utterly reversed in science, wherein we learn there is neither a personal God nor a personal man. But here do you say, you, "have taken away my Lord," and "I know not where you have laid him," I have lost my Maker and my own identity? Look away then from your body, and you will find them; let go the belief you live in matter, and you will grow as the bird that bursts from the ovum; personality will be swallowed up in the boundless Love that shadows forth man; and

Chapter IV. Creation.

beauty, immortality, and blessedness, be the glorious proof of existence you recognize. This is not losing man nor robbing God, but finding yourself more blessed, as Principle than person, as God than man, as Soul than sense, and yourself and neighbor one. This science of being lessens not the dependence of man on God, but heightens it; neither does it diminish the high obligations of man towards God, but greatly increases them; it deteriorates not in the least from every possible perfection in God, because ascribing all to the impersonal Life, Love, and Truth. Personal love is little better than personal hate; both bringeth a snare, for their foundations are error, viz., Intelligence in matter, and we cling to them, only because we have not reached higher; not that God is found in them, but that we are groping darkly for Him where He is not, when there is no place where His voice is not to be heard. Is there one individual putting off the "old man" and "putting on the new," who has not felt the loss of personal pleasures and pains? yes, and of personal friends, before he found what belongs not to person, namely, the enlargement of his being in Love and Wisdom that reaches beyond personal pain or pleasure. The loss of a friend has, perhaps, given you the explanation of this. Pain quickly informs us that personal pleasure is mortal, and that both are error.

A sinner believes, momentarily, he is happier for wrong-doing, and another man that he suffers for doing right; the one is a belief of personal pleasure, and the other of pain, but both are false. God is not the author of personal sense, or discord. Would existence seem blank without a personal friend? then the time cometh when you will feel this solitariness, and when this vacuum must be filled with Principle, instead of person, and with the Love that is God. When this hour for development arrives, you will suffer from personal enemies so severely it will cause you to approach more readily the science that destroys all personal trust and gives you higher joys, even as pain is salutary in taking away a belief of pleasure in sense. These are the footsteps of science, by which Truth amputates error. Our individuality is never lost; but the belief of Life, Intelligence and Substance in person is lost. Universal Love is individual also,

Chapter IV. Creation.

embracing every idea from infinitesimal to infinity. And so of joy that issues from Spirit, it is both individual and collective; you cannot be alone, for God and man are inseparable, and eternal, and the rich blessing of understanding your individuality in Spirit and not matter, as Soul, and not sense, is that you may learn how to follow Jesus in this saying, "I and the Father are one." This spiritual understanding of man tends not in the least to humanize Jehovah, but to turn man from the human to the divine, from the belief of Life in matter, to the Life that is truth; to raise the understanding above frailty, and to pass the barriers of sense into the impersonal evermore of being.

That man epitomizes the universe, and is the body of God, is apparent to me not only from the logic of Truth, but in the phenomenon, that is sometimes before my spiritual senses, and which the late celebrated naturalist, Agassiz, saw in his microscopic examinations of a vulture's egg. We had made the discovery through spiritual sense, that the body of Soul embraces the universe, and that man is the full idea of Life, Substance and Intelligence, before seeing this corroborative evidence of Professor Agassiz's discoveries, in which he saw the atmosphere, sun, moon and stars, represented in the ovum of a bird; the point where the so-called embryotic life is formed appearing as the sun. Intelligence outside of matter, embraces every idea of man and of the universe; this Intelligence is Soul, and man borrows all Life and intelligence from this, his Principle, even as the earth borrows light and heat from the sun. Water corresponds in figurative purity, to Love, out of which Wisdom produced the "dry land," that is, the condensed idea of creation. "And God divided the light from the darkness." Truth and error were distinct in the beginning, and never mingled.

The idea which reflects most Life and Intelligence is man, and corresponds to the meridian light; that of lesser effulgence to dawn and twilight, which are named the morning and evening of our day. All calculations of a solar day were out of the question in the record of first Genesis; the sun was not then created, and Wisdom

Chapter IV. Creation.

measured not time by matter; therefore morning and evening were figurative of the ideas of God; faintly appearing and then disappearing in belief, but soon to be symbolized by greater light, corresponding to the solar sun, or the meridian idea representing the Principle of man, and man this idea. "And God said, let there be a firmament in the midst of the waters, to divide them." The firmament was the understanding, that divided the waters into those "above," and those "below," into the spiritual and material, that we learn are separated forever; identity was given the idea, representing immortal man; the material, or mortal man, was belief. Firmament, or understanding, united Principle to its idea. Life and Intelligence this Principle; idea, the universe and man. "And God made the firmament." This shows that Life, Truth and Love produced the understanding and separated it from belief, and all was "good" that God made. Also, that understanding interpreted God, and was the dividing line between Truth and error; to separate the waters which were under the firmament from those above it; to hold Life and Intelligence that made all things, distinct from what it made, and superior to them, controlling and preserving them, not through laws of matter, but the law of Spirit. In this arrangement, "all was good;" it being the order of science. "And God called the firmament heaven," that is, harmony, even the result of understanding. The first day in Spirit, is when "He whom to know aright, is Life eternal," i.e., Life, Love and Truth, bring forth their idea. The second day, is to perceive, and the third to understand this idea, viz., heaven, earth, and man.

"And God said, let the earth bring forth grass, the herb, yielding Feed," etc.

Let the idea of creative Wisdom reflect its Principle of creation, showing that the seed yields not an herb, because of a propagating Principle in itself; for there is none, insomuch as Intelligence made all that was made; the idea was only to shadow forth what Intelligence had made. Science not only reveals this, but the Scripture repeats it, that God made every plant of the field, before it

Chapter IV. Creation.

was in the earth, and every herb of the field before it grew. Mathematically speaking, ten multiplied by ten produces one hundred; but the science of being assures us Intelligence produces the units, and multiplies them. Hereby we learn creations of Wisdom are not dependent on laws of matter, but on Intelligence alone; it was Spirit that moved upon the face of the deep, and brought out of chaos, order, a universe and man, as the infinite idea of God. Unfathomable mind had expressed itself.

"The earth brought forth grass, and yielded fruit," in obedience to Intelligence, and not matter; even as a picture is produced by the artist. The idea of creative Wisdom and Love was given its identity; but it was mind, first and last. The grass and tree grew from out the infinite thought that embraced, and expressed them. The artist transfers a landscape from Soul, to sense; but its only immortality is in the Intelligence that forms it. This most important idea of creation constituted the "third day," and was the third epoch; a number corresponding to the resurrection; the third and seventh periods reveal the advanced ideas, whereby Intelligence is seen the Life of the grass, the herb, the tree, etc., and every manifestation of Life understood not Substance but the idea of the creative Life and Intelligence, in no way contingent on organization or matter. This is manifestly the science of being brought to light in our Master's reappearing on the third day, when the idea named man, appeared to his students, independent of matter-conditions. And also the finished figure of creation on the seventh day.

"And God said, let there be lights in the firmament of the heavens, to divide the day from the night, and let them be for signs and for seasons, for days and years." Hereby we learn the continuance of vegetation, and the years or age of man are not contingent on seasons, measured by our solar years, or governed in the least by the so-called laws of matter, for the light of understanding was to govern every idea of Intelligence. There was but one law-giver, when the stars first sang together, and harmony was the anthem of creation.

Chapter IV. Creation.

"And God made two great lights, the greater to rule the day, and the lesser the night; he made the stars also." The sun is figurative of Soul, of the Principle of man, and the universe; of the Life and Intelligence outside of matter, that governs the entire creation. Stars represent scintillations of Truth, that appear in the twilight of understanding, or darkness of belief. Matter never represented God; geology cannot explain the earth, nor one of its formations, for these formations are dependent alone on Spirit, that gave them forth the eternal heavens, earth and man. Intelligence formed and peopled the universe. The scripture gives no record of solar light, until after time had been divided into day and night, and vegetation was formed; showing you light was the symbol of the Life-giving creator, and not a source of Life to the vegetable kingdom.

> "All are but parts of one stupendous whole,
> Whose body nature is, and God the Soul."

Spirit is inseparable from its idea, but never in it; one cannot exist without the other. Principle would be nonentity without its idea, and idea could not be without its entity, or Principle. Soul exists not without man and the universe, for it is never separated from the complex and reflex shadow of itself; but God, the Soul of all, is not in man or matter.

"And God said, let the waters bring forth the moving creatures that hath life," the ideas of God that represent Life outside of matter; "and God blessed them saying, be fruitful, multiply," etc. Here the difference is shown between Wisdom's approval of those things created by Spirit and the command for them to multiply, and the curse upon Adam's race that sprang from dust, matter. So far, Life, Truth, and Love, had "made all that was made" and pronounced it "good "; but we have no record of their creating sin, sickness, or death; all was good that was created by God. The same Truth that made man harmonious, will destroy, at length, the belief of Life in matter, or mortal man, and reveal man the forever idea of God; but this Truth is met with the malignancy of error in return for Love,

Chapter IV. Creation.

shedding its blessings unsparingly on all. Malice pursues the reformer through every avenue of society, and the evil that persecutes, and the pride that refuses aid, binds the hands and feet of philanthropy, and then calls for stronger proofs of active limbs.

"And God made the beasts of the earth after his kind, and cattle after their kind, and saw that it was good." The beast and reptile made by Love and Wisdom were neither carnivorous nor poisonous; Love never created hatred, nor Truth error. In the science of being, man preys not on his fellow-man, and his neighbor is as himself. One beast shall not devour another, and the lion shall lie down with the jamb, and the little child shall lead them. The Wisdom that handled serpents unharmed, and that made a staff as a serpent, held dominion over reptiles and over all the earth; this dominion was illustrated by Moses and the prophets, and afterwards by Jesus and his disciples, the very best examples to elucidate the Truth of being. Understanding this science, Daniel was safe amid the hungry lions, well knowing the Intelligence that formed the lion was superior to him; therefore lie took refuge from the belief of Life in matter ready to perish, in Life that was God, where safety and refuge lay, and thus demonstrated his control "over the beasts of the field." Understanding Life not at the mercy of death, and Spirit superior to matter, saved the prophet from the hungry lions. To conclude an animal is superior to man, that matter is power, and Life in the body, leaves man in the hour of danger a Samson with eyes plucked out his strength a spectacle of weakness. When immortality is better understood, there will follow an exercise of capacity unknown to mortals; man will become a hundred fold more a man, when he holds himself in the science of being, starting from the basis of Spirit. In Truth there is endless strength and immortality.

"And God said, let *us* make man in our image, after our likeness, and let *them* have dominion over the fish of the sea and over the fowls of the air and over the cattle and over all the earth." The "Us" used in this quotation referred to Intelligence, the creative Wisdom, and expressed plurality; therefore if God is a person it plainly

Chapter IV. Creation.

implied more than one God; but to gain the right interpretation, which is the spiritual sense of this saying, is to admit the "Us" referred to, Life, Truth and Love; even the triune Principle that reveals the Life that is Truth, and the Truth that is Life, and both God, and God, Love. "Let them have dominion," also signifies plurality, for man was the generic name of mankind; in contradistinction to the belief that God made one man, and man made the rest of his kind, science reveals the fact that He made all. The photographer transfers the likeness of one or more objects, according to the number present, and we admit the likeness of three is not one, and *vice versa*; therefore, as man is the likeness of God the plain expression, "let us make man," and "let them have dominion," is conclusive evidence that God made man the idea of infinite mind, and was the plural, Life, Love and Truth; not a plural person, but Principle that gave the infinite idea. There could be no second creation after "all was made that was made," nor ever a man formed since the full idea of God was given. "So God created man in His own image, male and female created He them."

Hereby we learn, man was a generic name; also that he reflected the Principle of male and female, was the likeness of "Us," the compound Principle that made man. Male and female cannot be one in person, but are one in Principle, and if God is a person his gender would be both male and female, these being the likenesses of Him, as the Scripture informs us; but for these different personalities or sexes to be found in one person, would be deemed monstrous; hence, male and female being the likeness and representation of God, we learn that person is not the image of Him; much less can He be in person, inasmuch as he is Principle embracing the masculine, feminine, and neuter, represented by the universe and man. Gender is embraced in Spirit, else God could never have shadowed forth from out Himself, the idea of mile and female; this idea comes from Soul and not body, from Principle and not person.

Which, again, furnishes the proof that an egg is not the origin of man, that seed never produced a plant, etc. Intelligence "made all

Chapter IV. Creation.

that was made," and every plant, before it was in the ground; every mineral, vegetable, and animal, were ideas of the eternal thought. Supreme and universal mind embraced every form of the universe and gave it forth, as Spirit and not matter, and nothing was left for man or for matter to create, after Spirit had created all. This is science, and it underlies the harmony of God and man. The Scriptures declare "God is Love;" that "God is Spirit, Life, and Truth;" now these are not person; also there are many persons, and but one God; hence Deity is not person but Principle. Judging from Paul's rule, to learn the "invisible by the things He hath made," the ideas that express God, render it impossible for that to be one person which produces feminine, masculine, and neuter. The expression of God's gender is Principle and not person; the entire universe and man represent God as Principle, and not person; the infinite "Us " that embraced every idea of the universe, shadowing forth each from out itself; the unavoidable result of Intelligence that said, "Let there be light," that is, let the Infinite be expressed.

"In the beginning was the word, and the word was with God, and the word was God; all things were made by Him, and without Him there was nothing made that was made." "In Him was Life," etc., and then to conclude in the face of this infinite logic, that an egg is the starting point of Life, that seed produces germination, etc., is to forget this is mythical, and a belief that usurped the prerogative of understanding, starting an Adam from dust, calling itself Life in matter, and resulting in mortality, the very opposite of Truth.

After "all was made that was made," nothing could be added to the infinite expression of infinite Intelligence, and person is not the image and likeness of Intelligence, or matter of Spirit; therefore, these do not represent the plural "Us" in one Principle, nor the generic man, or male and female, created by Principle. We have not as much authority in science, for calling God masculine as feminine, the latter being the last, therefore the highest idea given of Him. The belief that the form of man is the body of the supreme Being, or that He is in a body, is the error of supposed Life and Intelligence in

Chapter IV. Creation.

matter, that bore the fruit of sickness, sin, and death; even the "tree of knowledge" reversing the science of being, by supposing Soul in body, Spirit in matter, and substituting personal sense for Soul, having dominion over man, instead of man's dominion over matter. This belief embraces all that is finite, sinful, and mortal; but recollect it is Adam, the error, that sprang from dust, nothingness, and by edict of Wisdom, will return to it. Man originated in God; he is the product of Spirit; hence, he is idea, and not Substance, even the body of Soul; his Intelligence is Spirit, not brains; mind not in matter, God not in person. Love is spiritual, joy-giving and eternal, a forever assurance that "God is Love;" personal attractions that originate in the body are fraught with change and death, impure, transient and mortal. The curse causeless came not to Adam, the original sin or error, in other words, to this belief of Life and Intelligence in matter. Spirit originating in matter, and Intelligence inserted afterwards, Soul pushed into a body, matter intelligent, and the body named man where personal sense takes the lead of Soul, is a myth. God was and is; and man was and is, His reflex shadow.

In Genesis, the spiritual record of the universe and man is lost sight of, it was so materialized by uninspired writers; the creations of Spirit are spiritual; for they cannot be material; they are ideas of Principle thrown off from Soul, instead of sense, and their Substance is their Principle. The bride of Spirit is the idea of Love, the lamb revealed to John in spiritual vision, not a mere belief or personal attachment; this idea came down from the New Jerusalem, the exaltation of Spirit over matter; it was the unselfish, pure and immortal. "We worship we know not what," when we "worship in temples made with hands," even our bodies, and from the standpoint of matter, instead of Spirit. "God is Love," and man the idea image and likeness of Him. Love's ideas are spiritual; its male and female are ideas of Soul instead of sense, expressed by the flower as well as man and woman, even those that God bath joined together, and mortal belief cannot put asunder. "And God blessed them, and said unto them, be fruitful and multiply and replenish the earth, and subdue it and have dominion over every living thing that moveth on

Chapter IV. Creation.

the earth." All blessings and power came with the creations of Spirit, and as such they were to multiply and replenish the earth on this basis of being, and subdue it, making matter subservient to Spirit, and all would be harmonious and immortal; in contradistinction to the generations of Adam, or the belief that matter subdues Spirit.

In this science of being, man "held dominion over the earth, and every living thing that moveth on the earth"; he knew neither Life nor power outside of Spirit, the governing Principle of the universe and man; and this Truth of all being, namely, that Intelligence is the only Life and Principle of all, brings to light the harmony and immortality of man. Error claims Life in matter, hence the creator a propagating vitality in vegetable and animal; and this error was the original sin, it being a belief of God in matter, or matter without God. This was the Adam, so totally depraved, insomuch as it claimed Life, Intelligence and Truth, that alone was God. Thinking to put Intelligence and Life in matter reversed the order of science, giving matter dominion over man. Intelligence multiplies the ideas of God only by destroying the belief of vitalized matter, for one is science and the other sense; one the Truth of being, the other its error; creative Intelligence was never transferred from Soul to sense, or from God to man.

We learn from the science of being that Spirit, independent of the so-called laws of matter, throws off its idea in every formation that is real or immortal. There is no material law that creates and governs man, or that man should obey; obedience to spiritual law is all that God requires, and this law abrogates matter, and makes the body idea, and as such harmonious and immortal.

"And God said, behold, I have given you every herb bearing seed, which is upon the face of all the earth, and every tree in the which is the fruit of a tree yielding seed," (the good fruit was not Substance but the idea of God,) "to you it shall be for meat." To understand that Life is Spirit, is this idea, and it consisteth not in the things man eateth; it is the Truth of man that makes man immortal.

Chapter IV. Creation.

But the poor belief that Life is supported by bread or meat, makes matter his masters and man mortals however much he may eat. Truth is the immortality of man, and error the only mortality; immortality is Soul, and not sense; matter can neither give nor take away Life. The Scripture saith, "Man liveth by every word that proceedeth out of the mouth of God," and this is not material bread, but that which comes from heaven, harmony, giving its idea, immortality. We know the belief of Life in matter is sustained by eating, drinking, etc., because it reverses the order of creation, and predicates Life on matter instead of Spirit.

"And every herb bearing seed, and every tree in the which is the fruit of a tree, was given man." The idea of God (and this was man) was superior to earth, because it was the supreme idea, that embraced the entire universe in itself, and to which all others were subordinate. In this science of being, the herb bore seed and the tree fruit, not because of root, seed, or blossom, but because their Principle sustained these ideas, not as Substance, but idea, for Intelligence held dominion over matter. Reproduction is the result not of seed or soil, but the Principle of man and the universe, that produces through Intelligence. "And to every beast of the earth, and to every fowl of the air, etc., wherein is Life, was given every green herb for meat." Unto every belief of Life in matter, the green herb symbolizing the immature and imperfect was apportioned, for this belief was error and must draw its nutriment from the "tree of knowledge," whereof if a man eat he should die.

"And God saw every thing that He had made, and behold it was very good." Mark the distinction between the things produced by Spirit, and those supposed to be material products. Adam was sinful and mortal; in other words, he was error, and this error the belief that Life and Intelligence are in matter. The first product of this belief was Cain, a murderer, and earth brought forth thorns and thistles according to error, Adam; and man must live by bread, and earn it by the sweat of his brow. The belief of Life in matter entailed nothing but discord; therefore this belief was error, and error

Chapter IV. Creation.

illusion; science says man has neither birth, growth, decay nor death; man is idea and not Substance, and spiritual instead of material. God "saw all that He had made," inasmuch as Intelligence understands all; hence the harmony and immortality of its ideas and of man as idea, and not Substance, and governed by mind instead of matter; mind that comprehends and sustains man, not as matter, but idea. Soul understands this science of being, but sense does not, and the less sense and the more Soul is brought out will man appear the glorious idea of immortality. Soul alone comprehends immortality; personal sense says, when the eye loses sight of him forever, man is dead.

"Thus the heavens and earth were finished, and all the hosts of them." Here the Scripture repeats again the science of creation, namely, that all was complete and finished, therefore that nothing has since been made; that Intelligence embraced all from the forever, and that all is perfect, infinite and eternal. This assurance, even, is self-sustaining, but to understand it, is to gain our harmony and immortality; no geological speculation can change or mar the fact that Intelligence, the Soul of man, embraces the universe and man in idea, and holds them thus, forever. As matter-substance, all is lost, but as Principle and idea, all is eternal. Never a mineral, vegetable or animal, was formed of dust; Spirit alone fashions all things. Birth, decay and death, are a personal sense of things, not their idea; man and the universe are complete and eternal in Intelligence, and nothing can exist out of that.

"And on the seventh day God ended His work, which He had made." This corroborates the statement in science, that Truth, Life and Love had fully wrought out the infinite and eternal idea named the universe and man; also, that error the opposite of Truth, was about to claim a work independent of God, in which matter instead of Spirit should be the creator. The Truth, and science of being were already recorded, but error was now to make a reversed statement of man and the universe, viz., that Life, Intelligence, and Substance belong to matter, that Soul is in body, God a person, man a second

Chapter IV. Creation.

Intelligence, and evil a third. This error was belief, and belief not mind, but a supposition of mind, not Soul, but what is termed personal sense, not Spirit, but intelligent matter, all of which is a myth. "These are the generations of the heavens and the earth, when they were created, in the day that the Lord God made the earth and heavens," in other words, when Spirit was the creator. Generations signified the manifold ideas of Intelligence, and Life.

"And God made every plant of the field before it was in the earth, and every herb of the field before it grew, for the Lord God had not caused it to rain on the earth, and there was not a man to till the ground." Here, again, is the undeniable statement that Intelligence is the only creator; also, that it produces vegetation, not through processes of culture or in obedience to what are termed laws of nature, but in obedience to Spirit; God made the plant before it grew; no partnership with matter is here acknowledged, and man was the idea of Spirit, and this idea tilled not the ground for bread; the Life of idea was its Principle; hence man could not die of starvation, or dyspepsia. The time cometh when we must all learn this science of being, in order to gain its harmony and immortality, even as we have already learned that the opposite belief of Life and Intelligence in matter, produces mortality, it being a belief of sin, Sickness and death.

The record of creation in Genesis repeats three times, "In the clay that the Lord God made them," indicating there was a time coming when another creation should declare itself the author of man. That creation was the history of Adam and his progeny, or mythological life in matter. After God created man, "there was not a man to till the ground," because there was no necessity of it ; the earth brought forth spontaneously, and man lived not because of matter, and earth was blessed for his sake, so unlike the curse that came with Adam, error. Spirit was the producer of harmony only, and Life self-sustained; therefore man was not to live because he ate much or little, giving no opportunity for gluttony or poverty, to mar the work of Wisdom. Man needed not to cultivate the soil, that

Chapter IV. Creation.

matter might produce itself, nor to presume himself on the prerogative of creator. Spirit was the Life and creator of all, and its work was complete, and beyond the power of matter to destroy; all things were made when comprehended by Intelligence. Soul had all in its own possession, and there was no personal sense to do the work of Wisdom. Life was not in matter, and there was no existence except to Spirit. Nothing is new to Intelligence; the infinite understanding is not creating the universe or man anew; these ideas were forever, without beginning and without end.

Matter has neither capacity, right nor power to create or to destroy; all is in the hands of Spirit, that hitherto hath wrought independently before belief claimed, through material law, to create and govern mineral, vegetable and animal. Intelligence made all that was made, and was not in the things it had made. Spirit never passed into matter to produce a world; heaven, earth and seas, and all things therein came from the eternal thought, and mind no more produces matter than matter produces mind. This is science, that God governs the universe and man. That matter propagates itself through seed and germination is error, a belief only, and not the Truth of being, and belief has its penalty, for, admitting mineral, vegetable and animal things of sense, instead of Soul, and dependent on matter for their ephemeral existence, makes them mortal. Not so with the universe and man, born of Spirit; they are harmonious and eternal.

"But there went up a mist from the earth and watered the whole face of the ground."

Truth created through the understanding, saying, "let there be light," but error came through darkness or belief, the figurative mist of earth, that which started from a matter basis; Adam was the belief of Life in matter that rose from the dust, saying man depends on material structure, and vegetation on the rain and dew. "And the Lord God formed man of the dust of the ground, and breathed into his nostrils the breath of life, and man became a living Soul." This statement of a second creation contradicts the first one, in which

Chapter IV. Creation.

Spirit said, "Let 'Us' make man." The first record was science; the second was metaphorical, and mythical, even the supposed utterances of matter; the scripture not being understood by its translators, was misinterpreted. After God had declared "all was made," and the creation "good," Wisdom never repented, or repeated what it had done; there was no second creation, and on a new plan. Had the record divided the first statement of creation from the fabulous second, by saying, after Truth's creation we will name the opposite belief of error, regarding the origin of the universe and man, it would have separated the tares from wheat, and we should have reached sooner the spiritual significance of the Bible. We are repeatedly assured in the second chapter of Genesis, that God had finished His work before Adam was created; that male and female, together with all the hosts of heaven and earth, were already made; therefore we have the authority of scripture for denying a second creation, or a single formation by matter. The harmonious creation was ended, and all was "good" that God created. Life, Truth and Love never made inharmonious man.

"God saw everything that He bad made, and behold, it was very good." Admitting He created Adam, Cain, and every other mortal error, He was the author of evil as well as good; but this is contradicted by the prophet Jeremiah, who saith, "Out of the mouth of the Most High proceedeth not evil and good"; and what did the Evangelist mean when he said, "All things were made by Him, and without Him there was nothing made that was made," "In Him was Life," etc.? Simply this, that Life never created death, nor Truth error; it is error alone, that produces error. The belief of Life in matter, named Adam, brought sickness, sin and death into the world, and God denounced this error, or Adam, and said it was mortal; "For dust thou art, and unto dust shalt thou return." This was not spoken of Soul, nor of man created by God; Life which is God, never entered into sin and death. Spirit was not the component part of Adam, or mortal man. The history of Adam is allegorical throughout, a description of error and its results, opposed to the Truth of being, and contradicting the divine economy; it makes

Chapter IV. Creation.

Intelligence, Life, and Substance, matter instead of Spirit, saying, "Believe in me and I will make ye as gods;" more than one God was its starting point. Truth gives the immortal idea or man from Spirit, but error, the mortal belief from matter. The express image and likeness of God was immortal man, and there is none other, or ever a man since created. Through a belief of pain and sorrow, error claimed to create man, but Truth gave its idea of God in joy, blessing, and dominion. Error's process of creating, bases Intelligence on matter, or would put Intelligence in matter; either of which is impossible, insomuch as it would make Intelligence both God and devil; i.e., both good and evil; this belief is proved error, in that it produces sickness, sin and death, hence the sentence of Wisdom, "Thou shalt die." The science of being never produced sickness, sin, or death, but destroys them.

The symbol of error was the "tree of knowledge " which God, the Truth of being, forbade man; it symbolized the belief of Life and Intelligence in matter, of which Truth said, partake not, lest ye die; but error replied, Truth is at fault, if you acquire knowledge, "your eyes shall be opened and ye shall be as Gods, knowing good from evil," i.e., men shall be intelligences, Gods! and these Gods, matter, called men, to distinguish them from another personal God. Is not this Idolatry, and walking over the spiritual law, "Thou shalt have no other Gods before me?" Spirit in matter and Soul in sense, makes "lords many and Gods many"; theology, materia medica, mesmerism, and every other 'ology and 'ism under the sun, originated in this very error. Intelligence and Life is God, omnipotent and eternal, and God never in matter, but producing spiritual, harmonious, and immortal man. There is but one God, one Life and Intelligence, one Principle of being, and this heals the sick, gives sight to the blind, destroys error instead of creating it, preaches the gospel to the poor, and is measurably explained in this science of being; the followers of Christ, Truth, were not the Rabbis, for it came to its own and was not received. Knowledge never enabled man to judge between good and evil, therefore it was a falsehood from the beginning, as Jesus said, "You were a liar from the

Chapter IV. Creation.

beginning, and Truth, Life, abode not in you," for Truth was never in matter, and mortal man is matter, and knowledge was his projenitor; mortal man is a belief of Life and death, of pain and pleasure, sickness and health, good and evil, mixed in one mass, called intelligent matter or personal sense. Adam impersonated this error, and Adam illustrated simply a belief, which we have endeavored to explain in its nothingness, together with the reality it would falsely make of the impossibility of Life and Intelligence in matter.

This error, or belief, shrinks from the voice of Truth calling to man, "where, or what, art thou, Soul or personal sense? art thou Spirit or matter? and belief replied, "I heard thy voice and was afraid." Fear was the first manifestation of the belief of Life in matter, for "the wicked flee when no man pursueth"; fear founded sickness said death. Error was naked, but it could not bide from the eye of Wisdom; and Truth replied, who told thee thou art naked? and error fell back on personality, saying, "She gave me of the fruit of knowledge," (a medical work, perhaps.) Woman, that was taken from my rib, (as if man was less the origin of her fault because she was not back again under that rib); told me I was in my body, and that Life and sensation are in matter. But when Truth questioned woman regarding the "knowledge" that said matter is intelligent, and personal sense is man, she replied, "The serpent beguiled me, and I did eat." Woman was the first to see out of the difficulty, owning this knowledge a serpent; as she is the first to lay down the belief that Life Originates materially. A serpent hung on the "tree of knowledge," metaphorically, to show its subtilty, and the Master bade his students be wise as the serpent, i.e., never allow the belief of Life and sensation in matter to put to silence the opposite, science of being. Woman was a higher idea of God than man, insomuch as she was the final one in the scale of being; but became our beliefs reverse every position of Truth, we name supreme being masculine, instead of feminine. Woman first perceived reason was beguiled by knowledge. Truth's question to Adam, error, viz., "Is Life and

Chapter IV. Creation.

Intelligence in matter?" rebuked and exposed this would-be material consciousness.

"The Lord formed man of the dust, and breathed into his nostrils the breath of Life, and he became a living Soul," put Truth in error! Intelligence in matter! made the body mortal embrace the Principle of being that embraces man! Did the Infinite enter matter through man's nostrils? did God, the Truth and Life, enter the Pick, sinning, and dying body? then Deity would be man, or man Deity, and Life mortal! this absurd belief is atheism. "When God, who is our Life, shall appear, then shall we be like Him." Man will be perfect, sinless, and eternal, when Spirit permeates man. Principle never entered its idea, nor Spirit matter. We have no record in Genesis that God gave Adam, error, dominion over the earth, and yet, to belief, error holds this away. Adam was a product of belief, and Eve, of Adam, and both were beliefs of Life in matter; we say beliefs because that is not the Truth of being. Principle, and not person, Spirit and not matter, Truth and not error, God and not man, made male and female.

"And the Lord said, behold, the man is become as one of us, to know good from evil, and now lest he put forth his hand and take also of the tree of Life and live forever, therefore the Lord sent him forth from the garden of Eden, to till the ground whence he was taken." No one can doubt this scripture is allegorical, pointing out the results of a belief of God in man, or Intelligence in matter; we cannot accept it in a literal sense without impugning the Love that made man, and gave him earth for a possession, and blessed it for his sake. A literal acceptation of this quotation implies malice, withholding from man the opportunity to reform, lest be should become better; but this is not our God, and so contrary to Love and Wisdom, we must accept it only as the pagan opinions of those re-writing the inspired word. The true interpretation of this scripture is its spiritual sense. Beginning in person instead of Principle, to explain God, we express him after the manner of man, the nature of personal sense and on the basis of error instead of Truth, drawing all

Chapter IV. Creation.

our conclusions from a material, instead of a spiritual standpoint, hence the discord, theoretically and practically, that follows the belief of intelligent matter. "Behold, the man is become as one of us." Error and not the Truth of being, said that; man is not God, therefore he did not become as one of "Us." Intelligence is not in matter, therefore it is not personal sense; Spirit in matter would make God mortal man, and Intelligence and Life, person instead of Principle, and body instead of Soul. That this error be not reckoned Truth, or as one of "Us," and claim the prerogative of Intelligence, God said, let all that produces sickness, sin, and death, " till the ground;" i.e., be understood as proceeding from a material, and not a spiritual basis, and therefore an error that returns to dust, primitive nothingness.

Let material things be understood forever, as apart from the spiritual; think not to blend matter and Spirit, for this is not the science of being, and will result in discord and death. From the sweat of the brow to derive Life or happiness, started with Adam, error; it was from the "tree of knowledge," so unlike the harmony and immortality of man created by Spirit. Lay not up for yourselves treasures on earth, is the better understanding of Life. Whatsoever proceedeth from Spirit, is harmonious and immortal, deriving all it is from God; but what cometh from matter, is mortal, dependent on sense instead of Soul. Material man, and a world of matter, reverse the science of being, and are utterly false; nothing is right about them; their starting point is error, illusion, therefore sin and sense are at home in this world, and mortal error stalks boldly forth on firm footing until the waiting hand of science shall strike it down. Truth has literally no foothold on such an earth, and with such views, for they accord neither place nor privilege to God. Error "tills" the entire ground here, working on a material platform, therefore Wisdom said, let Adam, error, that is not the image and likeness of God, not the immortal mind reflecting harmonious Intelligence, but a belief of Life and Intelligence in matter, be set apart from the immortal, i.e., the idea of Truth, for this is the science of being, that Spirit and matter, which is Truth and error, never

Chapter IV. Creation.

blend. Instead of the Life, Truth, etc., that make man harmonious and immortal, the belief or error, named Adam, depends on personality and pardon, like a vain child that demands to be blessed when it must be punished, because it knows not the terms on which a blessing is gained, but in its blindness expects from matter and personality the good that comes from Spirit and Truth.

If God had made Adam and sin, they must have been "good," for "all was good that He made." The translators of that record, wrote it in the error of being, to wit, the belief of Life and Intelligence in matter, hence their misinterpretations; they spake from error, of error, and from the standpoint of matter attempted to define Spirit, which accounts for the contradictions in that glorious old record of creation. Science in no instance has a material basis; matter and personality are not man, neither God, Intelligence. Belief is all that claims Spirit in matter, and would make personalities of error, and Truth, naming one mortal man, and the other God. That God is a person, or Intelligence in matter, and man another Intelligence of evil, is "knowledge, prohibited by Wisdom;" it was not the tree of Life. Truth had but one reply to all this error, "Thou shalt surely die;" therefore mortality attends every phase of this supposed Life in matter, whether mineral, vegetable, or animal. Whatever germinates after the manner of matter, will meet the fate of error, namely, sickness, sin and death, until every vestige of this belief is self-destroyed, and man understood, shadow and not Substance, whose only Life or Intelligence is God.

"So he drove out the man, and placed at the east of the garden of Eden cherubims and a flaming sword which turned every way to keep the way of the tree of Life." Here is a clear and distinct separation of Adam, error, from harmony and Truth, wherein Soul and sense, person and Principle, Spirit and matter, are forever separate. The figure used in the New Testament, of the wise men coming from the East, was employed here, also, and prefigured the sun that symbolized Soul, even the Principle of man, therefore the Wisdom of man. The sword of Truth is represented as two-edged,

Chapter IV. Creation.

cutting each way to protect from error, or the belief of Life in matter. Also, the "tree of Life," symbolized the Truth of being, and the "tree of knowledge," error or personal man. Truth also guarded Eden, harmony, and the science of being pointed the way of happiness and Life. Error alone was sickness, sin, and death, because it was a belief that matter is intelligent, and evil a person, named Satan, working in and against man. The "tree of Life " was guarded from the touch of mortality, because it symbolized the Truth of man, and between this Truth and the opposite error, was placed the metaphorical word, or flaming warning to hold them forever apart; showing that Truth and error, or Spirit and matter never mingle. The great point in the science of being is to learn that Spirit and matter never unite, or dwell together; but are the wheat and tares that grow side by side, until the harvest, when matter is destroyed, and God learned our only real being.

The infancy of this science is lisping to an unconscious age the great Truth of being; and perceiving one idea, and not its correlative one, many will call that science which is only a portion of it; and again, it is difficult in this evil world to do as well as we know. If mathematics present a thousand different examples, and one of them proves the rule laid down for the others, are not all equally authenticated? When a single statement of this science is proved, it settles the question for the others; all are dependent on one, and *vice versa*, one cannot be disapproved without disuniting the general chain through which the Principle is reached; hence, the command not to add or diminish one word to that which is inspired, and demonstrable; but which personal sense cannot explain.

"And Adam knew his wife, and she conceived and brought forth Cain, and said, "I have gotten a man from the Lord." This record implies a new creation commenced, after God had finished His work; that Wisdom was entering into partnership with man, to create anew the whole human family; but the beauty, sublimity and science of the record is lost sight of here, if we enter this labyrinth of inconsistencies, unconscious it is the record of error opposed to the

Chapter IV. Creation.

Truth of being. Adam was a metaphor, showing the opposite of God's creation, and the original texts were written metaphorically at first, the only method of reaching the science of the scripture, hence, the Truth of the Bible is to rise to its, spiritual interpretation, then compare its sayings, and gain their general tenor, which enables us to reach the ascending scale of being through demonstration; as did prophet and apostle.

The scripture seems more obscure in Genesis and Revelations than other portions, solely because the original texts were not understood by those re- writing them. Three hundred years after the apostles, there was not a written text of the Now Testament; it had to be taken up at first, orally. The record of creation given in the first chapter of Genesis, is the science and Truth of being; but the opposite statement in the second chapter, where man sprang from dust, instead of Deity, is error's statement, even personal sense speaking in sin, sickness, and death, that would confine Life to matter-conditions, and limit Omnipotence. In this error and belief, the herb is not created without seed and soil, and man is the product of an egg. The first record embraces the Principle of harmonious man, even the Truth of being; and the second, the origin of the belief of Life in matter, which belief embraces also, sickness, sin and death, -- all that is mortal. To admit God made man of dust, and afterwards breathed Intelligence into matter, and it became a living Soul, is rank atheism, that would submerge supreme Wisdom in the things it creates; this statement of man and God, makes both mortal. "In Adam, (error,) all died," "and in Christ," (Truth,) "shall all be made alive."

The Truth of being casts out error, heals the sick, and raises the dead; understanding Life exempt from mortality, and no sensation, or Intelligence in the body, is the ultimatum of being; the way, the Truth and Life, that points out the footsteps of science. Life is not in matter, unless Truth is in matter; Life is God, as the scriptures declare, and God never germinated. He is the same yesterday, to-day, and forever; outside of all He creates, and the creator of all. If

Chapter IV. Creation.

God breathed into the body, into matter, Wisdom, then matter became Spirit, and the stronger rules out the weaker and matter is God; error claimed this when it said, "I will make you as Gods "; but Truth replied to this belief, "Thou shalt die." Life, Truth, and Love never formed their image and likeness of dust, nor breathed into dust, (matter), Truth and Love. We should naturally shrink from the error and belief, (if it were only understood) error presupposing another God, or that the Supreme Being entered man that He had made, or that matter embraces God. The statement that God made man of matter, and then put Himself, into personal sense and sin, should be understood the very opposite of the Truth of being; and if this was so understood, sin, sickness, and death would disappear.

Error makes man a slave to matter, but this error came from "knowledge," and was mortal. Truth gave man immortality and dominion over matter. The mist that went up from the ground, causing it to produce, was figurative of the belief that matter germinates, and man's Life is matter instead of Spirit. This belief takes the explanation of man out of the bands of science, wherein man is the product of Spirit, and gives it to personal sense; denying the express declarations of God, that man was made the image and likeness of Spirit. Truth said, partake not of this knowledge, it is error, denouncing it as fatal; but error replied oppositely, "In the day ye eat thereof ye shall become as Gods;" that is, there shall be more than one intelligence, for matter shall be permeated with Spirit, brains, nerves, etc., shall be intelligent of good and evil, and pain and pleasure, Life and death shall be mixed and named personal sense.

We cannot fail to see the great contradiction between the spiritual creation of the universe and man; and the so-called material creation of these through Darwinian evolution or propagation. Mortal and material man is purely mythical; this man started from what? "the ground," *i.e.*, his basis was matter; and woman was evolved from this man; mythologically stated, she came from his rib. Afterwards male and female physically were made the

Chapter IV. Creation.

foundations of man, making races and an egg the author of being. But this evolution or Darwin theory is false; there is no Life and Intelligence in matter, passing &like from vegetable, mineral and animal, hearing the while Wisdom's denunciation, so unlike the blessings and honor bestowed on man's origin in Spirit, and the offspring of God. Immortal man was sustained by Spirit, the mortal by matter and the sweat of his brow.

One held Life in Soul, the other in sense; one was "good" and blessed, the other accursed. A misconception of man pervades the whole statement of mortal, or material man, from his origin in dust, until be returns thither; his entire history is the origin and end of error, and not man.

"I have gotten a man from the Lord," was a falsehood, from the beginning; for this man was a foul murderer, and Truth and Love never created hatred and sin; supreme harmony never produced the Adam and his progeny; that which is not God, or His idea, is not only evil and mortal, but unreal, yea illusion. A wrong version of the scriptures, has hidden their Truth. The Prophet Isaiah is recorded to have said, "God creates peace and he makes evil"; but turn to Jeremiah, and you find this contradicted. Jesus, also, takes the opposite grounds for the basis of his demonstration, showing that God casts out Kin, sickness, and death, instead of creating them.

What would we say of the musician whose harmony produced discord? Science gets right these knotty points, and renders to God the things that are His. We learn error by its results. Sickness, sin and death are the fruits of error; Truth gives harmony and immortality; thus Wisdom adjusted it, and "Thou shalt die" was not spoken in vain of what purports to be Life, Substance and Intelligence in matter, God in man, and Soul in body. Adam, made of dust, was not the image or likeness of God, Spirit; therefore partaking of "knowledge" never lost his first estate, but was the result of it. Man, originating in God, never fell into sin or death; he is forever happy, harmonious, and immortal, inheriting this

Chapter IV. Creation.

birthright alone from Spirit. The so-called man that is sinning, sick, and dying, is not man, but a dream of Life, and Intelligence in matter; "dust to dust," nothingness.

"And Cain went out from the presence of the Lord and dwelt in the land of Nod, and Cain knew his wife," etc. This second fabulous creation originated man first in dust, woman in a rib, and the rest of humanity in an egg. Up to that no mention was made of another woman save Eve, the mother of Cain. Eve, in the Hebrew, signifies beginning, and the question is naturally suggested, whence came the wife of Cain? This, however, is unimportant in the evolution of matter whereby Intelligence and man are supposed to be developed, subject to propagation, growth, and depth. This false theory or Adamic error, was ruled out from the presence of God, Truth, to dwell in the land of Nod, the land of dreams and illusion. Error, named Adam, was the foundation of this mythical creation, and the belief still continues, namely, that man is matter, hence the image of God mortal. Spirit created all things. Man created from matter is mythological; with dust, a rib, and Cain's mother for his wife, alas! who shall say that a monkey was not our great-great-grandfather?

Far be it from us, with thought or expression, to touch profanely the glorious record of the Bible, where alone we may gain the understanding of man's immortal basis; and meager were all earth's possessions, disinherited of the inspired page. But the understanding of scripture is what we need, to restore the harmony of being and gain its Principle, the Father's house, where the prodigal returns, and the perfection of man appears. Christ said, "Believe me that I am in the Father and the Father in me, else believe me for my works' sake", i.e., understand that I am Intelligence, and not matter, and that Intelligence is God, (there is no evil Intelligence) else believe this for the demonstration it brings, healing the sick, and casting out error. We cannot doubt the inspiration that opened to us the spiritual sense of the Bible, when it lifted us from disease and death, giving us triumph over the body. Standing at the threshold of scientific being, and there beholding the falsity of earthly things, "the Spirit

Chapter IV. Creation.

and bride say, come, and whosoever will, let him drink of the waters of Life, freely." Humbly, as fervently, we join grateful issue with the Truth of being, that separates Adam, error, forever from the presence of God, and says to the body, no personal sense, no Life, Intelligence or Substance in matter. In the atmosphere or mind of Soul, man is seen the image and likeness of goodness and perfection, and cannot lose this estate, he being the only heir to the abundant affluence of Life, Truth, and Love, that said, "Let us make man in our own image."

Mortal, and material man, is simply a belief of Life in matter; we say a belief, because he is not the reality of man, and never can reach Life that is outside of matter, where alone is our real, because our harmonious being. Looking and thinking from a material point only, we never shall gain the science of being. In the dark ourselves, how can we see the darkness or the light even. The belief of sin and sickness, or of death, or Life in matter, hides man's Life in harmony, that is Soul and not sense; but who will "believe our report, to whom the arm of the Lord hath not been revealed." The sun, that is light and heat, gives little warmth or brightness until the clouds pass from before it; thus the science of being is seen only as sense is hushed, and Life is learned spiritually. Every agony of mortal man wafts him onward over the billows until error is finally destroyed, and "There is no more sea." This is the new birth, the travail of error before it is self-destroyed, and man is born of Spirit and not matter. In the allegory in Genesis, error said, "Believe me, I will make you as Gods." But Truth replied, to this belief "I will greatly multiply thy sorrow and conception; in sorrow thou shalt bring forth, and thy desire shall be to thy husband and he shall rule over thee." The first intimation of sickness, sorrow, and man's tyranny, came with the belief of Life and Intelligence in matter. "My son, give me thy heart," restores concord to all the dependencies and relations of being. Our Master's impotent foes, were the world of sense; but he feared them not; that which killed the body but was not able to destroy Soul, the Life and Principle of man, had no terrors for him.

Chapter IV. Creation.

Treating of the growth of eggs, Prof. Agassiz said, "It is very possible that many general statements current now, about birth and generation, will be changed with the progress of information." Had the great naturalist gained through his tireless researches the scientific basis of being independent of growth and organization, the blessing of that ardent mind would have continued longer with us; history is greatly indebted to his labors and genius, for facts relating to the belief of Life in matter. His discoveries brought to light important points in what is termed embryotic life; the butterfly, bee, etc., propagating their species without the male element; and this corroborates science, proving plainly that the origin of the universe and man depends not on material conditions. The spiritual understanding of Life, embraces neither sensuous formations nor conditions of matter. All that hag a beginning has an end; what we name life germinating in an egg, and expanding thence to adult being, will finally go out, which proves it never was Life, and nothing, in fact, but a belief of Life, and this belief, mesmerism and not man. Animals of lower organisms combine three methods of reproduction; they multiply by eggs, buds, and self-division, proving the conditions of Life become less imperative in lower organisms, or where there is less mind and belief on this subject. Prof. Agassiz says, "Successive generations do not begin with the birth of new individuals, but with the formation of the egg whence these individuals proceed; and we must look upon the egg as the starting point of the complicated structure of man." His deep researches into material structure culminate here in logical conclusion, and with less hypothesis and more observation than generally attend such theorems.

His discovery aids the science of Life; he has bearded error in its den, proved clearly the origin of mortal man to be matter, and not Spirit; the product of an egg, instead of God, and that a belief of structural life is the sole progenitor of what is termed mortal man; even as Truth is the origin of immortal man and the universe. But what availeth it to investigate this so-called life, that germinates, matures, and decays; that is found to end even as it began, a

Chapter IV. Creation.

nameless nothing, starting in dust, or an egg, and ending in dust. This belief and error the source of sickness, sin and death, hides the real harmony of Life. When it is learned that God is our Life, man will be immortal, sinless, and perfect, and never until then. Spirit is without beginning and without end; but admitting the false premises of Life in matter, whence to draw our conclusions of man, we may infer the discord and confusion consequent on this error and belief with but one signification, viz., "dust to dust."

Error of thought leads to error of action; a constant contemplation of sin will produce it, and the ever-present belief of existence in matter, drops the standard of man in dust. Contemplate Life as it is, neither man nor matter, but God, that which is Intelligence, purity and harmony, and we gain its happiness. If Life has a starting point, immortality is a myth; commencing at a given point, signifies &terminus. If Life has a beginning, it has an end also, and there is no immortality. Life is spherical, without beginning or end; the form of the globe typifies it, and the Principle of the universe is Life, Truth, and Love. Life is cause and not effect, universal, infinite, omnipotent, producing all that really is, and never inside its productions. An egg were a narrow boundary for God! and matter cannot produce matter, much less can it produce Spirit, or Spirit permeate matter. For Spirit to enter matter would be to destroy it, and all would be found Spirit; the immortal destroys mortality, and death would be swallowed up in Life. That like produces like, is not only true in homeopathy, but holds good in the science of being. Embryology affords no instances of one specie producing another; of a serpent germinating a bird, or a lion a lamb; this would be gathering grapes of thorns, and figs of thistles. Such amalgamation would be deemed monstrous, and out of the order of things. A pure fountain sendeth not forth impure streams, and *vice versa*. Then how can Spirit germinate matter, the holy the unholy, and the immortal, mortality.

The difference is not as great between the opposite species, as between matter and Spirit, so utterly unlike in substance and

Chapter IV. Creation.

Intelligence. That Spirit propagates matter, or matter Spirit, is morally impossible; science repudiates the thought, and personal sense alone, must father it, because it is unnatural, unreal, and impossible. Germinating Intelligence is germinating God; how very absurd! Intelligence in matter would make matter the circumference of mind. Intelligence produces, or is produced, which is it? Is matter first and mind afterward? matter the primogenitor of mind, or does Intelligence germinate non-Intelligence? Like produces like; Intelligence is Spirit that germinates idea, and not matter; therefore matter is neither effect nor cause. All is mind; matter is but a belief, and error. Natural history shows that each specie produces its like only the bird is not the father of the beast; the egg germinates the parent stock, and the seed the original plant; hybrids are rapes upon nature, and not the common order. Harmonious and immortal man is the offspring of Intelligence, of the unerring and infinite understanding that said, "Let us make man," hence the scientific certainty of his continuance. All that is discordant is mortal, and without Principle or understanding. Mind produces mind; Intelligence produces the idea of Intelligence; and the mortal and material, the beliefs of belief. One is Truth, the other error; one real, the other unreal; the material produces only the mortal, its basis is belief, and not Truth.

Professor Agassiz argues, "man springs from races." Mr. Darwin has it, he comes up through all the lower grades of being, and must be a monkey before he can be a man. Mr. Darwin is right with regard to mortal man or matter, but should have made a distinction between these and the immortal, whose basis is Spirit. Animality produces animals, and what is good and pure mingles not with evil or the impure; these are two diametrically opposite sources and results; the good comes from God, from Spirit outside of matter, the evil is a belief of matter; hence, the less material the belief, the more transparent mind is for God to shine through, for all that is pure is harmonious and eternal; and the more is God, the Intelligence outside of matter, seen through man, but not from him.

Chapter IV. Creation.

Matter cannot produce Spirit, and *vice versa*. Truth cannot produce error, therefore it never made a mortal, sick or sinful man, nor error a spiritual, harmonious or immortal man. Error reflects error, and Truth is reflected only by Truth. Spirit gives forth only the image and likeness of itself, therefore the idea of God, pure and undefiled; a mortal and sinful man is the product of mortality and not of God, of error and not Truth; hence the scripture's statement of him, that he sprang from the ground, *i.e.*, from a material basis; and ours, that he is a belief only, and error; and Mr. Darwin's that his primogenitors are beasts; and Prof. Agassiz's, that he germinates from an egg. Our views will be accepted later than the others, only because they are more spiritual. Prof. Agassiz asked, "What can there be of a material nature, transmitted through these bodies, called eggs, themselves composed of the simplest material elements, by which all peculiarities of ancestry belonging to either sex, are brought down from generation to generation." Here we see the darkness and doubt creeping into the great mind of the great naturalist, because of the material base of his reasoning; starting from matter instead of God, for the basis of immortal man, who by searching can End out God?

A student said to us, "I understand your explanations of Truth, but I cannot understand error;" and why? because he made it something, and we, nothing; he gave to error a local habitation and a name, making it what it is not, even an entity and power. There is no mortal man, or reality to error; first, because man is immortal, and error is not the Truth, or reality of being; secondly, that these are neither God nor His idea; all that is real, is eternal. Pains or pleasures of personal sense are unreal, and the so-called life of mortal man is a myth. The belief of Life in matter is the so-called mind of man, that suffers because it is a belief of suffering, and dies because it is an error of belief. Searching into the origin of Life is vain; no beginning or end hath Life, for it is from everlasting unto everlasting. Life is Truth, and Truth is Life, act brought to light through error or sickness, sin, and death; Truth is immortality, not in mortality, for it is Soul, not in sense and sin. If Life starts in an egg,

Chapter IV. Creation.

it matter, and mortal; but matter cannot produce Intelligence; whence then is mind? All is mind; there is Do matter. Spirit destroys the belief of matter, as Truth destroys error. If possible for Spirit, God, to enter into a body of sin and death, then harmony enters discord, and discord destroys harmony; can good dwell in evil, or evil represent good?

The poor logic and lack of Truth that would blend Spirit and matter, immortality and mortality, sin and goodness in one body, and call it man, was the error Jesus argued against as the foundation of all discord, showing its falsity by parable and proof; Christ, Truth, casts out this error and heals the sick, beginning at once to destroy mortality with its own immortality. The wicked often return evil for good, when the Truth of being comes in contact with their error to destroy it; therefore the followers of Christ, Truth, must love their enemies and go forth as lambs among wolves. The sick sometimes pass through severe sufferings in the changes Truth produces, before it destroys the error or disease; and the chronic sinner, or hidden hypocrite suffers from the introduction into his mind of the science of being, and often hates its teacher. Man's immortality rests on a spiritual, and not a material basis, and his health on Soul and not sense. We have no foundation for man's immortality, if the perfect is not distinct from the imperfect; and what evidence have we of God, or perfection, where we admit imperfection germinates from God? The good we are, the order, beauty, and loveliness we behold, all assure us God is Life, Truth, and Love, and that matter embraces all error, while Spirit is perfect. Spiritual science reveals all matter inanimate, while personal sense would make it both animate and evil; but which is the standard of Truth, personal sense, or science?

That harmony, Intelligence and Life, are outside of matter, wholly apart and distinct from error, and mortality, even the leaf and flower, too beautiful to die, declare. A consciousness of Truth, Life, and Love, is Soul, not body. The Psalmist saith, "When I consider thy heavens the work of thy fingers, the moon and the stare which

Chapter IV. Creation.

thou hast ordained, what is man that thou art mindful of him? thou madest him to have dominion over the works of thy hands; thou hast put all things under his feet." Matter is as clouds, and Spirit the sun, that appears to us only as the clouds disappear. The sun is not in the cloud, but shines beyond it; thus it is with the Soul of man; when the belief of Substance, or Life in matter disappears, we take up existence as Spirit, and our body is transparent to Soul, and no longer a belief of substance-matter, or personal sense, but the idea of Intelligence, harmony, and Life. Truth separated Jesus, its idea, from the world of error, and the world of sense felt the effect of Truth, because it was tearing away the foundations of error, that could not understand the need there was of this; hence the unappreciated labor and love of Jesus, the great demonstrator of the science of Life. Had Jesus defended error, admitted its positions, and justified them, he would have been the world's favorite. But this was impossible to him who chose his master of Spirit. He could not destroy sickness with the Truth, that Life is God, and be a stickler for personal sense, and Life in matter. Had he believed with them on this point, he would have mingled amicably with hypocrites and the sensuous man, and not rebuked them, and been hated for it; but hypocrisy was more repugnant to goodness and Truth, than other forms of evil.

The fact that Christ was Truth, error soon found out, and the world of personal sense hated Jesus, for he rebuked it, and chose not an 'ism, or 'ology, to define Christianity, or to aid him in its practice. Had he believed as others did, he would not have so suffered from the world, or had he preached better than he practiced, he would have mixed error with error, and no chemical change, or separation from the world would have followed his preaching; but he could not and would not cast out devils with Beelzebub; he might have been a popular man, on this common bags, but then he could not have been a Christian; he might have talked well, and not been good enough for that goodness to prove itself, by making war on error, and he would have passed for a good man. The world of sense and error felt him, for he was destroying it; those whom he blessed, cursed him, yet he loved his enemies, and while they thought of him only to

Chapter IV. Creation.

condemn, his better thoughts answered theirs, healing them of sickness and casting out their errors. Such was the effect of his mind on all it touched, whether enemy or friend, and such will be the effect on mankind, of every real follower of Christ. His mind, pure and spiritual, touched theirs to higher issues, and restored harmony to the body. He knew that like produces like, that his higher being in contact with others, changed and lifted them higher, that Truth germinates Truth, and Spirit imparts spirituality, and not materiality; this was the science and the Principle of his consistent demonstration, that healed the sick, and cast out error. Any hypothesis of birth and death, is unworthy Intelligence. What is real is eternal, eliminated and sustained by Spirit alone, that matter cannot express, and much less control or destroy. All the formations of God are based on Spirit and immortality, and that which is formed by Soul, and not sense, is harmless, harmonious and eternal.

Heaven and earth, together with every animal, mineral, and vegetable that God hath made, are harmonious and eternal. The belief of Life in matter, produces its own kind, for it is predicated on error, that brings forth that which is sinful, ferocious, impure, and mortal. Vertebrates, articulates, mollusks and radiates are Simply what mind makes them. They are technicalized mortality, that will disappear when the- radiates of Spirit illumine sense, and destroy forever the belief of Life and Intelligence in matter.

The voice of Christian science crieth in the wilderness to-day, with scarcely an adherent on earth, but we also know, it is preparing the way for the Principle of being to be understood, and its demonstration given that casts out error and heals the sick. Death brings not at once spiritualization, nor is it the stepping stone to a distant day of final judgment, when a personal God shall paw sentence on man. The sentence of Truth against error is already passed; every loss and experience of the falsity of earthly things, pronounce it. Truth sentences error, now and forever, and the final judgment to which olden tenets pointed, is when the belief of Life or death in matter is destroyed. When the strong fetters of personal

Chapter IV. Creation.

sense are broken, man will be free to do God's, will, and then will we behold the "new heaven and new earth, for the former things shall have pawed away;" and the material given place to the spiritual; Spirit destroys matter. The harmonious and immortal heavens, earth, and man, will be revealed and understood when science shall take the place of personal sense, and error yield to Truth. The sharp experiences of earth, and the tender Wisdom that take away idols, help to hasten this hour, and to destroy the belief of happiness in personal sense. Why the pleasure-loving world cannot discern the science of Life, is "because carnal man cannot discern spiritual things." When personal sense yields up the ghost, and Life is found, Soul understood, it will be the resurrection of man in Truth; but Spirit can never be apprehended until matter is understood a myth. Life, that is Spirit, is not reached until all error is destroyed.

The belief that death is the door to spirituality and Life, is the error that prevents a better understanding and improvement of being, by which alone, immortality is won. We gain immortality through the footsteps of science that reveal Truth, Life, and Love, to our understanding, in which we learn there are no physical laws, no necessary fulfillment of material conditions, no sin, sickness, or death, in Life that is Soul. That death is a step towards Life, is error that begets mortality; for belief fulfills the conditions of a belief, and therefore will continue to die until the falsehood and error of Life or death in matter, is destroyed. Death is but the stepping stone to other mortal conditions of belief; it never procured Life, for this is God, and God must become our practical Life, before man is found immortal. We see in the vegetable kingdom that the seed must rot to propagate anew, and the poor germ is doomed to this game experience also; it must rot again, according to material law. The answer to the ancient question, which is first, the egg, or the parent that takes care of the egg? is given when you admit the parent is developed from an egg, for that is first which produced the parent; but an egg never propagated man.

Chapter IV. Creation.

"We have no right to assume that individuals have grown, or been formed under circumstances that made matter conditions essential to their maintenance and reproduction, or important to their origin and first introduction, unless we dismiss reason and revelation utterly. That earth was hatched from the egg of night was anciently argued, and this absurdity is less than to conclude Spirit produces matter, or that it is in matter. Pursuing the varied hypotheses of man, we think as a child, but putting away childish things and asking more earnestly after God, we shall be answered from Soul, and not sense, and Spirit, instead of matter, will guide our conclusions. Heathen philosophy, modern geology, zoology, physiology, anatomy, etc., deal with other or different phenomena from those proceeding from the Supreme Being. The first proceed from belief only, but the latter are reflections of Spirit; these are the ideas of God coming to the understanding, but the former are beliefs of matter. The proof requisite to sustain assumptions diametrically opposed to personal sense, is just what Jesus taught, namely, the fruit they bear, otherwise the demonstration they bring; if you contradict sense with science and abide by the rules of the latter, you will demonstrate harmony, and prove your position the right one. Our experience of what is called Life germinating from an egg, corresponds with that of Job, that it is of "few days and full of trouble." From this material source flow all sorrow, sin, and death, and the power is not in its origin to "deliver us from the body of this death," consequently our next appeal is to something higher that to matter, drugs, 'ologies, or 'isms. We may call on God to heal our sicknesses, and though we pray seven times a day, and our clergyman and physician pray for us, we may not gain the blessing; Dot faith, but understanding, brings the blessing.

To know that God is not the author of sin or suffering, and that " his band is riot shortened, or car heavy," but that error produces error, is to learn what error is, and how destroyed; then shall we find our remedy for sickness and sin, is to "work out our own salvation." On this point mankind need much enlightenment, for the science of being alone solves the problem of man harmoniously. God giveth

Chapter IV. Creation.

not a stone for bread; when we ask earnestly and strive for health to be useful, able to do good to ourself and others, why does he withhold it? These are unanswerable questions, irreconcilable with Wisdom until we learn God is not person, but Principle, and that we must understand this Principle, to direct our being in harmony with it; and then shall we be able to govern the physical and mental. All depends on mind: matter holds no power over man to create or to destroy him. Sickness and death are errors of belief arising from an ignorance of our origin and immortal being, and to be harmonious and immortal we must understand the science of Life, that changes our reckonings of Life from body to Soul, and from matter to Spirit. Knowing we are Intelligence, and not intelligent matter; Soul and not sense, is the Truth that destroys all sickness, sin, and death. Once perceiving the mental hallucination that embitters existence, we shall unmake what mind has made. God sends not one of our diseases, and matter cannot create sensation, nor can it govern mind. Error alone, produces error, and all sickness, and every discord of earth is error.

Thought, let loose somewhat from the old basic theories amalgamates with other forms of belief, and changes them; this we see prototyped in the floral kingdom, in blended tints of leaf and flower. The metaphysical, however, will end as the physical, when, according to Agassiz, "the intermixing of different species, urged to its final limits, results in the distinct original species." Error must be destroyed at its fountainhead, or it will resume its old proportions and relations. Mind must settle down on an improved basis, even the Truth of being, or health will never be universally established, and when this is done, harmonious and immortal man will be the only man. Prof. Agassiz has given the origin of mortal and material man; he has traced what we term animal existence, through various stages of its embryology, and with most important observations that ought to awaken thought to the higher and purer contemplation of man's origin that must precede the understanding of being. Man is not the offspring of sense, but Soul, and co-existent with God. The fact that modern researches prove animal existence in some instances free

Chapter IV. Creation.

from its lowest instinct, is worthy our philanthropy, and points to the future footsteps of the science of being.

The great point, is to understand the Principle of being, -- the Life that is eternal, without beginning and without end, and this study will absorb the attention of sage and philosopher at a not far-distant day; but the Christian alone will fathom it, for he it is that understands better the Life that is God. We cannot reach this Principle unless it be understood; man's immortality even, hangs on understanding the science of being. Because God is the only Life and Principle of man, that which is good is all that is immortal; but to prove our ignorance of this, we have only to point to the tenacity with which we cling to beliefs of sickness, sin and death. Had we the understanding of our God-being or the omnipotence of Truth, we should have no fear of matter, and having none, our bodies would become harmonious and immortal; a belief of Substance-matter would then give place to the understanding of Substance-Spirit; for the spiritual body is the only real one, and tangible as the material. Ontology receives but little attention from the working- day world, and the signification of psychology is shockingly perverted. The science of Soul is not mesmerism, by any means, and is less understood than all other questions; little justice is done metaphysics by a utilitarian people where the race is to the swift.

The domestic economy of the bee, and its method of multiplying, foreshadows the understanding of being yet to come. That mind produces mind, and our beliefs of matter re-produced beliefs only, is the conclusion that accords with natural history and the science of being. Again, we state, all is mind; there is no matter, and this needs only to be understood to establish harmony perpetual. Mind is the only actor, and produces mind, viz., the Truth or error of man; matter is not an entity or reality. From the deep sleep that fell upon Adam, Eve was produced. In sleep, cause and effect are beliefs only, that which seems, and not that which really is. This was the advent of mortal and material man. Sickness, sin and death, had no real basis, for they originated not with God, Spirit, but were beliefs

Chapter IV. Creation.

of matter, hence the very opposite of understanding, and without Principle or immortality, therefore they proceeded not from the creative Wisdom. All that originated in Adam (that supposed addenda to creation) was not "good," it was illusion, the offspring of a dream; hence it was a belief only, and not the reality of being. Sin, sickness, and death were embraced in this belief of Life in matter, and are the dream, and not the reality of Life. We classify-belief error, insomuch as it embraces all that is mortal discord; it changed the stand-point of being from Spirit to matter, from understanding to belief, yea, from God to man. Adam was the impersonation of error, but man was the type and image of Truth. Adam constituted matter and mortality; man represented immortality and Spirit; but the dream or belief of Life in matter is, that Adam is man, and that error is Truth. There was no more foundation for calling sin, sickness, and death, man, than for saying, "I will make man as God."

Should universal mind or belief adopt the appearing of a star as its formula of creation, the advent of mortal man would commence with a star. The belief regarding the origin of mortal man has changed since Adam produced Eve, and the only reason a rib is not the present mode of evolution, is because of this change, and more mortal opinions to contend against now, than when error first said, "Believe in me." Conditions of matter are conditions of mind instead, therefore the supposed conditions becomes imperative as mind only. Error, named Adam, is the belief, or alpha and omega of what is termed Life in matter. When mortal belief says an egg produces man, this condition becomes as fixed and imperative as the original one of a rib. That we must breathe in order to live is another belief, whereas the reality of being is Life, and its phenomena not dependent on matter. Do you say man was formed before knowing his origin, then wherefore any belief on this subject? But Eve embodied the maternal egg, and was the offspring of Adam's dream, the germ of belief, and mortals since appearing are these beliefs. There is no mortal man; the sleep of Adam was what to-day we term mesmerism, in which belief creates, and controls all it creates. In mesmerism matter is made not to appear solid, and the harmless

Chapter IV. Creation.

stick becomes a serpent; according to what mind says of matter, it appears, hence we learn all material things are formed by mind, first and last. Belief may adopt any condition whatever, and that will become its imperative mode of cause and effect. The infinite and all-wise Maker condemned this creation, but let it have its experience before the sentence of our God was executed upon it.

A mortal body is but a belief of Life in matter, and controlled by this belief; its original requirements were less than its educated ones. Consciousness rises above the horizon of personal sense, starting first unconscious thought, and reaching what we falsely term conscious matter, before its demands proceed from the body. 'Tis safe to conclude man exists, though he has lost his lungs, or any other portion of organism; if he has reached the science of being, his existence is understood and eternal, and man is immortal only whose Life is Soul, and not sense, God and not matter. We must have the sense and consciousness of being that is independent of matter, self-existent, self-sustaining and eternal; for this is the Science of Life that casts out error and heals the sick. We know these statements jar on what is called personal sense; but we disregard that altogether; our only sorrow is not to be understood, or be thought irreverent of God, until Christendom learns how important what we say is to follow the rich example of our Master in healing the sick, preaching the gospel to the poor, etc. To-day our religions preach to the rich, and depend on matter, instead of God, to heal the sick.

The persecutions Truth met over eighteen centuries ago, and the demonstrations it gave in destroying sickness, sin, and death, and bringing to light immortality, it would be well to remember at this date; and if our readers understand what is written in this book, they will be able to prove to themselves, it reproduces, however faintly, the same proofs; shall it not then, be accepted, on the ground our Master said, "For the work's sake." Every new idea of Truth, that comes out from the infinite Spirit, and touches the ragged shores of belief, has been met with derision and chains, scourged out of synagogues at first, but afterwards pardoned and received.

Chapter IV. Creation.

To the pulpit we appeal. Judge not this science until you prove whether it be Truth or error; test its Principle by the rules laid down, and then will you learn God is the life of man, and that materia medica, or theology, never can take the place of the science of God, in healing the sick, and casting out all error. The beliefs that form the body mortal are not destroyed at once; "it is not all of death to die." After what is named death, the belief of sickness, sin and death continues, until the science of being is reached, and man's Life is found Soul, and not sense.

Adam being created before Eve, proves the maternal egg never propagated him, and Eve being formed of Adam's rib, shows her origin was not that; "knowledge " defined man falsely then, even as at present; although physiology has since been grafted into the forbidden "tree." An infant a few hours old was said to be immersed in water, to test the possibility of making him amphibious; and this daily ablution continued until the infant could remain under water, and the ordinary functions of lungs be suspended twenty minutes at one time, playing the while and enjoying the bath. The infant is wholly controlled by its parents' belief; addressing the mother mentally, we have stopped the moaning and restlessness of her babe, but could not affect the child, except through its mother.

This should furnish a hint to parents to control their offspring mentally; beginning in the science of being to govern their bodies; employing mind instead of matter, to heal them, and also to prevent their being sick. We should be able at the bedside of a mother, without medicine or applications of any sort, to prevent the pangs of child-birth; labor should be painless, and this dreaded hour be without suffering and joyful, even as the opening of the buds, or the development of the flower. Mind controls embryology without pain to the universe, and why not the same with woman? The parent's mind develops the infant before and after birth, until the mother says, my child can take care of itself; at this period the human species, bird and beast, dismiss their offspring from their immediate maternal eye, and commence educating them to what is termed, self-dependence; but alas! on the ground that Life depends on matter, and this destroys the Self-reliance that science would give.

Although the advancing stages of human development require the higher order of parental mind to guide their offspring aright, we regret to say, the human species make shocking work of it. The peculiar traits and characteristics of progenitors are transmitted from generation to generation; but this is a transfer of belief only, the parent's mind passing to their offspring. The poisonous reptile, bird of prey, beast carnivorous, and mortal man, are products of mortal belief, of error and not Truth, of Sense instead of Soul. The belief that Life and Intelligence belong to the body, is the source of all wrong-thinking, and wrong- acting; it takes away from Soul and gives to sense, and is the fountain of sickness, sin, and death. All formations are shadows of being, and we their Soul and Substance; but this fact of science detracts nothing from God, the universal Intelligence; and because this statement, understood, brings forth good fruits, heals the sick and destroys error, we have the Master's rule for its correctness, insomuch as the tree is known by its fruit. Life is the forming and governing Principle of all things, and by no means the frailty that the foot of man crushes out. Soul is the immortal basis of man and the universe, the Truth of all things, and the Principle that holds the very winds in its fist.

Substance is Intelligence, yea, Spirit, not matter. "I am the resurrection and Life," are the words of him who spake as never man spake; and knew all about it. But this understanding of Truth is to-day a voice crying in the wilderness of error. All is discord in mortal man; the good he would do is held back, by sickness, sin or death; if he works to benefit his race, he sinks into a premature grave, with softened brain, or something of this sort. Mental labor should strengthen man; mind is capable of endless action and immortal harmony; but incessant action will destroy matter. Searching into the science of being will never soften a man's brain, or produce disease of any kind, but is known to cure disease. And the only difficulty in proving this, is the utter ignorance of its principle. But taking an old

Chapter IV. Creation.

belief by the throat is surely no small task; somehow like the phoenix, it rises from its own ashes. The influence one mind exerts involuntarily over another is little understood; all our thoughts are moulded more or less by others; the body is governed by mind, notwithstanding our utter ignorance of this, and involuntary submission to it. If to-day the general thought embraced the science of being, man's longevity would increase ten-fold, and immortality be brought to light; the years of man will be extended as the belief of intelligent matter is destroyed, until at length a full recognition of Truth shall destroy all sin, sickness, and death. Error will continue seven thousand years, from the time of Adam, its origin. At the expiration of this period Truth will be generally comprehended, and science roll back the darkness that now hides the eternal sunshine and lift the curtain on Paradise, where earth produces at the command of Intelligence, and Soul, instead of sense, govern man.

CHAPTER V

PRAYER AND ATONEMENT

THOUGHTS unuttered are not unknown to the infinite Intelligence comprehending them, to whom a desire is prayer, and no loss can occur from trusting God with our desires, to mould and make higher before they are evolved in action. But prayer has its motives, and what are they? To make him better that prays, or to benefit his hearers, to inform the Infinite of what he is ignorant, or to be heard of men? First, are we benefited by praying? Were God a person to be moved by the breath of praise, or less than Infinite in understanding, or changing in Love and Wisdom, He might do more good because of our petitions, and grant them on the ground of the petitioner, in which case lip-service were an advantage not to be overlooked. But God is Love, and do we ask Him to be more than this to man? God is Intelligence, and can we inform the infinite Wisdom, or tell of our needs, the infinitesimal part already comprehended? Do we hope to change perfection in one of its arrangements, or shall we plead for more of the open fount, pouring in all we will receive, and more cannot be given? Does prayer bring us nearer the divine source of all being and blessedness? then it is the prayer of works and not words; asking to love God never made us love him, but this desire, expressed in daily watchfulness and assimilation to the divine character, moulds and fashions us to His image.

The danger of audible prayer is, that we fall into temptation through it, and become an involuntary hypocrite. First, by uttering what is not a real desire, and secondly, consoling ourself under sin with the recollection we have prayed over it. Hypocrisy is fatal to Christianity, and praying publicly, we often go beyond our means, beyond the honest standpoint of fervent and habitual desire; if we are not yearning in secret and striving for the accomplishment of all we ask, ours are "vain repetitions, such as heathen use." If our petition is sincere, we shall labor for what we pray, and be rewarded

Chapter V. Prayer and Atonement.

by "Him who seeth in secret and rewardeth openly." No expression of them can make our desires more, or less, nor gain the ear omnipotent sooner by words than thoughts. If every petition in prayer is sincere, God knows it before we tell Him, and letting it remain honestly before Him we incur no risk of overtalking our real state.

Prayer is sometimes employed, like a catholic confession, to cancel sin, and this impedes Christianity. Sin is not forgiven; we cannot escape its penalty. Being sorry for its committal is but one step towards reform, and the very smallest one; the next step that Wisdom requires is, the test of our sincerity, namely, a reformation. To this end we are placed under stress of circumstances where the temptation comes to repeat the offence, and the woe comes for what has been done until we learn there is no discount in the law of retribution, and we must pay the uttermost farthing. The measure we have meted will be measured to us again, full and running over; Christians and sinners get their full measurement, but not here; a follower of Christ, for centuries to come, must drink his cup; ingratitude and persecution will fill it to the brim, but God pours the riches of joy into the understanding, and gives us strength as our clay. Sinners flourish as the green bay tree, but looking farther, David saw their end.

Prayer cannot change the science of being, for goodness alone reaches the demonstration of Truth. A petition for another to work for us, never does the work required of us. To address Deity as a person, perpetrates the belief of God in man, which impedes spiritual progress and hides Truth. We reach the science of Christianity only through demonstration, but here, our good will be evil spoken of, and falsehood will war against advancing Truth. Principle should govern man; person can pardon but not reform the sinner. God is not a separate Wisdom from the Wisdom we possess, and the talent He hath given to be used we must improve; therefore, to call on God to do our work for us, is vainly supposing we have little to do but to ask for pardon and re-commit the offence. If prayer

Chapter V. Prayer and Atonement.

cherishes the belief sin is forgiven, and man better because he prays, it is asking amiss; for he is worse if the punishment sin incurs is kept back, or he thinks himself forgiven when he is not. Prayer is impressive; it gives momentary solemnity and elevation to thought, but does a state of ecstacy produce lasting benefit? Looking deeply, and metaphysically into these things, we find a reaction takes place, unfavorable to understanding and sober resolve, and the wholesome perception of God's requirements; also that personal sense, and not Soul, produces these moods of feeling. If spiritual sense guided men at such times, there would grow out of those ecstatic desires, higher experiences and a better life; self-examination, and more purity. A self-satisfied ventilation of ecclesiastical fervor never made a Christian; verbal prayer embraces too much error to forward this great purpose. First, it supposes God a person influenced by man, making the divine ear a personal sense instead of the all-hearing and all-knowing Intelligence, to whom every want of man is understood, and by whom it will be supplied.

Again, what we desire, and ask to be given, is not always best for us to receive, in which case the infinite understanding will certainly not grant our request; therefore what avails it with God bow much a man prays? When we pray aright, we shall "enter into the closet;" in other words, shut the door of the lips and in the silent sanctuary of earnest longings, deny sin and sense, and take up the cross, while we go forth with honest hearts laboring to reach Wisdom, Love, and Truth. This prayer will be answered, insomuch as we shall put in practice our desires. The Master's injunction was to pray in secret; to desire to be better, and let our lives attest the sincerity of that desire. Are we really grateful for the good we receive? then we shall have more, and never until then, and avail ourselves of the blessings we have, and this will thank God more than speech. >From the Intelligence that numbers the very hairs of our heads, we cannot conceal the ingratitude of barren lives by thanking Omnipotence with our lips, while the heart is far from Truth. When we vainly imagine gratitude is a mere expression of thanks, we had better examine our hearts and learn what is there,

Chapter V. Prayer and Atonement.

and this will show us what we are, and is the only honest expression of ourselves.

How empty are the conceptions of Deity that admit theoretically, the omnipotence and omnipresence of God, and then would inform the supreme mind, or plead for pardon that is unmerited, or for blessings poured out liberally. If we are not grateful for Life, Truth, and Love, but return thanks to them, we are insincere, and incur the sharp censure bestowed upon the hypocrite. The only acceptable prayer in this case is to put our finger to our lips and remember our blessings.

Praying for humility with however much fervency of expression, is not always to desire it. If we turn away from the poor and set aside their judgment, we are not fit to receive the reward of that which blesses the poor. When confessing to a very wicked heart, and asking to have it laid bare before us, do we not know more of this heart than we are willing our neighbor should know, and if a friend informs us of a fault, do we listen to the rebuke patiently and credit what is said, or rather join in thanks that we are not as other men? It is many years that I have been more grateful for a merited rebuke than for flattery; the only real sting is the unmerited censure, the wicked falsehood that does no one any good.

Do we love our neighbor as ourself, or because we do not, should we pray to be given this love and expect it because of asking, while we pursue the old selfishness satisfied with having prayed for something better, without a single evidence of the sincerity of this request by living consistent with that prayer. If selfishness gives place in us to Love, we shall love our neighbor and bless them that curse us, but can never meet this great demand by asking for it; there is a cross to be taken up, before the reward is given.

Do we "love the Lord our God with all our heart, Soul, and strength?" This includes much, even the surrender of all personal affections and personal worship; it is the ultimate of being, the

Chapter V. Prayer and Atonement.

science of Life that recognizes only the consciousness, Spirit, wherein Soul is our Master, and sense without a claim. Are you willing to leave all for Christ, Truth, and be reckoned with sinners? Have you reached this point? No. Do you really desire to attain it? No. Then wherefore make long prayers about it, and ask to become Christ-like, when these are the footsteps of our dear Master; if unwilling to drink his cup, wherefore pray with the lips to be partakers of it? The only consistent prayer is, to do right so far as we understand the right, and to walk in the light so far as we receive it, even though it be with bleeding footsteps, and let our real desires and works be rewarded by the Father who, seeth in secret. The whole world will not understand Christianity for centuries to come.

When we are good enough to take His cup of earthly sorrows, we shall have it, and until we are, and do drink of it, all the vain repetitions that heathen use can never reach the demonstration that Jesus gave and instructed his followers to give, as the test of Christianity, saying, "And these signs shall follow you." We learn in science the necessity for Christians to suffer in this wicked world of sense, insomuch as they oppose it, and are helping to destroy it, therefore it would destroy them. Anciently, in Japan, they conveyed a praying-machine through the streets, stopping at the doors to earn a penny grinding out a prayer. But in the belief of higher civilization, we pay for prayers in lofty edifices. Experience teaches that we receive not the good we ask for inaudible prayer. Petitioning a personal Deity is a misapprehension of the source and means of all good and blessedness; therefore it cannot be beneficial, and we receive not, because, as the scripture saith, "We ask amiss, to consume it on our lusts."

Suffering for sin is all that destroys it; every supposed pleasure of personal sense, will furnish more than its balance in pain, until the belief of Life and Intelligence in matter is ultimately destroyed. We are not rid of mortal experiences, of sin, sickness, or death, at the change called death; we cannot reach heaven, the harmony of Life, except we understand the Principle of harmonious being, that

Chapter V. Prayer and Atonement.

alone destroys personal sense and error. Seeking is not sufficient to destroy error; striving to enter into the straight and narrow way of science, is all that will enable us to do it. Spiritual attainments are the preparation for heaven, and that which opens the door to a higher understanding, even the Life that is God. The petitions to a personal Deity bring to man only the results of his belief; they cannot obtain Truth, Life, or Love. We know that a desire for holiness is requisite to gaining it, but if we really desire this above all else, we shall lay down all for it; first learn your willingness to do this, and then you may calculate safely on the only practical way of reaching holiness. Prayer cannot change the unalterable Truth, or give us the understanding of it; but a desire to know and do the will of God is necessary, and also a symptom that we are growing wiser; but this desire needs no expression from the lips; our lives express it.

Asking God to heal the sick has no effect to gain the ear of Love, beyond its ever-presence. The only beneficial effect it has, is mind acting on the body through a stronger faith, to heal it; but this is one belief casting out another; a belief in God casting out a belief of Sickness, and not the understanding of the Principle that heals being. Jesus said, a kingdom divided against itself cannot stand; a belief is not the science of being that heals the sick, and casts out sickness on the ground that sensation and Intelligence are not in matter; the Truth of being is what destroys error. Exchanges of the same commodity are the mere merchandise of mind, and not science. Deity interposes not in behalf of one, and not another, who adopts the same measures in prayer. If the sick recover on the platform of prayer, it is the result of individual belief. All may avail themselves of God in science as a present help in trouble. Love is impartial, and universal in its adaptation and bestowments; the open fount, that saith, "Ho! every one that thirsteth, come ye, and drink."

Prayer to a person, affects the sick as a drug that has no efficacy of its own, but borrows its power from faith and belief in matter. The drug does nothing in the case, insomuch as it has no

Chapter V. Prayer and Atonement.

Intelligence. The Principle of man, and not a person, produces all good.

Seeking the Science of Life, and not content with a material sense of things, gives hungerings and thirstings after righteousness, because it reveals the perfect Principle on which Life and immortality are Avon. A wordy prayer may afford a sense of quiet and self-justification, but this makes the sinner a hypocrite. We never despair of an honest heart, but those spasmodically face to face with their wickedness, and always seeking to hide it, are the indexes that correspond not with contents, the counterfeits of true manhood, that hold secret fellowship with their own sins. Such are spoken of in the scripture as whited sepulchres full of uncleanness, "making long prayers," etc.

If the author of much apparent fervor and many prayers is sensual and insincere, what is the mental comment of those understanding the science of being? That if be had reached the standpoint of his prayer, this would not be the case. If our silent thoughts support the conclusion that we feel all the aspiration, humility, gratitude and love they pour forth, this is enough to know of our Christian estate, and it is greatly wise not to deceive ourselves or others; nothing is hidden that shall not be revealed. Professions and prayers, we regret to say, cover a multitude of sins. Christians rejoice that the secret beauty and bounty of their being, though hidden from the world, is known to God; self- abnegation, purity and Love, are a constant prayer. It is the practice and understanding of our God-being, that gains the ear and right hand of Omnipotence, and calls down blessings infinite. Trustworthiness is the only foundation of faith; without a fitness for holiness we shall not receive it, nor yield faithful adherence to it.

"God is Love;" more than this we cannot ask; higher we cannot look; beyond this we may not go. To regard God a person that forgives or punishes sin, according as His mercy is sought, or unsought, is to misunderstand Love, and institute prayer as the

Chapter V. Prayer and Atonement.

safety-valve for wrong-doing. Do we ask Wisdom to be merciful to sin, then "We ask amiss to consume it on our lusts;" and to forgive sin without punishment, allows the sin to multiply, and this is neither mercy nor Wisdom. A magistrate may remit a criminal sentence; but this is no benefit morally to the criminal, and has only saved him from one form of punishment. The moral law that alone is capable of justifying or condemning, still demands man to go up higher, or meet the penalty of a broken law that punishes to compel this progress. Personal pardon of sin -- and there is none other -- for Principle, never pardons sin, leaves man free to commit anew the offence; if indeed he has not suffered sufficiently from sin, to turn from it with loathing. Truth entertains no pardon for error, but wipes it out in the most effectual manner.

Asking God to pardon sin, is a "vain repetition such as heathen use." Habitual goodness, is praying without ceasing, in which motives are made manifest by the blessings we bestow, whether these are, or are not acknowledged, and attest our worthiness to be made partakers of Love. We cannot pray aright, and believe that God, who is the same yesterday and forever, is changeable or influenced in the least by a mortal sense of what man needs. He who is immutably right, will do right, without being reminded of it; and the wisdom of man is insufficient to select from God. We would not stand before a blackboard, and pray the Principle of mathematics to work out a problem for man; nor should we ask the Principle of all good to do a work already clone, and which we have only to avail ourselves of, that is, to understand, in order to receive its blessings. The Principle of man must be reflected by man, else he is not the image and likeness of the patient, tender, and true, yea, the one altogether lovely; and to go higher than this, and understand "God is Love," is the work of eternity.

"When thou prayest, enter into thy closet, and when thou hast shut the door pray to the father which is in secret, and thy father which seeth in secret shall reward thee openly."

Chapter V. Prayer and Atonement.

The closet signifies the sanctuary of Spirit, its door opening on Soul, and not sense, opening to Truth, God, and closing on error. The father in secret is the Principle of man, unseen to personal sense, the infinite Intelligence that knows all things, and rewards according to motives, regarding mind only and not speech. The "prayer of the righteous" that "heals the sick," is after the manner our Master taught, when he bade his students enter into the Spirit of prayer, the door of personal sense closed, lips mute, and man in audience with his Maker, where, Spirit instead of matter, and Soul instead of sense are understood the standpoint of being, even the Principle thereof, that destroys sickness, sin, and death. Thus the power of Life, Love and Truth, will destroy sin, sickness, and death, and enlarge the capacities of man, revealing his God-given dominion over earth; but remember, also, that "none but the pure in heart shall see God"; shall be able to take this scientific position of prayer, in which personal sense is silenced, and Spirit the master of man. After a momentary cessation in the belief and dream of Life in matter, whereby Life, that is God, unfolds itself, comes the understanding and consciousness of dominion over the body that casts out error and heals the sick, and you speak as one having authority. We have taught our students the footsteps to this prayer; let them answer to-day, have they followed them. A great relinquishment of material things must precede this advanced spiritual understanding; 'isms but retard it, and mediumship more than most things. This prayer is not faith; it is demonstration; it heals the sick and advances man in the scale of being; it recognizes the falsity of personal sense and the Life that is Soul.

Only as we rise above sensuality and sin, can we reach its standpoint. Prayer addressed to a person, prevents our letting go of personality for the impersonal Spirit to whom all things are possible. We cannot serve two masters, if we are sensibly with our body and consequently our words, and regarding Omnipotence a person, whose ear we would gain, we are not Soul, Life, Love and Truth, and therefore not in the harmony of being and oneness with the Father, "In demonstration of the Spirit and power." Make it a

Chapter V. Prayer and Atonement.

conscious reality for a single moment, that Life and Intelligence are not in the body, and you are without sensation in the body, and if sick, will find yourself well; sorrow is turned into joy, when we become conscious Soul, able to govern the body with Life, Truth, and Love; hence those words of our Master, "I and the Father are one," that wrought such blessed works, and "greater works than I," (in the flesh) "ye can do, because I go to the Father." The scientific position of Intelligence is Soul triumphing over sense.

Absent from the body and present with the Lord is not ecstacy or trance, but a realization of the science of Life, as laid down in this volume; it is obedience to the law of God, governing the body by Spirit instead of matter; therefore our Master said: "After this manner pray ye"

> Our Father, which art in heaven,
> Hallowed be thy name;
> Thy kingdom come,
> Thy will be done on earth as it is done in heaven.
> Give us this day our daily bread,
> And forgive us our debts as we forgive our debtors,
> And lead us not into temptation, but deliver us from evil,
> For thine is the kingdom, and the power, and the glory forever."

The following is the spiritual signification of the Lord's Prayer:

> Harmonious and eternal Principle of man,
> Nameless and adorable Intelligence,
> Spiritualize man;
> Control the discords of matter with the harmony of Spirit.
> Give us the understanding of God,
> And Truth will destroy sickness, sin, and death, as it destroys the belief of intelligent matter,
> And lead man into Soul, and deliver him from personal sense,

Chapter V. Prayer and Atonement.

For God is Truth, Life, and Love forever.

Atonement is oneness with God; it is Life, Truth, and Love fulfilled, whereby sickness, sin, and death, are destroyed. Jesus of Nazareth explained and demonstrated his oneness with the Father, for which we owe him endless love and homage, although at the time of his labors he received less gratitude and honor than other men. His mission was both individual and collective; he did Life's work right in justice to himself, and to show us how to do ours, but not to do it for us, or to relieve us of a single responsibility in the case. He taught us the way of Life, its Principle and proof, demonstrating what He taught, that we might understand its Principle; how it healed the sick, cast out error, and triumphed over death. Jesus was more the idea of God than a man can be whose origin is less spiritual than his, therefore he demonstrated higher than others the Principle of being, even his oneness with God. He understood the science of those sayings of his, "I am the Truth and Life," "I and the Father are one." Any reference to himself was made to Christ, the Principle of the man Jesus, for he called not Intelligence man, but God. It was not to a person, but to Truth, Life, and Love, he looked to destroy sickness, sin, and death. The mission of Jesus was to demonstrate the science of Life, he was its idea, even the chosen of Principle to prove God, and what God does for man.

Belief had established the false conclusion that God was in matter; that Truth and Life were in man, and man was mortal, sinning, sick, and dying. He wished to show, this belief was the very opposite of Truth, and that Spirit was not in matter, hence the death of the cross and the re-appearance of Jesus according to his scientific statement of Life, namely, "Though you destroy this temple (body) yet will I (Spirit) build it again." "I," the Life, Substance, and Intelligence of the universe, and man, am not in matter that you can destroy. His beautiful metaphors and parables of the tree and its fruit; the fount and stream; the tares and wheat; the sower and husbandman, etc., explained Intelligence and Life not mingled with sin and death. He laid the axe of science at the root of

Chapter V. Prayer and Atonement.

the "tree of knowledge" to cut down all that embraced opposite doctrines; hence error's hatred of him, and Truth's approval. This more pure, and spiritual idea, named Jesus, destroyed the beliefs of Life in matter, and gave to man the understanding of the Principle of being. Those students who followed his instructions and example, loved and honored him, and those who did not, hated and dishonored him. The former cast out error, and healed the sick with Christ, Truth; the latter, only in the name of Truth. Of the seventy he taught, but eleven remained faithful, showing how far the science he taught and demonstrated, was apart from the acceptance of the world of sense. And when Christ, Truth, cometh again, will he find faith on earth? Over eighteen centuries ago, "He came to his own and his own received him not." Those professing Christ are sometimes the first to reject Truth, if it collides with their beliefs; even its severest persecutors have been of this class. The honest fishermen who bad little to leave, were those who left all for Christ, Truth, until progress compelled the change, and the learned Paul stepped forth for Truth.

When a teacher of music demonstrates by some masterly performance, the harmony of music, he gives the proof of a Principle that the learner must understand; but if this demonstration included also a nameless sacrifice, we should admit, the Principle of it was not only harmony, but Love. This was the precious import of our Master's teachings and demonstration; he proved the science of being not only by destroying sickness, sin, and death, but the significance of Life without death, and in this proof was embraced big Love. Error had hoped to destroy Truth, and kill Jesus. Those for whom he laid down all worldly honors, and bore their infirmities that through his stripes they might be healed, were his accusers. So will it be to-day, Christian martyr; he who best understands the Truth of being, will be most falsified, pursued, and condemned.

The teacher of music, who demonstrates for the benefit of others, has by no means relieved them from giving the proof requisite to show where they stand in science; he rather does this, for

Chapter V. Prayer and Atonement.

their example that they may understand that which they should demonstrate. Implicit faith in the teacher, whose self-abnegation and toil have bestowed blessings on man, will never make Musicians of the learners; they must go and do likewise, or they are not improving their talents, which, unimproved, condemned them. We must understand the Principle Jesus taught, at whatever expense, and practice it, or we are not Christians.

The science of Life that our Master demonstrated, was not a theory, doctrine, or belief; it revealed a Principle that brought its proof with it; and this proof was not forms, or systems of religion, but the science of being, that brought out all the sweet harmonies of Life. Jesus informed John what the proof of Christ's coming was, saying, "Go and tell him the things ye see and hear; how the sick are healed, the lame walk, the deaf hear, the blind see, and to the poor the gospel is preached." Tell him what its demonstration is; and the spiritual John will at once perceive God is its Principle. Materia medica professed the ability to heal, also, and the Pharisees to teach Christ, Truth, but they only hindered the success of Jesus' mission; many of the seventy he had taught, stood in his way also, together with one who boldly betrayed him into the hands of his enemies. If our Master had never had a student, he would not have come to the death on the cross; but his mission would have been unfulfilled, and his history lacked its sweetest pathos. Through his unmerited persecutions we see the fate of science in a world of error, and the reception a sensuous world gives the Principle that contradicts personal sense with Soul.

At the same time that I love Jesus more than all men of the past or present ages, treading alone a path of thorns, up to the throne of Wisdom, in speechless agony exploring the way for others, yet I cannot see that he has spared us one individual experience, or that we have not the "cup" to drink in proportion to our fitness to drink it and demonstrate God, above others. To keep the commandments of our Master and follow his example, is our proper return, and only evidence of gratitude for all he has done for us; but this is not a

Chapter V. Prayer and Atonement.

personal worship, nor reward to a person; it is to understand the Principle Jesus taught and proved, and follow, as much as in us lies, his example; to separate ourselves from the world of error and press forward to the Life that is Truth and Love. The pleasures, frowns, or flatteries of earth, are but ghosts of nothingness, compared to the prize set before us, "And laying aside every weight and sin that so easily beset us, let us press forward to the high calling of God in Christ," putting aside personal self and sense, for Soul, the Principle of being.

Every pang of repentance, every suffering for sin, (accompanied with reformatory efforts) and every good deed, stones for sin. But if the sinner is sorry, and continues to pray, and to sin and be sorry, he hath no part in the at- one-ment. TO understand God, "Whom to know aright is Life eternal," is to do the will of Wisdom; and none hath part in Him, who demonstrates not, in part, the Principle embraced in the teachings and practice of our Master. If not obeying the science of being according to its Principle, God, we should have no confidence in man's safety, because God is good, and man repents. But if we are growing spiritual, and error is yielding to Truth in our demonstrations of being, and our daily walk and conversation, we shall say at length, "I have fought the good fight and kept the faith;" for I am a better man. This is having part in the at-one-ment. If a man stands still, praying, and expecting because of another man's goodness, sufferings and triumphs, he will reach his harmony and reward; that man will vibrate, a pendulum, between sin and the hope of forgiveness; selfishness and sensuality winding him up to this action, and his growth will be slow. An at-one-ment with Love and Truth, is to apply the meaning of the Life, and not death of Jesus, to deeds and a Christian character, and not to cover, or forgive sin, but to destroy it in the most effectual manner. When Truth lays the axe at the root of error, saying, cut it down, then comes the experiences and sufferings that cause one, even as a drowning man, to make vigorous efforts to save himself, and these efforts are what save him.

Chapter V. Prayer and Atonement.

"Work out your own salvation," is the demand of Life and Love; and to this end God worketh with you. "Occupy until I come," i.e., wait for thy reward and grow not weary in well doing. Although your endeavors are against fearful odds, receiving no present reward, go not back to error, nor become a sluggard in the contest, and you will find your reward when the smoke of battle clears away, so that you discern the good you have done, and your gain from experience. Love often delays to deliver from temptation, that it may try, and prove you as by fire. If you understand the science of being sufficiently to have faith in the right, and no faith in wrong, you will work more earnestly, though more silently, perhaps, in persecution than amid applause, for your labor is more needed; and the reward of your self-sacrifice is great, though it be never here. Final deliverance from error, whereby we rejoice in immortality, boundless freedom, and sinless sense, is not won through smooth footsteps, nor through doctrines, or pinning one's faith to personality. Whoso believeth wrath is righteous or appeased by the unmerited death of a good man, cannot understand God. Justice requires no propitiation but from the sinner; mercy cancels without pay or sacrifice, and revenge is inadmissible in Love. The wrath that is appeased is not destroyed, but indulged, and may require another sacrifice, one being found insufficient; but these are the traits of heathen Deities, and not of our God, the Principle that is Love.

God's wrath vented on his only son, is without logic or humanity, and but a man-made belief. The beautiful import of this hard place in theology is, that suffering is an error of personal sense that Truth destroys, and sin falls, a broken reed, at the feet of Love. The Rabbinical teachings said, "He that taketh one doctrine firm in faith, has the holy ghost dwelling in him." But this receives a strong rebuke from our Master, who said, "Faith without works is dead." Faith, as a belief, is but a pendulum between nothing and something, holding on to no foundations; but the advanced understanding that is sometimes misnamed faith, is the evidence gained from spiritual sense that rebukes the belief of personal sense, and brings out of experience the Life that is God. In Hebrew, Greek, Latin, and

Chapter V. Prayer and Atonement.

English, the word "faith" embraces two meanings, viz., "trustfulness" and "trustworthiness." The first trusts all to another, and the second understands and relies on one's self. "Lord, I believe, help thou mine unbelief," expresses the helplessness of a blind faith, whereas "Believe, and you shall be saved," is self-reliant, trustworthy faith that implies the understanding that brings its own reward. The Hebrew gives the following signification of the verb, "to believe:" "To be firm, lasting, constant," and this certainly applies to Truth understood; for firmness in error will never save man from sickness, sin, or death. An acquaintance with the original texts, together with a willingness to give up beliefs founded on dynasties and the wont passions of men, for the advanced views of civilization and the spiritual sense of Truth, makes the scriptures a chart of Life to man.

Christ and God are words synonymous. Christ signifies the Soul and Principle of the man, Jesus. The manner of expressing him in Scripture gives the meaning of this relationship, viz., Jesus, the son of God, i.e., the idea of Principle, and the offspring of Soul, and not sense.

Publius Lentulus wrote to the conscript fathers at Rome,"The disciples of Jesus believe him the son of God." Those who were taught by him the science of being, reached the glorious perception that God is the only author of man. The virgin mother first conceived this idea of God, and named it Jesus; the illumination of spiritual sense had put to silence personal sense with Mary, thus mastering material law and establishing through demonstration that God is the father of man. The science of being overshadowed the pure sense of the virgin mother with a full recognition that Spirit is the basis of being. The idea we call Substance, and Mary named Jesus, dwelt forever in the bosom of the Father, in the Principle of man, and woman perceived it because of her more spiritual nature. The belief that Life originates with the sexes, is strongest in the most material natures; whereas the understanding of the spiritual origin of man cometh only to the pure in heart. Man and woman, as ideas of

Chapter V. Prayer and Atonement.

God, i.e., Spirit, meet Soul's expectancy, and are immortal evidences that Spirit is harmonious, and man eternal. Jesus was the offspring of Mary's self-conscious God-being in creative Wisdom; hence he was more spiritual, more the idea of God, and demonstrated the science of Life, as others cannot, whose origin is material. This idea of Truth came to rebuke Rabbinical error; to point out the way of Truth and Life, and to demonstrate, as it did, throughout the whole earthly career of Jesus, the difference between the offspring of Soul, and of sense; of Truth, and error; Christ was God; therefore the Principle of the man, Jesus, otherwise his Father; Jesus acknowledged no ties of flesh, saying, "Call no man your Father upon the earth, for one is your Father which is in heaven." Again, "Who is my mother, and who are my brethren, but they that do the win of my Father." We have no record of his ever calling a man father. He recognized God the only Principle of being, therefore, the Father of all.

Referring to the materiality of the age, he said – "The time cometh and now is that they who worship the Father shall worship Him in Spirit and in Truth." Again, foreseeing the persecution that must attend the introduction of this science, he said, "The time cometh that whosoever killeth you will think he doeth God service." "And these things will they do unto you because they have not known the Father or me." In other words, are ignorant of the Principle of being; their father, on earth and in heaven, being personality instead of Principle; ignorant, also, of the origin of man, his nature and true existence. The world of error is blind to the Truth of man, and the world of sense, to Life that is Soul. Jesus was neither understood in his origin, his nature, or works; not one component part of his being did the world of sense get right. Even his righteousness and purity hindered not the accusation, he is Beelzebub, the chief of sinners, a glutton, and the friend of the impure. Christian martyr of the nineteenth century, does it wrong thee one half as much? then remember, it is enough for thee "that the servant should be as his Lord," and that you be found worthy to unloose the sandals of thy Master's faith. To conclude persecution

Chapter V. Prayer and Atonement.

for righteousness' sake belongs to the past, and that Christianity today is at peace with the world, honored by sects and societies, is to mistake its Very nature. History will repeat itself; the trials of prophet, disciple, and apostle, those of whom "the earth was not worthy," await, in some form, the pioneers of Truth.

Scripture informs us, Jesus read the thoughts of man, discovering the hidden springs of action, and construing them according to motive. Perceiving their thoughts, as he walked with his students, he answered, unasked, questions that needed explanation. This mind-reading was not clairvoyance, it was absence from the body, a spiritual insight wherewith he shew the woman of Samaria her error, and convinced her of his superiority over man, and she went away, saying, "Is not this the Christ," the Truth of man that discerns the error? His marvellous works are readily accounted for when we remember, Christ is God, and that Jesus held all that he was, God, and wrought from the standpoint of his God- being, and this was the science of being.

A magistrate who lived at the time of Jesus, wrote, "His rebuke is fearful," and his strong language in scripture regarding hypocrisy, confirms this saying, but the stronger evidence that his reproof was pointed and pungent, is the necessity there was for it when he cast out devils and healed the sick. The only civility Truth exchanges with error is "Get behind me, satan." There is too much animal courage, and not sufficient moral courage in Society. Christians take up arms against error at home and abroad, grapple with sin in themselves and others, and continue this warfare until they have finished their course, and thenceforth receive its reward.

If you have triumphed sufficiently over the errors of personal sense for Soul to hold the balance of power in your being, you will loathe sin and rebuke it, under whatever mask it appears; and you can bless your enemies only in this way, but they may not so construe it. We cannot choose but work out our own salvation on the Principle Jesus taught and demonstrated, viz., casting out devils,

Chapter V. Prayer and Atonement.

healing the sick, and preaching the gospel to the poor. A moral coward is unfit to bear the standard of Truth, and God will never place it in his hands.

A member of the Methodist Church once said to us, "I hope, when you write your work on science, you will dwell much on the atonement." After reading these pages, if the "arm of the Lord is revealed" to that mind, anew she will commence her own work, and with the unction of primitive Christianity, heal herself and others, and thus gain the liberty of the sons of God. This is regeneration, and to have part in the atonement, and to understand wherefore Jesus suffered and triumphed. But Truth, lifting its voice above 'ology and 'ism, and requiring a reconstruction of man, must be persecuted, and those not having touched its garments and felt in their body it has healed them, will persecute it.

If all those partaking of the sacrament intended to commemorate the sufferings of Jesus, had drank "his cup," they would have revolutionized the world; or if all who partake of these symbols today, were Christians, taking up their cross, healing the sick, casting out error and preaching Christ, Truth, to the poor, it would establish the millennium.

But all who eat bread and drink wine in memory of Christ, are not ready or willing to drink his cup, and to leave all for Christ, the Truth and Life, that is God. Then wherefore ascribe to this willingness with a dead rite, before showing forth in your body, that the Truth has come to your understanding, that heals the sick, and makes the body holy and acceptable, that Paul said, was "our only reasonable service." And if Christ, Truth, has come to us in demonstration, no commemoration is requisite, for it is "God with us."

"And as they were eating, Jesus took bread, and blessed it, and brake it, and gave it to the disciples, and said, 'Take eat, this is my

Chapter V. Prayer and Atonement.

body.' And he took the cup, and gave thanks, and gave it to them, saying, 'Drink ye all of it.'"

The glorious sense or proof of that hour is lost spiritually, when confined to a literal sense, or the use of bread and wine. The disciples were eating when he prayed and gave them bread. Now this would have been improper in a literal sense; but in its spiritual, it was natural and beautiful. Jesus prayed; was "absent from the body and present with the Lord." His followers silent, humble, patient, self-sacrificing, and strong, anticipating the approaching hour of their Master's betrayal, sat eating the manna, that before had fed the persecuted followers of Truth in the wilderness. Their bread came down from heaven; it was the great Truth of spiritualized being, that often had healed the sick, and cast out error; their Master had broken, explained it to them before, and now it was feeding, sustaining them; they also had borne it from house to house, "breaking," explaining it to others; and now it comforted them. For this Truth their Master was about to suffer violence, and his cup of sorrow he must leave to them; he had drank it even with thanks, after a momentary weakness that said, "Let this cup pass from me," and now remembering also the cross and crown it bore, he said to his followers, "Drink ye all of it." Professors of Christ, are you drinking this cup? has the blood of the New Testament, the sufferings and persecutions that attend a new understanding of God, been shared by you? have you drank this cup? If not, have you commemorated Jesus in his "cup?" When the human struggled with the divine, our great exemplar said, "Not my will but thine be done"; not personal sense, but Soul be represented by me. This new understanding of the Love that is impersonal, gives up all for Christ, Truth, blesses them that curse it, heals the sick, casts out error, raises those dead in belief, and preaches to the poor.

The rabbi and priest taught a material law, and it was "An eye for an eye," and "whose sheddeth man's blood, by man shall his blood be shed "; not so did Jesus, the new testator of God, copy his will; his law was Love, and "Greater love hath no man than this, that

Chapter V. Prayer and Atonement.

he lay down his life for a friend," but he did this for his enemies, showing the Love, the Life and Truth, that is the at-one-ment with God.

First on the list of Christian duties, he taught his followers to heal the sick; he attached no importance to dead ceremonies; it was the living Christ, the Truth, that is Life, that made him the resurrection and Life to all who follow him. Thus keeping his precious precepts and following his demonstration in its understanding, we shall indeed drink his cup and be baptized with his purity, until we sit down with him anew in a fuller understanding of the Principle of that man, Jesus. "For as often as ye eat his bread and drink his cup, ye do show forth the Lord's death till he come."

A belief can never show forth the works of understanding, and has never yet followed Jesus in his demonstration; to do this we must consecrate our lives to the Principle for which be was crucified, and be willing to drink of the cup it brings. "But for this cause many are weak and sickly among you, and many sleep."

Rites fetter the pinions of Soul, they materialize, and prevent the Spirit, by holding us to the body; for matter separates from Spirit. We speak of the atonement of Christ reconciling God to man; but Christ is God, and God propitiates not Himself, and there is nothing higher to conciliate. Again, Love and Truth are not irreconciled to the idea of God, and man is this idea. But man being the shadow of Almighty, cannot exceed Him in Love; or reconcile Truth to error. His students understood the sufferings, teachings, and demonstration of their glorious Master better than all this. When Jesus gave up the body material to be slain, and afterwards presented it to his students unchanged, he had proved what he had taught, showing them he was act dead, and they knew it was proof of the Principle he had before taught, and disproved our opinions of a future resurrection, or a spiritual body at the change, called death; his body was a belief of matter, as before, until he rose to Spirit above the reach of personal sense, and triumphed over the last enemy, death, as before he had conquered sickness and sin, and this was what his followers were to commemorate in their lives, so far as they understood his teachings and demonstration; hence the saying, "The works that I do ye shall do, and greater."

Theology explains the crucifixion of Jesus, a pardon ready for all sinners; Spiritualism finds his death necessary only for the presentation, after death, of the personal Jesus; calling this "a spirit's return." We differ from both, and while we respect all that is good in the church, and outside of it, our later consecration to Christ has been on the ground of demonstration, and not profession, yea, to follow the commands he gave to those he sent forth. For conscience's sake we dare not cling to the old belief, insomuch as understanding somewhat the Principle of his proof, the Life, and not death, that Jesus showed forth, raised us from hopeless disease, and gave us a triumph over sickness and sin, we never had gained from our former beliefs and profession of religion.

The efficacy of the crucifixion of Jesus is the practical Truth it demonstrated for our understanding, and that ultimately will deliver mankind from sickness, sin and death. This Truth he had before spoken in their midst; but until they saw it triumph over the grave the disciples were not able to admit and demonstrate so fully its Principle. Thomas, beholding the idea of it in Jesus, (after his supposed death) was forced to acknowledge how entire was the proof. From all the disciples had seen and suffered, they became more spiritual, therefore could better understand what the Master had taught them. This, therefore, was the resurrection, for it raised them from the blindness of a belief in God to the understanding of Him, "Whom to know aright was Life." They needed this, for soon their dear Master that had just risen to their comprehension would rise again, higher in the spiritual scale of being, and so much beyond them in reward for all his faithfulness, he would disappear to their more material thoughts, and Biblical history would name it the ascension. Ancient prophets who wrought before Jesus, foretold his coming, and the reception the world of sense would give Truth; also

Chapter V. Prayer and Atonement.

there is a connection inseparable between their experiences, and those of every Christian who perceives the idea and accepts the understanding of God. Jesus, born of a virgin mother, was more of a miracle to that age, than to this; for even the naturalist is now furnishing reports of embryology in some species wholly without the male element. The Bethlehem babe was the nearest approximation since the record in Genesis to the science of being, in which Spirit makes man; for man born of woman, was the usual advent of mortal man, and this material belief was what entered Mary's spiritual conception of Jesus, which accounts for the struggles of Gethsemane, but it made him the mediator between God and mortal man; this lack of entire science in the advent of Jesus, produced its discord, and met its fate in death. Had his origin and birth, however, been wholly apart from mortal belief, Jesus would not have been recognized by mortal man; and "he was the light that was to lighten every man that cometh into the world;" therefore he must be the mediator, or interpreter of Truth to error that destroyed error and rebuked personal sense with the Principle of being.

Jesus never ransomed man, by paying the debt sin incurs; whosoever sins must suffer. This Christian martyr suffered for the Truth, that destroyed error, and while it blessed the whole world, was that for which it hated him; even the sinner must learn Truth, by the things he suffers. Love is no compromise with sin, and pays no debt of its contracting; but it can and does point out the way to escape from it and reach the harmony and science of being. The blood of that righteous man shed by sinners, was a crime that affords no ground for further sin or a belief of its pardon, it was an injustice to humanity that the beat man should be sacrificed by the worst men. Jesus taught the way of escape from sin, but that all that sinneth shall die, in other words, that sin must be destroyed. Wisdom punishes, instead of pardons, sin. The terrible effect of our false views regarding the atonement, is to make a sinner less fearful to sin, believing a tear or a prayer will secure its pardon; this heightens hypocrisy and suffocates conscience. The time is not far distant when our theological views of atonement will undergo as radical a change as those have already done regarding a bottomless pit, burning with fire and brimstone, and the election and fore-ordination of a portion to be saved or be lost. But for these false views regarding the forgiveness of sin, ministers and laymen would never break the commandment, "Thou shalt not commit adultery," and then talk of their love for God, and Christian experience.

The sweet and spiritual significance of the death on the cross, is Love laying down all of earth to instruct its enemies the way to heaven, proving what heaven is, and how obtained. We speak of the blood of Jesus as efficacious to save sinners; it is the efficacy of the Truth and Love that Jesus taught and demonstrated, which alone can destroy sin; and sinners are never saved. The blood of Christ was an offering of Spirit and not matter, a pledge of undying Love. O! highest conceptions of spiritual sense tell us, what is Love.

CHAPTER VI

MARRIAGE

WHEN our great Teacher went to John to be baptized, not having reached his motive, the good patriarch was astounded, and reading his thoughts, Jesus prefaced his purpose saying, "Suffer these things to be so now, for thus it becometh us to fulfill all righteousness," that is, yield obedience to common forms, until you reach the understanding of their spiritual significance. Marriage is the only legal and moral form among the higher species, for generation, and until the spiritual creation is discerned and the union of male and female apprehended in its Soul-sense, this rite should continue under such moral regulations as secure increasing virtue. Infidelity to the marriage covenant is the social scourge of all peoples; the pestilence that wasteth and walketh at noon-day. The commandment, "Thou shalt not commit adultery," is not less imperative, than "Thou shalt not kill." Virtue is the basis of civilization and progress; without it there is no true foundation to society, and it were utterly impossible to attain the Science of Life; but virtue should be recognized; and the fear to take responsible posts of duty lest the vicious misjudge you, be wholly removed. Owing to the shocking depravity of mankind, chastity is looked at suspiciously; it requires more moral courage for woman to meet the low estimates in society of virtue, than to help lift its standard from the dust.

The last infirmity of error that would fasten itself on society, to see it hop and hobble under a new burden of guilt, is named "free love"; wherein "they declare their sin as Sodom, and hide it not," but the boldness of depravity will show its deformity. A union of the masculine and feminine mind seems requisite for completeness; the former reaches a higher tone from communion with the latter; and the latter gains courage and strength from the former; therefore, these different individualities meet and demand each other, and their true harmony is oneness of Soul. Woman should be loving, pure,

Chapter VI. Marriage.

and strong. Man, tender, intellectual, controlling; the attraction between the sexes will be perpetual only as it is pure and true, and like the seasons, brings its sweet changes and renewal. Beauty, wealth, or fame is incompetent to meet the demands of the affections, and should never waver the balance against the more honest claims of intellect, goodness, and virtue. Happiness is spiritual, born of Truth and Love; it is unselfish; therefore it cannot exist alone, but requires an object to cherish. Our affections are not poured forth vainly, when meeting no return; they enrich the being, enlarging, purifying and elevating it. The wintry blasts of earth may transplant the flowers of affection, or scatter them to the winds; but sundering ties of flesh, unites us to God, where Love supports the struggling heart, until it ceases to sigh over earth, and folds its wings for heaven.

Marriage is blest or unblest, according to the disappointment it incurs, or the motive it fulfills. To happify existence by constant intercourse with those adapted to elevate it is the true motive for marriage; wedlock gives pinions to joy, or trails its drooping wings in dust. Notes are illy arranged that produce discord; tones of mind may be different, but they should be concordant, to blend harmoniously. Unselfish ambition, nobler motives for existence, increased harmony, happiness and usefulness, because the different elements of mind meet and mingle, finding in union there is strength -- is the true marriage. Let there be moral freedom in wedlock; never contract the limit of worthy deeds by a selfish exaction of all one's time and thoughts. With additional joys, benevolence should grow more diffusive, for the narrowness and jealousy that would confine a wife or husband forever at home, will not promote the sweet interchange of confidence that comes of love; while a wandering desire for incessant amusement outside the home circle is a poor augury for happiness. Home is the dearest spot on earth, and should be the center, but not the boundary of the affections. Said the peasant bride to her lover, "Two eat no more together than when they are separate," and this should furnish the hint, that a wife ought not to enter into vulgar extravagance, or stupid ease, because

Chapter VI. Marriage.

another supplies her wants. Wealth may obviate the necessity for toil or ill nature in the marriage relation, but nothing can shirk its cares. "She that is married careth for her husband, how she may please him," and this is the very thing it is pleasant to do. Matrimony should be entered into with a full recognition of its enduring obligations, and the most tender solicitude for each other's happiness and approbation should wait on all its years.

Mutual compromises preserve a compact that might otherwise become burdensome. Man should not be required to participate in all the annoyances and cares of domestic economy, or woman to understand political economy; but fulfilling the different demands of separate spheres, their sympathies may blend to comfort, cheer and sustain each other, thus hallowing the copartnership of interests and affection whereon the heart leans and is at peace. Tender words, and unselfish care for what promotes the respect and happiness of thy wife, is more salutary in prolonging her smiles and health, than stolid indifference, or jealousy; husbands, hear this, and remember how slight a thing might have spared the old trysting times. It is too late after marriage to grumble over disparities of dispositions; a mutual understanding should exist before, and continue ever after this union. Deception is fatal to happiness. The nuptial vow is never annulled so long as its moral obligations are preserved, but the frequency of divorce shows the sacredness of this relation losing its puritanical character, and that some fatal mistake is undermining its true basis. A separation takes place when the motives for marriage are not suited to individual progress and happiness. The science of being inevitably lifts us higher in the scale of harmony, and will ultimately shake off all shackles that fetter the mind, ripe for advancement. Therefore, to avoid a disruption in the marriage relation, mutual tastes, joys, and aspirations are necessary to form a happy companionship. The beautiful, is the good in character, that clasps the indissoluble links of affection.

A mother's affection cannot be separated from her child, embracing as it does, purity and Truth, both of which are immortal,

Chapter VI. Marriage.

therefore it lives on under all difficulties. From the very logic of events, we learn the selfish and impure are all that is fleeting, and that Wisdom will ultimately separate what it hath not joined together.

Marriage should improve the species, become a barrier to vice, a protection to woman, a strength to man, and a center for the affections. This, however, in a majority of cases, is not its present tendency; and because the education of our higher natures is neglected for other considerations, frivolous amusements, adornments of the person, passion, display, and pride. An ill-attuned ear calls discord harmony, not apprehending concord; so personal sense, discerning not the true happiness of being, places it on a false basis; but science corrects the discord and teaches us Life's sweeter harmonies. Soul hath infinite resources wherewith to bless mankind, and happiness were more readily attained and secure in our keeping if sought of Soul. The higher order of enjoyments are all that satisfy the cravings of immortal man; we cannot circumscribe our happiness within the limits of wealth or fame. The good we possess should have ascendency over the evil, and the spiritual over the animal, or happiness is never reached. This would improve progeny, diminish crime, give higher aims to ambition, and prepare the way for science. The offspring of such parents would inherit more intellect, better balanced minds, and sounder constitutions.

If some fortuitous circumstance places in the arms of gross parents a more spiritual offspring, the beautiful child early droops and dies, like a tropical flower dropped amid Alpine snows; or marrying reproduces in the helpless offspring the grosser traits of her ancestors. What hope of happiness, or noble ambition hovers around the child inheriting propensities that must be overcome, or reduce him to a loathsome wreck. For propagating the human species, is there not greater responsibility than for your garden culture, or the stock of your flocks and herds? Nothing should be transmitted to offspring unworthy to perpetuate. The formation and education of even mortal mind, must improve before the

Chapter VI. Marriage.

millennium. The most important education of the infant is to keep it mentally free from impurity, and let mind develop the body harmoniously; mind, and not matter, should govern the physical. For parents to create a desire in their child for incessant amusement, always to have some demand on hand to be fed, rocked, tossed, or talked to, and afterwards complain of their child's fretfulness, or in after years of Its frivolity,- all of which they have occasioned, is art error.

Yielding one's thoughts to contemplate physical wants surely produces them. A single requirement beyond what is necessary to meet the most modest needs of the babe is hurtful. The condition of the stomach, bowels, food, clothing, etc., is of no serious import to your child. Your views regarding them will produce the only result they can have on the health of your child. The daily ablution of an infant is not more natural or necessary than to take a fish out of water and cover it with dirt, once a clay, that it may thrive better in its natural element. Cleanliness is next to godliness, but washing should be only to keep the body clean, and this can be done with less than daily scrubbing the whole surface.'

Giving drugs to infants, noticing every symptom of flatulency, or constantly directing your mind to them, laden with beliefs of disease, laws of health, sickness, and death, conveys your mental image to their bodies and stamps it there, making it probable at any time to be reproduced in the disease you fear. Your child can have worms if you say so, or whatever fear the mind holds, relative to that body; it is thus you lay the foundation of disease and death, and educate your child into discord and. out of harmony. The entire education of children should be only such as will form habits of obedience to moral and spiritual law; there is no physical law to be consulted.

Taking less thought "what ye shall eat or what ye shall drink," will do much more than you are aware of for the health of rising generations. Children should be allowed to remain children in

Chapter VI. Marriage.

knowledge, and become men and women through the understanding of their spiritual being. We should not think for a moment a law of matter outside of ourselves can harm our babe, for it cannot. Intelligence outside of matter, that forms the bud and blossom will regulate the body, even as it clothes the lily, if we do not interfere by some belief. The higher nature of man is not governed by the lower; this would annul the order of Wisdom; the false views we entertain of being, hide the eternal harmony and produce the ills of which we complain. Because the belief of intelligent matter is accepted, and the opposite science of mind rejected, shall we submit it is true, or that, the so- called laws of sense are superior to laws of Soul? You would never conclude a flannel is better to ward off pulmonary disease than the Intelligence that forms the body, if you understand the science of being. Man is the offspring of Spirit; the beautiful, good and pure are his ancestors; his origin is not brute instinct, nor does he pass through material conditions up to man. Spirit is his primitive and ultimate being, and God his Father.

The rights of woman are discussed on grounds that seem to us not the most important. Law establishes a very unnatural difference between the rights of the two sexes; but science furnishes no precedent for such injustice, and civilization brings, in some measure, its mitigation, therefore it is a marvel that society should accord her less than either. Our laws are not impartial, to say the least, relative to the person, property, and parental claims of the two sexes; and if the elective enfranchisement of woman would remedy this evil without incurring difficulties of greater magnitude, we hope it will be effected. A very tenable means at present, is to improve society in general, and achieve a nobler manhood to frame our laws. If a dissolute husband deserts his wife, it should not follow that the wronged and perchance impoverished woman cannot collect her own wages, or enter into agreements, bold real estate, deposit funds, or surely claim her own offspring free from his right of interference. A want of reciprocity in society is a great want that the selfishness of the world has occasioned. Our forefathers exercised their faith in the direction St. James taught, " To visit the fatherless and widows,

Chapter VI. Marriage.

and keep yourself unspotted from the world "; but ostentation, the master of ceremonies, and stereotyped belief have ruled out primitive Christianity, so that when a man would lend a helping hand to some noble woman, struggling alone with adversity, his more prudent wife saith "'Tis never beat to interfere with thy neighbor's business."

Again, a wife is withheld from the ready aid her Sympathy and charity would afford, by some domestic tyrant. The time cometh when marriage will be a union of hearts; and again, the time cometh when there will be no marrying or giving in marriage, but we shall be as the angels; the Soul rejoicing in its own mate wherein the masculine Wisdom and feminine Love are embraced in the understanding. Because progeny needs to be improved, let marriage continue, and permit no breaking down of law whereby a worse state of society is produced, than at present.

Puritanical honesty and virtue should be the stability of this covenant; Soul will ultimately claim its own, and the voices of personal sense be hushed. Marriage should be the school of virtue, and offspring the germ of man's highest nature. Christ, Truth, should be present at the altar, to turn the water into wine, giving inspiration to understanding, whereby man's spiritual origin and existence are discerned. If the foundations of affection are consistent with progress, its vows will be strong and enduring. Divorces inform the age that some fundamental error in this union is the source of its discord. To pin the science, hence the harmony of this relation, we should regard it more metaphysically and less physically.

The broad-cast power of evil so conspicuous to-day, is the materialism of the age struggling against the spiritual era, that advances; beholding the world's lack of Christianity, and the powerlessness of promises, to make good husbands or wives, mind will at length demand a higher affection, and ferment on this and many other subjects, until it settles down on an improved understanding. But the fermentation of fluids is not pleasant, during

Chapter VI. Marriage.

this nondescript stage, and matrimony that was once a fixed fact, is not so desirable on a slippery foundation.

The mental chemicalization that has brought infidelity to the surface, will as surely throw it off, and marriage will settle down purer after the scum is expelled. ‚Sweet are the uses of adversity, which like the toad, ugly and venomous, wears yet a precious jewel in his head." They teach us not to lean upon earth, it is a broken reed, that pierces to the heart. We do not half remember this in the sunshine of joy and prosperity. But sorrow is more salutary, and points us from the cross to the crown prepared for those who pass to their reward through much tribulation. Trials are but proofs of God's care for his children. When spiritual development takes place it germinates not from seed sown in the soil of earthly hopes; rather do these decay to propagate anew in Spirit those higher joys that have no taint of earth, and thus our experiences go up higher, and a point is won in progress.

In conjugal felicity, it is well to remember how fleeting are the joys of earth, and be grateful for them. In conjugal infelicity, separate not if there is no moral demand for this; far better &wait the logic of events, than for a wife precipitately to leave a husband, or a husband his wife, for if one is better than the other, this other pre-eminently needs good company. Socrates considered patience salutary under such circumstances, making his Xanthippe a discipline for his philosophy. Sorrow has its reward, and never leaves man where it found him; it is the furnace that separates the gold from the dross, and gives back the image of God. The cup our Father hath given, shall we not drink it? and learn the lesson He inculcates.

When the ocean is stirred by a storm, the clouds lower, the wind screams through the straitened canvas, and waves lift themselves to mountains, we ask the helmsman, "Do you know your course, and can you steer your vessel amid the storm?" Even the dauntless seaman is not sure of his fate, well knowing the science of

Chapter VI. Marriage.

navigation is not equal to the Science of God; but acting up to his highest understanding, firm at the post of duty, awaits the issue. Thus should we deport ourself in the seething ocean of sorrow, hoping and working, stick to the wreck, until the logic of events precipitates the doom, or sunshine gladdens the wave.

The possibility that animal natures give more force to character than the spiritual, is too absurd to consider, when we remember the exemplar of man healed the sick, raised the dead, and commanded even the winds and waves to obey him, through the ascendency of the spiritual over the material. What we avail ourselves of God, is as potent with us as it was with Jesus, and our want of spiritual strength speaks the rebuke it deserves; and our limited demonstration puts to shame the labor of centuries. We should hold our body not so much in personal, as spiritual consciousness, even as the orange we have just eaten, and of which only the idea is left, then would there be neither pain nor sin. Systems of physic and systems of doctrines treat of the pleasures and pains of personal sense; but Christ takes them all away, and the epoch approaches when to understand this Principle of being, will form the basis of all harmony and progress. At present we live ridiculously for fear of being thought ridiculous; are slaves to fashion, appetite, and sense; in the future we shall learn Soul is an architect that makes men and women beautiful, noble, and not to be blotted out. We ought to weary of the fleeting and false, hence, of personal sense, and cherish nothing that hinders our highest self-hood.

Frugality is essential to domestic prosperity, and so is affection; but to silence the voice of conscience to gain wealth, is trade without profit. The genius of woman shrinks from controversy with a knave, or a fool. A man respects the reputation of a woman, but a mouse will gnaw in the dark a spotless garment. Culture and refinement are not things of the toilet, but reflections of head and heart. Innocence is a gem, worn unconscious of pick-pockets. Husbands that dissipate care in the club, are poor stocks in ready markets. A husband is the best friend, or worst enemy of his wife. "Favor is deceitful, and

Chapter VI. Marriage.

beauty vain, but a woman of Wisdom, should be praised." A bad woman is a loathsome leprosy, dangerous to all that approach her. In marriage, avoid disparity in ages, tastes, or education, and make choice only of those qualities that wear well. Jealousy is the grave of affection; mistrust where confidence is due touches with mildew the flowers of Eden, and scatters to the four winds the leaves of love. A bridal altar is the verge of a new existence; wherein the old is fading out of the experience, to admit the new; two beings mingling into one; be not in baste to take the vow, "until death do us part," but consider well its obligations, responsibilities, and relations to all your future happiness; "judge before friendship, then confide till death."

CHAPTER VII

PHYSIOLOGY

BECAUSE science reverses the positions of personal sense, human reason acts slowly in accepting it, contesting every inch of ground it occupies, while error, self-complacent and applauded, sneers at the slow marches of Truth. Physiology is a name in our land. Institutions honor it, and materia medica bows the knee, but notwithstanding this, it has not improved mankind. We shall yet open our eyes to this fact in theodicy, that depending on matter for what Intelligence is responsible, is a mistake with grave consequences. The fundamental error of mortal man, is the belief that man is matter, but theorizing from mushrooms up to brains, amounts to little in the right direction, and much in the wrong. Classifying the different species of man, mineral, vegetable, and animal, an egg is the author of the genus homo; but we perceive no reason why man should begin thus sooner than in the more primitive state of dust where Adam commenced. Brains are beneath the craniums of animals; then to admit brains are man, furnishes a pretext for saying he was once a monkey, which is met with the reply, if this be the case, he will again be one, according to natural history.

What is man? brain, heart, or the entire human structure? If he is one, or all of the component parts of his body, when you amputate a limb, you have taken away a portion of man, and a surgeon destroys manhood, and worms are the annihilators of man. But losing a limb or injuring structure, is sometimes the quickener of manliness, and the unfortunate body presents more nobility than the statuesque outline, and we find, "a man's a man, for a' that." Admitting matter, blood, heart, brains, etc., and the five personal senses, man, we fail to see how anatomy makes out the different species of brute and human, or determines when man rises above his progenitors, for both possess these constituent parts, and must, to some extent, be mortal man, if he is matter. According to accepted theories, the

Chapter VII. Physiology.

genus homo ranges from dust to Deity, the latter having its origin in matter, while the different varieties of man are mineral, vegetable, and animal; but the spiritual is not a link in this chain of so-called being, and is seen only as it disappears. If man was first dust, he has passed through every form of matter, until he became man, and if the material body is man, he is matter, and the dust that returns to dust. But this is not man, the image and likeness of God, but a belief of Soul in sense, and of Life in matter, that Wisdom consigned to annihilation. Anatomy makes man a structural thing; physiology continues this definition, measuring his strength by bones, sinews, etc., and his Life by material law. Phrenology makes him a thief or Christian, according to the development of bumps on the cranium; but not one of these define immortal man. The tendency of all true education is to unfold the infinite resources of being, but to measure our capacities by the size or weight of our brains, and limit our strength to the use of a muscle, holds Life at the mercy of organization, and makes matter the status of Man.

Physiology is like fiction in which debauchery is toned down to fascinate, and mankind are in danger of catching its sentiment. The very opposite teachings of physiology, are all that will open again the gates of paradise that beliefs have closed, and reach the personification of Spirit, in which man is upright, pure, and free, having no need to consult calendars or clouds to learn the probabilities of Life, or brainology, to know how much of a man he is. Mistaking his origin and nature, we call man both matter and Spirit; the latter sifted through the former, Soul put through personal sense, carried on a nerve, and subject to ejection at the hands of matter; the intellectual, moral, and spiritual, that exist as Soul outside the body, subject to the body]

Unless civilization embraces heathenism, why should man, in the nineteenth century, bow down to fleshbrush, flannel, bath, diet, exercise, air, etc., when matter is not capable of doing for him what be can do for himself? The idols of civilization are more fatal to health and longevity than the idols of other forms of heathen

Chapter VII. Physiology.

homage; they certainly call into action less faith than Buddhism in Intelligence governing man. The Esquimaux restores health by incantations, as effectually as the modus operandi of the schools.

Physiology is anti-Christian; it teaches us to have other gods before "Me," the only Life of man. The good it claims is positive evil, because it robs man of his birth-right from God. Truth governs it not, and the inharmonious condition that calls for physiology, is the result of physiology, or our beliefs of matter.

Did the teachings of Jesus comprehend the economy of man, less than those of Graham or Cutter? They alone embrace the Principle of man's harmony; but our theories do not. "He that believeth in me shall not see death," contradicts, not only the systems of man, but points to that which is self-sustaining and eternal The demands of God are wholly spiritual, and reach the body only through Spirit that controls matter; there are no physical laws; all are mental. The best interpreter of man's needs said, "Take no thought for the body, what ye shall eat or what drink."

Putting on the full armor of physiology, obeying to the letter, the so-called laws of health, statistics show, has not diminished sickness, nor increased longevity; diseases have multiplied and become more obstinate; their chronic forms more frequent; the acute more fatal and death more sudden, since man-made theories have taken the place of primitive Christianity.

Explaining man a physical being evolved from matter, is a Pandora box opened on mankind, whereby hope escapes, and despair alone remains. If matter laws prevent disease, what causes it? not the laws of God, surely, for Christ, Truth, heals the sick, and Mugs to light immortality; but not through obedience to physiology. Laws of matter are nothing more or less than a belief of Intelligence and Life in matter, even the procuring cause of disease, and God its cure. Not more sympathy exists between physiology and Christianity, than God and Belial. Failing to recover through

Chapter VII. Physiology.

adherence to materia medica, physiology and hygiene, the despairing invalid drops these, and turns in his extremity -- sometimes to God, the *dernier resort* of mortal man, and one in which he has even less trust than in drugs, air, exercise, etc., showing we have other Gods before Me. The balance of power is given to matter, by every theory of the schools, whereas Spirit at last asserts its mastery over man, and holds the body harmonious and immortal.

To understand the Principle that embraces the harmony of being, is beyond burnt offerings or sacrifices. If the recovery of the sick is submitted to a personal God we shall reach no higher than faith; understanding will be wanting, therefore man's existence as Soul instead of sense, will not be comprehended. We comprehend Life in science or the harmony of being, only as we deny personal sense. The relative claims we permit Intelligence and matter, determines the harmony of our existence; our health, longevity and Christianity. We cannot serve two masters, and must reach God through science, and not with sense, or material law. The source of all Life and perfection, we should not offset with drugs, laws of health, etc. When man would be both good and- evil, he will grow no better, and the result of this error will make him grow worse; so it is with an attempted compromise between Spirit and matter. Even in healing the sick, to gain the advantages of Spirit, we must lose our faith in matter.

The severest part of teaching or learning the science of being, is to empty the mind of the thousand and one beliefs that war against Truth; for you cannot fill a vessel already full. After laboring long with the well or ill-stored mind, to shake its faith in matter, and give it a crumb of faith in God. viz., the capacity of Spirit to make the body harmonious, we have thought yearningly of our Master's love for little children, and understood how, "of such is the kingdom of heaven."

Chapter VII. Physiology.

We admit mind influences the body somewhat, but conclude matter, blood, nerves, brain, etc., hold the balance of power; in accordance with this belief, we continue the old routine, and this deprives us of the available superiority of mind over matter. We cannot control our body, mentally, with a negative position. Spirit works against matter, and *vice versa*. They can no more unite in action than good and evil, and it is wise not to take a halting, or half-way position on this subject, or think to work equally with right and wrong. there is but one right way, and this we should learn to-day, is Spirit and not matter. To govern the body scientifically, we must admit only mind, and you will find it impossible to gain control over the body on any other ground; a conservative position on this point, or faith strongest in matter, will never do it.

If you manipulate your patients, you lean on electricity more than Truth, and it is matter more than mind you employ to heal the sick, while science teaches you success is on the side of Intelligence, and that you only weaken your power with matter. It is useless to say you manipulate patients, but lay no stress on this manipulation; then why do you do it? We answer for you -- because you are not sufficiently spiritual to do otherwise; and if this is so, why do you call it science, explained in this work? If you are too material to understand the science of being, and rub the head as a substitute for living Truth, adopting words and manipulation instead of good deeds, then you adhere to error and flee to electricity because you have not science, and are afraid to trust yourself to heal with your God-being. "Adam, where art thou?" is your question here at every step. If you manipulate the sick, the more to satisfy them that you are doing something for them, this is not necessary, for they are generally satisfied when cured, and manipulation will retard your success. "Where your treasure is there will your heart be also." Having more faith in electricity than you have in your God-being, balances you on the side of matter, and your power as a mesmerist will diminish your achievements in the direction of science, and vice versa, and this should remind you where your treasure is. Casting out error with Truth shows your real position in science. The

Chapter VII. Physiology.

sensualist or dishonest man can never rely on Truth to heal the sick; they must depend on personal sense, and their only power is mesmerism and manipulation. Jesus cast out error and healed the sick, not with manipulations or drugs, but his God-being.

Food, fatigue, or sleeplessness, you say may cause distressed stomachs or aching heads, and then cudgel your brains to reproduce in memory what you think hurts you, when your remedy lies in getting the whole thing out of mind, for matter has no sensation and mind only can give pain. To reduce inflammation, dissolve tumors, or cure organic disease, mind is more potent than matter, and why not, since Intelligence is Life, and mind the seat of feeling or sensation, the body has nothing to do with it. When we say the stomach or head is disordered or pained, consider what art thou that repliest to Spirit? can matter speak for itself, or has it the issues of Life? Pain or pleasure belongs to mind alone. Matter has no partnership with Spirit. The head cannot ache, but believing it does, "as a man thinketh so is he." Mind is all that *feels*, that produces action or impedes it; but, ignorant of this, or shrinking from its responsibility, you throw the burden on matter, and lose conscious control over your body. Adjust a balance, and a single weight removed from one of the scales gives preponderance to the opposite one; so with body and mind; what you cast into the scale of matter to weigh for or against health, you take away from Intelligence, and its power to hold the balance against matter. Your belief weighs against your health while it ought to weigh for it. When the body is sick according to a belief of matter, you trust in drugs, laws of health and matter to heal it, when you have got yourself into the difficulty through these very beliefs of Intelligent matter. Disease is caused and cured by mind alone; matter never did it; this you do not understand now, but must before you are immortal. To lay aside our God-being as of little use in sickness, seems anomalous; to depend on matter then and put Truth aside for the hour of health, is to learn it can not do as much for you then as in sickness.

Chapter VII. Physiology.

Because materia medica and physiology say man is sick and useless, suffering, or dying, in obedience to laws of God, are we to believe this? despite his laws to the contrary are we to believe what Jesus proved false? he surely did the will of the Father and healed sickness instead of producing it. The demands of God relate to mind alone, but the claims of physiology and what are termed laws of nature, rest upon the body only. Which, then, are we to accept as legitimate and capable of producing most harmony? We cannot obey them both, for one works against the other, and will be supreme in the affections. Spirit and matter are opposites, and we cannot work from the standpoints of both; attempt it and we shall find ourself cleaving to one and forsaking the other.

Heal your body with the science of being if you can, adhering to the old regimen, taking drugs, or yielding your mental control to laws of matter. Obedience to what you call material law, prevents obedience to the spiritual law that enables you to handle deadly serpents unharmed, and put matter under your feet. Like a barrister that would strengthen his plea, introducing the text, "Wo unto you, lawyers, for you shut up the kingdom of heaven against man;" you plead for recovery of God, and then abut out the aid of Spirit through your material means; thus working against yourself, and suffocating your own strength and ability. The plea for matter, medicine, laws of health, etc., goes against the science of mind over matter, and *vice versa*. There is this clause in the statue of Truth to which we call your attention at such times, viz., that sin, sickness, and death are not governed by laws of God. Error produces error, sin and sickness, for both are errors of belief, and what causes disease cannot cure it, unless it be the homeopathic dose where matter is destroyed and mind says this. Admitting sickness a condition of matter over which God has no control, makes Omnipotence, on some occasions, null and void. The law of Christ, Truth, finds all things possible to Spirit; but the so-called laws of matter find Spirit of no avail, and demand obedience to them, reversing the basis and economy of being; to matter we deny the support of law; our beliefs

Chapter VII. Physiology.

of matter are not correct, as Jesus clearly demonstrated healing the sick, raising the dead, etc., contrary to them.

Can the agriculturist produce a crop without first sowing the seed and awaiting its germination, according to laws of nature? Yes; if as the Bible says, error caused man to till the ground, for in this case, obedience to Truth, would remove this cause. God never made a necessity for error, or a law to perpetuate it. The opposite of harmony are supposed laws of nature, and by these you mean laws of God, therefore, it is not in harmony with Truth to be well. As you would construe them, laws of nature annul the law of Spirit; But the law of Christ demands man's entire obedience, heart, Soul and strength, which admits no reservation, or obedience to aught else, and we should have no other God. Truth is Strength, and error weakness. Physiology is one of the fruits of the "tree of knowledge," that said, I will open your eyes, and make you as Gods, but instead, closes them to man's God-given dominion over earth. Christ, Truth, cast out physiology and every law of health, giving sight to the blind, hearing to the deaf, etc., contrary to them. If these explanations dishonor the schools, they honor God, and there is no other Truth to honor.

What we term laws of nature, are simply laws of belief regarding matter, the premises whereof are error; therefore their conclusions are such. The All-wise has made no laws regulating sickness, sin, and death, these are errors, that Truth destroys. Belief produces the results of belief, and the penalty it affixes will be as positive as the belief that causes it; therefore, our remedy lies in reaching the bottom of the thing, in finding out the error or mind that produces the discord we see on the body, and not to honor it with the title of law, and then yield obedience to it.

Truth, Life, and Love are the only demands that rest on man, and the only laws that govern him. We say my hand hath done this; but what is the "my" in this case, but mind, the universal cause whence proceedeth all harmony and inharmony. Discord is not a thing, but a

Chapter VII. Physiology.

belief, and the action of our hand is either produced by Intelligence or belief, by harmony or discord. The so-called voluntary and involuntary action of the body is governed by mind, and not matter. And, controlled by Intelligence, the body is governed by the Principle of being, in which man is harmonious and immortal; but governed by man's belief, it is discordant and mortal. Under extreme cold, heat, fatigue, etc., we say, the body suffers, but this is belief only, and not the Truth of being; matter cannot suffer, mind alone suffers, and not because we have transgressed a law of nature, matter, but a law of belief. Our proof is, that if you destroy the belief in regard to the suffering, it disappears, and the effect of what you term broken law, producing catarrhs, fevers, consumptions, etc., goes with the belief. A lady whom we cured of consumption, breathed with great difficulty when the wind was east; we sat silently by her side a few moments, and her breath came gently, the inspirations becoming deep and natural; we then requested her to look at the weather-vane; she saw it was due east; the wind had not changed, but her difficult breathing had gone; therefore it was not the wind that produced it, and our explanations broke this mental hallucination, and she never suffered again from east winds. Here is testimony on this point.

I was suffering from pulmonary difficulties, pains in the chest, a hard and unremitting cough, hectic fever, and all those fearful symptoms that made my case alarming. When I first saw Mrs. Glover, I was reduced to such a state of debility as to be unable to walk any distance, or to sit up but a portion of the day; to walk up stairs gave me great suffering for breath. I had no appetite, and seemed surely going down the victim of consumption. I had not received her attention but a short time, when my bad symptoms disappeared, and I regained health. During this time, I rode out in storms to visit her, and found the damp weather had no effect on me. From my personal experience I am led to believe the science by which she not only heals the sick, but explains the way to keep well, is deserving the earnest attention of community; her cures are not

Chapter VII. Physiology.

the result of medicine, mediumship, or mesmerism, but the application of a Principle that she understands.

JAMES INGHAM
East Stoughton, Mass.

Mortal man is divided into five points of sensation, called personal sense; these five points constitute pleasure, pain, sin, sickness, and death; what would be left of man at the mercy of personal sense? Spirit is superior to matter, and the body that is ours, should be under our control; settle the question then, which Shall be master, Soul or body, but do not think to serve both, for you cannot. Soul, owns man now and forever; let the owner of man then govern him, and the body will be harmonious and eternal. Neither a blade of grass appears, nor a spray buddeth within the vale, nor a leaf unfolds its fair outlines, nor a flower starts from its cloistered cell, without the Principle of man, even that Intelligence which the winds and sea obey, hath clone it; naught but universal Soul, that numbers the very hairs of our head, and marks the sparrow's fall, can govern man. Sin, sickness, and death are inharmonies; they are not identity, action, or being, they are matter-beliefs, that appear and disappear, governed alone by mind, but without the reality or support of law or Spirit.

That God is the law of discord, is morally impossible, or that Wisdom instituted penalties to protect us from what is without law, except to belief, is again impossible. Wisdom never made matter to subdue Spirit; to say it did is like concluding it made Hades to get ready for sinners; but there were so many sinners they had to make their own Hells. God is too pure to behold iniquity, "in Him was Life," etc.; and harmony never produced discord, or Life death. Goodness makes its own heaven, sin its own hell, and belief its own sufferings. A dream seemeth a reality while it lasts; a falsehood is true to those that believe it, and sickness is real to such as have it, but mind and not the body is responsible for it all. Pain and pleasure are mind, not matter; the body has no sensation of its own. Discord is unreal, harmony is real; admitting the same reality to discord we do to harmony, one has as high a claim on confidence and obedience

Chapter VII. Physiology.

as the other. If evil is as real as good, error is as real and immortal as Truth. What we name diseased action is discord, but harmony is the reality of being; hence the former is a belief only, and not the Truth of being; if death is as real as Life, immortality is a myth, and if pain is as real as the absence of pain, it will be immortal, and harmony is not the order of being. Personal sense discords, and is therefore a belief only; matter has no sensation; the action proceeding from Soul is harmonious and eternal.

In Mohammedan belief, a pilgrimage to Mecca was salutary to save man's Soul, and in still another belief, inanimate matter is able to save man; one is paganism, the other materia medica. Disease germinates in unconscious mind, until it reaches what is termed conscious matter, or the body, named personal sense, but there is no conscious matter; therefore disease is mind still, named matter; thus the belief of sickness is developed as a germ, rising above its soil, and we have a crop abundant or scanty, according to the variety and strength of soil, the mind full of materia medica, laws of health, physiology, etc. The diagnosis of disease helps more than most things to cultivate the seeds of disease, causing them to take deeper root in the patient's mind, 9.nd to spring up, bearing fruit "after its own kind." Doctors deport themselves, generally, as if there was no law of mind; at least, they regard not this law, or they would sooner administer poison in matter than mind. They fight disease with matter and admit it with mind, and this makes it a certain thing. They propagate it mentally, and then consider a thing of mind should be dosed with matter; but after all, 'tis faith in drugs, etc., that cures, mind is their remedy at last.

Faith is all that ever made a drug remedy the ailments of a man. Mortal mind is belief, the immortal is understanding, the latter is Spirit, the former personal sense; we must learn to bold immortal and mortal mind or belief separate. The cause and cure of disease is solely mental, and to understand this renders mind less productive of disease, and able to destroy it. Matter has neither action nor sensation of its own; mind moves the body, and feels for it. We

Chapter VII. Physiology.

cannot retain the old positions diametrically opposite to metaphysical science, and conquer disease with mind. And because physics must eventually yield to metaphysics, it will keep the old schools fighting science for the next century. Ignorance, superstition, or avarice will shut the door on health and harmony not obtained through their systems. When there were fewer doctors and less thought bestowed on sanitary subjects there were better constitutions and less disease.

In olden times, who ever heard of a case of dyspepsia; if one had chanced to appear it would have yielded at once to benevolence, or hard work; people had little time then to be selfish, or to think of their bodies, and for sickly after-dinner-talk. The exact amount of labor the stomach could perform was not mapped out in mind by physiology; therefore a man's belief was not a law to his digestive organs. The action of mind on the body was more harmonious before the "tree of knowledge" had taken deeper root in man's belief. The primitive privilege was to take no thought about the bowels, or gastric juices, letting these act in obedience to Truth, instead of error. A ghastly array of diseases was not constantly kept before the mind by works on physiology, hygiene and materia medica; hence the greater longevity and more harmony of man. Before these got the floor, dyspepsia, consumption, spinal diseases, etc., were not heard of in all the land. The duties of man were thought of, and the naturally undisturbed mechanism of man not interrupted by sorrow, cares, or materia, medica, went on harmoniously. Damp atmospheres, and freezing snows, empurpled the cheeks of our forefathers; but never reached the refinement of inflaming bronchial tubes; they were as ignorant as Adam, before informed by his wife, of bronchial tubes, or troches for bronchitis.

But, alas! the nineteenth century would load with disease the very airs of paradise, and hunt mankind down with airs in dress and airs of heaven. Metaphysics hold mind the only friend or foe to man, and Truth destroying error, the great panacea. It is important to learn the exact belief that has produced disease, if you would destroy it,

Chapter VII. Physiology.

unless your spirituality is equal to this by holding a balance over matter; when you destroy disease in mind it disappears on the body. A surgeon must hit the ulcer with his lance to cure it, unless he is able to destroy it without the sharp point; and you must reach the mind by argument, unless the Spirit reaches it without speech. A strongly material, bigoted, or opinionated man yields more slowly to scientific treatment than the more liberal and logical mind, but the spiritual is more easily affected than either.

Do you say, let an M.D. attend to the real malady, and the metaphysician take up hysteria and imaginary disease? But facts are stubborn things; we have found in healing the sick on the Principle herein stated, severe and acute disease yields more readily than the chronic. This method of healing is far from temporizing with disease, or unsafe in cases difficult and dangerous; ignorance of science and the force of education, are all that would lead to such a conclusion. A physician who understands the science of being is the only one I would venture to conduct a dangerous or difficult case. We had tried all others and failed to recover before learning this "more excellent way." Many great and good men have passed away within the two years we have been writing this work, that might have been saved by the science of which it treats.

An accident once happening to us, would have proved fatal, but for the Truth herein stated, that saved us; hundreds of cases given over by materia medica, and the minor hosts of Esculapius, we have since cured by it. Had we depended on materia medica, or used the means ordinarily employed in such emergencies, or allowed the weight of our former beliefs regarding structural and organic life, or the opinions expressed regarding the fatal nature of our case, to balance the scale of Mind at the time the accident occurred, we should have passed away, or survived only to be a hopeless invalid and cripple. The Principle of science herein explained, saved us, and the triumph we achieved over our body at that time made us stronger in the Truth, and consequently more healthy ever since. A supreme moment, more than ordinary circumstances, tests this science

Chapter VII. Physiology.

insomuch as it proves more clearly than others the superiority of mind over matter, drugs, and material law. Ignorance of the relations of mind to the body, and the superiority of the former over the latter, are all that occasion skepticism regarding mental pathology

A physician said to us, "I know mind affects the body somewhat, and advise my patients to be hopeful and take less medicine, but there are organic diseases that mind cannot affect." To this we replied, it is poor logic that facts contradict; we have many cases on record of cures wrought through mind alone, that materia medica had failed to reach. You admit death has occurred from fright, and this proves every function of the body controlled by mind; death covers the whole ground, it stops the action of brain, heart, blood, lungs, etc., and if all organic action can be stopped by mind, it is controlled by it, and can be cured also. Mind produces what is termed organic disease, as directly as it does hysteria, and cures it as readily; the demonstration we have given of this removes the question beyond cavil. We predicate this science on proof, and have not more evidence of our existence, than we have gained of the utter control mind holds over the entire organization and functions of the body. Through mind alone we have cured organic disease of the lungs, liver, heart, brains, bones, muscles, etc., that defied physiology and materia medica to heal.

But to govern the body harmoniously with mind, you must understand the science of being predicated on mind and not matter. Few will admit that what is termed involuntary organic action is governed alone by mind, or that mind unconsciously controls the body, but man presents this phenomenon every moment, who comprehends not his own being, for this proves ignorance of mind's action on the body. Supposing a dose of poison be administered through mistake, and physician and patient are looking for favorable results when the patient dies, -- did mind produce this? As surely as if it bad been consciously done Mind is ever active, for action signifies mind and the remote and predisposing thought furnishes a link to the present, although what we term personal sense knows this

Chapter VII. Physiology.

not. Accordingly, the thought that has risen above the verge of unconscious mind is the only one recognized, but it has acted before, and effects have followed this action all the same as when the thought became conscious. The mortal body, of matter, is but a grosser strata of mortal mind.

When darkness is over the earth, personal sense cannot say where the sun is, or that there is a sun; our antipodes must tell us this, or we must learn it of science. Thus it is with mind; the very reverse of what we are thinking at present, is often the remote cause or belief that has produced the inharmony of the body, and we must learn this belief of its opposite thought or the effect oil the body, or submit its character and relations to science. We are willing to leave the explanation of light and its effect on the earth, to science, and because sense takes no cognizance, a portion of the twenty-four hours, of the sun, never say it has no effect on the earth, or deny there is a sun, or that the earth borrows light and heat from the run. No more should we deny the effect of mind on the body because the belief that produces this effect is below the mental horizon, not having risen yet to recognition. The valve of the heart, opening and closing for the blood, is not less obedient to mind than our hands, that perform the offices of our will; but because mind embraces one action consciously and not the other, we say the cause is physical and not mental. Stop the action of mortal mind wholly, by what is termed death, and every function of the body mortal ceases; proving organic action produced by mind and not matter. Brains are totally ignorant of thoughts; matter has no consciousness of its own, and its propelling power is mind; all mechanism is controlled by mind.

Personal sense is a supposition that matter is conscious, that brains are competent to say how much mind a man has; that heart, lungs, stomach, etc., are capable of determining his harmony and continuance. Soul is not heard in all this; the immortality of man is silenced with utterances of mortality, Intelligence mute before non-Intelligence. This personal sense is the source of sickness, sin and death; but there is no personal sense; matter has no Intelligence, and

Chapter VII. Physiology.

Soul is incapable of error. Life goes on scientifically in Soul, undisturbed in its harmony, but personal sense has no recognition of Soul or Truth. All discord is error, belief; the Truth of being is harmony and understanding. Destroy the belief or error, and the discord disappears.

The metaphysician understanding this, in case of decaying lungs, destroys in the mind of his patient this belief and the Truth of being and immortality of man assert themselves over the error and belief of decomposition, and the lungs become sound and regain their original proportions.

Physiology has never explained Soul, and had better not undertaken to explain body. Truth has no beginning, and therefore no end. Life was, and is, and ever will be, for Life is God, and its idea was, and is, and ever will be, and this idea is man, that Spirit has made, and matter cannot unmake. Our body is as dead that ,we call living as ever it will be, and when dead, as much alive as it ever was. Life is Spirit, not matter, and if you understand the law of Spirit you understand bow to make the body immortal. Physiology is like the drugs we say make man suffer because he took too little of them; it causes sickness, and then to cure it we double the dose. "Take no thought about the body what ye shall eat or what drink or wherewithal it shall be clothed, and the body, or matter, will give you no intimation of its own wants, for it has no requirements of its own. Happiness or misery belongs to mind and not body; sensation is mind and not matter, and mesmerism proves this when belief is seen to determine sensation.

Every new method of obtaining health has its advocates, and when you get the consent of mind to this method as preferable to others, the body will demand it and be benefited by it so long as this belief lasts. You can educate a healthy horse to take cold without his blanket, but the wild animal left to his instincts, snuffs the wind with delight. Epizootic is an educated finery that a natural horse has not. The principle of being reveals the immortality of man, on the basis

Chapter VII. Physiology.

of Spirit; but personal sense defines him as matter, hence the mortality of this man.

We have discerned some diseases approaching, weeks before they made their appearance on the body, and because they were latent things of mind before they appeared as matter, that grosser strata of mind, and never in a single instance, were mistaken in results. Again, during an aggravation of symptoms that occur in the changes, or chemicalizations that sometimes alarm the patient, we have seen the mental signs that assured us the danger was over, and said to the patient, you are healed, sometimes to his discomfiture, when he was incredulous of the fact, but it always proved as we foretold. We name this merely to explain the mental, instead of physical origin of disease, therefore, that rules of health, taking strong hold of the belief of the patient, beget and foster disease, by keeping mind on this subject, fearing and trying to avoid sickness. The faith reposed in drugs had better remain in one's self; understanding the control mind holds over the body, we should have no faith in matter. Science reveals the origin of disease wholly mental and not physical, also that it is cured through mind and not matter. However much we trust the drug, or medium through which this faith is exercised, it is the faith and not the medium that heals the sick. The spirituality that enables us to read the minds of patients, enables us to heal them also, for the action of Spirit on matter is to restore the harmonious relations of mind and body.

Healing the sick through mind instead of matter, enables us to heal the absent as well as the present. The spiritual capacity to apprehend thought, is reached only when man is found not having on his own righteousness, which is the law, but the righteousness which is of God. Science fits us to read the mind of the sick, and heal them through mind; for having learned man is governed by Spirit that understands all things, we know Spirit is that to which all things are possible. The approaches to this great affluence of Truth that heals the sick, are made through the footsteps of our Master. Christianity alone is its basis, and physiology, that pins our trust to

Chapter VII. Physiology.

matter instead of God, its very opposite. Ignorant of the footsteps and foundation of this science, the world may call it mesmerism, trance, mediumship, electricity, etc., but not one of these in the least express it, and whoever reaches the science of being in the high sense of its sudden cures, learns it is by taking up the cross and following Christ. We are scientific only as we let go material things, drugs, manipulations, etc., for the spiritual, and leave all for Christ, trusting only Truth to heal the sick. Our beliefs are not spiritual, they are from the hearing of the ear, from personal sight and sense.

Spirit never believes in God because it understands Him. Power is a belief of matter, a blind force, the offspring of will and not Wisdom, of the mortal, and not the immortal mind, -- yea, of error, and not Truth. The headlong cataract, the devouring flames, the tempest's breath, the lightning and storm, together with all that is selfish, dishonest, and impure, represent power. Might belongs to Spirit, the very "winds are in His fists;" and, controlled by Spirit and not matter, they are harmonious. Error is the prototype of will; and willing the sick to recover, or man to do this or that, infringes on his rights; it is mesmerism capable of all evil, instead of the science of being. Christ, Truth, stills the tempest and is the "peace be still" to destructiveness or disease.

To personal sense opposites affinitize; but not so in science, the mind of Soul, where Truth never mingles with error or the So-called mind of the body, and therefore is able to cast it out. Spirit is Intelligence; matter is not; there is a mind of Soul, but not of body, of God, but not man. The mind of Soul is the aroma of being, the atmosphere of Intelligence thrown off by Spirit; but the so-called mind of man is the belief that a pulpy substance under the skull contains mind, yea, that matter is Intelligent, and this belief is false, the mocker of Intelligence, even error calling itself Truth. This is the scientific statement of mortal man, but man is immortal, therefore this is not man, but a belief anatomized metaphysically. To classify Spirit and matter thus, that Spirit is distinct from matter but must pass through it to be identified, is a mistake. The limitless would

Chapter VII. Physiology.

destroy limits if it entered them, and Spirit cannot be limited. It is a dream and illusion that Soul is in body and matter the medium of Spirit. We are not aware it is a dream, the terrible nightmare, that makes suffering or enjoyment just as the dream chances to run. We would prefer the suffering that makes one willing to be aroused from this dream, to the pleasure that tends to hold it.

We frequently heal the sick who are absent from us, without the least consciousness of it on their part, except from their recovery. Now reverse the case, and mathematically you prove that if mind eschewing laws of health, dietics, physiology, etc., restores the sick, an opposite mind crammed with physiology, etc., might make them sick. This proof we gain of our body, for such mind causes us what are termed the physical sufferings that matter is powerless to do and could not produce. Whenever we have taken charge of a practice to establish a student, it was not necessary for us to see the patients to heal them; we could do this without seeing them; if the student was not advanced spiritually, we failed to benefit the sick so much in connection with him. Mind acts mesmerically or scientifically; it is will in mesmerism, and Truth in Science, that heals the sick. I can have no effect on the sick through manipulation, and cannot affect them mesmerically. Cases of healing the sick without seeing them, we record as proof of our statement. Mrs. Sarah Crosby, of Albion, Maine, sent for our aid, in case of an injury to her eye. At the time of writing she was hundreds of miles away, but after receiving her first letter, as soon as the mail could bring it, we received another from her, of which the following is an extract: --

"Since the accident to my eye, it has been so exceedingly sensitive to the light, I have shaded it, unable to do any writing or sewing of any note. The Sunday I mailed you a letter I suffered a great deal with it; Monday it was painful until towards night, when it felt better; Tuesday it was well, and I have not worn my shade over it since a week ago Monday, and I have read, sewed, and written, and still all is well. Now you may form your own conclusions. I told a friend the other day you had cured my eye, or perhaps my fear of

Chapter VII. Physiology.

my eye, and it is so; though I am sure, for the life of me, I cannot understand a word of what you tell me about the possibility of a spirit like mine having power over a hundred and seventy pounds of live flesh and blood to keep it in perfect trim."

The following is a case of heart disease described in a letter from a lady at New York.

"Please find enclosed a check for five hundred dollars in reward for your services, that can never be repaid. The day you received my husband's letter I became conscious, for the first time for forty-eight hours; my servant brought my wrapper and I rose from bed and sat up. The attack of the heart had lasted two days, and no one thinks I could have survived but for the mysterious help I received from you. The enlargement of my left side is all gone, and the M. D.'s pronounce me entirely rid of heart disease. I have been afflicted with it from infancy, until it became organic enlargement of the heart and dropsy of the chest. I was only waiting, and almost longing, to die; but you have healed me; and yet how wonderful to think of it, when we have never seen each other! We return to Europe next week. I feel perfectly well. L. M. ARMSTRONG."

Mr. R. O. Badgeley, of Ohio, wrote: "My painful and swelled foot was restored at once on your receipt of my letter, and that very day, I put on my boot and walked several miles." He had previously written me, "A stick of timber has fallen from a building on the top of my foot, crushing the bones somewhat."

A lady at Louisiana wrote: "Your wonderful science is proved to me. I was a helpless sufferer six long years, confined to my bed, unable to sit up one hour in the long, long twenty- four. All I know of my cure is this; the day you received my letter I felt a change pass over me, I sat up the whole afternoon, went to the table with my family at supper, and have been growing better every day since; I call myself well. JENNY R. COFFIN."

Chapter VII. Physiology.

The following is from a lady in Lynn: "My little son, one year and a half old, was a great sufferer from disease of the bowels, until he was reduced to almost a skeleton, and growing worse constantly; could take nothing but gruel, or some very simple nutriment. At that time the physicians had given him up, saying they could do no more for him, but you came in one morning, took him up from the cradle in your arms, kissed him, laid him down again and went out, In less than an hour he called for his playthings, got up and appeared quite well. All his symptoms changed at once. For months previously nothing but blood and mucous had passed his bowels, but that very day the evacuation was natural, and he has not suffered since from his complaint, and it is more than two years since he was cured. Immediately after you saw him, he ate all he wanted, and one thing was a quantity of cabbage just before going to bed, from which he never suffered in the least. L. C. EDGECOMB, Lynn, Mass."

We were called to Mr. Clark, in Lynn, with hip disease, saw him in the afternoon for the first time; his physicians had probed the ulcer that day, and informed us the bone was carious; the patient had not been up nor turned on his couch for months. On entering the house we were told he was dying; his wife stood over him weeping. We stood at his bedside a moment; he sank to sleep; woke presently, saying, "I feel like a new man, my suffering is all gone." In a few hours he rose from his bed, dressed himself, and that afternoon took supper with his family. The next day we saw him in the yard, and have not seen him since, but are informed lie went to work in two weeks, and is now well. Hundreds of similar cures might be named, that we wrought contrary to what are termed laws of nature regulating disease and recovery, but prefer you should learn the Principle of these cures and be able to do your own work. Experience also has taught us the greater the moral or spiritual distance between us and an individual, the more they persecute us; as with individuals so with the general thought, those cures remote from the comprehension of the age, have only afforded our enemies new opportunity for detraction.

Chapter VII. Physiology.

Theories admit the limbs are matter and moved by mind, but the fact is, all is mind of different admissions and constructions. Mind increases or retards action, causing sickness or health; but this is not because of physical action, for it is effect and not cause. You say man cannot exist with a headless trunk, or consumed lungs; but man was never for a moment despoiled of his fair proportions; it is matter you are talking of, and not man. Nerves have neither consciousness nor sensation; the body has no life; Spirit is the only Life and Principle of man; but never for a moment enters matter, or is destitute of its idea or man. Hearing is not because of the ear or its mechanism; if the construction of the ear or auditory nerve is destroyed, man is not deaf. Intelligence is left, and hears, sees, etc., independent of matter or organization. The error or belief of Life in matter should give place to this understanding of Spirit's indestructible faculties, that cannot be lost, because they exist without the necessities of matter; otherwise, they were mortal.

Again, a change of belief changes all the reports of personal sense, and man sees, hears, etc., independent of the organs that you say determine the existence of these faculties. If the mesmerized subject whom you call man, accepts the belief that he sees, with closed eyes, or from the top of his head, or hears without sound, such will be the case. To him sight is not confined necessarily to organization, and is only what his belief says of a thing. Change his belief of cold and heat, pleasure or pain, and cold is to him heat, and pleasure pain, and *vice versa*. Here you perceive nerves bear a changed report with a change of belief; therefore personal sense is not a standard, nor is sensation dependent on organization; it is not matter, but mind that determines sensation. Science reveals to spiritual understanding the body without sensation, and man the reflex shadow of Soul, and Soul embracing all the faculties of being, having no lack of emotion, speech, sight, or sound; and possessing the consciousness of all things, its blessings are not at the disposal of organization, that accident or disease can destroy. All being is spiritual and not material, for this is the scientific statement of being, the basis of immortality, and we shall all ultimately learn this. Nor

Chapter VII. Physiology.

can we begin to understand Life a day too soon. Every theory opposed to this prolongs sickness, sin and death, making that which is immortal in understanding, mortal in belief. When the belief of Life and Intelligence in matter disappears, its physical manifestation will cease, and mortal man return to dust, and why? because be was simply a belief, and this belief an error, instead of the reality of being; for man is not matter, and never dies. To prove the body called mortal man error and not Truth, we have only to find it mortal. The belief of Life and Intelligence in matter is destroyed; but Life and man, still are, and ever will be.

Matter is not the medium through which Spirit acts, or is manifested. Spirit is never individualized, and there is no medium for it. Spirit is infinite, because it is Intelligence, what then can limit it? Again, to Spirit Intelligence alone is Substance, and there is no matter. If the body was intelligent, it could never return to dust, for mind dies not, and Intelligence never developed from matter.

Physiology makes man both Spirit and matter; and this error would make man mortal. If brains are mind matter is mind; and a stone, a lesser degree of man. To admit Spirit is not in matter, and then say it is manifested through it, contradicts facts, for matter manifests mortality only, and Spirit is immortal; not a glimpse or manifestation of Spirit is obtained through the erring or decaying. Spirit is positive to all things, and if it passed through matter it would destroy it, or become negative to it. Metaphysical science, dry and abstract though it appears, should not be overlooked for the transient and mortal sense of things; health, harmony and immortality are gained through spirituality only; and this will be understood sooner or later. Truth has but, one department for its students, and but one branch of education, viz., the science of being. Studying into the nature of matter, that embraces sin, sickness and death, hath no real advantage; and matter-laws of health lay the foundation of sickness. Knowledge embraces neither Life nor Truth; but when we define the material with the spiritual, and look from nature up to nature's God, learning is profitable. Prof. Rudolph's

Chapter VII. Physiology.

astronomical explanations are of this sort. The researches and experiences of our great minds are of the utmost importance, when given thus.

Astronomy, Natural History, Chemistry, Music, Mathematics, etc., as ideas of a Principle, are nine-stones in the pathway of science; but when we attempt to put Principle into these ideas, we give them the interpretations of personal sense, that mislead our conclusions. Let spiritual sense give the last, because the highest explanation of all things, and "the last shall become first, and will be final." If material man was really man, when this body is destroyed man would be annihilated; identifying man through matter you have no authority for saying, he lives after that is destroyed. Education is all that develops sense, but it cannot develop Soul; Casper Hauser, without this education, manifested less Intelligence than a mouse, was unable to feed himself, even knew less than the lower species, guided by instinct. The infant boy, incarcerated in a dungeon where neither sight nor sound could reach him, at the age of an adult, was not a man, -- showing years make not men -- he was an infant still and a belief of Life in matter, that proved itself neither Intelligence nor the idea of God, but in reality nonentity. Thus mortal man for whom laws of health are conjured up from the abyss of condemned "knowledge," is just this material nothingness, "dust to dust;" therefore, what availeth it to plant him deeper in matter-belief, whence he sprang and was accursed.

The least thought or said of physical structure, laws of health, etc., the higher will become manhood and woman-hood, the fewer diseases appear, and less harm be derived from change of climate, unwholesome diet, laying aside flannels, severe mental labor, sedentary habits, heated rooms, and all the *et cetera* of physiological rules based on man as a structural thing, whose life is at the mercy of circumstance. The scriptural warning against "knowledge " ought to be heeded, but it is not; the stronger constitutions of our forefathers compared with this age, should furnish a hint, but they do not; the difficulty lies in our nameless theories; sin, sickness, and

Chapter VII. Physiology.

death, all over the land, are the fruits of the belief of Life and Intelligence in matter.

The simple food our forefathers ate would not cure dyspepsia to-day; with rules of health in the head and the most digestible food in the stomach, there would be dyspeptics; the effeminate constitutions of this period will never grow robust until the science of being takes the place of materia medica, physiology, etc. The ignorance of our forefathers of the knowledge that to-day walks to and fro in the earth, made them more hardy than our physiologists, and more honest than our politicians. We by no means deprecate learning, deep research, original thought, history, observation, invention, science and understanding; it is the scheming barbarisms of learning, the mere doctrine, theory, or nauseous fiction, we deplore. Novels, remarkable only for exaggerated pictures of depravity, works on materia medica, hygiene, or laws of health, remind you of Aesop's mountain in labor with a mouse; introduce but a scandal and humbug and you please society. What I wish to know is, if this taste be not a fault of our systems of thinking and writing. All is mechanical; nature is suffocated; the core of mankind is not reached, and its coverings thickly inlaid with foreign devices. Let us be individually what we are; not swallowing camels for popularity, or mincing at gnats in the shape of honest ideas, because they come from the Soul of man. If knowledge is power, it is not Wisdom, but blind force, whose material origin is made known by losing in time, what it gains in power.

To eschew error would usher in a new era, pulling down the bars of sects, and the conventionalities of knowledge, would build up spiritual foundations, whereby we take God into our experiences, and become healthy and harmonious, noble men and women, instead of despairing invalids and matter-automata. The less we have of personal sense, the more we have of Soul; and the fewer laws material, the more longevity and spiritual understanding. Learning all was vanity "in the flesh," made Solomon a wise man, that before had been the fool of sense.

Chapter VII. Physiology.

Ancient theories separated a personal Satan from man by horns and hoofs; modern opinions compromise; eschewing his satanic majesty in such proportions, they retain a sinful and mortal man, the opposite of God's idea, at war with his Maker, and swaying his own destinies in defiance of Him, yet supposed to have God dwelling in him! Whatever is sinful, sick, or dying, is not man, but that which Paul described "without hope, and without God in the world," and the psalmist said, was "a sleep, and dream that is told." "He that dwelleth in the secret place of the Most High shall abide under the shadow of the Almighty." Relinquishing the belief of Intelligent matter, man abides in Spirit and is harmonious; but this is a most high, and most secret place to personal sense, that knows nothing about it.

When the relation between Soul and body, and God and man is understood in science, we shall become harmonious mind and body, and never until then.

If Life is affected in the least by exercise, food, clothing, etc., God is discordant, the harmony of Spirit beclouded, and Life at length put out. Physiology and materia medica, direct us not, as David did, to God, "a present help in time of trouble," but change the tones of Life to a minor key that flattens into discord, while the science of Life that sharpens its sweet tones and conscious harmony into immortality, asks in vain for a hearing. That "old things shall paw away and behold, all things shall become new," I for one, anticipate with joy, willing, if need be, that Truth shall cut off right hands and pluck out right eyes, in amputating error. We perceive the "irresistible conflict" that awaits the ages when Truth shall overturn the beliefs of man.

Let the science of Life be taught in our institutions of learning and taken up by pulpit and press; give it but the place of physiology and it would eradicate sickness, sin and death, in less time than these have been increasing on the old systems and stereotyped plans to beat them. Simply to understand the nothingness of error, saves a

Chapter VII. Physiology.

Don Quixote warfare with windmills, and we gain the immortality and liberty of being, by control over our bodies. Since man "hath sought out many inventions," he has not learned that knowledge can save him from the dire effects of knowledge. Many a hopeless case of disease has been induced by a single post-mortem examination, not because of virus taken into the system, (one condition of blood is as harmless as another if mind says so, but not otherwise,) it is some fatal belief that is admitted, that does the harm. Mind alone affects the secretions of the body, gives action, and increases or diminishes it; a simple blush or fright tells us this. When the unconscious mental conception of disease takes place, its symptoms and locality appear on the body the same as in optics, when the image is formed on the retina that becomes visible to personal sense. The error of talking over sickness and peering into the symptoms of disease to conjure up from the dark depths of discord some new discovery, is little understood. When a physician names an ailment, describing its Symptoms and their danger, he has committed an unconscious offence against being, against his patient's happiness and liberty, and will make a sure job for himself, if not a fatal one for his patient.

A lady was etherized and died while under its effects, her physicians affirming it was not safe to perform the surgical operation without ether. The case was brought to trial, the evidence found conclusive, and the verdict returned that death was occasioned, not by the ether, but her fear of taking it. Her sister testified the deceased protested against inhaling the vapor, saying it would kill her, but after this, was compelled by her physicians to inhale it. Had those surgeons understood the action of mind on the body, they would have allayed her terror before administering the ether, or much sooner have risked a severe surgical operation than the effects of fear. Such ignorance, yea, cruelty, should arouse the community; diplomas give no more claim to a dupe or a victim, than the assassin's steel. Inert matter taken wholly into account, and mind disregarded! when the sequel proved the patient died of mind instead of matter.

Chapter VII. Physiology.

Books that would rule disease out of the mind instead of impressing it more strongly on the belief, would abate sickness ten per cent. in a short period. Instruct your patient that he is not an involuntary subject of disease, but can resist it, and overcome it too, with mind that is superior to matter. To understand their God-given dominion over the body, would reassure and encourage the sick and impart healthy action to the body. Knowing their mental power, they would meet sickness as fearlessly as we encounter a swarm of insects that flee before us.

Science and personal sense are antagonists, bearing very different reports of man, but demonstration proves science right and personal sense wrong, and that mind instead of matter controls matter. Doctors examine the body to ascertain the exact power matter is bringing to bear on man to kill him, and render judgment accordingly. Giving all precedence to discord, they poison the minds of patients with the belief they have no defense, mentally, over their bodies, when the fact is, mind produces all action, whether it be sickness or health. Reverse the case, and when the symptoms of disease appear administer to the mind and not the body; teach the patient that pain, swelling, ulceration, morbid or acute action, etc., appear on the body only because they are mapped out in mind, for the latter transfers its images to the body. Ask the patient what he thinks of the ailment; and what his mind admits on the subject is what you must destroy in order to relieve the obedient body of discord. Go to the fountain head to heal your patient.

But what a task! say you, to teach the present age mind's control over the body. Admitting it changes the stand-point of old theories, turning them upside down, and the sick may not understand your sayings at first, still they will produce an effect on their minds, and this will affect their bodies. This is the science of being, that Truth, brought to bear on error, begins to destroy it. You will heal the sick with Truth despite the odds against you, and inaugurate a perception of science that will be for "the healing of the nation." You may be quite sure that not understanding your metaphysical process of

Chapter VII. Physiology.

healing, your patients will have little faith in it until they feel its beneficial effects, showing you their faith is not what heals them. Your demonstration must be the only proof of what you say. The sick are sooner restored by Truth than error, and through mind than matter. The mental cure is higher proof of power, because it is made against fearful odds, even the weight of universal opinion in favor of matter, and the preconceived views of your patient working unconsciously against themselves and the metaphysical cure.

Physiology insists the body is diseased independent of mind, and despite its protest; that its functions are interrupted without the co-operation of mind, and that matter-laws control the body. This error is quite as palpable to us, and will be to others at some future day, as the rejected tenet of theology, that "all are lost who are not elected to be saved."

The body is our servant, obedient not only to mind in one instance, but in every case. The shocking theory that man is governed all his days, and killed at last by his body. is too absurd to last another century. Our press sends forth, unwittingly, many a plague spot an the human family, in treatises on disease, hygiene, and therapeutics; giving names for maladies and long explanations regarding them, affects people like a Parisian name for a new dress; every one that can, will have it. A minutely-described, long-syllabled name for disease has cost a man all his earthly days of usefulness. What a price for knowledge! but not exceeding its original market value, when God said, " In the day thou eatest thereof thou shalt die." A doctor's belief in disease harms his patients more than calomel, morphine, ether, or the forceps; mind is more potent than matter. A patient hears the doctor's verdict like a culprit his death-sentence. He may seem calm under it, and to exercise fortitude worthy a better cause, or an occasion more real, but he is not calm; fear is mastering the case and developing the disease.

Chapter VII. Physiology.

The mind's power to harm the body, reversed in action, would heal it, and the sick would triumph over the disease they resign themselves to suffer on the ground of inevitableness. If mind can kill, as has been proved, it has power to cure also. Ah! patient, or impatient sufferer, may your eyes be opened to behold your way of escape from sickness; to this end we have pledged our endeavors, and labored since God raised us up from hopeless disease and unspeakable sufferings. The doctor is the artist that delineates in mind most distinctly the image of disease, and causes belief to fill up his outlines on the body. Possibly discus had appeared before you saw your doctor, but it could not be so positive or defined as afterward; you must have felt the influence of his mind, his belief in disease affected yours, even if be said nothing, and but for this it might have gradually left your mind and you would have recovered.

We would not deny to physicians, as noble men and women, great philanthropy of purpose; we only urge them to make their endeavors more effectual by changing their basis of action from body to mind, and from personal sense to science. If the science of being was familiar to them as the edicts of the schools, blessings numberless would flow from such high sources. In every case of disease, or of health, to heal the one or preserve the other, the science of Life is all that is necessary. But the various methods of healing have not been science, else disease would have disappeared ere this remote period since Adam, error, first introduced it. The so-called laws of health are not science, for the latter delivers man from their penalty and destroys the law, establishing a higher law, even the superiority of Soul over sense, and of Spirit over matter. It annuls the oppressive bondage that our theories enforce on man. The law of God is opposed to laws of matter, and entitled to more obedience and respect. His law is Intelligence, that recognizes no higher law, and if this be not apparent to more than myself. why appeal to God to restore the sick, when the so-called laws of health are of no avail. God should control man at all times, and under all circumstances; and controlled thus, he is harmonious and immortal. Sickness, sin, or death will never trouble man, or the body

Chapter VII. Physiology.

controlled by Soul and not sense, Spirit and not matter. If the law of Truth, Life and Love, produced sickness, no law of matter could destroy it, and it were morally wrong to employ means acting against this government; the law of God is the only admissible authority in the universe, but this law pertains to mind and not matter. What, then, is left to physiology but crossbones and skulls? Man will never be learned in harmony and immortality until the error of physiology is destroyed by Spirit triumphing over matter.

Because the muscles of a blacksmith's arm are strongly developed, it does not follow that exercise did this, or that he whose habits are sedentary must be fragile. If matter was the cause of action, and muscles without mind used the anvil and smote the nail, such an inference might be true; but muscles act in obedience to man, hence the fact that mind and not matter enlarges and strengthens them only through the demand man makes on them, and the corresponding power he supplies, and not because of exercise or muscles, but the blacksmith is the strength of his arm.

Man moves his own body and develops it in whatever direction mind determines; whether consciously or unconsciously, it matters not. The feats of the gymnast are proofs that the latent powers of man are unknown to him; mind fixing on some achievement, makes its accomplishment easy. Had Blondin believed he could not walk a rope over Niagara's abyss of waters, to accomplish that feat would have been impossible; but, understanding it could be done, be lost his fear and gave his muscles flexibility and power that was attributed, perhaps, to a lubricating oil. When Homer sang of Grecian gods, how dark was Olympus compared with Sinai. David expressed the science of being when he said, "Thou madest man to have dominion over the works of thy hands; thou hast put all things under his feet."

CHAPTER VIII

HEALING THE SICK

NOTE. The learner will derive more benefit from studying this science with its author, than is possible to gain from teachers in other departments of education. The metaphysical requires the elucidations of spiritual sense, and personal sense cannot apprehend the explanations of soul; hence a mere classical education leaves Spirit much out of the question, and educates man only from the personal standpoint of matter.

OBSERVATION and experience teach us, those scorning to swerve from a direct line of duty, or vainly to stoop to personal aggrandizement at the sacrifice of conscience, and make popularity paramount to Truth, are traduced by many whom that line of duty touches. In warfare with error, you attack with intent to kill, and the wounded or cornered beast bites you if he can; the sin you assail turns on you and succeeds in getting the world to condemn you, that it may justify itself. It being found necessary to uncover sin to destroy it, you must tell a sinner what his sins are before you can do him good, and if he hates you for it, it is because he is unwilling to reform. Those we attempt to raise give us their whole weight to lift, and when we let go to have them take hold, sometimes fall back on us. Teaching the bigoted, reforming the licentious, or exposing the hypocrite, who shall escape without censure? We commenced our labors in the simple faith that all whom we healed would acknowledge it, and those we taught would live up to our teachings if from no higher motive than to promote their success in healing; but this has not always been the case. Although it is plain the foundations of the science of being are Truth and spirituality, and the seed that brings forth much fruit, must fall into the "good and honest heart," yet all who know this are not willing to yield to it.

Chapter VIII. Healing the Sick.

Truth stirs man to a better, or, temporarily, to a worse condition that afterwards leaves him better; it affects error the same as it does sickness, causing it to intermit before it yields and is destroyed.

The humanitarian is above the arrows in the quiver of ignorance, envy, or malice; they fly beneath his feet, until spent of their fury, they fall to the ground. Such as are identified with a cause, until that cause is understood, are not understood; in its birth they have travail and sorrow; in its infancy, toil and sacrifice; but clasp their nursling more tenderly when menaced, knowing when he is a man he will speak for himself and mother.

Nothing but a lack of spiritual discernment, or dishonesty, could prompt one who in the least comprehends this science, to call it mesmerism, or to practice mesmerism and call it science. When those bidden of old to the feast of Truth came not, our Master accepted such as did come. In like manner, to-day "the servant must be as his Lord," exercising no choice of his own, but laboring for posterity, bearing all blame and scorn, and counting his victory in the far-off years. Healing in science has its reward even here, but the task of teaching the science of being is quite another thing. Pains of personal sense often make the sick willing to part with its errors, but those in health and at ease in their possessions are reluctant to change masters, hence the more thankless and toilsome task of teaching, compared with healing. We instruct students to recommend their patients to avoid, as much as possible, contact with minds filled with opposite physics, hygiene, etc., while under treatment of metaphysics, for it retards their recovery; but they forget the same right belongs to a teacher, and the same necessity exists for students to avoid contact with certain minds that hinder their advancement. Institutions have their by-laws to restrain the evil passions of those under their care, but we have had no such necessary protection in teaching.

Not to admit God the Principle of the science of Life, is to be ignorant of this science; and to say God is its Principle, and the

Chapter VIII. Healing the Sick.

discoverer, teacher, and demonstrator of the science is not taught of God, is contradictory.

Students may dwarf, or destroy for the present, their position in scientific healing through error, with falsehood, dishonesty, or sensuality; in which case their demonstration advances no higher, and their practice, if they have one, become mesmerism and no longer science. Such students can never reinstate themselves aright except through repentance, reformation and restitution. We should welcome back the penitent and support the weak, but to him that covereth his sins and rejoices in his iniquity let the reward of his hands be given; an accumulated debt more to be feared than his creditor's account. The wickedest or the best man is not understood by the age in which he lives; both are beyond its appreciation. The wickedest man commits his sins knowingly and in secret, having not grown sufficiently to be punished by Wisdom, he hides his evil in the manner we shall name; and the best man is hidden from the present age in the Wisdom of future ages. When separating tares from the wheat the mills of God grind slowly, and if the tares that Wisdom casts away, predominate we see little results, but if there be much wheat, stores are garnered because of the grinding. "Whomsoever He loveth, him he also chasteneth."

There is but one possible way of doing wrong with a mental method of healing, and this is mesmerism, whereby the minds of the sick may be controlled with error instead of Truth. Whoever has witnessed the effects of mesmerism, has seen it make a joint stiff or a limb lame, proving beyond a doubt it can affect the body injuriously. Whispering into the minds of the sick falsehoods, will do their bodies harm if Truth poured into their minds does the body good. We have witnessed the proof of both these statements. For years we had tested the benefits of Truth on the body, and knew no opposite chance for doing evil through a mental method of healing until we saw it traduced by an erring student and made the medium of error. Introducing falsehoods into the minds of the patients prevented their recovery, and the sins of the doctor was visited on

Chapter VIII. Healing the Sick.

the patients, many of whom died because of this; cases that the Truth of being would have healed, his own error rendered hopeless. Witnessing these terrible results was our occasion for learning their cause, or discovering this mal-practice, and our students are well aware we have no difficulty in tracing the mental cause of disease. But before we discovered this mal-practice and its motives, the evil bad reached so far, and held such sway over the patient's minds, when we informed one she was not recovering and had better return home, she answered with indignation, "My doctor says I am recovering," but died before she reached her earthly home. Wholly unconscious of his secret method of turning the minds of those he manipulated, against his benefactor, or of its effects on their bodies, the patients asked us if the doctor had lost his power, not understanding it was his loss of Truth, and the hidden evil of his course that injured the patients. A student of science cannot practice mesmerism honestly, therefore successfully, as a Newton, who knows no higher method of healing. But the mal-practice we allude to was more terrible than simply a change to mesmerism; it chose darkness rather than light because its deeds were evil.

Such a practitioner putting aside our moral precepts retains that portion only of our teachings which relates to the patient's belief of disease and the method of destroying this belief by the doctor's opposite, verbal, and mental argument. This is the very least of the science of being, and yet the only part the mal-practitioner can avail himself of to heal the sick. The patients have no recognition of how much error he may also mingle with this argument of Truth that will affect their minds and bodies together, and to bad results as well as good. If the sick recover from the effects of the doctor's mental argument opposed to theirs, it proves, on the ground of science, he has changed their belief with regard to their disease, or the body would not have responded thus; and now comes his opportunity to do evil; for, if be can change their belief relative to sickness, he can also change it with regard to an individual, or upon any subject. But, remember, it is only the manipulator and mal-practitioner that can do this, and not those who heal with the Truth of Science. First,

Chapter VIII. Healing the Sick.

because the latter do not manipulate the head; and secondly, because their source of healing is science and Truth, and if they should attempt to control the mind with error, they would not affect the sick, while the mal-practitioner's principal power is to do evil, and a crumb of science is all he has wherewith to heal; and his want of better success is the result of his wickedness.

We have actually stood in awe at the absolute might of Truth, when witnessing the effect a little has on the sick, and sadly remembered how much could be done by the truly wise, "who put oil in their lamps" and have not the power to abuse the science of being. Since witnessing the evil one student did in the name of science, we have utterly objected to students rubbing the head. The mal-practitioner's sin standeth "in holy places." It is a crime against the highest tribunal of Soul, commending wrong and condemning right, it tramples on every law of justice and Truth.

In defence of mesmerism is urged, that Dr. Quimby manipulated the sick. He never studied this science, but reached his own high standpoint and grew to it through his own, and not another's progress. He was a good man, a law to himself; when we knew him he was growing out of mesmerism; contrasted with a student that falls into it by forsaking the good rules of science for a mal-practice that has the power and opportunity to do evil. Dr. Quimby had passed away years before ever there was a student of this science, and never, to our knowledge, informed any one of his method of healing.

The only practitioners of this metaphysical science to-day, have been our students; but through wrong doing some have dimmed their pure sense of Truth, while others stand firm in "the hope set before them."

We should condemn a physician for adulterating his medicine and then claiming it was genuine. The medicine in scientific healing is mind; and shall dishonesty, revenge, falsehood, or impurity, be

Chapter VIII. Healing the Sick.

the stronger ingredient or quality of his mind, and the practitioner say he heals with Truth, and the science of Life? Worse than poisonous drugs is the mental evil imparted through inoculation of mind. Such a practitioner is the most effectual circulator of error on earth. Even though he may change a belief of sickness to a belief of health, he has not the power to destroy error with Truth.

There are but two methods of healing, one is matter, the other, mind. The scientist heals with Truth; therefore rubbing the head, or manipulating the body is no assistance to impart Truth to heal the sick. To do evil in science is not more possible than in prayer to God. We will consider, briefly, some points of the mal- practice alluded to.

First, as a weapon of revenge. The modus operandi of the mal-practice is as follows: The doctor rubs the heads of his patients, communing with them mentally as he does this, but instead of speaking to them only Truth, and that which promotes harmony, he takes this opportunity to introduce into their minds side-issues, such as suit his sinister purpose, imparting his own likes and dislikes to the patients, either from vengeance or ambition. It the doctor helps the patients through head-rubbing, it is through their belief he does it, and mind is controlled either with Truth or error. And a bad effect can as certainly follow this practice as a good one, but the patients are wholly unconscious of this, or how it is produced. If be has imparted error he certainly will deny it, but if he had not done this we should never have learned what this mal-practice was. Through an erroneous influence on their minds the patients are made, in a day, worse physically, while to him whom they owe this state, even the author of it, all unconsciously they turn to be healed. We have learned this mal-practice is impossible in science, and is mesmerism demoralized. Had it been possible for us to control mind through this subtle, criminal agency, we could not have been tempted to do it, even in self-defence; the temptation, even, could not reach us, and we resorted to our pen to expose this evil that reached, for the first time, our apprehension.

Chapter VIII. Healing the Sick.

Some newspaper articles falsifying the science, calling it mesmerism, etc., but especially intended, as the writer informed us, to injure its author, precipitated our examination of mesmerism in contradistinction to our metaphysical science of healing based on the science of Life. Filled with revenge and evil passions, the mal-practitioner can only depend on manipulation, and rubs the heads of patients years together, fairly incorporating their minds through this process, which claims less respect the more we understand it, and learn its cause. Through the control this gives the practitioner over patients, he readily reaches the mind of the community to injure another or promote himself, but none can track his foul course; the evil is felt but not understood. It can demoralize a community, and the mal-practitioner be undiscovered in his work and claim fidelity in mental healing -- a sacred and solemn trust. Controlled by his will, patients haste to do his bidding, and become involuntary agents of his schemes, while honestly attesting their faith in him and his moral character. Talking one way and acting another, he occupies a position the very opposite of Truth. This is no idle picture of pen or imagination, but a faint portraiture of facts discovered through the victims of this mal-practice; facts that we submit to others for proof. Try it, whoever will, manipulate the head of an individual until you have established a mesmeric connection between you both; then direct her action, or influence her to some conclusion, arguing the case mentally, as you would audibly, and mark the result. You will find, the more honest and confiding the individual, the more she is governed by the mind of the operator. But learn the lessons of the science of Life, and through these go up higher, to the discovery of this great Truth, and do this if you can; it would be as impossible as for light to be darkness.

If you had the power that mesmerism gives to influence minds wrong as well as right, the science herein explained would take it away. To control minds with sinister motives, or in any but a right direction, would destroy your position in science. Influence the minds of others from motives of selfishness, revenge, impurity, or any bad motive, and you would lose your ability to heal in science,

Chapter VIII. Healing the Sick.

and never regain your position until you had suffered sufficiently from this error, to forever destroy it, and not venture again on ground so dangerous. A mal-practitioner can never reach the standard of scientific healing. It would be as impossible as for a camel to go through the eye of a needle.

To prevent the evil of this criminal outlawry growing without let or hindrance, the community should understand it; this error can lift its giant proportions above common modes of doing evil, and hold more arbitrary sway over minds than any other past or present power of sin. The science of healing is incapable of evil, but this opposite practice is as clearly proved capable of great mischief, and even crime; able, while it lays high claims to right, secretly to work out a hidden wrong against humanity, justice and Truth. Malice will sometimes show itself and defeat its own purpose; falsehood, uttered aloud, is met with rebutting testimony; but this method of injuring others by a silent, and subtle impregnation of falsehoods and prejudices in the minds of individuals, to be spoken by them to others, is "Satan let loose," the sin that "standeth in holy places." Law cannot restrain, or punish it as it deserves, and community will be slow to acknowledge the heinous crime, until they learn its power to work iniquity, and note its workings; "more subtle than all other beasts of the field," it coils itself about the sleeper, fastens its fang in innocence, and kills in the dark. We thank Wisdom, that revealed this great error to us before these pages went to press, that the years we have labored to bless our fellow-beings be not wholly lost through this trespass upon the blessing of mental healing.

We knew of no harm that could result from rubbing the head, until we learned it of this mal-practice, and never since have permitted a student, with our consent, to manipulate. We gained the little we understand of the Truth of being through our own experiences and proofs, and learned this opposite error standing face to face with it, through another's mal-practice; shall we deny the ability of the mathematician to say wherein the mistake lies of

Chapter VIII. Healing the Sick.

examples wrought incorrectly, or say to the musician who gives the true tone, you are not able to say what is the discord?

Because we never manipulate the sick, the opportunity to learn any evil possible to head-rubbing was not afforded us until years after our first investigations of science. The doctor that depends on manipulation (and he cannot employ it honestly without such dependence), works from a matter basis, whence come all the evil deeds and inventions of Satan. A cure wrought in science is the spiritual predominating over the material; Truth mastering error; the very opposite of mesmerism and the mal-practice aforesaid. In science mind must rise above matter to admit the fuller effluence of Spirit, God, that heals the sick and casts out error, but manipulation prevents this result. The multitudinous minds a physician has access to, enables him, through this medium to do much good, or much evil, throughout the community. This should be regarded when employing a manipulator of the head, that moulds mind and controls it, though less publicly and suddenly, not less surely than the mesmerist who comes more honestly before the foot-lights with his performance. Through his mesmeric control over minds, the mal-practitioner can hold his patients and practice, whether he heals the sick or not, and he moulds some of them into a belief they are healed, but others he must keep moulding, that is, continue to treat, or they will relapse. There are certain self-evident facts; this is one of them. A student of science, understanding its high requirements, cannot be unfamiliar with the fact that the teacher must have reached it worthily who has grown to its discovery, for this cannot be without pursuing faithfully the straight and narrow path that leads to Truth.

Therefore, to know this and acknowledge it, is honesty and understanding on the part of a student, and not to know it, or acknowledge it, ignorance or dishonesty, and every true student will bear testimony to this statement. Paul said, "Live peaceably with all men inasmuch as in you lies." This is wholesome counsel, and a most desirable thing; but could he Eve peaceably with all men, when

Chapter VIII. Healing the Sick.

"that which is perfect" had come to his understanding, and that which is imperfect was to be done away? Not the learning of a Roman student spared him when he girded on the armor of Truth and rushed to battle with the age. When be "fought the good fight" and kept the faith, he passed from the forum into toil and dishonor, and from a dungeon to a scaffold and a crown.

If virtue forgives vice, it cannot love it; if charity overlooks a multitude of sins, it hath no fellowship with sin; and if honesty endures patiently and long the abuses of dishonesty, it hath the prudence at length to get out of its hands. These are separate qualities of character, that circumstance or duty compelling to meet for a time, must part company through a law of being, and often with a tremendous explosion.

The exhibitor of mesmerism startles you with his power, but you are satisfied to conclude it is ridiculous, and you are not its subject; his experiments, however, are honorable, being open, and illustrative of the influence he has through it over the thoughts and actions of others. But the dishonest mesmerist of which we speak, is the mal-practitioner, who claims to take a place in science, but sinks to a secret assassin in society. So important are the rules of mental scientific healing, that even repeated they do good, but we gather not grapes of thorns, the tone of the individual's mind inculcating them, overshadows them, and if his mind be not in accordance with them, it imparts its own hue to the patient; then who shall say which effect is strongest, the good he says, or the evil behind it that he imparts. If the mal-practitioner says mentally to the patient, as he rubs his head, "be healed!" and she recovers, or is improved morally, influenced in that direction, you say this is a moral and physical gain, and behold the proof that he practices very wisely. But suppose he says to her mentally, as he rubs her head, something wrong to do, or believe, and designates this wrong, directing her thought and action in that channel, and she unconsciously obeys him, feeling this hidden spring to action as readily as the other. What, then, are your conclusions of this practice? that you should be subject to evil

Chapter VIII. Healing the Sick.

because you are sometimes subject to good? Never trust human nature in the dark, if this nature is so dark it covers its footprints.

Manipulating the head, we discovered, establishes between patient and practitioner a mental communication not in the least understood by the patients or the people. Through this medium the doctor holds more direct influence over their minds than the united power of education and public sentiment. Mesmeric power is stronger for evil, than good, in contradistinction to the enlargement of the intellectual, moral, and spiritual being that science imparts to individuals, elevating the capacity to do good, above others.

In proportion to the mal-practitioner's power to govern the minds of his patients from selfish motives, is his ability in science diminished. Whoso doeth evil that good might come, incurs the sentence, "his damnation is just."

Witnessing this abuse of metaphysics, a friend anxiously said to us, "You discovered metaphysical healing, and have also discovered this abuse of it, and the evil done through mesmerism; now why do you not forestall this wrong by controlling the minds of individuals or the community to disbelieve its falsehoods?" To this we replied, "We have neither divine authority, nor the power to control minds for any other than their own benefit, and we are giving the results of our moral, spiritual, and metaphysical researches to the world as fast as possible, but the footsteps of falsehood and error are swift, those of honesty and Truth slow, and strong. The community must understand the science of being to appreciate it, and they must detect the wicked mal-practice to appreciate that; therefore the true verdict is not yet given, and Truth can wait, for it is used to waiting. Will should be impotent except in 'good will to man,' and this involves open action and upright conduct; science is not a blind Samson, shorn of his strength."

The silent argument used in his own behalf, as be manipulates the head, the mal-practitioner would blush to make audibly. Suppose

Chapter VIII. Healing the Sick.

he has a juror for a patient, and establishes the mesmeric connection between them, he can influence more than law or evidence, the verdict of that honest juror. If a bargain is to ratify, or a purpose to accomplish for himself, or his reputation at stake, be looks out for an opportunity to manipulate the bead of some party concerned, and controls their actions or conclusions to suit the occasion and meet his desires. Friendship is not too sacred for his depredations; the friends of many years he separates, covering all recognition of his villainy and raising himself in the esteem of those very individuals to whom he has done irreparable injury.

Our rebuke to a false student elicited his revenge, and through this we discovered the mal-practice we expose. We have seen manipulating the head form a habit more pernicious than opium-eating, in which the treatment must be continued, or the patient go back to a worse condition than the first.

It is more difficult to heal the sick, subject to this mal-practice, than under treatment of drugs; and yet the patients are strangely attached to their doctor. We have started patients at once out of disease on the road to recovery, on whom this mal-practitioner has produced a relapse.

Scientific treatment fills the mind with Truth that heals the sick, but the mal- practitioner impregnates it with error that produces new disease; rubbing the head, he keeps his cases constantly on hand, because of the struggle between the little Truth he brings to bear on the case, and the error he introduces. To have barely sufficient right to make the wrong plausible, is more fatal to science than the unmasked error. No enthusiasm or praise is as zealous or fullsome as this mal-practitioner can elicit, while nothing is more relentless and unyielding than the prejudice he can arouse; but mesmerism governs them both, and enables the doctor to gain his point in sin, but not in science. Surely "the fool hath said in his heart, no God." Manipulating the head, even to a thinness that would reveal the brains, can never heal the sick in science. This mental mal- practice

Chapter VIII. Healing the Sick.

is a shameless waste of time and opportunity, an abuse of ignorance or good nature inconsistent with science, the economy of Soul and the harmony of man. This secret trespasser on human rights manipulates the bead to carry out, on a small scale, a sort of popery that takes away voluntary action instead of encouraging the science of self-control, and sets himself up for a doctor who is a base quack. Far intermeddling with what should be the independent functions of society, the mal-practitioner gets his fee, but the involuntary agents of his schemes get bad pay for their services.

Conservatism or dishonesty, either in the statement or demonstration of science, is clearly impossible; where Principle is concerned there is no secret; explanation and proof are required, and no concessions made to persons or opinions. The relation of Truth to man, improving him physically and morally, we have stated as we discovered it, and submit our statement to proof. Having first convinced ourself through demonstration of the Principle of our discovery and its ability to heal the sick and bring out the harmony of being, we deem it worthy the name of *science*. Healing disease on this basis, we learned beyond a doubt, that mind governs the body and is more potent than matter to heal the sick.

To admit personal sense a source of pleasure is to deny it is a source of pain also, and *vice versa*, for "the same fountain sendeth not forth sweet and bitter waters."

Personal sense embracing both sin and happiness, sickness and health, Life and death, according to the teachings of Jesus, contradicts itself, and therefore destroys its own existence. Jesus cast out error and healed the sick through his God-being, well-knowing that harmony cannot produce discord: hence he denied personal sense, and admitted but one Intelligence, and this, not the author of evil. To suppose evil and good, discord and harmony proceed from the same fountain, is contrary to revelation. The common acceptation of Truth is that whatever produces sin, is error. Then wherefore admit that materia medica, physiology, anatomy, etc., are

Chapter VIII. Healing the Sick.

science when they take the opposite ground that insists on personal sense governing man, whence cometh all discord.

God is not the author of sin; Soul is not the source of sickness, sin and death; rather does it destroy these to make man immortal. The body defined as personal sense, is mortal; and that which is mortal is error. That sin proceeds from personal sense, we know, and this proves the fountain evil, and the streams evil also, therefore Wisdom never produced either; hence, God is not the author of personal sense. We say food sustains the Life of man; and again, that a heavy meal kills him. Here the old theory that opposed Christ, Truth, is reproduced in affirming the same fountain sendeth forth sweet and bitter waters. If the All-wise hath a law demanding food to preserve the Life of man, He hath no law by which food can destroy him. We must take the opposite ground of personal sense in regard to sin, Sickness and death, to fully destroy them; a physical demand is not to be admitted, but destroyed, only the demands of Soul are to be heard; the body cannot speak for itself, being unintelligent.

Is it mind or body that declares undigested food irritates the nervous tissues producing a terrible sense of pain, faintness, oppression, etc., and that your remedy is to expel the food, or digest it? This is mental testimony, and there is none other, 'tis a law of belief, mis-named a law of matter; the body cannot define cause and effect.

A case of extreme suffering from food, came under our observation. The lady had said, but a few moments before we came to her assistance, "I shall die unless the food is expelled," and in ten minutes thereafter was rid of her sufferings, and when questioned in regard to her feelings, replied, "I have no pain now, and would like to eat again." By contending mentally against a physical position you can change it and destroy it through mind, even as you have produced it thus. The sick argue for their own suffering, by admitting its reality; they are ignorant of this fact, however, or that

Chapter VIII. Healing the Sick.

their mental position is what produces the physical, and their friends often strengthen this error and quarrel with you for trying to help them out of it.

Mind, and not matter, embraces 0 suffering; we prove this when removing the suffering on this basis, or through mind. Our Principle heals the sick, therefore it produces a better physical effect than the opposite views that make sickness; then why not adopt it, or judge of it by our Master's rule, the "fruits." If you understood the science of being, your body would be harmonious and immortal. The balance adjusted by science falls on the side of happiness and Life.

Delirium tremens embraces error of two sorts; the plea of personal sense for strong drink, and the belief that it diseases the brain. Both these mental positions are mastered with metaphysical science; first, because there is no pleasure in intoxication, or produced by matter, and secondly, that matter, or the brain, is not inflamed. The belief of pain is more easily eradicated than an appetite, or belief of pleasure, owing to the strong desire the patient has to be rid of one, and his reluctance to pad with the other; both of which we the self-inflicted positions of mind, and not matter. Disputing the grounds of personal sense, that alcoholic drinks intoxicate the brain, giving pleasure or pain to matter, and rising above this error, Soul, versus sense, gets the case and relieves the patient. But the severer task is to destroy the belief of the inebriate with regard to the so-called pleasure of sense in drunkenness, while this is all that will reform him. Destroy the belief that pleasure is derived from intoxicating drink, and the habit yields at once, but until this is done, it intermits and lingers, proving intoxication a mental, and not a physical error. Here are two points we desire you to note; first, the moral advantage this healing has over other methods, and the falsity of the arguments of personal sense, assuming drunkenness enjoyment. This admission, however, is not more false than to conclude a liquid distilled from matter is capable of destroying body and brain.

Chapter VIII. Healing the Sick.

The belief that pain and pleasure, good and evil, God and devil, fraternize, is a hoary mistake meeting us at every point. Pleasure or pain in matter is a self- evident falsehood. Lifting yourself, somewhat, to the understanding of the Life that is Wisdom, Love, and Truth, you will break the spell of personal sense. The Truth of being, coming to their consciousness, opens the prison doom to the sick and affects the body as nothing else can. One mind, partly rid of the errors of personal sense, touches another with the science of being that reproduces harmony, causing what we term a chemical change in the body that goes on to form a new basis of being; even as when an acid and alkali meet that form a neutral salt. But remember, the opposites that destroy each other are without spiritual affinity. To admit the positions of personal sense, would never destroy them. To reform the drunkard, or heal the sick, or turn the sinner from his way, we must argue against their positions; nothing else destroys them.

That mind controls matter, is the fundamental strength of morality, for it gives man control over sin, sickness, and death, whereas the old systems take it away. To understand that brains never killed a mart would prevent his ever having disease of the brain; but this result is not gained, simply repeating this fact to the sick, or to one's self; it must be a mental conviction reached through science and admitted only because it is understood. If a doubt exists in regard to a patient's recovery, there should be none about the method of promoting it; no fears entertained that Intelligence is not sufficient to govern the body and make it harmonious. The fact seems to us self-evident, that the body cannot destroy the body, or consign it to dust, and so put out the image of Soul. Besides, there is no justice in law that punishes a man for doing good, for honest labor, or deeds of kindness. Through the eternal law of right, we are exempt from all sentences not passed on sin.

When the sick are made to realize the lie of personal sense the body is healed. Faith generally lies in the direction of material means; therefore the suffering or sick are apt to overlook the fact,

Chapter VIII. Healing the Sick.

that science heals them, and impute their recovery to some extraneous circumstance. The action of mind on the body is not more perceptible to personal sense than the origin of the wind, or the chambers of the hail. Turn to the eighth chapter of John, and you find the following reply to the testimony of personal sense. "Ye are of your father, the devil, and the lusts of your father ye will do; he was a murderer from the beginning" (referring to Cain, the first offspring of Adam, error), "and abode not in the Truth; when he speaketh a lie he speaketh of his own, for he is a liar and the father of it."

If there be any mystery in healing the sick on this platform laid down by Jesus, it is the mystery of Godliness, ambiguous only to the sinner, or to personal sense. Time alone is required to bring out the practical proof of our statements; and because they are riot understood to-day, it is no sign the time for their appearing has not arrived. Truth comes when it is needed, and not because of a personal demand.

Anew birth is the work of ages instead of a moment. Until the belief of Life, Intelligence, and substance in matter is destroyed, man has not "passed from death unto Life." A change of being's basis from sense to Soul requires time and understanding; it is nothing short of man's perfection, and what Jesus said was requisite to see the kingdom of heaven. The reign of harmony that science will establish, will explain the great difference between the moral effects of the present mode of healing and that of science, and the different receptions they have met from the world of sense and sin.

First comes the apprehension in science, of Life that is Soul, wholly independent of the body or sense. Next, its demonstration is commenced in living more of God, and having sounder bodies and purer minds, until we go up through higher understanding even as Elijah, to the Life that is God and knows no death. But we are little in danger of such goodness and its demonstration in this century. Loosing worldly approval indicates not only true Christianity, but

Chapter VIII. Healing the Sick.

the approach of this scientific stage of being; therefore we should welcome it as our dearest hope and highest aim. The only link to Life is through science; Life is never gained through death. The chemical changes that Truth introduces into the body through mind, is what destroys error and brings to light immortality. The works of our Master convinced Nicodemus their origin was God, the Principle of harmonious man. So when he inquired of him how he healed, this was the reply, "Except a man be born again, he cannot enter into the kingdom of heaven;" except he understands Life outside of personal sense he will never gain the harmony of being. But this was not the Pharisee's Christianity, nor the Rabbi's choice; to them sense was more desirable than Soul; matter had more claims than Spirit, and man, than God. Said the Master, "Because I tell you the Truth, ye believe me not, but he that is of God heareth God's words," i.e., the truly spiritual will understand the things that belong to Spirit, but the more material find this very difficult.

When Jesus introduced Christianity that cut off right hands land plucked out right eyes, demanding the control of our bodies and a nobler existence, they said, "He is a Samaritan and hath a devil," i.e., we know his origin, and for him to claim, "I and the Father are one," indicating he is God, is imposition. Pride said, then as now, Truth must come from the rulers, be clad in soft raiment, and nothing else should be found Truth. But Wisdom foreseeing this error, said, "Out of the mouth of babes hast thou perfected praise," and except you become as a little child, you cannot enter into harmony; i.e., unless we yield our educated opinions and beliefs, and reject the positions of personal sense, we shall neither discern our true being, nor understand the omnipotence of Spirit.

Standing at the bed of death, we need these words and their meaning to re- assure us and raise up the dying. "He that believeth in me shall never see death." The little trust we have in Spirit, and the strong faith we hold in matter, will meet us at this point with the inquiry. "Adam, where art thou," cherishing the belief of Life in matter, or holding firmly on to Life that is Spirit ? and the answer

Chapter VIII. Healing the Sick.

we honestly give will show us where we stand. The last enemy to be overcome is death; therefore much is to be understood before we gain this great point in science. Laying aside the beliefs that so easily beset us, we should not regard a condition of matter able to destroy man, mind or body, for both are immortal. A wasted form lies before you; the doctor calls his disease consumption, but the scientist finding no identity in discord, regards the disease a belief, and cures it thus; for understanding in part the Life that is Soul, he will destroy this belief of sense with the science of being. Never consent to the death of man, but rise to the supremacy of Spirit over matter, and denying the claims of personal sense, prove what it is to be a Christian whose Life is "hid with Christ in God;" therefore wholly spiritual. What if the lungs are ulcerated or decayed, mind has done this; action is produced by mind and not matter; Change, therefore, your belief in the case, combat the error and belief of Life in matter, with the Truth that Life is Soul and not sense, and you will form the lungs anew, and they will resume their healthy functions. We know this to be true, and state it because we have proved it. Disease is a belief, its origin mental instead of physical, and it matters not what the body indicates, in reality all is mind, there is no matter, and mortal things are beliefs, and not the science of man in which he is immortal.

That pain or pleasure, Life or death, belongs to the body, is but a belief. Immortal Soul is the producer of all things, and never made out of itself, mortality, or a suffering body. Speak to disease as one having authority over it, having Soul, and not sense, on your side, and you will master this belief; and immortality, which is the Truth of man, will assert its claims over mortality, and the sick recover. God, Spirit, is your stronghold in this extremity, and you feel how vain a thing is death pitted against the immortality of Soul and body. Life is the law of Soul; and personal sense, or matter, has no law. Holding on to the Truth of being is your only hope whereby to destroy its error. The science of being raises the dead; fear ye not, therefore, death; you may raise up the dying if minds around you are not strongly opposing this Truth, so little understood to- day; and

Chapter VIII. Healing the Sick.

sometime over this wave of the troubled sea, your God-being, that destroys all error, sin and death, will walk fearlessly; showing how real is Life, and how unreal, death. But there were some people so bigoted or material they even hindered the Master doing many mighty works because of their unbelief.

When healing the sick make your mental plea, or better, take your spiritual position that heals, silently at first, until you begin to win the case, and Truth is getting the better of error, then your patient is fit to listen, and you can say to him, "Thou art whole," without his scorn. Explain to him, audibly, sometimes, the power mind has over the body, and give him a foundation in the understanding to lean upon, that he may brace himself against old opinions. The battle lies wholly between minds, and not bodies, to break down the beliefs of personal sense or pain in matter, and stop its supposed utterances, so that the voice of Soul, the immortality of man, is heard. The belief of Life and sensation in matter is the source of all suffering and sin. The science of being reveals Life, conscious Soul and not sense, Spirit and not matter, and this leaves man safe in Soul, where there is no recognition of sickness, sin, or death. To raise the dead, restore the sick, or reform the sinner, we should understand science in its first statement, namely, that nothing is real but God, and His idea; aught beside is illusion, error and belief, that disappear. Recognizing the nothingness of sickness, sin, and death, is all that will ever bring out the harmony of man, or enable him to conquer them. With this scientific starting-point we shall master disease and temptation, or blush to be conquered by what is unreal. Understanding discord unreal, and harmony the only reality, emboldens us to fight the good fight.

Never admit error real as Truth, for if you do you will have more difficulty to get right than you need have. To turn a sinner from his error or belief, is more difficult than to turn the sick from theirs; for the latter, weary of suffering from it, yearn to relinquish it, and when the sinner reaches this point he is reformed. If science destroys not sickness, sin, and death, they are immortal. The only remedy for sin,

Chapter VIII. Healing the Sick.

sickness, or death, is obedience to the law of Life, and if Christ, Truth, be insufficient to cure sickness and destroy death, man is mortal. If we learn in part, even, the science of Life, it begins at once to destroy mental and physical discord.

The demonstrations and explanations of Jesus embraced all the theology or materia medica necessary to heal the sick or make Christians, and because he never recommended materia medica, hygiene, physiology, etc., we infer these methods are anti-Christian. If, as the Scripture saith, and science confirms, Jesus did the will of God, we are not doing his will who follow not his example, but resort to methods all our own.

"Herbs for the healing of the nations" typified the "balm in Gilead" and a physician there, even Soul the healer, and science the balm, which was Spirit triumphing over matter. Truth neither destroys Truth, nor creates error to be destroyed. Life never destroys Life, nor creates death to destroy it. Truth, or Life, is not the author of sin or death, and there is neither power nor Intelligence in matter. Sickness and death are the opposites of harmony and Life, and no law can support what Christ, Truth, destroys. The only law in existence, or that we should acknowledge, is God, the Principle of man, controlling man and matter. Spirit is not personality, nor persons that have passed away; and nature is God, hence it is Spirit and not matter. Intelligence governs man and the universe, but never instituted material law to govern them, and Spirit never produced matter. The Bible contains all our recipes for healing, and this is one of them:

"Agree with thine adversary quickly, while thou art in the way with him, lest at any time the adversary deliver thee to the judge, and the judge deliver thee to the officer, and thou be cast into prison; verily I say unto you, thou shalt not come out thence till thou hast paid the uttermost farthing."

Chapter VIII. Healing the Sick.

This was one of our Master's rules for casting out error and healing the sick. It referred, however, not to legal proceedings, or processes material, but to a mental tribunal and judgment. The adversary was not man, but error; and the directions, how to proceed with sin or sickness that would impose through belief a penalty for transgressing law that is not law, insomuch as justice is the moral signification of law, and injustice implies its absence. Shall a teacher pay the penalty of sickness for performing well and faithfully her tasks? or a great mind, because of the good it has done, fall soonest a prey to disease? must man suffer at the hands of God, for steadfastly doing right? Shall the mother droop, or suffer, because of maternity, if such is the design of her being? Because of fatigue, exposure to cold, or some supposed infringement of the so-called laws of health, we ignorantly admit there is danger of being sick, and this mental position decides the physical one; therefore, "agree with thine adversary quickly;" say to this belief, " Get behind me, satan, for thou savorest not the things that are of God, but those that are of man;" it is not a broken moral law to which your penalty is attached, but a condition of matter, a demand from something wholly unintelligent and incapable of justice. God has no law of injustice, wrong proceeds from belief, and not Truth.

To conclude quickly on the treatment of error, was the rule our Master left for casting it out. He never recommended laws of health to our knowledge. On a law that is not God's, we have a moral right to pass judgment, and to commute its sentence; every instance of matter, or the body, governing man, is justly condemned, and morally impossible insomuch as it manifests a want of Wisdom that renders it null and void. The only hope in sickness or sin, is to agree quickly with thine adversary; that is, if tempted, or if disease appears, to banish the temptation, or the disease, at once from the mind, and suffer it not to plead in its own behalf lest you fall a prey to your belief in the case. On this mental basis, when the first symptoms of disease appear, knowing they gain their ground in mind before they can in body, "agree quickly with thine adversary," i.e., dismiss the 6rst mental admission that you are sick; dispute

Chapter VIII. Healing the Sick.

sense with science, and, if you can annul the false process of law, alias your belief in the case, you will not be cast into prison or confinement. The sick must never plead guilty; in other words, admit they are sick, for then are they subject to sentence and imprisonment, according to the law of belief. Take the ground of science in the first instance, never admit sensation in matter, or that the body can be pained, or has any claims of its own, or power to make man suffer; adhere to this scientific position and battle the old belief with it until you destroy it, and you will get well.

To agree quickly with thine adversary in the first instance of sickness, is to take antagonistic grounds to it, and prove your superiority over it. Not to admit disease, is to conquer it; and if you understood the science of being, you would admit no reality to aught but God and his idea. When you say, "I am sick," you plead guilty, that is, you admit matter has sensation and will be delivered to the judge, in other words, into the hands of this belief that will deliver thee to the officer (disease), the ruler of mortal man that casts him into prison and fetters his entire being. But disease has no Intelligence of its own, or law, whereby to do this. You sentence yourself unwittingly, therefore, "agree with thine adversary quickly;" meet every circumstance as its master, and watch your belief, instead of your body; think less of laws material, that you may appreciate better the spiritual law of being, yea, the dominion of man over matter. Meet every adverse circumstance with science, instead of the beliefs of sense, and you will master it.

Error is a coward before Truth, and death is but another phase of the dream of Life in matter, wherein we meet at every point the consciousness of continued existence, with the same beliefs to conquer, and the same errors of sense to master through science. We must understand our way out of difficulties, or we never in reality are out, and the harmony and immortality of man are never understood until every error of sense is destroyed. To apprehend the economy and capacity of man's being, metaphysics must take the place of physics, and mind, instead of matter, be consulted in

Chapter VIII. Healing the Sick.

sickness. Fear, and its effects on the body are involuntary. Fear of disease and love of sin are the foundations of man's enslavement; but for these he could triumph over his body. Mind acts on the subject before disease becomes apparent on the body; but the individual has no recognition of his belief producing disease until it is developed physically. We look to personal sense for the evidence of disease, but there is no personal sense, unless matter is intelligent and holds the issues of Life. Because mind acts unconsciously to sense, the sick say how can mind have caused disease, "I never thought of the disease until it appeared on my body." But mind is first, and causation; nothing commences in matter; the plant springs from the eternal Intelligence --before we call it matter; but our mortal blindness and its sharp consequences, prove our need to understand the action of mind and its effects; we should study mind more and matter less, if we would avail ourselves of Soul in its control over sense. We can destroy sickness, the same as sin, by learning its origin and nature in mind, instead of body, and finding the belief that occasions it.

You can prevent or cure scrofula, hereditary disease, etc., in just the ratio you expel from mind a belief in the transmission of disease, and destroy its mental images; this will forestall the disease before it takes tangible shape in mind, that forms its corresponding image on the body. The science of being destroys the errors of sense with the Truth of man, and this is "casting out devils and healing the sick." Unconscious matter cannot dictate terms to conscious mind, causing either pain or pleasure; and matter is unconscious. The belief that our body forms conditions of its own, independent of mind, is the error of mortal man that makes him mortal.

You say the body feels, but the fact that pain is not felt without mind, and can be removed through it, proves mind the origin and cause of suffering. All the diseases on earth, (and there are none in heaven), never interfered for a moment with man's Life and its harmonious phenomena. Man is the same after, as before a bone is broken, or a head chopped off. Casualties has no reality to Soul; it

Chapter VIII. Healing the Sick.

exists only as belief, and is apparent only to personal sense. Accidents are unknown to God. It the science of Soul was reached, immortality would be gained, and there would be no chance for suffering. Soul and body are inseparable and eternal; if one is indestructible, so is the other. Understanding this, exempts man from disease and death, that anatomy and physiology regard positive claims on Life. Denying the Truth of being, measurably prevents its benefits on the body, by hindering its action in mind. It is not faith, but understanding, we need in science, and, "whosoever shall deny me before men, him will I also deny before the Father." This beautiful text refers not to a person, but the Principle of man that embraces the Truth of being, that casts out error and heals the sick. Reason discounts on revelation when it denies God the things that are His, and contradicts the omnipotence of Soul over sense; but whose reasons aright on this point, and hesitates not to declare his-views, i.e., ,to confess me before men," becomes harmonious. When reason accords with the declaration of Scripture that man has dominion over earth, we shall recognize this, and turn in triumph from the seemingly impossible, to "all things are possible," and demonstrate this.

"He that denieth me before men," refers to a denial, or an open acknowledgment of our honest convictions that effectually hinders or aids man's progress. Because the science of being is not yet understood, and the age is not yet awake to this subject, if we but half desire to understand it, and conceal this desire, we shall be unable to demonstrate it. A hypocrite or liar has no part in the science of Life; whosoever overlooks moral honesty for worldly policy, has not gained an insight into science sufficient to heal through it. If be has learned its rules, he has not understood them, and must have gained them of one whose experiences have gone up higher.

For a broken bone, or dislocated joint, 'tis better to call a surgeon, until mankind are farther advanced in the treatment of mental science. To attend to the mechanical part, a surgeon is

Chapter VIII. Healing the Sick.

needed to-day, but let the scientist see that inflammation, or long confinement, do not ensue. The time cometh when science will be our only surgeon, but, "suffering these things to be so now," let a bone be set, after the manner of men, then let science facilitate the knitting process, and re-construct the body without pain or inflammation as much as possible in these days of ignorance.

The time approaches when mind alone will adjust joints, and broken bones, (if such things were possible then), but in the present infancy of this Truth so new to the world, let us act consistent with its small foothold on the mind. We greatly mistake the nature of being to conclude that which is real, is inharmonious or mortal. Sickness is not real, from the very fact it is discord and mortality, and these, errors and beliefs, things of sense that constitute the dream of Life in matter, but have no reality to God, the Soul of man. Meet discord and death with the opposite Truth of being, and it wakens, in part, from the dream of Life, to the realization of Life whereby we learn all discord is illusion. We say sickness is something to be feared; but this belief regarding it is what does the harm. Disease must be admitted in mind before it appears as matter; for body manifests only what mind embraces, whether it be fever, consumption, or theft. The doctor tells his patients their symptoms are feverish, and they vibrate between this opinion and its belief, until the physician says the fever is established; then the sick are confirmed, and go into confinement and serve out this mental sentence executing the body, more surely than the sentences of our courts.

Because science contradicts personal sense and sickness, you have no more moral right to dispute the proof that science is right, than of a rule of mathematics; and yet you will, for such is the case with all new discoveries. Cures wrought in science, are naturally misconstrued by sense, imputed to something besides the Principle producing them; hence, they must be understood to be appreciated. We may understand, perfectly well, how we heal the Pick, but because others do not, hey may interpret our cure on some other

Chapter VIII. Healing the Sick.

basis; and this not only works against the recovery of the sick, because it is antagonistic to Truth, but prevents their perception of it.

Jesus, wiser than his persecutors, said, "If I by Beelzebub cast out devils, by whom did your fathers cast them out?" knowing they acknowledged the prophets, but not the carpenter; this question was difficult to answer because the prophets healed as he did, and he introduced the comparison on account of this. Those calling the demonstration of the science of being demoniac over eighteen centuries ago, might to-day tone down the judgment to imposition. Jesus, reasoning clearly on this subject, although misapprehended by the materialistic age, introduced the following comparison to explain his healing. "How can one enter into a strong man's house and spoil his goods, except he first bind the strong man, and then he will spoil his goods." In other words, how can I cast out devils without bearding error, attacking the beliefs that produce all this discord through ignorance of Soul and body, and then are you sometimes "offended because of me."

Jesus employed neither technicalities, the logic of the schools, nor formulas of medicine to heal; be knew, if others did not, Soul's superiority over matter, to heal the body, and that harmony is reached, only as we understand its real basis, Spirit, and not matter, Soul, not sense; and acknowledge the supremacy of Intelligence. Personal sense is the strong man that the Truth of being binds, before destroying error. It being impossible to heal on the Principle of science, and admit the grounds taken by personal sense; therefore, bind this strong man bold sense in subjection to Soul, and pain, as much under control of mind as a temptation to sin; then can you despoil his goods, i.e., prevent sin and suffering.

When the mental control we hold over our bodies for good or evil, touching sickness, sin, and death, has been preached one-hundredth part as long as man's salvation through faith, we shall have men and women approaching to the image and likeness of God. Until personal sense is doubted, it will never be controlled.

Chapter VIII. Healing the Sick.

The ages may go on, admitting personal sense and its control over man, and fighting it with drugs, laws of health, etc., when, instead of pleasure, it utters itself in pain, but this will only sustain disease in mind, and then it will show itself in matter. Man will not be found harmonious until the belief of personal sense yields to the science of Soul.

Deplorable cases of passion mastering man, should arouse one to the responsibility of governing his body. A person whom we snatched from this oblivion of Soul, said to us, "I should have died, but for the Principle you teach showing me the nothingness and falsity of sense; medicine, and treatises on my case, only abandoned me to more hopeless sufferings, and slavery; adherence to hygiene was of no avail, and I was cured only when I learned my way in science."

At present we must accept the statements of science relative to personal sense, on the inductive method, admitting the whole, because a part, involving the entire Principle is proved. Pains of the body, or matter, are unreal, but not more so than its pleasures; both cheat man into a belief of their reality, but only as the mountain mirage that seemeth what it is not, or the terrible incubus from which he finds it difficult to awake. Admitting the entire grounds of the science of being, it quickly follows our poor demonstration looks us in the face; but to this we reply, enough has been understood and proved, to reveal it science, and to prove, measurably, the blessing it brings. When speaking of this subject to others, instead of admitting the proofs we have already given of its Truth, we are often met with demands for more proof; therefore, we recommend you to read carefully what we have written, understand for yourselves, and establish your own evidence through demonstration; at the same time the necessity, exists for a teacher of this science, the same as for music or mathematics, that must be explained to be understood, and understood to be demonstrated.

Chapter VIII. Healing the Sick.

Pioneering what is new, or of great value to the world, is like a traveller on the desert of Arabia in company with one who becoming alarmed, his beat and sufferings increase and his courage fails; but the explorer, despite the hardships, and convinced he will come out right, accepts the situation more calmly, and encourages his friend, assuring him the only danger is his fear, then points anew the path; at length they reach an oasis, where, resting and slaking their thirst, they are ready with new vigor to push on. But here the more helpless traveller turns to his guide, saying, are you not sometimes alarmed on this desert route? "Yes," is the ready response; but, replied the other, you told me my danger consisted in my fear, therefore you have no more practical Wisdom than myself; forgetting his guide carried the baggage, met the intricacies of the way, and was attacked by brigands, plundered, and hindered in his course, his fellow-traveller following not, until the danger was over. Bearing others' burdens, if you undertake more than you can well carry, and are tried or over-wrought, they name it a hopeless task, and desert you; few arms are extended to your support, until you can help yourself and others, and have no need of aid.

We learn in science, food neither helps nor harms man; admitting its power in one direction, we must in another. But here it were unwise to disparage the Principle, or proof of this statement, because you continue to eat, not having mastered the belief that Life depends on eating. This were like denying the Principle of harmony, because man is not yet harmonious, or saying Soul is not immortal, because Personal sense takes no cognizance of this fact. Man's Life is Soul, that eats not to live, and immortal man is the idea of Soul instead of sense. We have no evidence of food sustaining Life, except false evidence, even the belief of Life in matter, and this belief an error. A telegram announcing incorrectly the death of a friend, produces the same sorrow the reality would give; but you say your anguish is occasioned by your loss, until another message arrives, informing you it is a mistake, and your friend lives. Now did you not experience the same sufferings the reality would have brought, and did you not say it was the death of your friend that

Chapter VIII. Healing the Sick.

caused these sufferings; but afterwards learn your mistake, realizing you suffered from a belief, and not a reality. Thus it is with all sufferings; belief and not Truth occasions them.

Had a scientist attempted to calm the grief of your supposed bereavement before the second news arrived, whereby you learned the sufferings were produced, by error and not Truth, would you have thanked your comforter, though she gave you relief, until this fact was made plain to your understanding. The body or matter never yet informed man of disease; a belief carries the telegram to the body, and the body manifests only the sufferings of mind. Never a formation of Truth was diseased, or needed to be destroyed; error is all that suffers, sins or dies. The body manifests only what mind embraces. The mortal body is mortal error, even a belief of Life in matter; Truth holds man immortal, and no portion of him lost; Science and Scripture declare this, "He that believeth in me shall never see death "; we are exempt from error or belief, and immortal only as we understand God. Giving heed to inharmony is personal sense that in its ignorance of God silences the voice of Soul; in other words is "total depravity." Soul and personal sense are antagonists, one disputes every position of the other -- which evidence do you accept? Reason instructs us immortality is the friend of man. Hear the opposite testimonies of personal sense and Soul.

Sense; I am intelligent matter, a body of sickness, sin and death that constitutes a mortal intelligence. The lungs, with alarming resonance, repeat this warning; the fevered throbbing of arteries tells how fast the sands of life are running; the failing pulse, that the places once knowing man shall know him no more forever; the inevitable law of Life is death; that aught is beyond this who knoweth. The evidence changes -- mortal man is in health, at ease in his possessions, and sense says, eat, drink, and be merry; what a happy life is this. I am unjust, and no person knoweth it, take vengeance on ray fellow beings, chest, lie, and propagate this species; am brutish, but this is obedience to the nature God hath given me. What a nice thing is sin, what a joy, sense; my kingdom is

Chapter VIII. Healing the Sick.

of this world, and I am at peace. But a touch, an accident, one wheel in the mechanism stopped, all is lost, for I am mortal!

Soul; I am the Spirit of man that giveth understanding, beauty and Omnipotence, full of unutterable perfections, height upon height of holiness, the wonder of being, imperishable glory, for I am God, grasping, and gathering in all bliss, for I am Love, giving immortality to man, for I am Truth, without beginning and without end, for I am Life, supreme over all, for I am Intelligence, and the Substance of all, because I Am.

Does an M. D. examine the body, feel the pulse, and look at the tongue, to ascertain the condition of Soul, the Life of man, or the condition of his body, alias matter, and according to signs material give his opinion of Life, God, and the prospect for his continuing? If man was before God, and matter superior to mind, such methods were consistent, but not otherwise. Mind, instead of body is the fount of all suffering; but we forget this in sickness, when the mental condition is not regarded and wholly unknown to patient or physician, while its physical effect alone is taken up. Opinions and theories have so misguided judgment on these points, the Truth of being is lost sight of, and illusion taken for fact. However much the schools insist that discord rules harmony, and laws of matter govern the Life of man; science reveals Life otherwise, and gives an opportunity for this proof. Laws of God were never known to kill man, for this would destroy immortality. Man is the image and likeness, therefore the reflex shadow of God, and if one is mortal, why not the other? If man is lost his Principle is lost, and God is not left. Doctors fasten disease on the body, mapping it out in mind; when the mental picture is complete the patient will be sick. A belief of disease is liable to be made manifest at any time on the body.

If disease is Intelligence that produces results of itself, or the body can make its own conditions, despite the mental protest, we will admit the superiority of disease over man, and its power to make him sick, or kill him, but not otherwise. Mind produces all effects on the body; personal sense has neither pleasure nor pain except to belief, which is all there is to it. A mental image of disease, fully formed, is already painted on the body, whereas another picture of mind we transfer to canvas; 'tis the patient's fear that draws the picture, and the artist, mind, executes it fully on the body, but the patient is ignorant of his fear, or what mind's images are, until they are drawn on the body. If no mental image of disease was formed, there could be no manifestation of disease. The belief that disease is a power or Intelligence superior to man, is ever ready to reproduce some image of disease before the mind, and this image causes the fear, and the fear quickens or retards action, producing inflammation or whatever the nature or type of disease that prevails in the general thought, and comes to you entirely unbidden, and with no particular association to call it up. Again, disease comes through association, even as thoughts appear. For instance, your mental condition is a fixed belief, that, exposed to severe cold or dampness, you take cold; hence, the circumstance being this, you suffer the effects of a belief through association. If fevers are abroad, you say, I am liable to have them; and this mental condition, through association, produces the result.

Disease comes after the manner that one thought calls up another. If her child is exposed to conditions deemed dangerous, the mother says, my child will be sick, and her belief reaches her offspring to this very end; but she calls it the circumstances. You say, I have eaten too much, and shall find it difficult to digest such a quantity of food; or, I have consumptive parents, hence am predisposed to this disease, and the result follows, in natural sequence. The conditions of your belief are re-produced on your body. The remote cause of all disease, is a belief in it, and a fear of it; the present, or exciting one, the circumstance you say will produce it.

Exposed to contagion, having consumptive parents, being over-wrought, mentally or physically, eating too much, fasting too long, etc., you say, are dangerous to health, and you are a law to your

Chapter VIII. Healing the Sick.

body in the case, for the body could not suffer from these without mind, and a mind, that did not embrace these beliefs, would not suffer; the seeds of disease, germinated by circumstances, are sown in mind, not matter. Even as thoughts on other subjects are reproduced by association, so are diseases; and your belief regarding disease, and net the circumstance, is what affects your body.

Parents, nurses, and doctors, not perceiving these vital points in science, throw their mental weight in the wrong scale, and injure those they would bless. Pursuing an opposite course, and ruling out all mental admissions of disease, they would save the sickness they now occasion. We should recollect suffering is no less a mental condition, than enjoying. When an accident happens, you think, or exclaim, "he is hurt;" but to prevent the result you fear, you should oppose your own, and the frightened one's admission he is harmed. Contending you are not hurt, your body obedient to mental control, will yield to this fact.

When destroying scientifically the sufferings of children, oftentimes the mother will revive in their memory what you are blotting out, and describe how badly her child was hurt; or how much disease she has, etc., little knowing the effect of this is like fire to a burn. We should inquire only into our fears and beliefs regarding sickness, and disregard all else.

Matter cannot give testimony, therefore we should not believe personal sense; mind alone reports physical conditions and produces them. The sick argue against themselves by saying, "I am sick"; the physical affirmative should be met with a mental negative; all discord is error, insomuch as harmony is the only Truth of being; we must take a mental position, the very opposite of the physical one, to control the body to a change of action. We inform the muscles how to move, and they act in obedience to the mind, or there would be no action; so does the entire system. The sick are frightened, whether they do, or do not understand this, and the body, like a frightened

Chapter VIII. Healing the Sick.

man, runs too fast or too slow, partially palsied, or inflamed with fear, the action is naturally increased or diminished.

To advance in the understanding of Truth, we must live up to our present perceptions of it; and improving the present, we need take no thought for the morrow, for the morrow will take thought for us, and afford more light as we advance toward the light. When you know already, dishonesty is error, discipline yourself to meet consequences rather than do wrong or hide a wrong. Truth is nearly worthless to him who seldom uses it.

When physical action is inflammatory, mind is the cause; some fear has taken possession of you, although this fear is not recognized by the sick, yet the physical effects show us it exists, and the results are the same as if it existed consciously. Disease, originating in mind before it can be manifested on the body, is arrested, or ruled out of the latter, by destroying the belief that occasioned it. Fear causes the face to grow suddenly red, or pallid, proving the circulation of the blood is controlled by this mental condition; the body becomes weak, or suddenly strong, through fear, showing that weakness or strength is the result of mind, instead of matter. A mother, informed of the imprisonment of her son, instantly falls dead; here organic action has stopped from no other than a mental cause, and yet we are so buried in the rubbish of supposed Life in matter, we cannot, or do not, let this falling apple point to the Principle it reveals. Fear changes the entire secretions of the system; not only controls the functions of the brain, but the internal vicera, and the entire mechanism of the obedient body. Remove the fear of disease, and disease will disappear; for the body is restored through a change of mind; fear exists when the mind is wholly unconscious of it, and produces disease involuntarily. We never knew the patient that (lid not recover when the fear of his disease was utterly destroyed. The stronger never yields to the weaker, except through fear, or voluntary choice; and mind is mightier than matter, and controls the body, whether we do, or do not, admit this.

Chapter VIII. Healing the Sick.

The ills we fear are the only ones that conquer us. The body becomes inharmonious through mind alone; no law, outside of mind, governs the body. The law of God is the only absolute or inevitable, and this law never produces sickness, sin, or death, as its consequences. There is no pain without mind; matter cannot suffer or produce suffering. Disease is a fear expressed physically, not by the lips, but the functions of the body. Mitigate the fear, and you relieve the affected organ; destroy it, and the body regains its healthy functions. However impossible this may appear to our educated views on this subject, it is, nevertheless, a fact in science that we have tested sufficiently to declare it, as unhesitatingly as any other demonstrable Truth. That man is unconscious of his fear, neither changes its effects on the body nor the mental fact; ignorance of the cause, or approach of disease, not in the least militates against its mental origin. More or less fear accompanies all ignorance; who that understands the power of mind over body, its impelling force, and how controlled, and this very ignorance, like walking in darkness on the edge of a precipice, is an ever-present involuntary fear.

We say, my body suffers, and mind has nothing to do with it; this is simply impossible. The martyr, burning at the stake, conquers his body with mind, and silences personal sense with Soul. So the opposite extreme of stolidity meets his punishment with less torture than a mind touched to finer issues. Death has occurred from imaginary phlebotomy; individuals have died of contagions, hydrophobia, etc., believing they had been exposed to them, when such was not the ewe. Many instances of the mind's control over body, producing death, prove this control absolute, instead of partial. Physicians are ready to admit mind affects the body somewhat; but this is but a small part of the fact; science reveals all action produced and controlled by mind, and a single instance of this proved, as when people die from mental causes, justifies this statement.

If mind is the only actor, bow do we explain mechanism, apparently acting of itself, or through what we term matter power.

Chapter VIII. Healing the Sick.

Simply that mind has constructed this mechanism and carries it on. A mill at work, or the action of water on a wheel, is secondary, and not the primary cause; mind caused the mill and constructed the machinery. The eternal mind first "divided the waters," and controlled the wave. Mind is the primitive, and the derivative would not continue without mind to put it in operation; perpetual motion in matter is a failure; but perpetual motion of mind is science. Intelligence is the motive power, or procurer of all action. Take away mind and the body is without action; therefore it is but logical to conclude mind produces its action; but when we go farther, and cure diseased action through mind, that medicine could not remove, we gain this undeniable evidence.

Mind, like a telegraph office, holds the message conveyed to the body, and to prevent any bad results we must be careful the telegram is from science instead of sense. Deprived of this despatch, the body returns no answer of inflammation or disease, from the fact matter has no Intelligence of its own. The body is not an independent sovereignty, or reigning autocrat over man; any supposed government matter holds over Intelligence, is wholly mythical. The belief our body is substance, is not more true than that it is Life and Intelligence. What a material world we address; but Truth must be spoken; if not at all times, at some time, and we seem destined to take the enemy's first fire, for speaking it this time. We have faith this book will do its work, though not fully understood, in the nineteenth century. The revelator read its history in the little book, "Sweet in the mouth, and bitter in the belly." Though but a hint in time, it is a tale for eternity. Materiality must and will go out, though it be slowly; the spiritual era advances when physical effects will no longer be attributed to physical causes, but discerned in their final spiritual cause.

When fear causes the blood to bound through veins and arteries, or languidly to move the palsied mechanism, destroy the fear, and the system regains its equilibrium; anodynes, counter-irritants, or depletion can never reduce inflammation like the Truth of being.

Chapter VIII. Healing the Sick.

Faith, or belief, is a poor equivalent for science; we must understand man metaphysically, before we can control him aright, physically. Ignorance, coupled with a smattering of metaphysical learning, is a shocking bore; the Truth of being reduced to a petty cross-fire on every poor cripple and invalid, sending into him the cold bullet, "nothing ails you," had better be unsaid until it be understood. If a boil appears suddenly, that you say is painful, does it ache? The boil does not ache, for matter has no sensation; it is mind that feels, and that boil bespeaks your belief of heat, pain, swelling, and inflammation, but you call it the boil. Heat is a product of fear; warmth is the normal condition of Truth, cold or heat is not; body bereft of mind is cold at first, and afterwards nothing. Fear produces the heat, and another phase of belief tries to expel it through yet another form of belief, called a boil, that now appears on the body, mind holding at the same time the conclusion that boils are painful, but prolong Life, alias Intelligence. An error of premises produces error in conclusion, mental error occasions all the discords of body.

Heat would pass off as painless from the body as gas expelled from boiling water, but for our opposite beliefs. Chills are the effects of beat; ulcers, boils, etc., are heat coming to the surface; but mind, and not matter, creates this beat and forms all the identity disease has. The invalid may conclude a humor in the blood causes boils, and when this humor is brought to the surface the system is relieved; but mind, and not matter, has formed this conclusion and its results. You will have these forms of disease so long as you regard them channels for disease, or inevitable results of matter, Cherish any particular belief of disease and you are in danger of reproducing it on the body. Reverse the case and destroy your belief in this modus operandi of matter, and your fear of disease will not engender the beat to be thrown off; and what you thought before was scrofula, bile, and physical causes, you will learn was fear and mind acting on the body.

Disease, destroyed in its origin, viz., mind, never reappears again, and is cured effectually; but matter can never destroy it. A

Chapter VIII. Healing the Sick.

mental position taken doubtingly, is a very weak one; you must understand these points in science, or you are never thoroughly persuaded in your own mind of the power of belief and its sad effect on the body; neither can you discern the Principle bringing out the capabilities and harmony of being, that enables you to hold what you understand. In the positive belief and fear of disease yourself, it were vain to attempt, mentally, to remove another's fear or disturbed condition; as soon attempt to destroy beat with fire. To succeed in the science of Life, you must be found in it, having not on a belief, but the garment of Truth, and this will give you self-possession, and ability to bring out the full amount of the Life that is Christ healing the sick. Eschewing the belief you are Intelligent matter, you gain the capabilities of Spirit and the freedom of the sons of God.

Men of business have said this science was of great advantage from a secular point of view. It not only enhanced their physical and mental endurance, but control of man and perception of character. They have told us they could meet better the exigencies of business, by meeting mind on its own grounds, perceiving thoughts and their relation to men's acts. The science of Life not only brings out latent possibilities and capacities, but extends the atmosphere, or aroma of mind, giving man vent in broader and higher being. An odor, confined by a stopper, is not so benevolent as when the stopper is removed and it scents the room. Remove the belief of Intelligence beneath a skull bone, of Soul in body, and matter the master of man, and there quickly follows more of a man or woman, because they understand themselves and others better. Getting outside the evidence of personal sense to judge of men and things, is a vast gain to manhood and Godhood. We are suffocated by beliefs and 'isms, whereas a living Soul is liberty and Life; understanding can grasp even the infinite idea. We are conscious of intelligent Spirit; then away with the dream of intelligent matter, or that Intelligence dwells in non-intelligence.

Soul and body are different, but concordant, and one cannot be lost and the other left. To apprehend completeness and perfection,

Chapter VIII. Healing the Sick.

we must reach them, and bring out our model thus. Thinking of sin, sickness and death is not the method to conquer them, and form your model of Life; destroy them in mind and they are gone forever; get rid of the fear of sickness, or the love of sin, and you are rid of these errors in physical manifestation. Action should proceed from Principle, not idea, from Soul, and not personal sense, and mind instead of matter; when this is so, we shall govern our bodies and bring out harmony. Principle controls its idea harmoniously, governed alone as it is by the supreme Intelligence, but for this, 'ology or 'ism would make a sick globe. The belief that Spirit dwells in matter, and that matter has Intelligence, causes all discord; man is not sick; for mind is not sick, and matter cannot be; a belief is the tempter and tried, the sin and sinner, disease and its cause, death and the dying. Shock this belief by some expression, or impression, of Truth, start it from its fixed centre, and it will relieve the body at once. A tooth ceases to pain you before the forceps, a greater fear having silenced, for a moment, the lesser, showing the effects of mind on the body, and that "our greater evils medicine the less."

A bigot's circumference of mind is very small; personality and matter he believes in, but talk to him beyond these, of Principle and idea, and you get no response. Ignorance is the greatest foe to metaphysical science.

Never converse on sickness, watch its symptoms, recommend matter remedies, or seek to learn its cause in matter; and you will find it easier for mind to destroy, and to enjoy health yourself, and help others to do go. The basis of all disease, is error or belief; destroy the belief and the sick will recover. To be cheerful in sickness is well, to be hopeful is better, but to understand the nothingness of disease destroys it utterly. An invalid is a deplorable instance of mesmerism, with which one belief controls another, and error re-produces error. We admit one mind can control another mind, and thereby control the body, but never calculate we do this daily with our own body. The mesmerizer causes his subject pain without any physical cause, proving he produces this sensation

Chapter VIII. Healing the Sick.

through the subject's belief, and not that it existed in the body; then, to the belief of pain were he to add a belief of disease in any part, and keep up this state of mind sufficiently long, the disease would certainly appear there. The mesmerizer makes a limb rigid by making his subject believe he cannot move it. Thus it is with the sick; they mesmerize their bodies unconsciously, through their beliefs, to conditions of stiffened joints, disease, and death, and the only difference is, the cause in one instance, is understood to be mind, or belief, producing the results, and in the other case, believed to be matter; hence mind is employed to remove one, and matter the other condition, whereas both have their origin in mind, and are removed through mind. The lame man mesmerizes his body through the belief an accident or disease caused him lameness, and so long as this belief lasts, his lameness continues.

Sometimes faith in medicine, or the lapse of time wears away fear to such an extent the belief changes with regard to the disease, sufficiently to remove the bodily ailment. Remove the belief that holds the limb rigid and it is restored. But, says one, no man can mesmerize me. This may be true, and because you mesmerize your body so positively, others are negative to you; but such an individual would be difficult to cure with other's mesmerism, or materia medica, unless he bad more faith in them than himself. Science would heal him more readily through the understanding, for such minds are generally self-reliant and assured, holding strong, if preoccupied grounds. There is no law of matter that governs Intelligence; mind alone is supreme law. What we term laws of nature, governing man, are nothing more or less than man's belief, producing the results of mind on his body and not matter. Life is not evolved, but evolves phenomena. Life is eternal, giving forth its representation as the sun emits its rays. That Life is supported by food, drink, air, etc., that it is organic, or in the least dependent on matter, or sustained by it, is a myth.

Soul has a body when all matter is destroyed; the mortal body is a thing of belief called man, an error from its origin to its end; the

Chapter VIII. Healing the Sick.

Truth of being is immortal Soul and body. Expose the body mortal to certain temperatures, and belief says it has colds and catarrhs; to severe labor, and fatigue follows; to prick a vein lets out Life, and this man is at the mercy of a bodkin! putting aside mind, no such results follow to man. So long as the belief remains that dampness or cold produces catarrhs, fevers, rheumatism, or consumption, these effects will follow, and the air of tropical climes will afford exemption from them; but change the belief with regard to this, and the effects will change, and you will find the body manifests only what mind says, on these, and all other points. Matter is governed by mind.

Man, pursuing zealously the conditions of his belief, (and this is all there is to mesmerism), if told how mind affects the body, and, to illustrate, you quote the evidence of this in mesmerism, replies, "no man can mesmerize me." And yet he calls his body this me, and that body is just what his parents first, and secondly himself, has made it; and these parents were not matter, but mind, as the body proves, that is no longer thy parent, if mind has departed.

When we reach the science of Life, we shall learn Truth casts out devils and heals the sick, also, that Jesus gave disease and devil one signification. Those fear not they shall murder, whose perceptions reach the average of goodness, and if our spiritual perceptions were up to the standard of Christians, we should no more fear sickness, sin, or death. It is not less wise to fear sickness than to fear we shall steal; both are admissions of moral weakness, and a loss of control over the body that we should not permit. Let the slave to a wrong desire learn the science of Life, and he never more will cherish this desire, but rise higher in the scale of being. Allowing Soul to govern sense, is science, wherein we are a law of Wisdom to our body, of Life and not death.

Let mankind study this science with half the avidity they peruse volumes on disease, and try the different drugs and drills for health, and they will advance not from one disease to another, nor to

Chapter VIII. Healing the Sick.

decrepitude and death, but beyond sickness into harmony and Life. When "in him we live, move, and have being," is it impossible to conclude God is equal to camphor or a sweat? Life is proved Spirit, and not matter; and the only possible objection to our eagerly accepting this munificence of being is, that it requires a better demonstration of Life. The centuries are slowly, but surely, tumbling down the old corner stones, and building on better foundations. Not far distant, the hour looks down on us when sickness, sin, and death will be admitted error, and the Truth that destroys them sought instead of drugs.

Mind is the only alterative of the body; every secretion and function of the human system depend on mind and are controlled by it. The pallid invalid supposed to be dying from a bad state of blood, is restored to strength and health by changing her belief on this subject; it matters not whether she knows or does not know the working of mind and its bad effect on her body, she will recover when mind is set right on the physical question, and the blood will circulate naturally and healthily. The Oxford students furnished this precedent, who caused a felon to die of the belief he was bled to death; when not a drop of blood had flowed. This single case proved the superiority of belief over matter and blood, to kill a man. The belief that Life is contingent on matter, or that certain conditions of the blood and organic structure are fatal to man, must be met and mastered, before Life is understood, or found immortal. Mind causes all conditions of the body, and you can change them effectually and permanently only through this medium. To heal the sick with science, has this advantage over physiology, drugs, mesmerism, etc.; it is the Truth of being opposed to its error, by which man goes up higher in the scale of being; other methods are error opposing error, that have a temporary advantage only. Belief is on their side to be sure, for error coincides with error, strengthens it and weighs against the science of Life; but this has no advantage in the scale of Truth. The perception of man's possibilities enlarges his being, giving higher aims and broader scope to manhood. If there were no other

Chapter VIII. Healing the Sick.

and higher motives for acquainting ourself with God, the Principle of man, than to be rid of sickness, this would seem sufficient.

A student once said, "this science has made me all I am," and that was saying more, perhaps, than he was aware. There is infinite room in the science of man, for here the limits of personality confine not Intelligence.

Disease is one of the beliefs of personal sense that Truth finally destroys. No scientific work can treat of disease as an identity, or power. Any allusion to disease, or confession that you are sick, should be avoided, as you would shun telling ghost stories to children in the dark. Shut out from the light, a child suffers from thoughts of danger, and so does the adult who comprehends not his own being; the child must be taken out of darkness to get rid of his fear, and the suffering it occasions, and so must the man. The universal belief that suffering is physical, and not a creation of mind, produces suffering, owing to our ignorance of its origin. That Life is not dependent on matter we prove when Life goes on and matter is destroyed. Spiritually, I cannot perceive sickness, sin or death; and recognize these only as beliefs of matter. Sickness is error, its remedy Truth; and the science of being reveals that our body is sensationless, and that Spirit sees, hears, feels, acts, and enjoys, but cannot suffer; and this makes Soul and body harmonious and immortal. To conclude our body is Life, Substance, or Intelligence, and this body matter, that sees, hears, feels, sets, enjoys and suffers, makes sickness, sin and death autocrats over Soul, and man a slave to personal sense.

To Soul there is neither matter, sickness, sin, or death; but to personal sense these are realities, that even govern Spirit; what a mistake! we know this is error, and error a belief, destitute of understanding; and change the belief, the error changes, destroy it, and the error is gone. You see through solid walls, hear without sound, Walk over water, and have your body with yon in clairvoyance; but in the opposite belief of sense, your body remains

Chapter VIII. Healing the Sick.

in statu quo, and your mind goes without a body. Let the mesmerizer experience what we term the fears of personal sense, its pains or its pleasures, and his subject has those same sensations, which proves they are produced by mind and not matter, and are beliefs instead of the reality of things. Sickness is not imagination; it is more than this, it is a belief, a conviction of mind instead of a fancy. One animal looking another in the eye may cause a quarrel; but notice the superiority of Soul over sense, when the eye of man fastened fearlessly on the beast, starts him away with terror. This illustrates the effect of Spirit looking disease steadfastly in the face to destroy it, compared with our physiological drills, drugs, and mesmerism, which is the quarrel between beasts. When we submit to personal sense that we admit is the author of sickness, sin and death, we do not govern our bodies; we must turn to spiritual sense for happiness and immortality. Thinking less of what we term substance-matter, and more of substance in Spirit, we become a law to our bodies of Life, and not death, of harmony instead of discord, and of Truth instead of error.

I pity him more who is sick than him who is a sinner, for we rely on God to help man in the latter, but not the former case. If sense masters man in sickness, it may in sin, and Soul is out of office. Because personal sense reports you poor, it may tempt you to steal; or exposed to fatigue, or cold, say you must be sick; but should you believe it in one case more than in the other? in both cases it misguides and deludes. The belief that sickness is a necessity, or the master of man, disappears in science where our normal control over the body reappears. Bathing, friction, dietetics, air, exercise, electricity, etc., never yet made man harmonious; drugging or pounding the poor body to make it sensibly feel well, that ought to be insensibly well, is a sorry equivalent for the control of Spirit over matter. Has brains, blood, heart, lungs, stomach, bones, nerves, drugs, whiskey or sin, reduced thee to the slave of matter; remember these are not as strong as thou, and rise to thy God-given dominion; man is not the tool of personal sense, the Truth of being declares this. Sickness, as well as sin, is error, and can matter err? Sickness is

Chapter VIII. Healing the Sick.

a jar, an abnormal action, inharmonious, and what is the corrective of this ? matter cannot resuscitate, without mind, it cannot act of itself. We say it can; that certain combinations, gasses, secretions, acute or morbid conditions of matter produce inharmony, and bodily sufferings also; but this is not so, if the body causes pain it can also cure it, but matter neither caused nor cured disease; not a gas accumulates, or a secretion takes place, or a combination occurs without mind. We admit the voluntary action of mind controls muscles, bones and nerves, but conclude, when these please to rebel against mind, as in case of lameness or contraction, they will not obey, however much we desire it, and mind has no more control over them; but this makes muscles and bones superior to man in one instance, and in another his servant, which is unnatural and not equal to the economy of human governments. If muscles are capable of action without the mind, we might say they are capable of inaction also, on this same premises, but not otherwise; and if they are able to inact of themselves at any time, they are at all times, and man has no control over them, and one state is as much their normal condition as the other; hence a stiffened joint or paralyzed limb is as natural as its opposite.

But if mind controls muscles in one case, it does in all cases, When Shakespeare said, "Throw physic to the dogs," I have some faith he added to the cast-aways, the belief of intelligent matter. Sometimes in fevers, consumptions, etc., the patient seems full of courage, and we say, "bow calm he is; how can he be suffering from fear; his body is the victim of disease, but the mind is unmoved." Mind that in sickness we deem tranquil, is frightened with its own images; fear heats the insensible body and dashes the blood in mad currents; but Christ, Truth, stills this tempest, with its "Peace be still." If disease can attack and control the body without man's consent, so can sin; both are error to be destroyed; dare you admit Spirit cannot govern the body when error of any nature takes it in hand? Destroy the belief of fever and the fear it occasions, and blood will circulate again mildly, and the body be at peace. Personal sense takes no cognizance of what is going on in mind; it is blind to the

Chapter VIII. Healing the Sick.

cause of effects; to comprehend our explanation of man you must perceive its Principle in science, that demands understanding and demonstration; whereas personal sense requires belief only.

The metaphysical physician looks for effects where the physical doctor thinks he finds causes. The former finds all causation mind, the latter looks for cause only in matter; the former heals on the scientific basis of being, whereby mind governs the body, the latter through the belief that matter controls man. Metaphysical pathology rests on psychology, or the science of Soul; but the signification of psychology is perverted whenever construed mesmerism instead of science. The metaphysical method of healing the sick labors under this disadvantage, that mortal belief apprehends matter only, and not Spirit; and disparages the metaphysical, and gives the physical precedence in all things, throwing all the weight of belief in the scale of personal sense, and on the side of matter. Meeting the affirmative to disease with a negative, neutralizes the positive belief and its effects on the body, making discord become negative to harmony, and introducing the science of being. A patient thoroughly booked in physiology, materia medica, etc., is more difficult to heal with science, than one having never bowed the knee so methodically to matter.

In case of insanity you argue, mentally and verbally, against the belief that brains are diseased, the same as in other cases of physical disorders, for all physical inharmonies proceed from mental causes; insanity is but another form of mental error. We could afford to scorn a bold denial of personal sense if proof was wanting; but when it is not, and this reversed idea of man restores harmony to mind and body, as nothing else can, we must admit it science. Did riot this Truth of being silence personal sense and the so-called laws material, man were lost, and discord, sin and death, immortal. Insanity is a very interesting case to treat metaphysically, it being a clearer case, and affords better evidence of the effects of mind on the body. The only good effect you can produce on body or brain is the result of mind instead of matter, through the Truth of being that

Chapter VIII. Healing the Sick.

destroys error; but you cannot introduce the science of being that restores health, through manipulation; as soon teach man mathematics by rubbing his head. If the physician is scientific he is morally and practically fit for healing, without manipulation or medicine, and speaks as one having authority, possessing the Truth that destroys error. Under some circumstances it is well to converse with the patient audibly, explaining to him the science of his course; but under others, it arrays him and his sect against you and thus retards his recovery. Should a nurse or the friends of the sick think lightly of metaphysical healing, or despair of the patient's recovery, you should inform them as much as they cart comprehend, of its basis and results, requesting them, for the sake of the sick, to leave the patient out of their thoughts as much as possible, that the influence one mind holds over another may be obviated. You have as much better opportunity to be heard mentally, when speaking alone, as physically; we admit one cannot be heard when others are speaking louder than himself, or talking on other subjects; and this is why the physician needs to be alone with the patient, when mentally healing him.

A scientific practitioner never converses on other subjects when he is treating the sick; yon cannot gain the spiritual sense of your patient if you are addressing his personal senses, by manipulating him; besides you need to learn your patient's mind, and to do this you must be silent and still; manipulation, or conversation on other topics are injurious. The spirituality that abstracts all attention from the body, never manipulates and is the only positive position of scientific healing. The demonstrator of the science of healing is today an Atlas with the world on his shoulders, and the only reason he heals in one or a majority of cases is, not that law material or a single opinion or prejudice is in his favor, but because it is the Truth of being demonstrated by its fruits. Understanding the science of music, we have firm reliance on our ability to practice it; so with the science of Life, the only difference is, the latter demonstrates God controlling man, and the former, God controlling music; but the

Chapter VIII. Healing the Sick.

latter meets with more opposition because it tends to destroy all error, and is not understood at present.

The Scientist sees more clearly the cause of disease in mind, than the anatomist can in body; the latter examines the body to learn how matter is committing suicide, and the former reads mind to find what beliefs are destroying the body. The scientist is a law to himself; he would not do wrong knowingly, and if he has not reached this standpoint, he cannot give the more wonderful demonstrations of healing. Whosoever justifies an evil-doer, and does not expose his iniquity, is a partaker of his sin, and will have his reward. Whenever we have discovered a dishonest student claiming to be scientific, we have first explained to him his error, and next, rebuked him; and if neither explanation nor rebuke are heeded, and he does not reform, he becomes our enemy. The greatest hindrance this science can meet will arise from backsliding students, those claiming to practice it who do not adhere to its moral obligations, who have not yet realized until the fountain is purer, the stream will be turbid; mind must be right or its action on others will be inharmonious.

A mental condition, or error of belief unknown to both patient and physician, is not readily removed, and to gain a scientific perception of it, or apprehend the mental condition of the sick, you must hold the reins over your own body. Our Master knew the thoughts of others, solely because of his goodness and spirituality; therefore, mind-reading, with him, was very far from clairvoyance. To be able to discern the cause of sickness after the scientific mode of our Master, depends on your spirituality, obedience to your higher nature, after acquiring the rules of science that guide you aright. If you are becoming spiritually minded, you will discern the things that belong to Spirit; and in the ratio that you are not carnally minded, and according as you surrender error, will your spiritual discernment increase.

Chapter VIII. Healing the Sick.

Mental healing may be done both right and wrong; the wrong method is capable of evil, and is mesmerism, of which the lowest natures are capable. The scientific method is without power to do evil; it is Soul, not personal sense, or manipulation that destroys belief and fear and heals the sick, in which mind- reading is not Only found important to your success, but especially characterizing the demonstration. When once you understand disease has no identity, you will perceive sickness is but a belief. You should instruct the sick that Soul is Substance, and body its idea; that disease is not in the idea of Soul or immortality, nor can it exist in shadow, the body of Soul, therefore it has no existence.

The mental co-operation of the sick will promote their recovery. To move mind from its central error, viz., that Intelligence and Life are in the body, and matter is the master of man, is the great point in metaphysical healing. Every invalid has an especial fear, in which some disease and its approaching symptoms are more alarming than others; not because the disease is more dangerous, but more feared; remove the fear, and the danger is gone, for mind will master the disease. Physical phenomena epitomize the mental, in which a fearful object troubles us until it is removed from our observation. Disease is an image of mind, that must be removed from mental sight, or the fear it occasions will increase, and this will increase the inflammatory or morbid symptoms. A belief is the seed within itself that propagates all physical, because all mental discord. We know this is difficult to admit before it is understood, when the proof is ample; demonstration is all that convinces us of this fact, and until this proof is made, you cannot be safe. Conversing on disease, reading, or thinking about it, should be sedulously avoided. If doctors knew one half the harm clone by medical books they would abandon works on disease, and never speak again of sickness to their patients. Thinking of disease and pointing out its character makes it liable to appear on the body; such conversations or ruminations should be repugnant as obscene thoughts or words.

Chapter VIII. Healing the Sick.

Mind engenders all disease, in which case your only hope lies in thinking and hearing less about it, or in understanding the science that absolutely prevents it. When you employ a material remedy you must have more faith in it than the disease, and believe you are getting cured with more tenacity than you believe you are growing worse, that the balance of your faith in recovery or the remedy, may restore you; this condition of mind, neutralizing the effects of your fear, relieves the body. The whole is a mental operation, and matter has nothing to do with it.

The mortal body is but a phenomenon of mortal belief. Watch, then, mind more, and the body less. In case of sickness, or sin, to destroy the one, or remedy the other, we should begin in mind instead of matter; "pluck the beam out of our own eye, that we may see clearly to cast the mote out of our brother's eye." Unless we are rid of blindness ourself, we are the blind leading the blind, whereby both fall into the ditch.

The study of materia medica, physiology, etc., should give place to metaphysical research, whereby we gain an insight into the power mind holds over matter. Mental power, governed by science instead of personal sense, by Truth instead of error, makes man eternal, and will destroy sickness, sin and death; while the material methods for reaching the ultimate harmony of man, have failed to accomplish this. The attention given medicine, laws of health, and saving souls, bestowed upon the moral elevation of man, or the metaphysical understanding of him, would usher in the millennium. Jesus understood this, but the Rabbis did not; hence their scorn of the glorious Nazarene and his demonstration above theirs. Soul takes care of the body in science, where God is an ever-present help in times of trouble. Keeping the body, or,, the outside of the platter, clean," is only done by keeping the mind right. Bathing and brushing to remove exhalations from the cuticle, receive a useful hint from Christianity, and another from the Irish emigrant, who is in health, although in filth; showing that the physical must correspond with the mental. When dirt gives no uneasiness, body and mind are equally

Chapter VIII. Healing the Sick.

gross, and the result is not so chafing. Filthiness that harms not the filthy in mind, could not be borne with impunity by the refined or pure; but what we need is the clean body and clean mind, and the body rendered pure by mind and not matter, for the latter can never do it permanently. One saith, "I take good care of my body," and repeats his decalogue with all the zeal of a devotee; but the scientist knows he has taken best care of his body who leaves it most out of his thoughts; hence the demand, absent from the body and present with God.

John Quincy Adams, and hundreds of others were instances of health and physiology; so the tobacconist who has taken poison for half a century, assures you it preserves his health; but does this assertion make it so, or establish the fact that tobacco is a good thing, or prevent the conclusion he would have been better without it? Such instances only prove the power of belief over the body, and fasten our conclusions in science, "as a man thinketh, so is he." Mind decides the effect of drugs, regimen, physiology, etc., on the body; for man is governed by mind instead of matter. The only condition of health and happiness, is ignorance of the so-called laws of matter, and understanding God, hence more confidence in Soul governing sense, and rising above selfishness, or mere personal considerations, in which pleasure or pain of the body is taken so largely into account, into the atmosphere of Spirit instead of matter.

A highly opinionated man, booked in the old school systems, has little room for enlarged reasoning; metaphysical science being intangible to touch or taste, he casts it overboard. His treasures laid up in sects, pride, person, or popularity, are in earthen vessels, that yield little space to God. The man of avoirdupois is shocked at our small estimate of exquisite viands; the diminutive intellect, alarmed at our exclusive appeals to mind, and the man of sense, sad at the prospect of Soul only! thus, when the world is bidden come to the feast and Truth of being, one has a farm, another a merchandise, and another a wife, therefore they cannot come; but ere long Truth compels us to come in ways we least expect. When sickness

Chapter VIII. Healing the Sick.

overtakes man, he is weak with all his imaginary strong-holds of matter, having nothing but material law to lean upon, and this, he owns he has transgressed, where can he look for immortality? Is it to person or Principle, to matter or Spirit, to body or Soul, he finally flees?

If matter is the identity of man, existence is but a continuation of personal sense that proves itself the source of pain. To contend for personal sense, and against mind's control over the body, is like the defendant arguing for the plaintiff, and in favor of a law that sentences him to suffer. Sin, sickness, and death, would destroy man; then why should we sustain these by a supposition of their inherent power and control over man, making him amenable to laws that destroy him. Until metaphysical science becomes popular, the weal, or vain will never advocate it, however much they are benefited by it. Those of a very different mould are commissioned for its hours of depreciation and struggles. The final proof that all is Spirit hastens. Life will be demonstrated ere long according to our statement of it, viz., Spirit and not matter; then shall we marvel at the tenacity of opposite opinions, that with the law and prophets and science, we must at length learn Truth of the things we suffer. Because science is in advance of the age we should not say, "adhere to personal sense to-day, for our present life depends on matter." If this is the case, man is mortal; but it is not so, and we cannot advance in science until we lose this belief.

Error is not a necessity at present or in the future, and to-day is the acceptable time of Truth; the present, even as the future, demands the science of being. To stop utterly eating and drinking until your belief changes in regard to these things, were error; get rid of your beliefs as fast as possible, and admit the Principle, for it is the platform of health, joy and immortality. To reach this proof by degrees, and only as we are capable of doing so with increasing health, harmony and happiness, is the only proper method. We would not, for we could not transform the infant at once to a man, or keep the suckling a life-long babe. Man need not spend his days in

Chapter VIII. Healing the Sick.

ignorance of the science of Life, expecting death will make him harmonious and immortal, for it will not; we advance to Life understandingly, therefore we cannot step at once from death to Life, or from matter to Spirit. Only as we understand the Principle of being, and reach perfection, are we Spirit, and eternal.

Death cannot advance man but one step towards a higher existence, insomuch as it changes not his belief but in one thing, namely, that he died, and of the disease he supposed was killing him. Mortal man is the same after as before the change called death; his body is the same belief of man, the same supposed personal sense, Substance in matter, and Life in the body, as before death; and so long as this error remains, mind being the same, the body remains mortal. We are never Spirit until we are God; there are no individual "spirits." Until we find Life Soul, and not sense, we are not sinless, harmonious, or undying. We become Spirit only as we reach being in God; not through death or any change of matter, but mind, do we reach Spirit, lose sin and death, and gain man's immortality; hence the need to commence Life's lesson to-day. We gain no higher experiences from death except to learn we die not, and this we gain of Life only and not death. The science of being reveals Substance, Intelligence and Life, not matter but Spirit.

Herein also we learn the immense disparity between the belief of Life in matter and the reality of being. Science makes the demonstration of Life perfection; and this we all must show before we have any grounds to say we understand Life, or are Spirit. Instead of this science requiring too much of man, at present we do not perceive one half the rightful claims it has upon us, or we should urge them at once on our own acceptance. The Scriptures inform us man liveth "not by bread alone, but by every word that proceedeth out of the mouth of God." Truth is the Life of man, but the age objects to making this practical, which is generally the case with all high requirements. We ask, consistently with the demands of God, and to-day, that less thought be given to what we shall eat, drink, or wear, that we live more simple and primitively, for this will increase longevity and morality. If we admit food can disturb the harmonious functions of mind and body, either the food or the belief must be dispensed with before man is harmonious. The belief that matter governs the Life of man must be met and mastered on some basis before man is learned immortal. Sickness is abject slavery; an invalid haunted by the belief of physical suffering that masters him at all points and on all occasions, is the most pitiful object on earth. Laws of health constitute a government of matter over man wholly unnatural; they attach penalties to our best deeds.

We ought to learn from history and experience the less we believe these so-called laws the less we suffer from their infringement, and the better we obey God's spiritual law. People who know nothing of physiology, hygiene, or materia medica, until missionaries give them of this "tree of knowledge," suffer not as we do from the so-called laws that we say must be obeyed or they kill us, and they enjoy better health than those obeying them. What, then, shall we say of law "more honored in the breach than the observance?" Slavery must yield to innate right, and destroyed in mind, it will die out of forms of government; ignorance of our inalienable rights makes us slaves. If we recognized all being, God, we would perceive our dominion over Sickness, sin and death; for governments oppressive and unjust Wisdom layeth its hand upon to destroy, and they fall forever before the might of understanding. The watchword of freedom from the bondage of sickness and sin is not taken up; it has no inspiration for mankind.

This is owing to the fatal belief that error is as real as Truth; that evil has equal power and claims with good, and discord is as normal and real as harmony; such admissions work badly. That matter is solid Substance, and Spirit essence inside of matter; that Spirit is Life, but dwells in decay and death; that Spirit is God, but cannot make man without partnership with matter; that man is not man until he is matter; are false admissions and contradictory statements that Seem too absurd to be permitted a place in reason. If man is matter, he is not mind, and dust is as intelligent as Deity. If Intelligence or

Chapter VIII. Healing the Sick.

Spirit is in matter, the infinite is in the finite, and Spirit is less than matter, for we cannot place the greater within the less. If man existed not forever, and before material structure, he does not exist after his body is disintegrated. If we live after death we lived before birth. Life has no beginning, therefore no end; all that is material must disappear before man is found immortal. How strange, then, to conclude man would have had no individual being unless he had been individualized through matter, an impossible beginning of Intelligence.

The body never affected the Life of man for a moment; eating never made him Eve, nor abstaining from food caused him to die. Do you believe this? No! Do you understand it? No! And this is the only reason that you doubt it; the cadaverous dyspeptic learning this, has a sweet face without a sour stomach, and is nearer the kingdom of heaven than you. We are attracted or repelled mentally without knowing the thoughts that lead to this. We weep because others weep, and laugh because they laugh, and have small-pox on this ground, for disease is not hereditary or contagious only through mind. The more spiritual we are, the more conscious to us is an error of belief. Surrounded by minds filled with thoughts of disease, constantly dwelling upon their bodies, and with some complaint always ready, the spiritual suffer greatly in this mental atmosphere; such involuntary agents of pain to themselves and others, must be reformed. When mental contagion is understood, these people will be avoided as we now avoid small-pox. To stop the manufacture of disease and give us a better mental atmosphere, is worthy the present age of progress. We would sooner risk our health, inhaling the miasma of a rice swamp, than be obliged to listen constantly to complaints of sickness, or through sympathy or society be kept in the mental atmosphere of the sick; some natures may stand it, but ours has a struggle.

We admit man is immortal, -- our only evidence of this, however, we gain from his harmony; discord, sickness or death never begat this conclusion. Immortality was never demonstrated to

Chapter VIII. Healing the Sick.

personal sense; but apprehending in the least, Soul and science, no man doubts his eternal existence. Physical effects proceed from mental causes; the belief we can move our hand moves it, and the belief we cannot do this renders it impossible during this state of mind. Palsy is a belief that attacks mind, and holds a limb inactive independent of the mind's consent, but the fact that a limb is moved only with mind proves the opposite, namely, that mind renders it also immovable. Medical works fill the mind with images of disease that are liable sooner or later to be re-produced on the body. The consent of mind must first be given that palsy is practical, then the circumstance said to produce it, and the result follows you have it developed.

Ossification, or any abnormal formation of bone, is produced by mind alone; for a bone never grew independent of mind, and the cause producing this can remove it. What the physician and others determine is fatal in a case, and above all what the patient believes regarding this, is the only obstacle in the way of the recovery. A condition of matter must first have been a condition of mind; hence to destroy the former we must begin with the latter, and when the cause is removed its effects disappear. We will suppose two parallel cases of bone disease, both produced similarly and attended by the same symptoms; for one we employ a surgeon, and for the other a scientist. The surgeon, believing matter forms its own conditions, entertains doubts or fears in regard to the case, and his state of mind is communicated to the patient, whether verbally or otherwise. While we vainly suppose the sick feel the effects only of thoughts expressed, they feel more surely the unexpressed fear, doubt, or anxiety, inasmuch as it is more intense. The scientist, understanding how mind alone forms every condition of matter, gives courage and strength to the patient while imparting to his understanding the Truth of being that destroys error, and restores the limb without stiffness, displacement, or unnatural formations; whereas the surgeon's similar case will terminate, if not fatally, in some unnatural condition of the joint. Understanding the cause of disease wholly mental, a scientist will never for a moment admit general

Chapter VIII. Healing the Sick.

opinions regarding it, or take physical symptoms into account, except as mental conditions or beliefs to be destroyed through mind.

Personal sense and science clash, of course, in this statement, for they are opposites and without affinity, and this quarrel will wax warmer until it is over, and sense yields to science. Pride, ignorance, prejudice or passion will close the door on science until future centuries open it wide to man, and he regains the harmony of being. If Life and Intelligence depend on organization, man is material; and stop the functions of the body, or let the body be spiritual, and man is annihilated; and there must be a new creation of man. If Life escapes from matter it is not Spirit, and must return again to matter, in which case there is no spiritual existence. If material existence is real, the spiritual is unreal, and *vice versa*; if Life is matter, or in matter, it cannot continue outside of matter; and material decomposition must reduce material man to dust. Even the worm begotten of death, springing from corruption, we name Life in matter; making Life a product of death and death a product of Life. When will the age awake to reason on being, as fairly as on other subjects.

We should object to natural history leaping thus the barrier of species. There is neither vegetable, animal, nor organic Life, if Life is Spirit, and the testimony of Scripture and demonstration of Life prove that it is. Called to the bed of death -- the Truth of being is your only resource to restore health and raise up the so- called dying; on its basis alone can you recognize immortality, and dispute personal sense or the apparent fact of death, with Soul; man is not dying if Intelligence is Life; man's being is mightier far than death, for Truth is mightier than error. Your privilege is to prove "He that believeth in me," i.e., understandeth the Truth of being, "shall never see death." Understanding Life, destroys death. We have demonstrated the effect of this statement of science on the sick sufficiently to establish its practical value. Though we admit man is immortal, we apprehend Life only as a thing material, or escaping from the body; this is not correct; personal belief and error is

Chapter VIII. Healing the Sick.

responsible for this wrong statement of God. Death is but another phase or belief of the dream of life in matter; and while there is no reality in either, both will continue until the science herein stated is understood. The obsequies of the dead are a pitiful part of this dream, when we remember Life has neither beginning nor end. The so-called dead, although liberated from their belief that Life has ended, or even changed to them, are separated from our opinions and recognition of them; and they have no more cognizance of the body we are disposing of than we of their actual existence; these two dreams of Life are separated never to unite again until we pass into their phase of belief, or at length reach the understanding of Life and yield the error of personal sense, or matter-man, for Life that is God.

Science reveals immortality in such a light it precludes the possibility of Life in mortality. The lessons of earth should lift the affections and understanding to a spiritual base whereby we lose error to gain Truth, for, "he that loseth his life for my sake shall find it." Electric currents never passed from Spirit to matter; Spirit evolves the idea of Life, and this idea has no fellowship with matter or decay; to this final understanding we are all hastening.

We will suppose a case on the docket of mind, in which a man is charged with liver complaint. The patient feels ill, ruminates, and the trial commences. Personal Sense is plaintiff; Man, the defendant; Belief, the attorney for Personal Sense; Mortal Minds, the jury, and Materia Medica, Anatomy, Physiology, Mesmerism, and Mediumship the judges. The evidence for the plaintiff being called, testifies:

"I am Laws of Health, was present on the nights the prisoner (patient) watched with the sick, and, although I have the superintendence of human affairs, was personally abused on those occasions, and informed I must remain silent until called for at this trial, when I should be allowed to testify in the cue. Notwithstanding my rules to the contrary, the prisoner watched with the sick every night in the week; ,when thirsty, he gave them drink, and when sick,

Chapter VIII. Healing the Sick.

and in prison, he visited them;" at the same time attending to his daily labors, partaking of food at irregular intervals, sometimes retiring immediately after a heavy meal, etc., etc., until he was guilty of liver complaint, that we construe crime, inasmuch as we deem it punishable with death; therefore I arrested the man in behalf of the State (body) and cast him into prison. At the time of the arrest he summoned Physiology, Materia Medica, Mesmerism, and a masked individual named Mediumship, to prevent his punishment or imprisonment. The struggle, on their part, was long; missives of matter were employed vigorously but unavailingly; Materia Medica, held out the longest, however, being paid for it; but at length they all gave up their weapons to me (Laws of Health) and I succeeded in getting Man into close confinement." The next witness being called, stated:

"I am Coated Tongue, covered with a foul fur placed on me the night of the liver complaint, Morbid Secretions, Irregular Appetite, Constipation, Foul Stomach, and Debility being witnesses. Morbid Secretions mesmerized the prisoner, took control of his mind, producing Somnolence, etc., making him despondent, also, the sooner to precipitate his fate." Another witness being called, took the stand and testified:

"I am Sallow Skin, dry, hot, and chilled by turns since the night of the liver complaint. I have lost my healthy hue and become bad-looking, although nothing on my part occasioned this; I have daily ablutions, and perform my functions as usual, but I am robbed of my good looks." The next witness testified:

"I am Nerves, generalissimo of man, intimately acquainted with the plaintiff, Personal Sense, and know him to be truthful and upright, while Man (the prisoner at the bar) is capable of falsehood. I was witness to the crime of liver-complaint; knew the prisoner would commit it, for I convey messages from my residence in matter, *alias* brains, to the body, and am on intimate terms with Error, a personal acquaintance of the prisoner, but a foe to Man."

Chapter VIII. Healing the Sick.

The name of this third person was called for by the court, and the reply was, "Mortality, governor of the state (body) in which Man is supposed to reside." In this state there is a statute regarding disease, namely, that Man upon whose person disease is found should be treated as a criminal and punished with death.

Judge. "Did Man, by doing good to his neighbor possess himself of disease, transgress your laws and merit punishment?" "He did." The deposition of Bowels was then read, they being too inactive to be present. Another witness took the stand, and testified as follows: "I am Ulceration; was sent for shortly after the night of the liver-complaint, by Laws of Health, who protested the prisoner had abused him, and my presence was required to make valid his testimony. One of the judges, (Materia Medica) was present when I arrived, endeavoring to assist the prisoner to escape from the hands of what he termed justice, alias nature's law; but my sudden appearance with a message from Laws of Health changed his purpose, and he decided at once the prisoner (patient) should die."

The testimony for the plaintiff (Personal Sense) being closed, Materia, Medica arose and with great solemnity addressed the jury, (Mortal Minds) analyzing the offence, reviewing the testimony, and explaining the law relating to liver- complaint, the conclusion of which was, that laws of nature render disease homicide. In compliance with a stern duty, Materia Medica said he must charge the jury not to allow judgment to be warped by the petty suggestions of Soul; to regard in such cases only the mortal evidence of Personal Sense against Man. As the judge proceeded, the prisoner (patient) grew restless, his sallow face blanched with fear, and a look of despair and death settled upon it. A brief consultation ensued, when the jury, Mortal Minds, returned a verdict of guilty, the prisoner being charged with liver-complaint in the first degree. Materia Medica then proceeded to pronounce the solemn sentence of death upon the patient, who, for loving his neighbor as himself, was found guilty of benevolence in the first degree, that led to the committal of the second crime, liver-complaint, that matter-laws construe

Chapter VIII. Healing the Sick.

homicide, for which crimes we sentence this man to be tortured until he is dead, and may God have mercy on his soul.

The prisoner, (patient) was then remanded to his cell (sick bed) and Theology sent for to prepare Soul that is immortal, for death! the body, called Man, having no friends. Ah! but Christ, Truth, was there; the friend of man, to open wide those prison doors and set the captive free. Swift on the wings of Love a message came, "Delay the execution! the prisoner is not guilty." Consternation filled the court-room, some exclaiming, it is contrary to law and order; others, "Christ walks over our laws, let us follow Him."

After much debate and opposition, permission was obtained for a trial at the bar of Spirit, where Science should appear as counsel for the poor prisoner. Witnesses, judges, and jurors of the Mental Court of Common Errors were summoned to appear at the bar of Truth. When the me for man *versus* matter opened, his counsel was regarding the prisoner with the utmost tenderness, but that solemn, serene look changed, the earnest eyes kindling with hope and triumph uplifted for a single moment, turned suddenly to the Mental Court of Common Pleas, and Science opened the argument by saying: "The prisoner at the bar has been sentenced unjustly his trial was a mocking tragedy, morally illegal; Man has had no counsel in the case; all the testimony was on the side of matter, and we will unearth this foul conspiracy against the liberty and life of Man. The only valid testimony in the cue proved the alleged crime was never committed, and the prisoner unworthy of death or of bonds. Your Honor, Materia Medica, has sentenced Man, the image of God, to die, denying justice to the body, has recommended mercy for Spirit who is infinite Wisdom and Man's only law-giver! Here you will please inform us who or what has sinned; has the body committed a deed?

Your counsel, Belief, argues, that which never sinned should die, while mind, that is capable of sin and suffering you comfort and commend to mercy. The body committed no offence, and man in

Chapter VIII. Healing the Sick.

just obedience to higher law, helped his fellow man, which should result in good to himself. The law of our Supreme Court decrees, whoso sinneth shall die, but good deeds immortalize man, bringing joy instead of grief, pleasure instead of pain, and life instead of death. If liver complaint was induced, trampling upon Laws of Health, it was a good deed, the witness is a usurper of man's liberty and rights, and should be consigned to oblivion. Watching beside the couch of pain in the exercise of Love, that fulfills the whole law, doing unto others as ye would they should do unto you, is no infringement of law, for no demand, human or divine, renders it right to punish a man for doing right. If man sins, our Supreme Judge of equity decides the penalty due to sin; but he can suffer only for sin, and for naught else can he be punished according to the laws of God; then what jurisdiction has your Honors, Materia Medica and Physiology in the case? 'Sittest thou to judge a man after the law, and commandest him to he smitten contrary to the law?' The only jurisprudence to which the prisoner shall be made to submit is Truth, Life and Love, and if these condemn him not, neither shalt thou condemn him, but shall restore to him the liberty against which you have conspired.

"Your principal witness (Laws of Health) deposed he was an eye-witness to the good deeds for which you sentence a man to die, and even betrayed him into the hands of your law, then disappeared on that occasion to reappear on this, against Man, and in support of Personal Sense, a known criminal. The Supreme Court of Spirit, *versus* matter, finds the prisoner, on the night of the alleged offence, acting within the limits, and in obedience to the divine statute, upon which 'hangs all law and testimony, giving a cup of cold water in my name,' etc.; and thus laying down his life, he should find it; such deeds beer the justification, and are under the protection of the Most High ruler. Prior to the night of the arrest the prisoner summoned two judges, Materia Medica, and Physiology, to prevent his committing liver-complaint; but they employed their sheriff, Fear, who handcuffed him and precipitated the deed you would now punish, leaving Man no alternative but to believe your law, fear its

Chapter VIII. Healing the Sick.

consequences, and be punished for all this. The judges struggled hard to rescue the prisoner from the penalty they considered justly due; but failing in this, ordered him to be taken into custody, tried and condemned, whereupon these abettors appear at the bench to sit in judgment against him, and recommend the jury, Mortal Minds, to find the prisoner guilty. Their Honors sentence Man to die for the offence they compel him to commit; construing obedience to the law of Love disobedience to the law of Life, claiming to wrest Man from the penalty of law at one time, and at another sentencing him by it.

"One of your principal witnesses, Nerves, testified he is a ruler of the State, (body) in which he says Man resides; that he is on intimate terms with the plaintiff, and knows Personal Sense to be just and truthful, but man, the image of God, a criminal. This is a foul aspersion on his Maker, unworthy a worm; it blots the fair escutcheon of Intelligence; 'tis a malice aforethought to condemn Man in defence of matter. At the Bar of Truth, in the presence of Justice the judge of our Supreme Court, and before its jurors, Spiritual Senses, I proclaim this witness, Nerves, destitute of Intelligence, without Truth, possessing no reality, and bearing the messages of Error only. Man self-destroyed, the testimony of matter respected, Intelligence not allowed a hearing, Soul a slave recommended to mercy, whose body is supposed to be executed-are the terrible records of your mental Court of Common Pleas."

Here the opposite counsel, Belief, called Science to order, for contempt of court, and their Honors, Materia Medica, Anatomy, Physiology, Mediumship, and Mesmerism rose to the question of expelling Science from the bar, for high-handed treason, and stopping the judicial proceedings. But Justice, the judge of the Supreme Court of Spirit, overruled their motion on the ground that parliamentary usages are not allowed at the bar of Truth, that holds jurisdiction over the petite Court of Error.

Science then read from his own statute, the Bible, remarking it was better authority than Blackstone, extracts from the Rights of

Chapter VIII. Healing the Sick.

Man. "And I give you power over all things that nothing shall by any means harm you." "Let us make man in our image, and let him have dominion over all the earth." "Whoso believeth in me shall not see death," etc.; proving the witness, Nerves, a perjurer, and instead of a governor of the state, (body), wherein man was falsely reported to reside, an insubordinate subject, preferring false claims to office, and bearing false witness against Man. Then turning suddenly to Personal Sense, (by this time silent) Science continued, I order your arrest in the name of Almighty God, on three separate charges: perjury, treason, and conspiracy against the rights and existence of God's image and likeness.

Another testimony, equally unimportant, said that a garment of foul fur was spread over this witness, by Morbid Secretions, on the night of the liver-complaint, while the facts in the case proved this fur was foreign, and imported by Belief, the attorney for Personal Sense, who is in company with Error, and smuggles his goods into market without the inspection of Soul's government officers. Whenever the court of Truth summons Furred Tongue to appear for examination, he disappears, and is never more heard of. Morbid Secretion is not an importer or dealer in fur, but we have heard their Honors, Materia Medica and Mediumship explain how it is manufactured, and know they are on friendly terms with the firm of Personal Sense and error, receiving pay for their goods, and introducing them into market. Also be it known, that Belief, counsel for the plaintiff, Personal Sense, is a procurer for this firm; manufactures for it, keeps a furnishing store, and advertises largely for this firm. Ulceration testified he was absent from the state (body) when a message came from Belief, commanding him to take part in the homicide; at this request he repaired to the spot of liver-complaint, frightened away Materia Medica, who was manacling the prisoner under pretence of saving him, but this ignorance, not malice, was in fact an unconscious participation in the deed, for which Laws of Health has had Man, innocent of all crime in the case, imprisoned, tried and condemned to die.

Chapter VIII. Healing the Sick.

Science then turned from the abashed witnesses, with words like sharpened steel, pointed at the hearts of Materia Medica, Physiology, the felon Mesmerism, and the masked form, Mediumship, saying: God should have smitten thee, thou whited walls, sitting to judge in justice, but condemning in thine ignorance the prisoner who sought your aid in his struggles against the deed whereof you accuse him, then coming to his rescue only to fasten, through false testimony, an offence on the prisoner of which he is innocent; aiding and abetting that for which you would sacrifice man, declaring your executioner, Disease, to be God's servant and the executor of His laws, when our statute decides your witnesses, jurors, and judges condemned, by higher law, and only awaiting the executioner, Progress. We send our very best detectives to whatever locality you report your Disease, but visiting the spot, they learn it was never there, or it could not elude their discovery. Your Mental Court of Errors, at which you condemn or acquit man on the ground of disease, is the oleaginous machinations of your counsel, Belief, that Science arraigns before the supreme bar of Soul, to answer for his blood-shed. You taught Morbid Secretions to make sleep befool his reason, before sacrificing man to your gods; your jurors, Mortal Minds, were mesmerized by your attorney, Belief, and compelled to deliver man to his open-jawed packs. You would transform good deeds into crimes, to which you attach penalties; but no warping of justice renders disobedience to Laws of Matter, disobedience to God, or an act of homicide; for matter cannot kill what Spirit has made.

Even penal law construes homicide under stress of circumstances justifiable, and what greater justification hath a deed than that it did good to our neighbor, wherefore, then, we ask in the name of outraged justice, do you sentence Man for ministering to the wants of his fellow man, in obedience to higher law? You cannot walk over the supreme bench; Man is amenable only to God, who sentences for sin only. The false and unjust beliefs of your Mental Court of Errors enact a law of sickness, then render obedience to this law punishable as crime; such are the spurious enactments of

Chapter VIII. Healing the Sick.

"knowledge." In the presence of the supreme law-giver, standing at the bar of Truth and in accordance with its statutes, I repudiate the false testimony of Personal Sense, forbid his entering more suits against man to be tried at the bar of matter, and appeal to the just and equitable decisions of Spirit to restore the prohibited rights of the body.

Here the counsel for the defence closed, and the Chief Justice of the Supreme Court with benign and imposing presence, appropriating, comprehending, and defining all law and evidence explained from His statute, the Bible, how law punishing aught but sin is null and void. Also that the plaintiff, Personal Sense, is not permitted to enter suits at the bar of Soul, but required to keep perpetual silence, and in case of temptation, to give heavy bonds for good behavior. The plea of Belief we deem unworthy a hearing upon all occasions; therefore, let the things it has uttered, now and forever, fall into oblivion, unknelled, uncoffined, and unknown. According to our statute, Laws of Matter cannot bear witness against man, neither can Fear arrest him, nor Disease cast him into prison; our law refuses to recognize man sick or dying, but holds him the image and likeness of immortal Soul; reversing the testimony of Personal Sense, and the decrees of the Court of Error in favor of matter versus man, we decide in favor of man and against matter; therefore, we recommend that Materia Medica, Physiology, Laws of Health, Mesmerism and Mediumship be given a public execution at the hands of our Sheriff, Progress. The supreme bench decides in favor of Intelligence, and that no law outside of mind can punish man. Your personal judges of the Mental Court of Common Pleas are chimeras, your attorney, Belief, an imposter persuading Mortal Minds to return a verdict contrary to law and Gospel, while your plaintiff, Personal Sense, is recorded in our Book of books, a perjurer. Our Teacher of spiritual jurisprudence said of him, "You were a liar from the beginning." We have no trials for Disease at the tribunals of Spirit, and man is adjudged innocent of transgressing physical laws, because there is no spiritual statute relating thereto.

Chapter VIII. Healing the Sick.

The law of Christ, Truth, is our only code, and "will not the judge of the whole earth do right?"

The plea of Science closed, and the jury of Immortal Mind agreed at once upon a verdict, and there resounded throughout the vast audience chamber of Soul, "NOT GUILTY"; then the prisoner (patient) rose up strong, free, and glorious. We noticed as he shook hands with his counsel, Science of Life, all sallowness and debility had disappeared, his form was erect and commanding, his countenance beaming with health and happiness; dominion had taken the place of fear, and man no longer sick and in prison walked forth, "whose feet were beautiful upon the mountains."

The above allegory illustrates the effect of mind on the body, how the testimony of personal sense and the plea of belief would punish man; while the plea of Science commutes the sentence of error, with Truth.

When symptoms of sickness are present, meet them with the resistance of mind against matter, and you will control them. Life, that is Soul, must triumph over sense at some time, and it is wise to-day to learn this of scientific being. Silently or audibly, according to the circumstances, you should dispute the reality of disease on the basis of the explanations herein given; when healing mentally call each symptom by name, and contradict its claims, as you would a falsehood uttered to your injury. Here is a phenomenon I will state just as I discovered it; if you call not the disease by name when you address it mentally, the body will no more respond by recovery, than a person will reply whose name is not spoken; and you cannot heal the sick by argument, unless you get the name of the disease; but the higher method of healing in Christian science is, so to live that your Life, " hid with Christ in God," is the Life of Soul that destroys the errors of sense. Agree not with sickness, meet the physical condition with a mental protest, that destroys it as one property destroys another in chemistry; understanding this in science, your mind will

Chapter VIII. Healing the Sick.

neutralize the disease, destroy the fear, and the system will regain its equilibrium.

I have seen a dose of Truth, regarding disease, produce stronger physical effects than ever I witnessed from a dose of drugs. The opposite negative neutralizes the affirmative of disease, and thus destroys it. We have before told you all is mind; therefore, what you term physical effects, are purely mental ones. The mental admission produces what is named the physical effect; hence the fatal results of treatises, admitting, describing, or locating disease. Diagnosing symptoms physical, to learn the actual cause of bodily discord, when mind is the only causation, is error, proved already the procurer, instead of destroyer of disease. I never presume on statements diametrically opposed to personal sense, unless I have proved their Truth beyond a doubt. I have tested this mode of healing with scientific certainty, in many cases, and in no case has it failed to prove a benefit to the sick. The task, herculean, of introducing a science has before been tested by patient discoverers; but when the Truth of being is learned, it will be proved. It was said to us, "The whole world feels you, and why are you not more widely known?" Could they have seen the little time we have to be known, and how our work is done, in the closet with the door shut, "seen by Him who seeth in secret," they would have understood why. To make a specialty of healing is really impossible for us, when our time, means, and health are required for the fuller investigation of this subject; to teach, write, establish practices for students, or halt, perhaps, at measures to be adopted, because of persecution. None should reject Truth because it exposes some past poverty of opinion, or requires the surrender of present beliefs. Indifference to Christian science surprises one when we know it is the eternal right in which God holds the scales, and adjusts all harmonious balances. Even doctrines and beliefs are to-day reaching forth their hands for the science of being; and that which reveals Truth ought not to be misjudged because of ignorance or prejudice.

Chapter VIII. Healing the Sick.

Some of our present readers may wish to tone down the radical points in this work, others to cast them overboard; yet science will reproduce itself, and as mind changes base from matter to Spirit, there will be severe chemicalization. Truth cannot be lost; if not admitted to-day in its fullness, the error that shuts it out will occasion such discord in sickness, sin, etc., that future yews will point it out, and restore at length the fair proportions and radical claims of Christian Science.

FINIS

Resources

A Favor

If you enjoyed this book I would ask that you to go back to Amazon and leave an honest review of the "Science and Health, 1875 Edition". We are a small boutique publisher and reviews help us spread the word to the world more effectively. I appreciate your time and effort.
Thank you, Barry J Peterson, Publisher

Interesting Reads:

"Science and Health, 1875 Edition", Mary Baker Glover (Eddy)
www.ScienceAndHealth1875Edition.Com

"The Sickle" by William W. Walker   www.TheSickle.Org

"The Quimby Manuscripts"   www.TheQuimbyManuscripts.Com

Reading to the Dead, a transitional grief therapy for the living
www.ReadingToTheDead.Com
Author: Barry J Peterson

Neville Goddard: The Complete Reader
www.NevilleGoddardReader.Com
Author: Neville Goddard

www.AudioEnlightenment.Com

Gnostic Audio Selection:

To access the streaming audio book version of
"Science and Health, 1875 Edition"
please visit www.GnosticAudio.Com and follow the directions to access your free streaming audio version of this publication. This is streaming audio only; the audio book is NOT downloadable

Visit www.AudioEnlightenmentPress.Com
for the latest publications from the world of Metaphysics

www.ingramcontent.com/pod-product-compliance
Lightning Source LLC
Chambersburg PA
CBHW030134170426
43199CB00008B/58